A COMMENTARY ON
THE NEW
CODE OF CANON LAW

By THE REV. P. CHAS. AUGUSTINE, O.S.B., D.D.
Professor of Canon Law

VOLUME VII
Ecclesiastical Procedure (Book IV)
(Can. 1552-2194)

B. HERDER BOOK CO.
17 SOUTH BROADWAY, ST. LOUIS, MO.
AND
68, GREAT RUSSELL ST., LONDON, W. C.
1921

CUM PERMISSU SUPERIORUM

NIHIL OBSTAT

Sti. Ludovici, die 8 Mart, 1921

F. G. Holweck,
Censor Librorum

IMPRIMATUR

Sti. Ludovici, die 9 Mart, 1921

✠Joannes J. Glennon,
Archiepiscopus
Sti. Ludovici

WM.-BALLOU COMPANY
BINGHAMTON AND NEW YORK

587683

CONTENTS

CONTENTS

CONTENTS

CONTENTS

CONTENTS

CONTENTS

CONTENTS

THE NEW CODE OF CANON LAW

BOOK IV
ECCLESIASTICAL PROCEDURE

INTRODUCTION

There is no part of Canon Law which is so conspicuously based on, nay governed by, Roman Law as the book which we now undertake to describe and, as far as necessary, to explain. The reason for this phenomenon is not far to seek. For not only did the Roman Law rest on the principles of natural justice and equity, but through the influence of the Christian emperors it became familiar to the Church at large. Not only the soil on which it had grown, but its very terminology, had become the common possession of the Christianized nations, not even excepting the Teutonic race, though the Germanic law had not been influenced as largely as others. An exception, however, was the English law. The little island of Britannica had its peculiar laws, to which the nobility as well as the laity clung conservatively, whilst the bishops and the clergy, many of them foreigners, applied themselves to the study of the civil, *i. e.*, Roman and canon law.[1] But the clerical element was finally eliminated or forced to retreat to its schools and monas-

teries. Thus it happened that the English law has least
of all received the structure and outlines of Roman or
ecclesiastical law.   In its stead it has introduced a terminology which needs a special study of Anglo-Saxon and
old French.   This we state in order to make it plain that
some terms of Canon Law are not easily rendered into
English, but require circumlocution. Therefore time-
honored and concise terms shall be retained in their
original Latin. The essentials of the trial, being common to all civilized nations, are the same in English law
as in others.

The Code divides Book Four, which embodies the second book of the decretals, into three parts:

I. Trials, or Ecclesiastical Procedure.
II. Beatification and Canonization.
III. Procedure in Particular Cases.

1 Blackstone-Cooley, *Commentary* I, 18 f.

PART I
TRIALS

Can. 1552

§ 1. Nomine iudicii ecclesiastici intelligitur controversiae in re de qua Ecclesia ius habet cognoscendi, coram tribunali ecclesiastico, legitima disceptatio et definitio.

§ 2. Obiectum iudicii sunt:

1.° Personarum physicarum vel moralium iura persequenda aut vindicanda, vel earundem personarum facta iuridica declaranda; et tunc iudicium est *contentiosum;*

2.° Delicta in ordine ad poenam infligendam vel declarandam; et tunc iudicium est *criminale.*

Can. 1553

§ 1. Ecclesia iure proprio et exclusivo cognoscit:

1.° De causis quae respiciunt res spirituales et spiritualibus adnexas;

2.° De violatione legum ecclesiasticarum deque omnibus in quibus inest ratio peccati, quod attinet ad culpae definitionem et poenarum ecclesiasticarum irrogationem;

3.° De omnibus causis sive contentiosis sive criminalibus quae respiciunt personas privilegio fori gaudentes ad normam can. 120, 614, 680.

3

§ 2. In causis in quibus tum Ecclesia tum civilis potestas aeque competentes sunt, quaeque dicuntur mixti fori, est locus praeventioni.

Can. 1554

Actor, qui causas mixti fori ad iudicem ecclesiasticum deductas ad forum saeculare iudicandas defert, congruis poenis puniri potest ad normam can. 2222 et privatur iure contra eandem personam de eadem re et de connexis causam agendi in foro ecclesiastico.

Can. 1555

§ 1. Tribunal Congregationis S. Officii suo more institutoque procedit sibique propriam consuetudinem retinet; et etiam inferiora tribunalia, in causis quae ad S. Officii tribunal spectant, normas ab eodem traditas sequantur oportet.

§ 2. Cetera tribunalia servare debent praescripta canonum qui sequuntur.

§ 3. In iudicio pro dimissione religiosorum serventur praescripta can. 654–667.

The Roman Law constantly employs, not *processus*, but *iudicia* (judgments), which were divided into public and private. Our Code, too, speaks here of *iudicium ecclesiasticum*, which it *defines* as the lawful discussion and settlement before the ecclesiastical court of a disputed matter of which the Church is entitled to take cognizance.

Can. 1553 determines which *matters belong by inherent and exclusive right* to the ecclesiastical court. They are:

1.° All *merely spiritual matters* and such strictly connected with spiritual things. This is a very moderate vindication of a right which cannot be denied to any autonomous society. That the spiritual element is superior to the material or temporal, the divine to the human, the spirit to the flesh, should be evident. Yet it was necessary to repeat that truth against the encroachments of emperors and rulers who would pose as popes.[1] A conflict was inevitable. Undeniably there were exaggerations on both sides, especially at the time of Boniface VIII, when some writers vindicated to the Pope everything except creation.[2] Such unwarranted assertions could not fail to provoke resistance, from which it was but a short step to encroachments. But the rights of the Church needed no concessions, which indeed had voluntarily been made by loyal rulers who perceived the mighty influence of the Church over a semi-barbarous populace. The orderly procedure of the ecclesiastical courts gradually permeated the civil courts, to the gain of a more equitable and just handling of trials.[3] This of course can only be understood in the light of unbiased history. The ecclesiastical legislator vindicates to his court:

(a) All *spiritual matters*. Such are everything belonging to faith and morals, the Sacraments and sacramentals, divine worship and the sacred liturgy, dispensations from vows and oaths, ecclesiastical offices, rights and obligations of the clergy, beneficiaries and religious, the extent of, and exemption from, ecclesiastical jurisdiction, etc.[4]

(b) Matters which might *per se* be called temporal, but are *intimately connected with the spiritual*, such as

1 Cc. 3, 6, Dist. 10.
2 See Scholz, *Publizistik zur Zeit Philipps des Schönen und Bonifaz VIII.* (Stutz, *Kirchenrechtl. Abhandlg.*, 6-8, 1903); Alex. Carerius, *De Potestate Summi Pontificis,* 1601, still asserts what is said in the text.
3 Cfr. Hergenröther, *Kath. Kirche u. Christl. Staat,* 1872, p. 26 f.
4 Cfr. c. 34, *Venerabilem*, X, I, 6; cc. 2, 3, X, II, 1; 15, X, V, 31.

advowson, church revenues, ecclesiastical burial, legitimacy of children, real immunity, etc.[5]

2.° The ecclesiastical court may also claim cases of *violation of ecclesiastical laws* and all matters in which the question of sin is involved, in so far as the determination of guilt and the infliction of ecclesiastical punishments comes into play. It is evident that here especially the *leges plus quam perfectae* and *perfectae* are intended, *i.e.*, such as have an invalidating clause or a penal sanction attached. As to penalties inflicted upon transgressors they are more especially the censures and vindictive penalties which may be meted out not only to the clergy but also to the faithful. This is sometimes expressly mentioned in concordats, where also the punishment of public sinners and transgressors of the holydays of obligation are specially noted.[6]

The second clause, *viz.*, to take cognizance of matters which underlie the *ratio peccati*, is an allusion to a famous decretal of Innocent III, "*Novit*," in which this great Pontiff assures the King of France and John Lackland of England that he has "no intention to judge feuds, but to decide concerning sin, which undoubtedly belongs to him."[7] Hence our text only mentions guilt and ecclesiastical punishment. This power is called *potestas directiva*, and consists in wielding the spiritual sword or the functions of an authoritative teacher vested with ecclesiastical or spiritual weapons.[8] This power necessarily follows from the legislative power, inasmuch as the latter would be ineffective without the executive power

[5] Cfr. c. 3, X, II 1; c. 3 X, III, 30; c. 3, X, II, 10; c. 9, X, IV, 17; X, III, 28, *de sepulturis*; c. 4, 6°, III, 23; Wernz, *Ius Decret.*, Vol. V, 1914, 3. 223, n. 268.

[6] Cfr., for inst., can. 1428, 1512, 1527, and all the diriment impediments.

[7] Nussi, *Conventiones*, 1870, pp. 92, 105, 151, 185, 312.

[8] C. 13, X, II, 1; see Hergenröther, *l. c.*, p. 403 ff.

proper. Even a religious society cannot do without the rod.

3.° A third category of matters strictly belonging to the ecclesiastical court comprises a certain class of persons (*ratione personae*). Hence the civil as well as the criminal cases of the *clergy* and all those who share the clerical privileges of the forum are subject to the ecclesiastical court. These, *i.e.*, the clergy proper as mentioned under can. 120, the religious as per can. 614, and the members of pious communities, though not religious in the canonical sense of the word, as per can. 680. All these, says the text, are subject to the ecclesiastical judge in civil as well as in criminal matters.

Can. 1552, § 2 distinguishes two classes of procedure, *ratione objecti, i.e.*, by reason of the purpose. For if an individual or a corporation goes to law, they are supposed to have sustained an injury or a wrong, for which they think it worth while to demand satisfaction. This

Concerning the threefold power distinguished by authors we may here add the following: The *postestas directa* would represent the Pope as endowed with unlimited power in spiritual as well as temporal matters, although the temporal power he wields through the worldly rulers, or rather these wield it by his command. The *postestas indirecta* is differently explained, but in general features there is agreement: the Pope rules directly over spiritual matters, whilst over temporal things he has power only as far as the object of the Church requires it. Hence the Pope may not depose secular princes, but he may change the occupants or transfer kingdoms, he may not issue or nullify secular laws, but he may absolve the faithful from the obligation of observing them if they are contrary to salvation; he may not judge in temporal matters, as a rule, but only assume the office of judge in case of two rivals or in case there is no one to judge. (See Bellarmine, *De Rom. Pont.*, l. V, c. 6). The *potestas directiva*, too, is not always explained in the same manner. But what is said in the text comprises all explanations. The Church is the supreme spiritual and infallible director of every conscience, giving admonitions, explanations and counsels to high and low. But this is not all,—the Church, being an autonomous society, also enjoys the right of exercising the judiciary and executive power over her members. (See Hergenröther, *Kath. Kirche und Christl. Staat*, 1872, pp. 411 ff. J. Milita, *De Eccl. Potest. Indirecta*, Rome 1891.

wrong may affect the person or corporation only, *i.e.*, a private interest for which they seek redress. Take, for instance, can. 1534, where personal and real actions are permitted in case of unlawful alienation. It may be that the property unlawfully alienated is claimed, or it may be that the alienators can prove that they have observed the prescribed formalities and wish to have their acts justified and declared legal. But the interest around which the prosecution circles is private, touching the persons only. Such a proceeding is called *contentious* or civil, in order to distinguish it from the following. For it may be that the person bringing a suit has at heart not private interests, but the public order or the welfare of the community. This happens when a crime, a *delictum publicum*, is committed, which may also affect a person, inasfar as he or she has suffered an injury by the perpetration of the crime. Yet the accusation is made against the perpetrator not for personal revenge, but for the sake of the vindication or restoration of the public order that was disturbed by the crime. This is called *criminal proceeding*. It now-a-days concerns almost exclusively the clergy, *i.e.*, persons who enjoy the *privilegium fori*, as explained under can. 120.

§ 2 of can. 1553 and can. 1554 mention matters subject to a *mixed court*, *i.e.*, matters in which the ecclesiastical as well as the secular judge are competent to render a verdict. Such matters, as far as the civil procedure is concerned, are: (a) *contracts made under oath*, as far as the carrying out of the contract, not the oath, is involved; (b) *cases of widows, orphans, and other destitute persons* allowed to choose the forum; (c) cases of *legacies* made by laymen partly in favor of pious institutions or foundations; (d) cases of *dowry, tithes, advowson,* provided the fact of temporal possession or the right of possession is involved.[9]

As to criminal procedure, the cases subject to a mixed court are mentioned under can. 1933, § 3.

In such cases, then, subject to a mixed court, the ecclesiastical judge, provided he is otherwise competent, may preoccupy the jurisdiction of the secular judge, and *vice versa*. If a *plaintiff* should, therefore, venture to bring suit before a secular court in a matter which has already been brought before an ecclesiastical court, he may be punished by the lawful ecclesiastical superior, if scandal was given or the importance of the case requires a punishment; and that punishment may be meted out without previous warning or threat.[10] Besides, such a plaintiff loses the right of bringing suit against the same person in the same matter or one connected with the matter at issue. Formerly excommunication was decreed for such who declined to accept the *forum ecclesiasticum* in mixed matters, and other punishments were inflicted on ecclesiastical persons of higher and lower dignity who attempted a change of forum.[11]

Can. 1555 sets forth, in general terms, the *method of procedure:* (a) for the *Holy Office,* which must proceed according to the norms prescribed and in the manner customary with that sacred tribunal; the same rules must be observed by the inferior tribunals of the Roman Court, if they are called upon to judge in matters pertaining to the Holy Office. This is especially the case in matters

---

[9] A damage or libel suit, especially among or against clerics, belongs to the criminal court according to can. 1935 and can. 1938. Yet what is stated in the text is perfectly true, for even injuries and libel suits, when directed against the clergy, affect the State as such.

[10] Cfr. Reiffenstuel, II, til. 2, n. 151 ff. Can. 2222.

[11] Martin V, "*Ad reprimendas insolentias,*" Feb. 1, 1428 (*Bull. Rom.,* ed. Luxemburg, I, 306 f.).

of faith and morals, the validity of holy orders, and the matrimonial cases arising from the Pauline privilege, disparity of worship and mixed religion, if the case is tried in a judiciary way.[12]

(b) For all *other tribunals* the following canons form the rule of procedure. This is particularly the case with the *S. Roman Rota* and the *Signatura Apostolica*, which are mentioned later (can. 1597–1605). In trials for the *dismissal of religious*, canons 654–668 must be observed.[13]

12 Cfr. *Normæ Peculiares*, P. II, c. VII, Art. 1, n. 6 (*A. Ap., S., I, 78 ff.*).

13 See this Commentary, Vol. III, p. 396 ff.

SECTION I

TRIALS IN GENERAL

TITLE I

THE FORUM COMPETENS

Every trial consists of two elementary parts, the persons concerned and the process or trial itself.

The persons chiefly concerned are the judge, who in the first title is comprised under the term competent court, the plaintiff, and the defendant.

Besides these, there are persons who assist these main actors in the trial. Then there is the process itself.

The Code premises a canon which is no doubt intended to preclude a false idea concerning the Supreme Head of the Church, as if he were subject to human judges.

EXEMPTION OF THE POPE

CAN. 1556

Prima Sedes a nemine iudicatur.

The *first or primatial see is subject to no one's judgment*. This proposition must be taken in the fullest extent, not only with regard to the object of infallibility. For in matters of faith and morals it was always customary to receive the final sentence from the Apostolic See, whose judgment no one dared to dispute, as the

tradition of the Fathers demonstrates.[1]   Neither was it
ever allowed to reconsider questions or controversies once
settled by the Holy See.[2]   But even the person of the
Supreme Pontiff was ever considered as unamenable to
human judgment, he being responsible and answerable to
God alone, even though accused of personal misdeeds and
crimes.   A remarkable instance is that of Pope Symmachus
(498–514).   He, indeed, submitted to the convocation of
a council (the *Synodus Palmaris,* 502), because he deemed
it his duty to see to it that no stain was inflicted upon his
character, but that synod itself is a splendid vindication
of our canon.   The synod adopted the Apology of En-
nodius of Pavia, in which occurs the noteworthy sentence:
" God wished the causes of other men to be decided by
men; but He has reserved to His own tribunal, without
question, the ruler of this see." [3]   No further argument
for the traditional view is required.   A general council
could not judge the Pope, because, unless convoked or
ratified by him, it could not render a valid sentence.
Hence nothing is left but an appeal to God, who will
take care of His Church and its head.

RESERVED COMPETENCY

CAN. 1557

§ 1. Ipsius Romani Pontificis dumtaxat ius est iudicandi:

1.° Eos qui supremum tenent populorum principatum horumque filios ac filias eosve quibus ius est
proxime succedendi in principatum;

1 Zozimus, " *Quamvis Patrum
traditio,*" March 21, 418 (Migne,
P. L., 20, 676).
2 Boniface I, " *Retro maioribus
tuis,*" March 11, 422 (*ibid.,* col.
776).

3 See c. 14, C. 11, q. 3; c. 10,
Dist. 96; cc. 10, 13, C. 9, q. 3;
Reuben Parsons, *Studies in Church
History,* ed. 2, 1901, Vol. I, p.
351 ff.

2.° Patres Cardinales;

3.° Legatos Sedis Apostolicae, et in criminalibus Episcopos, etiam titulares.

§ 2. Tribunalibus vero Sedis Apostolicae reservatur iudicare:

1.° Episcopos residentiales in contentiosis, salvo praescripto can. 1572, § 2;

2.° Dioeceses aliasve personas morales ecclesiasticas quae Superiorem infra Romanum Pontificem non habent, uti religiones exemptas, Congregationes monasticas, etc.

§ 3. Alias causas quas Romanus Pontifex ad suum advocaverit iudicium, videt iudex quem ipsemet Romanus Pontifex designaverit.

CAN. 1558

In causis de quibus in can. 1556, 1557, aliorum iudicum incompetentia est *absoluta*.

It has been an ancient custom for the Roman Pontiff to reserve certain cases (*causae maiores*) to his own *exclusive tribunal*. These are:

(a) The cases of actual *rulers* of nations, their sons and daughters, and proximate successors, provided, of course, their cases are brought before the Supreme Pontiff, as often happened when rulers still called themselves Christian;

(b) The cases, civil as well as criminal, of *cardinals*[4] and legates of the Apostolic See;

(c) The criminal cases of bishops, titular as well as residential.

To the *tribunals of the Apostolic See* are reserved:

4 A famous instance is the Caraffa trial under Pius IV; see R. Ancel, O.S.B., "Paul IV, et le Concile," Extract from la *Revue d'Histoire Ecclés.*, 1907.

(a) The civil cases of residential bishops, with the exception mentioned in can. 1572, § 2;

(b) All cases of dioceses and other exempt corporations immediately subject to the Roman Pontiff, such as exempt religious organizations and monastic congregations. If the Roman Pontiff calls other cases before his tribunal, that judge is competent whom he designates. This happened in the case of the English Ladies founded by Mary Ward.[5]

The cases mentioned (in can. 1156 and 1157) are so reserved that every other than the judge or tribunal mentioned is *absolutely excluded,* no preliminary hearing or taking cognizance of the case is permitted, and any attempted sentence would be *ipso iure* invalid. This is called *absolute incompetency,* because competency means nothing else but the jurisdiction proper to a judge, not only concerning the matter at issue (*ratione causae*), but also with regard to the person (*ratione personae*),[6] and where both are wanting, as under can. 1556 and 1557, the incompetency is complete in every respect.

ORDINARY AND EXTRAORDINARY FORUM

CAN. 1559

§ 1. Nemo in prima instantia conveniri potest, nisi coram iudice ecclesiastico qui competens sit ob unum ex titulis qui in can. 1560–1568 determinantur.

§ 2. Incompetentia iudicis cui nullus ex his titulis suffragatur, dicitur *relativa.*

§ 3. Actor sequitur forum rei; quod si reus multiplex forum habeat, optio fori actori conceditur.

---

5 See Bened. XIV, "*Quamvis iusto,*" April 30, 1749.

6 Wernz, *l. c.,* Vol. V, P. I, n. 275, p. 227.

Can. 1560

Forum necessarium habent:

1.° Actiones de spolio, coram Ordinario loci rei sitae;

2.° Causae respicientes beneficium, quamvis non residentiale, coram Ordinario loci beneficii;

3.° Causae quae versantur circa administrationem, coram Ordinario loci ubi administratio gesta est;

4.° Causae quae respiciunt hereditates aut legata pia, coram Ordinario loci domicilii testatoris, nisi agatur de mera exsecutione legati, quae videnda est secundum ordinarias competentiae normas.

Can. 1561

§ 1. Ratione domicilii vel quasi-domicilii quilibet conveniri potest coram Ordinario loci.

§ 2. Ordinarius autem domicilii vel quasi-domicilii iurisdictionem in subditum, quamvis absentem, habet.

Can. 1562

§ 1. Qui peregrinus est in Urbe, licet per breve tempus, potest in ipsa tanquam in proprio domicilio citari; sed ius habet revocandi domum, idest petendi ut ad proprium Ordinarium remittatur.

§ 2. Qui in Urbe ab anno commoratur, ius habet declinandi forum Ordinarii et instandi ut coram Urbis tribunalibus citetur.

Can. 1563

Vagus proprium forum habet in loco ubi actu commoratur; religiosus in loco domus suae.

CAN. 1564

Ratione rei sitae pars conveniri potest coram Ordinario loci, ubi res litigiosa sita est, quoties actio in rem directa sit.

CAN. 1565

§ 1. Ratione contractus pars conveniri potest coram Ordinario loci in quo contractus initus est vel adimpleri debet.

§ 2. In actu autem contractus permittitur contrahentibus, obligationis declarandae, urgendae vel implendae gratia, locum eligere, in quo etiam absentes citari et conveniri possint.

CAN. 1566

§ 1. Ratione delicti reus forum sortitur in loco patrati delicti.

§ 2. Licet post delictum reus e loco discesserit, iudex loci ius habet illum citandi ad comparendum, et sententiam in eum ferendi.

CAN. 1567

Ratione connexionis seu continentiae ab uno eodemque iudice cognoscendae sunt causae inter se connexae, nisi legis praescriptum obstet.

CAN. 1568

Ratione praeventionis, cum duo vel plures iudices aeque competentes sunt, ei ius est causam cognoscendi qui prius citatione reum legitime convenit.

Forum is a Latin word and formerly signified a place for giving judgment. The *forum* or *comitium* of the old Romans meant jurisdiction, or the power of passing judgment. *Competent* means proper jurisdiction over the person and case in question.

The *person* who determines the *forum competens* is the defendant, according to the well known adage: "*Actor sequitur reum*," *i.e.*, the plaintiff follows the defendant's court. However, this is to be understood as a rule which has its exceptions. For the Code itself makes exceptions in can. 1560, 1567, and 1568. Whilst, therefore, the principle "*actor sequitur reum*" constitutes the ordinary or *voluntary* forum, because it depends on the defendant's will, the other three mentioned in the three canons may be called *extraordinary* modes of following the forum, although even this distinction [7] is not quite adequate, since the law itself establishes these exceptions. The Code has a proper name only for one forum, which it calls *necessarium*, and hence the other six might be called voluntary *fora*.

Canon 1559 states that no one can be sued in the first instance (*instantia prima*) except before the ecclesiastical judge who is competent in virtue of one of the seven reasons stated in can. 1560–1568. If none of these seven titles justifies the judge in hearing the case, his *incompetency is relative*, because it may be that he would be competent by reason of the person being subject to his jurisdiction. Then the general rule is reaffirmed: *Actor sequitur forum rei*. But an exception is admitted in case the defendant is sued on various counts, which permit a choice of judges. This choice is left, not to the defendant, but to the plaintiff. Thus, if domicile and contract are in question, the plaintiff may choose either Ordinary.

---

[7] Wernz, *l. c.*, n. 259, according to customary teaching, distinguishes: *forum legale — conventionale; commune — singulare; universale — particulare; ordinarium — extraordinarium*.

Can. 1560 constitutes a *forum necessarium* in the following cases:

1.° All actions concerning forcible deprivation or *disseissin,* of which more under can. 1698, where the term *spolium* recurs;

2.° All cases touching *benefices,* even though non-residential, which must be decided before the Ordinary in whose diocese the benefice is located;

3.° All cases of *administration,* which must be tried before the Ordinary in whose diocese the administration was conducted;

4.° All cases in which *pious* bequests or legacies are involved, must be tried before the Ordinary in whose diocese the testator had his domicile, unless the question should turn about the mere execution of a legacy, when it may be settled according to one of the following reasons of competency.

By reason of *domicile* or *quasi-domicile,*[8] under can. 1561, anyone may be sued before the local Ordinary, who in this case also has jurisdiction over an absent subject. This court is the chief, ordinary, and natural forum for trying the defendant, even though he be absent from the diocese. If the plaintiff be absent, the summons suffices to render him in contempt in case he does not appear.[9]

This forum concurs with any other mentioned,[10] except, of course, the one spoken of in can. 1560.

A peculiar right is vindicated to the *City of Rome* as the "mother and teacher of all churches." As under the Decretals,[11] so now by our Code (can. 1562) a *peregrinus, i.e.,* any clergyman or layman who is in Rome, even though only for a short time, may be summoned there

---

8 Cfr. can. 91 ff., and our Comment., Vol. II, p. 14 ff.

9 Cfr. cc. 11, 17, 19, X, II, 2; c. 3, X, II, 14.

10 Santi-Leitner, II, tit. 2, n. 10; Smith, *Elements of Ecclesiastical Law,* Vol. II, p. 63.

11 C. 20, X, II, 2.

as if he were in his own domicile; and since a summons constitutes the beginning of a trial (can. 1725), it follows that the whole process may be finished there. However, the right of having the case pleaded at home remains, wherefore such a one may ask for leave to appear before his own Ordinary.

The *ius revocandi domum,* as the commentators say,[12] is not the same as that of declining the forum. The latter supposes that the judge is not competent, whilst in the case of *revocatio domum* the competency is admitted. Formerly the favor of *revocatio* was granted if the pilgrim came to Rome for a just and necessary reason, as stated in the Decretals. Our text has no such conditional clause, wherefore the old law must be looked upon as corrected in this case. We may, however, admit what the same writers say concerning two other conditions for making use of the *revocatio.* They deny the right if delay would be dangerous and if the *peregrinus* has committed a crime in the City of Rome. Our text adds a new regulation in § 2, can. 1562: One who has lived in Rome for one year, has the right (not the duty) to decline the forum of his own Ordinary and to demand that his case be tried before the tribunals of the City.

However, if we mistake not, the whole of canon 1562 must be understood in conformity with can. 1560, and hence the *privilegium urbis* cannot be applied. This seems to be deducible from the fact that the favor is subsumed under " domicile "; since this is not applicable in the cases mentioned in can. 1560, can. 1562 may not be alleged against can. 1560.

Those who have neither domicile nor quasi-domicile, *i.e., vagi,* are tried in the place where they happen to

12 Cfr. Reiffenstuel, II, 2, nn. 108 ff.

reside, "there and then," even if they had made up their mind to settle in another place.[13]

Religious are subject to the forum of the place in which their house is located (can. 1563). Religious who have made perpetual vows, lose their domicile;[14] but not those who have taken only temporary vows. However, in our case the quasi-domicile must be considered sufficient to establish the competent forum for all religious. If one would be dismissed or dispensed, and leave the religious house, he would regain his former domicile or quasi-domicile, and therefore the ecclesiastical court of the diocese in which he originally had a domicile or quasi-domicile, and not the court of the diocese in which the religious house is located, would be the *forum competens* for him.[15]

By reason of res sita (can. 1564) or location of the litigious object, one may be sued in any place where a real (not a personal) action is brought against him, on account of the object being permanently located in that place. The disputed object may be movable or immovable, in possession of the litigants or not, but whether it must be permanently situated there, not merely *in transitu*, is a disputed question.[16] Thus, for instance, if two bishops should get into a dispute over a bequest, that bishop's court would be competent in whose diocese the property was located.[17] But the text permits only a *real action, i.e.*, one against the thing itself, not against the person. Hence the judge who is competent by reason of the location of the disputed object may not proceed against the defendant by censures, or by declaring him contumacious; nor can he,

---

13 Reiffenstuel, II, 2, n. 45.
14 Can. 585.
15 Cfr. can. 641; S. C. EE. et RR., May 2, 1864 (*A. S. S.*, I, 365 f.).

16 Reiffenstuel, II, 2, n. 99 f. favors the opinion that *in transitu* is sufficient, nor is our text against that opinion.
17 C. 3, X, II, 2.

properly speaking, summon the defendant if the latter does not belong to his territory. But he may, in case of contempt, put the plaintiff in possession of the disputed object.[18]

By *reason of a contract* (can. 1565) one may be tried by the local Ordinary in whose diocese the contract was made, or must be fulfilled. A *contract,* as generally understood, is any agreement which involves the fulfillment of an obligation, including guardianship or tutorship.[19]

Since contracts are generally determined as to obligations and circumstances, the Code permits the contracting parties to state in the contract itself the *place* where the obligation is to be fulfilled or urged. This also determines the forum to which the absentee must be summoned and before which he must be sued.[20] If no stipulation was made as to the place where the contract is to be carried out, the place where it was made determines the forum. And consequently in such a case the laws of the respective diocese or province must be followed (can. 1529).

By *reason of crime* (can. 1566) one may be tried in the place where he committed the justiciable act, no matter whether it was grievous or not. The law only says: "*delictum*," *i.e.,* an external crime committed against the public order. The *whole* crime must have been perpetrated in the diocese whose Ordinary is thus rendered competent, but it is not necessary that the effects should have followed in the same diocese. If a cleric were shot in diocese A, and died in diocese B, the Ordinary of diocese A would be competent.[21]

All clerics of whatever condition or rank (laymen are now tried before the secular judge), except those men-

18 Wernz, *l. c.,* n. 289, p. 242, note 138.
19 Santi-Leitner, II, 2, n. 13.
20 C. 17, X; II, 2.
21 Wernz, *l. c.,* n. 290, p. 244.

tioned in can. 1556, are here comprised. Therefore also
exempt religious (see can. 616).

But what if the *perpetrator is at large, i.e.,* absent from
the territory where the crime was committed? § 2 of our
canon, for which no previous authority of law could be
alleged, rules that even in this case the local judge is entitled to summon the criminal and to pronounce sentence
on him.

By *reason of connection* (can. 1567) or contents one
and the same judge may take cognizance of cases which
have some connection with one other, unless the law
expressly prohibits this. This may happen:

(a) When one suit *depends* upon the settlement of another, as the principal may depend on an incidental question. Thus, a matrimonial case which involved an inheritance, if the validity of the marriage were concerned,
could not be decided by a lay judge, and therefore the
lay judge would be unable to take cognizance of the whole
case, even though he were competent to judge of the right
to the inheritance. The law (can. 1553, § 1, n. 1) prohibits him to be judge in spiritual matters and matters
connected therewith.[22] But if the question would only
be whether the person was born in or out of lawful wed-
lock, the lay judge would be competent in the whole affair.[23]

(b) A *connexio causarum* also exists when a general
action is brought, *i.e.,* one which implies several suits or
causes by reason of one's main office or quality, for instance, a tutor, guardian, or general manager may have
several suits on hand on account of his official capacity,
and hence may be called to court by various Ordinaries
and may plead before one and the same judge cases otherwise belonging to several courts.[24]

[22] Cc. 5, 7, 9, X, IV, 17; c. 3,
X, II, 10.

[23] Santi-Leitner, II, 2, n. 21.
[24] *Ibid.,* n. 22.

By *reason of prevention* (can. 1568) one of several
otherwise equally competent judges may be entitled to
take cognizance of a case, because he was the first to issue
a lawful summons to the defendant. Can. 1553, § 2,
dealt with the case of a mixed forum, when the ecclesiastical judge preoccupies the case by a legitimate summons. But it may also happen that a criminal who has
changed his domicile is summoned by the judge of the
former domicile or diocese; the judge who first issues
the summons is the competent one.[25] Finally, prevention
may take place when several judges are competent jointly
and severally (*in solidum*), for in this case *regula juris*
54 holds: " He has the better title who was prior in
time." [26] However the summons must have been served
legitimately, *i.e.*, according to the rules laid down in our
Code; [27] otherwise exception might be taken to the judge's
competency.

25 C. 19, X, II, 2.
26 C. 8, 6°, I, 14; Reiffenstuel,
II, 2, nn. 43, 166 ff.

27 See can. 1711-1725.

TITLE II

DIFFERENT STAGES AND SPECIES OF TRIBUNALS

CAN. 1569

§ 1. Ob primatum Romani Pontificis integrum est cuilibet fideli in toto orbe catholico causam suam sive contentiosam sive criminalem in quovis iudicii gradu et in quovis litis statu, cognoscendam ad Sanctam Sedem deferre vel apud eandem introducere.

§ 2. Recursus tamen ad Sedem Apostolicam interpositus non suspendit, excluso casu appellationis, exercitium iurisdictionis in iudice qui causam iam cognoscere coepit; quique idcirco poterit iudicium prosequi usque ad definitivam sententiam, nisi constiterit Sedem Apostolicam causam ad se advocasse.

Can. 1561 mentioned a prerogative of Rome. Another is set forth in the following canon, which embodies a principle that has been acknowledged since immemorial time, *viz.*, the right of *appeal to the Apostolic See* from any inferior tribunal and at any stage of a trial. The Council of Sardica (343) clearly stated this right,[1] and there is no need to recur to the Pseudo-Decretals.[2] The right of appealing to Rome was practised in every cen-

1 Cfr. c. 36, C. 2, q. 6; Hefele, *Konsilien-Geschichte*, I, 341, 541 ff.; Reuben Parsons, *Studies in Church History*, 1901, I, p. 209 ff.
2 See cc. 4–8, C. 2, q. 6.

24

tury and in various and distant provinces, and the Feb-
rorian synod or meeting of Ems was probably the first
to demand that Rome should reject and abolish appeals.[3]
The right of accepting and deciding appeals rests on the
primacy of the Roman Pontiff,[4] and is coextensive with
his legislative and judiciary power. Hence our Code vindicates this right to the Holy See, to which any civil or
criminal case may be appealed in any stage or instance
and from any phase a trial may have taken in any part
of the Catholic universe.[5]

§ 2 of this canon says that *recourse* to the Apostolic See
does not suspend the exercise of the jurisdiction of the
ordinary or delegated judge, who has commenced a trial
by issuing the lawful summons. Suspension of jurisdiction is attached only to an *appeal* properly so-called.
Hence in case of mere recourse, the judge-in-ordinary
may proceed with the trial and pronounce final sentence,
unless he has been duly informed that the Apostolic See
has called the case before its own court. The difference
between appeal and recourse is explained in can. 1889.
For an apparent exception as to parishes and benefices
see can. 2146.

CAN. 1570

ORDINARY TRIBUNALS

§ 1. Exceptis causis Sedi Apostolicae reservatis aut
ad eandem advocatis, ceterae omnes cognoscuntur a
diversis tribunalibus, de quibus in can. 1572 seqq.

§ 2. Quodlibet tamen tribunal, quod attinet ad

---

[3] Pius VI, "*Super soliditate*," Nov. 28, 1786, § 4.

[4] *Conc. Vatic.*, Sess. IV, c. 3, *De vi et ratione primatus*.

[5] *Gradus* means stage or instance, as we say, "first or second in-

stance"; *status* implies the condition or status in which the trial
happens to be, for instance, after
the summons, before the closing of
the acts, after the interlocutory or
definitive sentence, etc.

partium et testium examen aut citationem, documentorum, vel rei controversae inspectionem, decretorum intimationem aliaque huiusmodi, ius habet in
auxilium vocandi aliud tribunal, quod normas pro
singulis actibus iure praescriptas servare debet.

CAN. 1571

Qui causam vidit in uno iudicii gradu, nequit eandem
causam in alio iudicare.

With the exception of the cases reserved to, or called
before the Apostolic See, *i.e.*, the *causae maiores*, which
are such either by reason of the matter involved or of
the persons concerned, all other cases are tried by the
several tribunals mentioned below (can. 1572 sqq).

Causae maiores are also excluded from the S. Roman
Rota and the Signatura Apostolica.[6]

Now these regular or ordinary tribunals may find it
difficult to examine or summon the parties and witnesses,
to obtain and examine the necessary papers, to notify
the decrees, and so forth, because the parties and witnesses may live in distant and separate dioceses, or even
in countries with which communication is difficult. This
happens especially in matrimonial trials.[7] What is to be
done in such cases? The Code rules that in such cases
the tribunal which is in a condition to furnish the necessary information or to procure the legal procedure, *must
assist* the tribunal which tries the case. Of course, the
court thus called upon to assist is held to obey the legal
norms prescribed in the Code.

This applies also to the *S. Romana Rota*. If the party

---

6 Pius X, "*Sapienti consilio*,"
June 29, 1908 (*A. Ap. S.*, I, 15);
Lex Propria S. R. R., can. 15
(*ibid.*, p. 24).

7 S. C. EE. et RR., June 11,
1880, n. 19; S. C. P. F., 1883, n.
XIX (*Coll.*, nn. 1534, 1586).

is not present in Rome and has no procurator there, the diocesan court may be told to assist the S. Tribunal, which issues either a letter — which is a mild form of command — or a decree to the Ordinary in question to supply the processual acts.[8] Sometimes a *iudex instructor* is selected from outside the *Curia* (sc. *Romana*), who has to gather the proofs from witnesses, experts, and documents. This is done by a letter called *litterae rogatoriae seu remissoriae*. Such letters are also sent to diocesan courts when the litigants reside outside of Rome and cannot be easily summoned.[9] It is evident that the diocesan courts are obliged to give information and to proceed according to judicial rules, for otherwise the parties might escape by making exceptions which would draw out the trial indefinitely.

The *iudex instructor,* as assistant of another court than the trial court proper, must not be confounded with the court of appeal, or court of second instance, because no sentence is given by the assisting court. Only if a case has been decided by a court in one stage or instance, the same case can not be decided again by the same court in another stage (can. 1571), because an appeal requires two different courts, one lower and the other higher.[10]

8 Cfr. *Regulae* S. R. R., Aug. 4, 1910, c. 14 (*A Ap. S.*, II, 788).

9 *Ibid.*, can. 106, can. 143 (*l. c.*, p. 818, 827).

10 Cfr. c. 35, X, II, 28. *Iudex instructor* is not easily translated into English, although it has been rendered "judge of inquiry," according to the Italian "*giudice istruttore*." However, the very term *judge* seems to convey too much, as if a sentence were implied; but as the Latin also uses the term *iudex* it may be accepted, although *auditor* would perhaps be better; cfr. Messmer, *l. c.*, p. 53.

CHAPTER I

THE ORDINARY TRIBUNAL OF THE FIRST INSTANCE

Art. I

THE JUDGE

Can. 1572

THE LOCAL ORDINARY

§ 1. In unaquaque dioecesi et pro omnibus causis a iure expresse non exceptis, iudex primae instantiae est loci Ordinarius, qui iudiciariam potestatem exercere potest ipse per se, vel per alios, secundum tamen canones qui sequuntur.

§ 2. Si vero agatur de iuribus aut bonis temporalibus Episcopi aut mensae vel Curiae dioecesanae, controversia dirimenda deferatur vel, Episcopo consentiente, ad dioecesanum tribunal collegiale quod constat officiali et duobus iudicibus synodalibus antiquioribus, vel ad iudicem immediate superiorem.

Aside from the cases excepted by law, *i.e.*, those expressly mentioned in can. 1556 and 1557 and those assumed or accepted by the Apostolic See (can. 1570, § 1), all cases must be tried by the *local Ordinary,* who may exercise his power personally or by proxy, but must invariably proceed according to the rules laid down in the following canons. This is the law, new as well as old,[1]

1 C. 1, X, I, 31; *Trid.,* Sess. 24, c. 20, *de ref.*

for every diocese. *Exempt religious,* of course, are bound to this tribunal only in cases expressed by law (can. 616); otherwise their competent judge is the respective superior (can. 1579).

If a case concerns the *rights or temporal property of the bishop,* of the *episcopal mensa* (revenues), or of *the diocesan court,* it may, with the consent of the bishop, be tried in a body by the diocesan tribunal, consisting of the official and two senior synodal judges, or it may be brought before the court of the immediate superior.

The *antiquiores* are those longest in office, and the immediate superior would be the metropolitan. If the latter is a party to the trial, the immediate superior is the Delegate Apostolic, provided his instructions give him that power; otherwise, Rome.

CAN. 1573

THE OFFICIAL

§ 1. Quilibet Episcopus tenetur officialem eligere cum potestate ordinaria iudicandi, a Vicario Generali distinctum, nisi parvitas dioecesis aut paucitas negotiorum suadeat hoc officium ipsi Vicario Generali committi.

§ 2. Officialis unum constituit tribunal cum Episcopo loci: sed nequit iudicare causas quas Episcopus sibi reservat.

§ 3. Officiali dari possunt adiutores, quibus nomen est vice-officialium.

§ 4. Tum officialis tum vice-officiales esse debent sacerdotes, integrae famae, in iure canonico doctores vel ceteroqui periti, annos nati non minus triginta.

§ 5. Sunt amovibiles ad nutum Episcopi; vacante sede a munere non cessant, nec a Vicario Capitulari amoveri possunt; adveniente autem novo Episcopo, indigent confirmatione.

§ 6. Qui Vicarius Generalis est idemque officialis, sede vacante, cessat quidem a Vicarii, non autem ab officialis munere.

§ 7. Si officialis eligatur in Vicarium Capitularem, ipse novum nominat officialem.

Our text insists upon the appointment of a diocesan *officialis*. This official is first mentioned in the Decretals[2] of Boniface VIII, whence we may conclude that the office was introduced after 1234. The *officialis* was, appointed or commissioned by the bishop, and his office was ordinary, though limited. Later it appears to have been absorbed by that of the vicar-general. Now the Code rules that *every bishop is obliged to choose an official* with ordinary judiciary power. This office is distinct from that of the vicar-general. Only in case the diocese is small and there is not much business, may the bishop entrust the vicar-general with this office. How small or how large a diocese should be to require an *officialis,* is difficult to say; it depends upon the territorial extent as well as upon the number of the Catholic people and clergy residing there.

The tribunal of the *officialis* and the bishop form but *one* tribunal. Consequently no appeal is possible from the one to the other, or *vice versa*. Besides, the *officialis cannot render judgment in cases* which the bishop has *reserved to himself*. There is no doubt some similarity between the offices of the vicar-general and the *officialis;* but there is also a difference, for the bishop cannot lawfully curtail the power of the vicar-general beyond the

---

[2] C. 2, 6°, I, 14. His *cognitio causarum* was general; but the *potestas inquirendi, corrigendi aut* *puniendi* was denied him; neither could he decree any removal from benefice, office, or administration

cases mentioned in law, whilst the power of the *officialis* is entirely subject to the good pleasure of the bishop. Of course, the bishop has to make it clear which cases he has reserved to himself; otherwise the *officialis* may proceed, because his power is ordinary.

The *officialis* may be given *assistants*, but their power is not ordinary, nor must they be looked upon as quasi-judges *in solidum*. At least this seems to us a natural assumption because otherwise there would hardly be any unity of government.

The *officialis* as well as the *vice-officialis* must be *priests* in good standing, doctors in canon law or otherwise experienced, and at least thirty years of age. They are *removable* at the bishop's pleasure. Their office does not cease during the vacancy of the episcopal see, nor may they be removed by the vicar-capitular (administrator). But they need ratification by the new bishop.

If the offices of vicar-general and *officialis* are held by one person, the office of vicar-general, but not that of *officialis*, ceases when the episcopal see becomes vacant. If the *officialis* is elected vicar-capitular (administrator), he shall appoint another *officialis*.

SYNODAL JUDGES AND COUNSELORS

CAN. 1574

§ 1. In qualibet dioecesi presbyteri probatae vitae et in iure canonico periti, etsi extradioecesani, non plures quam duodecim eligantur ut potestate ab Episcopo delegata in litibus iudicandis partem habeant; quibus nomen esto *iudicum synodalium* aut *pro-synodalium*, si extra Synodum constituuntur.

§ 2. Quod ad eorum electionem, substitutionem,

cessationem aut remotionem a munere attinet,
serventur praescripta can. 385-388.

§ 3. Nomine iudicum synodalium in iure veniunt
quoque iudices pro-synodales.

CAN. 1575

Unicus iudex in quolibet iudicio duos assessores con-
sulentes sibi adsciscere potest; quos tamen ex
iudicibus synodalibus eligere debet.

Among ecclesiastical persons were mentioned synodal
judges, whose election, removal from office, etc., was described in can. 385-388.[3]   The Code now rules that such
judges, elected either at, or outside of a synod, should
be not more than twelve in number for *every diocese*.
They must be *priests* of approved morals and experts in
canon law.   They may be chosen from another diocese
if, to use a colloquial expression, the necessary " timber "
is not to be found in the diocese itself.   Their office is
delegated by the bishop, by virtue of which fact they may
assist in handling ecclesiastical trials.

No discrimination is made between synodal and pro-
synodal judges because in law the latter are regarded as
synodal judges pure and simple.   One of their prerogatives consists in being assumed as *counselors* by the judge,
who is entitled to select two of them in every trial (can.
1575).   This is the rule inculcated by the Council of
Trent; but in course of time it seems that protonotaries
non participantes were often elected to the detriment of
the synodal judges.   Benedict XIV restored the Tridentine enactment by admonishing the patriarchs, primates,
archbishops, and bishops to entrust the synodal judges
with ecclesiastical trials.   Their number was to be in

---

3 Cfr. Vol. II of our *Commentary*, p. 418 ff.

proportion to the size and importance of the diocese, but no less than four, priests of knowledge and proved ability, should be chosen for each.[4]

COLLEGIATE BOARD OF JUDGES

CAN. 1576

§ 1. Reprobata contraria consuetudine et revocato quolibet contrario privilegio:

1.° Causae contentiosae de vinculo sacrae ordinationis, et matrimonii, vel de iuribus aut bonis temporalibus cathedralis ecclesiae; itemque criminales in quibus res est de privatione beneficii inamovibilis aut de irroganda vel declaranda excommunicatione, tribunali collegiali trium iudicum reservantur;

2.° Causae vero quibus agitur de delictis quae depositionis, privationis perpetuae habitus ecclesiastici, vel degradationis poenam important, reservantur tribunali quinque iudicum.

§ 2. Loci Ordinarius tribunali collegiali trium vel quinque iudicum cognitionem committere potest etiam aliarum causarum, idque praesertim faciat quando de causis agitur quae, attentis temporis, loci et personarum adiunctis et materia iudicii, difficiliores et maioris momenti videantur.

§ 3. Duo vel quatuor iudices qui una cum praeside tribunal collegiale constituunt, inter iudices synodales Ordinarius, nisi pro sua prudentia aliter opportunum existimaverit, eligat per turnum.

CAN. 1577

§ 1. Tribunal collegiale collegialiter procedere debet, et ad maiorem suffragiorum partem sententias ferre.

4 "*Quamvis paternae*," Aug. 16, 1741.

§ 2 Eidem praeest officialis vel vice-officialis, cuius est processum dirigere et decernere quae pro iustitiae administratione in causa quae agitur necessaria sunt.

CAN. 1578

Exceptis causis de quibus in can. 1572, § 2, Episcopus semper potest tribunali ipse per se praeesse; sed valde expedit ut causas, praesertim criminales et contentiosas gravis momenti, iudicandas relinquat tribunali ordinario, cui praesit officialis vel vice-officialis.

Canon 1576 concerns a modern [5] institution which the legislator prudently and seriously demands to be set up in every diocese. How seriously he wishes to be taken here may be judged from the very first clause, declaring " every *contrary custom* is *reprobated* and every *contrary privilege is revoked.*" This institution is a *collegiate board of judges,* consisting either of three or five ecclesiastics, who form, not a corporation, but what was formerly called a society or college, and hence go by the name of *collegiate tribunal;* they must meet in a body and all be present at the same time.

§ 1 rules that to a *board of three judges* are reserved the following cases: (a) civil or *contentious* causes turning about the bond of sacred ordination (*vinculum s. ordinationis,* see can. 1993), the marriage tie (not mere separation), and the rights and property of the cathedral church; (b) *criminal* cases which concern privation of an irremovable benefice, which we believe must also be applied to the case of privation (not the mere removal) of an irremovable pastor; or which concern infliction or dec-

---

[5] If we say *modern,* we mean in the sense of an ordinary stable tribunal; for several delegated judges are mentioned more than once in the Decretals; c. 13, X, I, 3; c. 21, 22, 34, X, I, 29.

laration of excommunication, which may also touch laymen.[6]

To a *board of five judges* are reserved all criminal cases which involve the penalty of deposition, of perpetual privation of the ecclesiastical habit, or of degradation.

§ 2 permits the Ordinary to entrust the collegiate tribunal of three or five also with the cognizance of other cases, especially such as are more difficult and important by reason of circumstances of time, place, or person, or of the matter involved, for instance, in a mixed marriage when satisfaction is to be decided and the persons concerned are of high social standing. The same rule may be applied to clerics who hold important offices and to tendencies which are peculiar to a whole province or generation.

§ 3 commands the Ordinary to choose the two or four judges who constitute the collegiate tribunal together with the president, who is no one else than the diocesan *officialis*, in turn, from among the *synodal judges*, as, for instance, is done by the Roman Rota, where three proceed *per turnum*. The *turnus* may be taken either by seniority, or one senior and one junior, etc. But the Ordinary may depart from this rule if he deems it advisable, and select ecclesiastics who are not synodal judges.

Can. 1577 determines the *mode of procedure* to be followed by the board of judges. They must proceed *collegialiter, i. e.,* in a body, and give sentence by majority vote. Thus, if there are three judges, including the *officialis*, there must be two votes cast either for or against a sentence; if five judges vote, at least three votes are required to pronounce either an interlocutory or definitive sentence.[7]

---

[6] The text draws no distinction between different kinds of excommunication.

[7] *Lex propria S. R. R.,* April,

1908, can. 31, § 5; *Regulae S. R. R.,* Aug. 4, 1910, § 176 (*A. Ap S.,* I, p. 28; II, 834).

We said, "including the *officialis*," for § 2 of can. 1577 rules that the *officialis* or *vice-officialis* is the *president* of the tribunal, whose duty it is to direct the trial and decree what is required for administering justice in the case. Of course he must follow the general rules prescribed by the Code. But, like any other judge, he may follow the dictates of reason as long as these do not clash with the essentials of justice.

Although the *officialis* or *vice-officialis* is *ex officio* the president of the trial, the *bishop* himself may preside, and, of course, also vote when a sentence is to be pronounced. However, since no one should be judge in his own case the bishop is precluded from presiding in all matters concerning himself or his diocesan court, according to can. 1572, § 2. Besides, according to canon 1578, it is highly advisable, that he leave the decision of criminal and contentious (civil) cases, especially those of importance and consequence, to the ordinary tribunal presided over by the official or vice-official, lest he incur an odium which might impair his authority.

Can. 1579

§ 1. Si controversia sit inter religiosos exemptos eiusdem religionis clericalis, iudex primae instantiae, nisi aliud in constitutionibus caveatur, est Superior provincialis, aut, si monasterium sit sui iuris, Abbas localis.

§ 2. Salvo diverso constitutionum praescripto, si res contentiosa agatur inter duas provincias, in prima instantia iudicabit ipse per se vel per delegatum supremus religionis Moderator; si inter duo monasteria, supremus Moderator Congregationis monasticae.

§ 3. Si demum controversia enascatur inter religiosas personas physicas vel morales diversae religionis, aut etiam inter religiosos eiusdem religionis non exemptae vel laicalis, aut inter religiosum et clericum saecularem vel laicum, iudex primae instantiae est Ordinarius loci.

If a dispute arises between *individual* exempt religious of the same order or congregation, the judge of the first instance is the *provincial,* or the abbot of an autonomous monastery, provided the respective constitutions do not ordain otherwise.

Unless the respective constitutions provide some other mode, a civil case pending between *two provinces* must be tried, in the first stage, before the superior general or his delegate; or before the abbot president of monastic congregations if the controversy is between two autonomous monasteries. If a quarrel arises either between individual religious, or between religious corporations of different congregations or orders, or between individual religious of non-exempt congregations or lay institutes, or between religious and secular clerics or laymen, the judge in the first instance is the *local Ordinary.* The last-named case, of course, supposes that both litigants are in the same diocese. If they are not in the same diocese, the other rules of competency are to be followed, *viz.,* those mentioned under can. 1564–1568 (location of the litigious object, contract, crime, etc.).

ARTICLE II

AUDITORS AND REFEREES

CAN. 1580

§ 1. Potest Ordinarius unum aut plures auditores, seu actorum instructores, sive stabiliter sive pro certa aliqua causa constituere.

§ 2. Iudex auditorem eligere potest tantummodo pro causa quam cognoscit, nisi Ordinarius iam providerit.

CAN. 1581

Auditores pro tribunali dioecesano, quantum fieri potest, deligantur ex iudicibus synodalibus; pro tribunali vero religiosorum deligendi semper sunt ex alumnis eiusdem religionis ad normam constitutionum.

CAN. 1582

Eorum est testes citare et audire, aliaque acta iudicialia instruere secundum tenorem mandati, non autem sententiam definitivam ferre.

CAN. 1583

Auditor in quovis litis momento ab officio removeri potest ab eo qui eundem elegit, iusta tamen de causa, et citra partium praeiudicium.

CAN. 1584

Tribunalis collegialis praeses debet unum de iudicibus collegii ponentem seu relatorem designare qui in coetu iudicum de causa referat et sententias in scriptis redigat; et ipsi idem praeses potest alium ex iusta causa substituere.

Auditor [8] in our text means one who prepares the acts of a trial (drafter or draftsman). He is therefore also called *instructor actorum*. Such a one, or more than one, may be appointed by the Ordinary either permanently or for any special case. But a judge may choose an auditor only for a trial which he himself conducts, unless the Ordinary has appointed one for the same case, in which hypothesis the judge has to accept the auditor appointed by the Ordinary (can. 1580).

Auditors for the diocesan court should, if possible, be taken from among the synodal judges. For tribunals of religious, members of the respective institute should be selected (can. 1581). Auditors play a conspicuous part in the Decretals. They were generally appointed by the Pope upon the demand, or at least petition, of the parties. They had to "hear" (from *audire*), to examine, to take cognizance of the matters entrusted to them, and take down in writing what seemed important. Besides, they were obliged to report minutely and conscientiously to the Pope, which act was designated by the Latin term "*referre*." [9] But they seldom or never pronounced judgment. This right was given them only after they had been established as a regular college, under the name of Rota.

Can. 1582 defines the duties of auditors. Their *office* consists in summoning and hearing witnesses, in preparing the judiciary acts or documents according to the tenor or wording of their commission or mandate. An auditor may also be called upon to draw up a *restrictus* or summary of the acts.[10] But he is never allowed to pronounce a final sentence.

---

[8] *Auditor* is sometimes taken as identical with *index instructor* or judge of inquiry; cfr., Messmer, *Canonical Procedure*, 1897, p. 53.

[9] Cfr. c. 3, X, II, 12; c. 15, X, II, 13; c. 3, X, III, 27; c. 18, X, III, 5; 16, 21, X, I, 6; c. 23, X, I, 29; c. 4, X, II, 12; Phillips, *K.-R.*, 1864, Vol. VI, p. 467 f.

[10] S. C. EE. et RR., June 11, 1880, n. 29 (*Coll. P. F.*, n. 1534).

Can. 1583 permits the judge to remove the auditor at any moment of the trial, provided he has a plausible reason for so doing, and the parties suffer no disadvantage.

Besides the auditor, a referee or *ponens*, taken from the board of judges, is appointed by the president. This official must report to the judges on the process of the trial and write down the sentence. This is generally given in the form of an answer to a query, e. g.: *"Utrum constet de nullitate matrimonii? Resp. Affirmative* (or *negative*, as the case may be). If the judge who is appointed as *ponens*, wishes to decline the honor (or burden), he may do so, but he should have at least the semblance of a good reason,[11] in which case the president may substitute one of the other judges to act as *ponens*.

ARTICLE III

NOTARY, PROSECUTING ATTORNEY, DEFENSOR VINCULI

At every process or trial there must be present a *notary*, who at the same time acts as secretary. No papers or acts are valid unless written, or at least signed, by him. This latter clause permits the use of a typewriter. A rubber stamp is not admissible for the signature.

The notary must take down in writing the depositions of the witnesses who are present, as well as the answers sent in from other courts, which were asked for by the *litterae rogatoriae*.[12]

The notary must be chosen by the judge, before the trial begins, from among the notaries lawfully engaged in practice — in Rome they have to undergo an examination and are formally admitted to practice — unless the Ordinary has specially appointed one for the case.

11 *Regulae S. R. R.*, Aug. 4, 1910, § 179; § 9 (*A. Ap. S.*, II, 835, 785).   12 *Ibid.*, § 114; § 144 (*l. c.*, p. 821, 827).

PROMOTOR IUSTITIAE AND DEFENSOR VINCULI

CAN. 1586

Constituatur in dioecesi *promotor iustitiae* et *defensor vinculi;* ille pro causis, tum contentiosis in quibus bonum publicum, Ordinarii iudicio, in discrimen vocari potest, tum criminalibus; iste pro causis, in quibus agitur de vinculo sacrae ordinationis aut matrimonii.

CAN. 1587

§ 1. In causis in quibus eorum praesentia requiritur, promotore iustitiae aut vinculi defensore non citato, acta irrita sunt, nisi ipsi, etsi non citati, revera interfuerint.

§ 2. Si legitime citati aliquibus actibus non interfuerint, acta quidem valent, verum postea eorum examini subiicienda omnino sunt ut ea omnia sive voce sive scriptis possint animadvertere et proponere quae necessaria aut opportuna iudicaverint.

CAN. 1588

§1. Eadem persona officium promotoris iustitiae et defensoris vinculi gerere potest, nisi multiplicitas negotiorum et causarum id prohibeat.

§ 2. Promotor et defensor constitui possunt tum ad universitatem causarum tum pro singulis causis.

CAN. 1589

§ 1. Ordinarii est promotorem iustitiae et vinculi defensorem eligere, qui sint sacerdotes integrae famae, in iure canonico doctores vel ceteroqui periti, ac prudentiae et iustitiae zelo probati.

§ 2. In tribunali religiosorum promotor iustitiae sit praeterea eiusdem religionis alumnus.

CAN. 1590

§ 1. Promotor iustitiae et vinculi defensor electi ad universitatem causarum a munere non cessant, sede episcopali vacante, nec a Vicario Capitulari possunt removeri; adveniente autem novo Praelato, indigent confirmatione.

§ 2. Iusta tamen intercedente causa, Episcopus eos removere potest.

Each diocese should have its *prosecuting attorney* and its *defensor vinculi.*

Benedict XIV, in his well-known constitution, "*Dei miseratione,*" Nov. 3, 1741, decreed *ex plenitudine potestatis,* that each and every diocese, no matter how small or how large, should have a defender of the marriage bond. To this task is now added another, *viz.,* that of defending the bond of sacred ordination, which forms, as it were, a spiritual tie between the clergyman in higher orders (*i. e.,* from subdeaconship upward) and the diocese to which he belongs.

The *prosecuting attorney (promotor iustitiae)* is appointed for civil cases which, though perhaps of a private nature, may, in the Ordinary's view, concern the welfare of the diocese or the public welfare (*bonum publicum*). Thus, for instance, a quarrel between two clergymen about the possession of a benefice or office may scandalize the whole diocese.

The *promotor iustitiae* also functions in *criminal cases* which, as already stated, almost exclusively concern clergymen.

If these two officials are not summoned to trials which

require their presence, all the *acts are null and void,* unless
the officials in question were actually present, even though
not summoned. Hence *actual presence* is required, not a
summons. In civil matters the *promotor iustitiae* may be
summoned by the *instructor processus,* but his absence
would not invalidate the proceedings, whereas in criminal
cases his presence is absolutely required. The presence
of the *defensor vinculi* is indispensable in all trials concerning the marriage bond or the validity of ordination.[13]

However, if the promoter and the defender were not
present, though summoned, at one or the other hearing,
the validity of the proceedings is not impaired, but these
officials may inspect the minutes afterwards, in order to
make, either orally or in writing, such remarks as they
may deem necessary or opportune.

One and the same person may be promoter and defender, unless a multiplicity of affairs and cases prevents,
as may happen in large dioceses, or when cases are tried
by several courts, or in different places at the same time.

The offices of promoter and defender may be held for
all cases that may arise (*ad universitatem causarum*) or
one may be appointed for each individual case (can.
1588). Those elected for all cases do not lose their office
during the vacancy of the episcopal see, nor may they be
removed by the vicar-capitular; they need, however, the
approval of the new prelate. Besides, the bishop may remove them from office for any just cause (can. 1590).
This rule Benedict XIV established concerning the *defensor.*[14] The same Pontiff also described the *qualities*
which a *defensor* should have. The Code is even more
explicit and, besides, strictly requires the priestly character. The promoters and defenders, therefore, should be

13 *Regulae S. R. R.,* Aug. 4,   14 "*Dei miseratione,*" Nov. 3,
1910 (*A. Ap. S.,* II, 819).   1741, § 5.

priests in good standing, doctors in canon law or at least able canonists, of tried prudence and justice.

In trials of religious the promoter must moreover be a member of the same institute.

ARTICLE IV

BEADLES AND COURIERS

CAN. 1591

§ 1. Ad acta iudicialia intimanda, nisi alia sit probata tribunalis consuetudo, constituantur cursores sive pro omnibus causis sive pro causa peculiari; item apparitores ad sententias ac decreta iudicis, eo committente, exsecutioni mandanda.

§ 2. Eadem persona utroque officio defungi potest.

CAN. 1592

Laici ipsi sint, nisi prudentia in aliqua causa suadeat ut eccclesiastici ad id muneris assumantur; quod vero ad eorum nominationem, suspensionem et revocationem attinet, eaedem serventur regulae quae pro notariis can. 373 statutae sunt.

CAN. 1593

Acta quae hi confecerint, publicam fidem faciunt.

Couriers (*cursores*) were formerly employed by the Apostolic Chancery to affix papal bulls on four well-known public places in Rome, namely, St. Peter's, the Lateran, the Apostolic Chancery, and the Campo de' Fiori. This act constituted official promulgation.[15] The Code

---

15 *Ibid.*, § 17.

wants them to be appointed either as regular employees of diocesan courts, or for individual cases, unless the respective diocese or tribunal observes some other satisfactory custom. These couriers have the duty of communicating the judiciary proceedings or acts, of serving summonses, etc.

The *apparitores* (beadles, constables) are employed to carry out the sentences and decrees of the court. The two offices named in this canon may be held by one and the same person. The acts of *cursores* and *apparitores* are official and must be so accepted by the public (can. 1593).

As a rule these offices should be given to *laymen;* but if prudence demands that in some particular case an ecclesiastic be entrusted with such a mission, it may be done. They are appointed, suspended, or removed like notaries.[16]

16 See can. 373.

CHAPTER II

CAN. 1594

§ 1. A tribunali Episcopi Suffraganei appellatur ad Metropolitam.

§ 2. A causis in prima instantia pertractatis coram Metropolita fit appellatio ad loci Ordinarium, quem ipse Metropolita, probante Sede Apostolica, semel pro semper designaverit.

§ 3. Pro causis primum agitatis coram Archiepiscopo qui caret Suffraganeis vel coram loci Ordinario immediate Sedi Apostolicae subiecto, fit appellatio ad Metropolitam, de quo in can. 285.

§ 4. Inter religiosos exemptos, pro omnibus causis coram Superiore provinciali actis tribunal secundae instantiae est penes supremum Moderatorem; pro causis actis coram Abbate locali, penes supremum Moderatorem Congregationis monasticae; pro causis vero de quibus in can. 1579, § 3, servetur praescriptum §§ 1, 2, 3 huius canonis.

CAN. 1595

Tribunal appellationis eodem modo quo tribunal primae instantiae constitui debet; et eaedem regulae, accommodatae ad rem, in causae discussione servandae sunt.

CAN. 1596

Si collegialiter causa in prima instantia cognita fuerit, etiam in gradu appellationis collegialiter nec a minore iudicum numero definiri debet.

Appeal from the court of a suffragan bishop lies to the metropolitan. If a case was tried in the first instance by the metropolitan court, appeal lies to the court of that local Ordinary whom the metropolitan, with the approval of the Holy See, has chosen once for all as court of appeal.[1] Can. 285 insists that archbishops who have no suffragans, and Ordinaries (including prelates or abbots *nullius* who are immediately subject to the Apostolic See) must choose the nearest metropolitan (*viciniorem metropolitam*) for conciliar or synodal purposes. This same nearest metropolitan is the court of appeals from the archbishops and Ordinaries, as mentioned above.

For *exempt religious* the second instance, in all cases tried by the provincial, is the superior general and in cases tried by the local abbot, the abbot president. For cases mentioned under can. 1579, § 3, the competent tribunal of appeal is the metropolitan or the suffragan approved by the Apostolic See, or the nearest metropolitan, also approved by the same Holy See. It depends on whether the local Ordinary has a metropolitan, or whether the case was tried by the metropolitan in the first stage, or whether the archbishop or Ordinary had to choose the nearest metropolitan.

The court of appeal must be established in the same fashion as the court of the first instance; hence the collegiate board with the official and vice-official must be constituted also in courts of appeal, and the same rules

---

[1] In the *Acta Ap. Sedis* there are now being published many such approvals.

proportionately must be observed in the proceedings. If the case was tried *collegialiter* by the first court, it must be tried *collegialiter* also by the court of appeal; if three judges functioned in the lower court, three must act in the court of appeal; if five in the first, also five in the second instance.

CHAPTER III

CAN. 1597

Romanus Pontifex pro toto orbe catholico ad norman can. 1569 iudex est supremus, qui vel ipse per se ius dicit, vel per tribunalia ab ipso constituta, vel per iudices a se delegatos.

On the history of the *S. Romana Rota* enough has been said elsewhere.[1] That Pius X has restored its ancient splendor, no canonist will regret. As to the *Signatura Apostolica* something will be said in Art. II, *infra*.

Although these two tribunals are constituted in *foro externo,* or for judiciary matter proper, it must be understood that the Roman Pontiff has not thereby unreservedly committed himself to them. He remains the supreme judge in all matters, especially of appeal, as laid down in can. 1569. Hence, instead of leaving a case to these tribunals, he may pronounce judgment himself or entrust trial to delegated judges, who then act in his name, according to can. 199, §§ 1, 2. However, as a rule, all affairs which do not belong to the class of *causae maiores,* are entrusted to the two ordinary tribunals.

1 Cfr. Vol. II, p. 267 f. of our *Commentary.*

Art. I

THE SACRA ROTA ROMANA

Can. 1598

§ 1. Tribunal ordinarium a Sancta Sede constitutum pro appellationibus recipiendis est Sacra Rota Romana, quae est tribunal collegiale constans certo Auditorum numero cui praesidet Decanus, qui primus est inter pares.

§ 2. Ii sacerdotes esse debent laurea doctorali in utroque saltem iure praediti.

§ 3. Auditorum electio Romano Pontifici reservatur.

§ 4. Sacra Rota ius dicit aut per singulos turnos trium Auditorum, aut videntibus omnibus, nisi aliter pro aliqua causa Summus Pontifex constituat.

Can. 1599.

§ 1. Sacra Rota iudicat:

1.° In secunda instantia causas quae a quorumvis Ordinariorum tribunalibus in primo gradu diiudicatae fuerint et ad Sanctam Sedem per appellationem legitimam deferantur;

2.° In ultima instantia causas ab ipsa Sacra Rota et ab aliis quibusvis tribunalibus in secunda vel ulteriore instantia iam cognitas, quae in rem iudicatam non transierint.

§ 2. Hoc tribunal iudicat etiam in prima instantia causas de quibus in can. 1557, § 2, aliasve quas Romanus Pontifex sive motu proprio, sive ad instantiam partium ad suum tribunal advocaverit et Sacrae Rotae commiserit; easque, nisi aliud cautum sit in commissionis rescripto, Sacra Rota iudicat quoque in secunda et tertia instantia ope turnorum qui sibi invicem succedunt.

CAN. 1600

Causae maiores penitus excluduntur ab ambitu competentiae huius tribunalis.

CAN. 1601

Contra Ordinariorum decreta non datur appellatio seu recursus ad Sacram Rotam; sed de eiusmodi recursibus exclusive cognoscunt Sacrae Congregationes.

The S. R. Rota now consists of ten prelates or auditors, chosen by the Roman Pontiff and presided over by the dean, as the first among equals. The auditors must be doctors of both civil and canon law, and priests. They form the ordinary court of appeals, and a regular collegiate board of judges, who sit in judgment by turns, each consisting of three auditors, or in full session, unless the Pope decrees otherwise in some particular case. They have their special rules or by-laws, which are not secret, but have been officially published.[2]

The *competency* of the S. Roman Rota is as follows:

1.° It passes judgment in the *second* instance on all cases tried by any court of Ordinaries in the first stage and lawfully appealed to the Holy See. Here it may be well to state that the Rota will not accept any case unless a sentence has been rendered by the first judge or in the first instance. Otherwise the S. R. Rota has to ask for a *sanatio* or return the acts, all of which causes delay.

2.° The Rota judges also cases which have already been tried by itself or by another court in the second or any

[2] See *A. Ap. S.*, I, 22 ff., II, 783 ff.

other stage, provided these cases have not yet passed as *res iudicata* or been definitively adjudged (cfr. can. 1902 f.).

3.° Finally, the S. Romana Rota gives judgment in the first instance on cases mentioned in can. 1557, § 2, and others which the Roman Pontiff, either of his own accord or at the demand of the litigants, has reserved to himself and entrusted to the Rota. The same cases may also, unless the writ of commission is worded otherwise, be tried by the S. Rota in the second and third instance by way of succeeding turns. For the ten auditors are divided into ten turns, the first consisting of the three last (or junior) auditors, the second and third, of the six preceding auditors, the fourth of the Dean and the two last auditors, who again have to take their turn, etc. Hence there is always one who did not sit with the same two auditors.[3]

From the competency of the Rota are entirely excluded the *causae maiores,* which are such by reason either of the persons involved or of the importance of the matter.[4] To this class belong the cases mentioned under can. 1556 and 1557, § 1.

Can. 1601 rules that an *appeal or recourse* to the S. Rota is admissible *against the decrees of Ordinaries,* because such cases are exclusively handled by the S. Congregations. Hence whatever a local Ordinary settles administratively, for instance, division of parishes, etc., and in general all *recursus in devolutivo* [5] *tantum,* must be addressed to the S. Congregations, not to the Rota, and the episcopal court must pass a sentence if the case is tried in a judiciary way and appealed to Rome.

---

[3] *Lex propria,* c. 12, § 1 (A. Ap. S., I, 22).

[4] *Ibid.,* can. 15 (l. c., p. 24).

[5] See can. 345; 513, § 2; 1340, § 3; 1395, § 2; 1428, § 3; 2243, § 3.

Art. II

THE SIGNATURA APOSTOLICA

CAN. 1602

Supremum Signaturae Apostolicae Tribunal constat nonnullis S. R. E. Cardinalibus, quorum unus Praefecti munere fungitur.

CAN. 1603

§ 1. Apostolica Signatura videt potestate ordinaria:

1.° De violatione secreti ac de damnis ab Auditoribus Sacrae Rotae illitis eo quod actum nullum vel iniustum posuerint;

2.° De exceptione suspicionis contra aliquem Sacrae Rotae Auditorem;

3.° De querela nullitatis contra sententiam rotalem;

4.° De expostulatione pro restitutione in integrum adversus rotalem sententiam quae in rem iudicatam transierit;

5.° De recursibus adversus sententias rotales in causis matrimonialibus quas ad novum examen Sacra Rota admittere renuit;

6.° De conflictu competentiae quem enasci contingat inter tribunalia inferiora, ad normam can 1612, § 2.

§ 2. Videt ex potestate delegata de petitionibus per supplices libellos ad Sanctissimum porrectis ad obtinendam causae commissionem apud Sacram Rotam.

CAN. 1604

§ 1. In causa criminali, de qua in can. 1603, § 1, n. 1, si forte locus sit iudicio appellationis, hoc obtinetur penes ipsum Supremum Tribunal.

§ 2. In casu suspicionis, Apostolica Signatura definit utrum sit locus recusationi Auditoris, necne; quo facto, iudicium ad Sacram Rotam remittit, ut, secundum suas regulas ordinarias, procedat, Auditore, contra quem exceptio mota fuit, in suo turno manente vel excluso.

§ 3. In casu querelae nullitatis aut restitutionis in integrum aut recursus de quibus in can. 1603, § 1, nn. 3, 4, 5, de hoc tantum iudicat num sit nulla sententia rotalis, num locus sit restitutioni vel recursus sit admittendus; et nullitate declarata aut restitutione concessa vel admisso recursu, causam remittit ad Sacram Rotam, nisi Sanctissimus aliter providerit.

§ 4. In examine supplicum libellorum Signatura, habitis opportunis notitiis et auditis iis quorum interest, decernit utrum precibus annuendum sit, necne.

CAN. 1605

§ 1. Supremi Tribunalis Signaturae sententiae suam vim habent, quamvis rationes in facto et in iure non contineant.

§ 2. Nihilominus sive ad instantiam partis sive ex officio, si res postulet, Supremum Tribunal edicere potest ut praedictae rationes exponantur secundum regulas Tribunalis proprias.

After the auditors of the papal household had been constituted a formal corporation or court of trials, they were withdrawn from the immediate entourage of the Pope, who was then served by chaplains, called *referendarii*. These had to examine the petitions submitted to the Pontiff and present those worthy of acceptance to the Pope for his signature. Among these petitions, of course, there were such as required judiciary procedure, in which the *referendarii* lacked competency. Hence they could only issue decrees to other Roman tribunals, which perhaps had refused to render a decision or to accept the case at all. Although, therefore, the *Signatura* was not a tribunal in the proper sense of the word, yet it decided the competency of other tribunals and enforced the acceptance of cases when refused. This was the office of the *Signatura Iustitiae*. Besides this, there was another, which had more especially to deal with favors that belonged neither to the *Dataria* nor to the *Poenitentiaria*. The persons that made up this college were called collectively *Signatura Gratiae*. When the distinction between the two bodies was clearly made, is uncertain, but it probably dates from the time of Innocent VIII (1484–1492). In course of time both *signaturae* were reformed, their rights and privileges more accurately determined,[6] etc. But after the year 1870 their significance waned. Pius X resuscitated the *Signatura* as one tribunal, under the name *Signatura Apostolica,* which now consists of four Cardinals, one of whom is prefect (can. 1602). Its *present ordinary competency* is described by the Code as follows:

1. It takes cognizance of any violation of secrecy or damage done by the auditors of the S. Rota in not rendering justice or doing an injustice, whether by fraud or through culpable negligence. In cases of such violation or damage which involve a crime, appeal may be made by the accused auditor to the supreme tribunal of the Signatura.

2. The Signatura is also competent in any case of *suspicion* pleaded against any of the auditors of the S.

6 See Phillips, *K.-R.*, Vol. VI, 498 ff.; Bangen, *Die Röm. Curie,* 1854, 391 ff.; Hilling (Engl. Transl.) *The Roman Court,* 1907, p. 127 f.; Benedict XV, "*Attentis expositis,*" June 28, 1915 (*A. Ap. S.,* VII, 325) restored the two colleges of *votantes* and *referendarii.*

Rota. In every such case the Signatura shall decide whether the exception is well founded or not, and leave it to the S. Rota to proceed according to the established rules.

3. Furthermore the Signatura is competent when the *plaint of nullity* is made against a rotal sentence, for instance, when a marriage has been declared null.

4. Also in cases of *restitutio in integrum* being demanded against a rotal sentence which has become a *res iudicata*.

5. Also in *recourses* against a rotal sentence concerning matrimonial cases which the S. Rota refused to reconsider.

In the three last named cases (3, 4, 5) the Signatura alone has to judge whether the rotal sentence was null and void (on account of technical errors), whether restitution is justified or recourse is to be admitted. After the Signatura has rendered judgment, the case must be remanded to the S. Rota, unless the Holy Father provides otherwise.

6. The Signatura is also competent when there is a conflict *of competency* between inferior tribunals (can. 1612, § 2). Finally, the present Pope has enlarged its competency by giving to the Signatura a *delegated power* by virtue of which it may take cognizance of petitions addressed to the Holy Father to the effect that the S. Rota may be entrusted with a case brought before his Holiness. The Signatura, after having gathered information and heard the parties concerned, decides whether and how far the petition may be favored.[7] The decisions or sentences of the Signatura, to be effective, require no statement of reasons as to fact or law, but the sacred tribunal either *ex officio, i.e.,* if it deems it necessary and opportune, or if the parties insist, may explain the reasons on which it based a decision, according to its own by-laws.

[7] " *Attentis expositis,*" l. c.

CHAPTER IV

CAN. 1606

Delegati iudices servare tenentur regulas statutas in can. 199–207, 209.

CAN. 1607

§ 1. Iudex a Sancta Sede delegatus uti potest ministris constitutis in Curia dioecesis in qua iudicare debet; sed potest etiam alios quoscunque maluerit eligere et assumere, nisi in delegationis rescripto aliud cautum sit.

§ 2. Iudices vero ab Ordinariis locorum delegati uti debent ministris Curiae dioecesanae, nisi Episcopus in aliquo peculiari casu ob gravem causam proprios et extraordinarios ministros constituendos decreverit.

Delegated judges must follow the rules laid down in can. 199–207 and 209. A *judge delegated by the Holy See* may avail himself of the assistance of the officials of the court of the diocese in which he is to judge; but, unless his rescript reads otherwise, he may also choose or take to himself whomsoever he pleases.

Judges delegated by the *local Ordinaries* are bound to employ the officials of the diocesan court, unless the bishop, for a weighty reason and in an individual case, decides to appoint special and extraordinary officials.

TITLE III

RULES TO BE OBSERVED BY ECCLESI-ASTICAL TRIBUNALS

After defining the cases that may be judged by ecclesiastical courts, and describing the various tribunals, higher and lower, in every stage, the Code now lays down some general rules which are to be observed in all trials. These rules concern the judges and officials of tribunals, the order in which cases should be tried, the delays in law, the time and place of judgment, and the persons that may be admitted to court. Note, however, that these are only preliminaries of the trial proper.

CHAPTER I

This chapter commences with the so-called *exceptio fori declinatoria,* when exception is taken to the person of the judge because he is regarded as incompetent to try the case at issue.

COMPETENCY AND SUSPICION

CAN. 1608

Iudex competens parti legitime requirenti suum ministerium ne recuset, firmo praescripto can. 1625, § 1.

CAN. 1609

§ 1. Iudex antequam aliquem ad suum trahat tribunal et iudicaturus sedeat, videat utrum ipse sit competens, necne.

§ 2. Eodemque modo antequam aliquem ad agendum admittat, cognoscere tenetur num is in iudicio possit iure consistere.

§ 3. Non est tamen necesse ut de his referatur in actis.

CAN. 1610

§ 1. Si exceptio proponatur contra iudicis competentiam, hac de re ipse iudex videre debet.

§ 2. In casu exceptionis de incompetentia relativa, si iudex se competentem pronuntiet, eius decisio non admittit appellationem.

59

§ 3. Quod si iudex se incompetentem declaret, pars quae se gravatam reputat, potest intra decem dierum spatium appellationem ad superius tribunal interponere.

Can. 1611

Iudex quovis in stadio causae se absolute incompetentem agnoscens, suam incompetentiam declarare tenetur.

Can. 1612

§ 1. Si inter duos iudices pluresve controversia oriatur quisnam eorum ad aliquod negotium competens sit, res definienda est a tribunali immediate superiore.

§ 2. Quod si iudices, inter quos exsistit competentiae conflictus, subsint distinctis tribunalibus superioribus, controversiae definitio reservatur tribunali superiori illius iudicis, coram quo actio primo promota est; si non habeant tribunal superius, conflictus dirimatur vel a Legato Sanctae Sedis, si adsit, vel ab Apostolica Signatura.

Can. 1613 '

§ 1. Iudex cognoscendam ne suscipiat causam, in qua ratione consanguinitatis vel affinitatis in quolibet gradu lineae recttae et in primo et secundo gradu lineae collateralis, vel ratione tutelae et curatelae, intimae vitae consuetudinis, magnae simultatis, vel lucri faciendi aut damni vitandi, aliquid ipsius intersit, vel in qua antea advocatum aut procuratorem egerit.

§ 2. In iisdem rerum adiunctis ab officio suo abstinere debent iustitiae promotor et defensor vinculi.

Can. 1614

§ 1. Cum iudex, etsi competens, a parte recusatur ut suspectus, haec exceptio, si proponatur contra iudicem delegatum in causa unicum vel contra collegium vel maiorem delegatorum iudicum partem, definienda est a delegante; si contra unum vel alterum ex pluribus iudicibus delegatis, etsi Collegii praesidem, a ceteris iudicibus delegatis et non suspectis; si contra Auditorem Sacrae Rotae, a Signatura Apostolica ad normam can. 1603, § 1, n. 2; si contra officialem, ab Episcopo; si contra auditorem, a iudice principali.

§ 2. Si ipsemet Ordinarius sit iudex et contra ipsum exceptio suspicionis opponatur, vel abstineat a iudicando vel quaestionem suspicionis definiendam committat iudici immediate superiori.

§ 3. Si exceptio suspicionis opponatur contra promotorem iustitiae, defensorem vinculi aut alios tribunalis administros, de hac exceptione videt praeses in tribunali collegiali vel ipse iudex, si unicus sit.

Can. 1615

§ 1. Si iudex unicus aut aliquis vel etiam omnes iudices qui tribunal collegiale constituunt suspecti declarentur, personae mutari debent, non vero iudicii gradus.

§ 2. Ordinarii autem est in locum iudicum qui suspecti declarati sunt, alios a suspicione immunes subrogare.

§ 3. Quod si ipsemet Ordinarius declaratus fuerit suspectus, idem peragat iudex immediate superior.

CAN. 1616

Exceptio suspicionis expeditissime definienda est, auditis partibus, promotore iustitiae vel vinculi defensore, si intersint, nec in ipsos suspicio cadat.

CAN. 1617

Quod ad tempus attinet quo exceptiones incompetentiae et suspicionis proponendae sint, servetur praescriptum can. 1628.

Since a judge is by virtue of his office appointed to administer *justice,* he is *not at liberty to refuse his services* to those who request it. Hence our Code (can. 1625, § 1) has established certain penalties against those who unreasonably fail to exercise their function as judges, when duly called upon. And the superiors have to see to it that they comply with their obligations, as Innocent III already enjoined.[1]

However, compliance with these obligations supposes *competency.* Therefore the judge, before he summons any one to his tribunal, and when about to take his seat,[2] must first ask himself whether he is competent, either by reason of his jurisdiction over the person, or by reason of the matter he is to judge. This is done by considering the various reasons which establish the competent forum. If he is a delegated judge he must, besides, be aware of the tenor of the rescript under which he acts, in order not to overstep the limits of his power.

Here the commentators refer to the famous law *Barbarius*[3] which offers the example of a fugitive slave

1 C. 17, X, II, 1.
2 The act of sitting is becoming to a judge, yet it is certainly not required for the validity of the sentence, as § 3 of can. 1609 makes evident, and can. 1877 seems to imply.
3 L. 3, Dig. 1, 14, *de officio praetorum.*

who acted as a judge, though he was no Roman citizen. All the glossators hold with Ulpian that the acts of such a judge would be valid, because this assumption is more human and in keeping with the public welfare. However an intruder, if the *titulus coloratus* (common error) were wanting, could not function validly.[4]

The judge must also consider whether those who seek his services are entitled thereto, that is, in general, whether they are persons endowed with the right of prosecution, of which more shall be said under title IV, ch. I.

It is not necessary, however, to put all this into the minutes (*in actis*) of the case.

If the defendant (*reus*) takes *exception to the judge*, on the claim that he is incompetent for one reason or another, he must state the grounds for his claim. Such a ground may be incompetency for lack of one of the reasons which establish a competent forum, as stated in can. 1560-1568 (relative incompetency). But if the judge declares that his competency in the case is established, no appeal is permitted from his sentence. There may be other reasons brought up by the defendant to establish the incompetency of the judge. Thus if the judge is delegated by another, it may be objected that he obtained his rescript by fraud.[5] Besides, the defendant may oppose the judge as being partial, because of aversion for the defendant and similar reasons. In that case the defendant may appeal to the higher court within ten days from the date of the exception made, provided the judge has admitted his incompetency and proof was furnished.

If the judge has found himself *absolutely incompetent*,

4 Reiffenstuel, II, 1, n. 200; Santi-   5 C. 38, X, I, 29.
Leitner, II, 1, n. 14.

i.e., by reason of the person to be judged as well as of the matter under adjudication, he is bound to make a declaration to that effect, no matter how far the trial may have proceeded (can. 1611).

The question of competency may be raised, not by the defendant, but by the colleagues or *co-judges,* as to which of them is entitled to hear the case. This quarrel should be settled by the immediate superior or next higher court, according to the rules of appeal. If the judges belong to different higher courts, the competent higher court is the one to which the controversy was first brought for settlement. If there is no higher court, the question is to be settled either by the legate of the Holy See or by the Signatura Apostolica.

Exception against the judge on account of *blood relationship and affinity* is extended by can. 1613 to the whole direct line and to the first and second degree of the collateral line. Besides, the judge may be interested in the case he has to judge for other reasons: he may be guardian or administrator,[6] he may be bound by the ties of friendship, he may be an enemy, political or personal, of the parties, or he may have a personal interest in the case, either of gain or loss, or he may have acted as attorney or proxy in the same case before. All these reasons militate against the judge, who therefore should not accept such a case for trial, though the Code does not state the nullity of the act. Exceptions must be heard and disposed of before the trial begins.

The same rules also apply to the *promotor iustitiae* and the *defensor vinculi,* who therefore should waive jurisdiction under such circumstances.

According to can. 1614, a plea of exception which arises

6 Thus c. 36, X, II, 28, which, however, mentions only a delegated judge.

not from lack of competency, but from *suspicion*, must be settled by the *delegans*, if one judge, or all the judges, or the greater part of the collegiate board of judges with delegated power are objected to as suspicious. If the suspicion is alleged only against one or the other of the board of judges, even though the suspected one may be the president, the question must be decided by the other, non-suspected judges. The Signatura Apostolica settles all questions with regard to a suspected auditor of the S. Rota. The bishop is competent to judge the plea of suspicion against his official. And if there is an auditor in any court, according to can. 1580, the exception is disposed of by the chief judge, who in the case of a collegiate tribunal would be the official, or the vice-official if he takes the place of the official.

If the *Ordinary himself* is judge, and the plea of suspicion is brought against him, he shall either abstain from judging the case, or first have the exception settled by his immediate superior, according to can. 1594.

If exception is taken to the *promotor iustitiae*, or the *defensor vinculi*, or another official of the acting court on the ground of suspicion, the president of the collegiate board is competent to adjudge the matter.

If the judge sole, or one or all of a collegiate body of judges, are *declared* to be suspect, they must be changed, but the stage or instance of the court remains the same; the Ordinary should replace the suspected judges by others who are beyond suspicion. Should the Ordinary himself have been declared suspected, his immediate superior, *i.e.*, the metropolitan, should replace him for this case by another judge. The plea of exception must be disposed of as *quickly as possible* in order not to conflict with can. 1620. When a case under that plea comes up, the respective parties must be heard, and also the promoter and defender, provided they are present and not suspected themselves.

The *time* within which these exceptions of incompetency and suspicion must be brought, is to be determined according to can. 1628.

DUTIES OF THE JUDGE

CAN. 1618

In negotio quod privatorum solummodo interest, iudex procedere potest dumtaxat ad instantiam partis; sed in delictis et in iis quae publicum Ecclesiae bonum aut animarum salutem respiciunt, etiam ex officio.

CAN. 1619

§ 1. Si actor pro re sua probationes quas afferre posset, non afferat, vel reus exceptiones sibi competentes non opponat, iudex ne suppleat.

§ 2. Si vero agatur vel de publico bono vel de animarum salute, eas supplere potest et debet.

CAN. 1620

Iudices et tribunalia curent ut quamprimum, salva iustitia, causae omnes terminentur, utque in tribunali primae instantiae ultra biennium non protrahantur, in tribunali vero secundae instantiae ultra annum.

CAN. 1621

§ 1. Excepto Episcopo qui per se potestatem iudiciariam excerceat, omnes qui tribunal constituunt aut eidem opem ferunt, iusiurandum de officio rite et fideliter implendo coram Ordinario vel coram iudice a quo electi sunt, vel coram viro ecclesiastico ab

alterutro delegato, praestare debent: idque ab initio
suscepti officii, si sint stabiles, aut antequam causa
agatur, si pro peculiari aliqua causa sint constituti.

§ 2. Etiam iudex a Sede Apostolica delegatus vel
iudex ordinarius in religione clericali exempta idem
iusiurandum praestare tenetur cum primum constituitur, adstante ipsius tribunalis notario, qui de
praestito iureiurando actum redigat.

Can. 1622

§ 1. Quotiescumque iusiurandum praestatur sive a
iudicibus aut tribunalis administris, sive a partibus,
testibus, peritis, semper emitti debet praemissa divini
Nominis invocatione et a sacerdotibus quidem tacto
pectore, a ceteris fidelibus, tacto Evangeliorum libro.

§ 2. Iudex partem, testem aut peritum ad iusiurandum recipiens, eum regulariter commonefaciat tum
de sanctitate actus et de gravissimo delicto quod ad-
mittunt iurisiurandi violatores, tum etiam de poenis,
quibus obnoxii fiunt qui falsum in iudicio iurati af-
firmant.

§ 3. Iusiurandum secundum formulam a iudice
probatam praestari debet coram eodem iudice aut eius
delegato, adstante utraque aut alterutra parte, quae
interesse iurisiurandi praestationi velit.

Can. 1623

§ 1. In iudico criminali semper, in contentioso autem
si ex revelatione alicuius actus processualis praeiudicium partibus obvenire possit, iudices et tribunalis
adiutores tenentur ad secretum officii.

§ 2. Tenentur etiam semper ad inviolabile secretum
servandum de discussione quae in tribunali collegiali

ante ferendam sententiam habetur, tum etiam de variis suffragiis et opinionibus ibidem prolatis.

§ 3. Imo quoties causae vel probationum natura talis sit ut ex actorum vel probationum evulgatione aliorum fama periclitetur, vel praebeatur ansa dissidiis, aut scandalum aliudve id genus incommodum oriatur, iudex poterit testes, peritos, partes earumque advocatos vel procuratores iureiurando adstringere ad secretum servandum.

CAN. 1624

Iudex et omnes tribunalis administri, occasione agendi iudicii, munera quaevis acceptare prohibentur.

According to the nature of different cases, the judge is to act differently, and although, like a praetor, he may be a judge by virtue of his office, yet in *civil cases*, which concern private interests only, he can proceed only upon the demand of the parties who seek his services. Otherwise the judge might commit excesses [7] and interfere in matters which are not in his power. Judgment supposes a plaintiff, and where there is no complaint, no judgment is required for private affairs. The case is different, of course, when the public weal and the salvation of souls are concerned, as in all *criminal matters*. Hence if the judge has obtained notice or a complaint that a crime has been perpetrated,[8] provided, of course, it is not mere slander or defamation, but based on facts, he is obliged *ex officio* to proceed (can. 1618).

Different also is the way the judge must proceed in civil and criminal cases, respectively. If the plaintiff in a *civil case* offers no proofs, or the defendant pleads no

[7] C. 1, X, V, 31. 1880, n. 11 (*Coll. P. F.*, n. 1534).
[8] S. C. EE. et RR., June 11,

exception, the judge is not supposed to supply the deficiency or put in an exception, but acts merely as judge between the litigant parties, and his knowledge is, as shall be seen under can. 1869, strictly judicial. This does not mean that he should act as judge even though he has no knowledge at all of the requirements of the office, for a judge culpably destitute of the knowledge required would not only commit a grievous sin, but be liable to all the damage caused by his judgment.[9]

In *criminal cases*, which concern the public weal or the salvation of souls, the judge *may* and *must*, if he can, *supply* deficient proofs, and use even his extrajudicial knowledge to ensure a fair and just judgment (can. 1619).

In order to prevent unnecessary and costly delays, which may cause considerable damage to the parties involved,[10] the Code emphasizes the duty incumbent on judges and tribunals, of *speedily finishing trials*. In the first instance a trial should not be protracted over *two years*, in the second, not over a year. However, speed is not haste, and a "hurry up" trial might involve injustice. Hence this rule must be understood *salva iustitia*.

To secure proper and conscientious trials and judgments the Code lays down another obligation for those who are engaged in a trial, including all the officials and assistants of the court, excepting the bishop, when he himself exercises judiciary power. It is the *oath*. This must be administered by the Ordinary or the judge who has selected them, to the other officials and assistants, or any one delegated by either of them, provided he be an ecclesiastic. Habitual judges must take the oath before they assume

9 Bouix, *De Iudiciis Ecclesiasticis*, 1855, Vol. I, p. 135 f.

10 Theologians justly maintain that a judge who culpably protracts a trial is held to indemnification; Bouix, *l. c.*, p. 136.

office, and judges selected *ad hoc, i.e.,* for one special case, must take it before the trial begins. Also a *judge delegated by the Apostolic See,*— including the bishop if he acts as delegated judge and the judge of exempt clerical organizations,— must take this oath before the trial commences, in the presence of the notary of the court, who shall put it down in writing (can. 1621).

The *manner of taking* this oath is as follows: The judge and the officials or assistants of the court, together with the parties, witnesses, and experts, must first invoke the name of God; the priests hold their left hand to the breast, the rest of the faithful touch the book of the gospels.[11] Before administering the oath, the judge should warn the parties, witnesses, and experts, of the sacredness of oaths, of the grievousness of perjury, and of the penalties established for perjurers.[12]

The *formula* of the oath must be approved by the judge and be pronounced in his presence or that of his delegate, and of both or one of the parties who should witness the administration of the oath (can. 1622).

To the conscientious and proper administration of justice also belongs the keeping of the *official secret,* which can. 1623 inculcates. This is always to be kept in *criminal* trials. In *civil* trials it must be observed if a revelation of the proceedings would be prejudicial to the

---

11 The formula used in the Roman Curia is (*Acta Ap. S.,* I, 41): "*In nomine Domini. Ego N. N. spondeo, voveo ac iuro, fidelem et obedientem me semper futurum B. etro et Domino Nostro Papae eiusque legitimis successoribus; ministeria mihi commissa in hac S. Congregatione (Tribunali aut Officio) sedulo ac diligenter impleturum; munera mihi in remunerationem, etiam sub specie doni oblata, non recepturum: et secretum officii re-*

ligiose servaturum in iis omnibus, quae sacri Canones aut Superiores ecreta servari iusserint, itemque, quoties ab Ordinariis id postulatum fuerit, et quando ex revelatione alicuius actus praeiudicium partibus aut Ecclesiae obvenire potest. Sic me Deus adjuvet, et haec sancta Dei Evangelia, quae meis manibus tango."

12 Cfr. can. 1757, § 2, n. 1; can. 1795, § 2.

parties, either in a spiritual or material way. Therefore the judges as well as all other officials and assistants, must hold their tongue. The same persons are bound by an inviolable secret concerning preliminary discussions held by the board of judges before the final sentence is pronounced. They must also observe strict secrecy concerning the various ballots and the views pronounced at the balloting. Besides, if the nature of the case or of its proofs is such that a revelation of the proceedings (minutes) or arguments (proofs) would endanger the reputation of others, or cause contention or scandal, etc., the judge may command the witnesses, the experts, the litigant parties and their lawyers or proctors to keep the secret under oath.

A final obligation set down in can. 1624 is the *refusal to accept gifts*, no matter how small or great, whether of a consumable nature, such as drinks, eatables,[18] etc., or of a pecuniary or other kind, as a service, recommendation, etc. This prohibition obliges the judge and all the officials acting at a trial. Then the text says: *occasione agendi iudicii*, which certainly means, not only on the occasion of a trial, but also with respect or reference to the same, because the object is to preclude bribery, which the divine and ecclesiastical laws forbid.[14]

This is so true that even if the litigants have equally strong proofs in their favor, the judge is not allowed to accept money in favor of one against the other.[15]

---

18 C. 11, 6°, I, 3, permits acceptance of *poculenta* and *esculenta mera liberalitate oblata*, but our text excludes even these.

14 Cfr. Is. 1; Mich. 3; Bouix, *l. c.*, p. 137.

15 S. O., *Prop. 26 damn.*, Sept. 24, 1665 (Denz., n. 997).

CAN. 1625

§ 1. Iudices qui cum certe et evidenter competentes sunt, ius reddere recusant, vel qui temere se competentes declarant, vel qui ex culpabili negligentia aut dolo actum nullum cum aliorum detrimento vel iniustum ponunt aut aliud litigantibus damnum inferunt, tenentur de damnis et ab Ordinario loci vel, si de Episcopo agatur, a Sede Apostolica, ad instantiam partis aut etiam ex officio, congruis poenis pro gravitate culpae puniri possunt, non exclusa officii privatione.

§ 2. Iudices qui secreti legem violare vel acta secreta cum aliis quoquo modo communicare praesumpserint, puniantur mulcta pecuniaria aliisque poenis, privatione officii non exclusa, pro diversa reatus gravitate, salvis peculiaribus statutis, quibus graviores poenae praescribantur.

§ 3. Eisdem sanctionibus subsunt tribunalis officiales et adiutores, si officio suo, ut supra, defuerint, quos omnes etiam iudex punire potest.

In order to give weight to the preceding laws, the legislator adds a penal sanction, which consists partly of a natural, or at least moral, consequence, and partly of a penalty to be imposed.

1. The *moral* or theological *penalty* consists in the obligation of making restitution or *paying the damages* that may arise from unqualified actions. These may be committed by:

a) *judges* who certainly and evidently are competent on every score, as provided in can. 1560–1568, but refuse to render judgment after complaint is made; [16]

16 C. 8, X, III, 149.

b) those who rashly declare themselves competent, be-cause rashness inculpates the judge; [17]

c) those who by culpable negligence or deceit proceed invalidly to the detriment of others, by omitting the neces-sary formalities or requisites as to the proceeding or hearing of witnesses; [18]

d) those who act unjustly, for instance, by inflicting a censure on innocent parties, or by bribery and avarice; [19]

e) those who injure the litigants in any other way, against their own conscience, through human respect or hatred.[20]

2. The *penal sanction,* which is, judicially speaking, also contained in the first clause, consists of *proportionate* penalties, which may be inflicted upon the demand of the injured parties, or *ex officio:*

a) By the *local ordinary,* if the judge is subject to his jurisdiction, or

b) By the *Apostolic See,* if the guilty judge is a bishop. This penalty may even be privation of the office of judge.

§ 2 threatens a pecuniary fine and other penalties, even privation of office, for judges who dare to *violate the law of secrecy* or communicate secret proceedings to outsiders in any shape or form.

The punishment must be proportionate to the guilt, and may be even severer if particular statutes provide severer penalties.

The same theological and penal sanctions threatened against judges may be inflicted by the judge on guilty officials and employees of his court.

---

17 C. 49, C. 11, q. 3.
18 C. 11, X, II, 19; c. 2, 6°, II, 1.
19 Cc. 8, 88, C. 11, q. 3; c. 1, 6°, II, 14.
20 C. 1, 6°, II, 14.

CAN. 1626

Cum iudex praevidet actorem probabiliter spreturum esse sententiam ecclesiasticam si forte haec ipsi sit contraria, et idcirco conventi iuribus non satis consultum iri, potest, ad eiusdem conventi instantiam vel etiam ex officio, actorem adigere ad congruam cautionem praestandam pro ecclesiasticae sententiae observantia.

If the judge foresees that the plaintiff will not heed the ecclesiastical sentence in case it is against him, and that, therefore, the rights of the defendant will not be guaranteed, he may, either *ex officio* or upon the demand of the defendant, oblige the plaintiff to give bail or security to the effect that he will abide by the ecclesiastical sentence.

It is customary and required, when cases are brought before the S. Roman Rota, to deposit a certain sum of money for the expenses and as bailment.[21]

[21] *Regulae S. R. R.*, Aug. 4, 1910, § 3 (*A. Ap. S.*, II, 795).

CHAPTER II

CAN. 1627.

Iudices et tribunalia tenentur causas ad se delatas eo ordine cognoscere quo fuerunt propositae, nisi aliqua earum celerem prae ceteris expeditionem exigat, quod quidem peculiari decreto a iudice seu a tribunali statuendum est.

CAN. 1628

§ 1. Exceptiones dilatoriae, eae praesertim quae respiciunt personas et modum iudicii, proponendae et cognoscendae sunt ante contestationem litis, nisi contestata iam lite primum emerserint aut pars iureiurando affirmet eas tunc tantum sibi innotuisse.

§ 2. Exceptio tamen de incompetentia iudicis absoluta a partibus opponi potest in quovis statu et gradu causae.

§ 3. Pariter exceptio excommunicationis opponi potest in quolibet iudicii statu et gradu, dummodo ante sententiam definitivam; imo si agatur de excommunicatis vitandis, aut toleratis contra quos sententia condemnatoria vel declaratoria lata fuerit, ii ex officio semper excludi debent.

CAN. 1629

§ 1. Exceptiones peremptoriae, quae dicuntur *litis finitae*, veluti exceptio rei iudicatae, transactionis, etc.,

proponi et cognosci debent ante contestationem litis;
qui serius eas opposuerit, non est reiiciendus, sed condemnetur in expensis, nisi probet se oppositionem
malitiose non distulisse.

§ 2. Aliae exceptiones peremptoriae proponi debent
post contestatam litem, et suo tempore tractandae sunt
secundum regulas circa quaestiones incidentes.

CAN. 1630

§ 1. Actiones reconventionales satius statim post
litis contestationem, utiliter quovis iudicii momento,
ante sententiam tamen, proponi possunt.

§ 2. Cognoscantur autem simul cum conventionali
actione, hoc est pari gradu cum ea, nisi eas separatim
cognoscere necessarium sit aut iudex opportunius
existimaverit.

CAN. 1631

Quaestiones de cautione pro expensis iudicialibus
praestanda aut de concessione gratuiti patrocinii, quod
statim ab initio postulatum fuerit, et aliae huiusmodi
videndae regulariter sunt ante litis contestationem.

CAN. 1632

Quoties, proposita principali controversia, quaestio
praeiudicialis suboriatur, id est eiusmodi ex cuius solutione pendeat solutio quaestionis principalis, illa ante
omnia a iudice cognoscenda est.

CAN. 1633

§ 1. Si ex principali controversia quaestiones incidentes nascantur, cognoscantur prius eae quarum
solutio viam sternat ad aliarum solutionem.

§ 2. Quod si nullo nexu logico inter se cohaereant, quae prius ab alterutra parte propositae sunt, illae antea definiantur.

§ 3. Si de spolio incidat quaestio, haec ante omnia est dirimenda.

This chapter contains general rules for the judge, instructing him how to proceed. These rules concern the order of time in which cases must be tried, exceptions and reconventions, the giving of bail, and the logical or casual interdependence of cases.

1. First the Code rules (can. 1627) that judges and tribunals must try cases in the order of time in which they are proposed (*prior in tempore, prior in iure*). Hence a judge is not at liberty to give preference to one case over another, unless he is convinced that one should be disposed of as soon as possible.[1] But this view should always be objective. The inversion of the regular order, if deemed necessary, requires a special decree by the judge or the tribunal.

2. Next the Code lays down the rules for taking cognizance of so-called *exceptions*. These are statements or assertions of the defendant against the plaintiff, made in order to postpone or weaken his purpose. They are *dilatory*, if they defer action only for a time, and may, as can. 1628, § 1 says, regard either the persons concerned in the trial, *i.e.*, the judge or plaintiff, or the mode of the trial, for instance, the order in which it is conducted.

These exceptions must be proposed and disposed of *before the litis contestatio;* after that has taken place, exceptions are admissible only if they were raised after

---

1 For instance, a case of *matrimonium consummatum* on account of sinful occasion should be given preference to a case of *matrimonium contrahendum*.

the issue in pleading, or if the party declares under oath that they became known to him only after the *litis contestatio*. Thus it may happen that suspicion is created only after the plaidoyer, or that a relationship existing between the judge and the plaintiff becomes known to the defendant only after the *contestatio*.

However, exception may be taken to the *competency* of the judge at any phase or stage (instance) of the trial, provided his alleged incompetency is *absolute, i.e.,* comprises the persons at law as well as the question proposed. This means that even if an incompetent judge has already given an interlocutory or final sentence, he can still be rejected on the plea of absolute incompetency.

A privileged exception is that of *excommunication* against the plaintiff. This claim, says our text, may be made at any stage or instance of the trial, up to the final sentence. This favor was granted in order to make ecclesiastical censures more respected. However, Innocent III as well as Gregory IX enacted that a defendant who deliberately omits to oppose the plea of excommunication, though it is to be admitted in the first instance, must be condemned to bear the expenses caused by protraction of the trial.[2] The Code is silent about this fine, and more probably does not sustain it.[3]

Those who are under a condemnatory or declaratory sentence of excommunication (either as *vitandi* or *tolerandi*) must be excluded from ecclesiastical trials *ex officio. i.e.,* by the judge or board of judges, or by the president or the local Ordinary. This exception may be raised even against the judge or judges.

Another species of exception is that called *peremptory,* which entirely quashes the action or intention of the plain-

[2] C. 12, X, II, 25; c. 1, 6°, II, 12.

[3] We say "more probably," by reason of comparing sect. 3 of can.

1628 with sect. 1, can. 1629 where the expenses are clearly stated.

tiff. These are *litis finitae,* for instance, the proof that the matter at issue is already adjudged, or an agreement concerning a doubtful matter (*transactionis*), prescription, or payment made.[4] Such exceptions must be proposed and settled before the *litis contestatio.* But they may not be rejected even after the trial has entered that phase. However, unless the defendant can prove that his omission to oppose this exception sooner, was not intentional or malicious, *i.e.,* designed to vex or fatigue his adversary, he is to be condemned to pay the expenses caused by the delay.

Other peremptory exceptions, which amount rather to incidental questions, must be proposed after the *litis contestatio* and are considered under Title XI.

3. The Code next considers the counter-plea or *reconventio, i.e.,* an action or suit which the defendant may put in against the plaintiff before the same tribunal, for instance, when a wife sues her husband for separation, and the husband sues her for divorce, or the one pleads desertion and the other cruelty. Such counter complaints may be proposed from the *litis contestatio* to the moment before the final sentence.

The plea proposed by the plaintiff and the counter-plea opposed by the defendant should be tried at the same time, *pari gradu,* and by the same judge. But the plaintiff is to be heard first and the defendant must make answer to his allegations; whereupon the counter-plea of the defendant must be discussed. Thus the question may be settled at once.[5]

4. Questions concerning the bailment or *security* for defraying the expenses of the trial, or a gratuitous defence asked for at the beginning of the trial, and other

4 Engel, II, 25, n. 1, 6.
5 Cfr. c. 1, X, II, 4; c. 2, X, II, 10; Santi-Leitner, II, 4, n. 4.

similar questions should as a rule be settled before the *litis contestatio* (can. 1631).

5. Finally the Code considers the *logical or causal connection* of dependent or related cases or controversies. If an apparently principal question depends on the solution of the prejudicial controversy, the so-called side-issue must be settled first.   For instance, when a wife demands that her husband be restored to her, but the husband claims that blood relationship exists between them, the question of consanguinity, though *praeiudicialis*, must be settled first.[6]

Similarly a connection may exist between several *incidental questions* or countercharges that may be brought up. These must be settled so that the solution of one paves the way for the solution of the other. Thus, if an election is attacked, and the electors assert there was a conspiracy or censure, the question of conspiracy or censure must first be disposed of, even though it is purely incidental.[7]

If there is no *logical connection* between several questions the one which was first proposed must be settled first. When disseissin (*spolii*) is alleged, this charge must be disposed of first.

6 Cfr. c. 1, X, II, 10; c. 5, X, I, 9.   7 C. 19, X, II, 1.

CHAPTER III

CAN. 1634

§ 1. *Fatalia legis* quae dicuntur, idest termini perimendis iuribus a lege constituti, prorogari non possunt.

§ 2. Termini autem iudiciales et conventionales, ante eorum lapsum, poterunt, iusta intercedente causa, a iudice, auditis vel petentibus partibus, prorogari.

§ 3. Caveat tamen iudex ne nimis diuturna lis fiat ex prorogatione.

CAN. 1635

Si dies, pro actu iudiciali indicta, sit feriata nec in decreto iudicis dicatur expresse tribunal vacaturum nihilominus causis cognoscendis, terminus intelligitur prorogatus ad primam sequentem diem non feriatam.

The Code wishes trials to be terminated within a reasonable time so that peace may be restored between the litigants. However, delays may be granted in order to enable the judge to obtain a fuller knowledge of the case and to pass judgment with greater security. For this purpose so-called *dilationes* or delays are granted either by law or by the judge, or agreed upon by the parties.

1. The delays which are granted by law concerning the time for appealing, or at least for finishing, an action, are called *fatalia legis*. They cannot be prorogued,[1] except, of course, by the supreme judge.

1 Cfr. c. 4, Clem. II, 12; Santi-Leitner, II, 8, n. 2.

Judiciary delays, granted according to the prudent discretion of the judge, or the *conventional* delays agreed
upon by the parties, may be prorogued if there is a just
reason for such action and the parties were heard and
asked for delay.   However, the judge must always watch
that the prorogation is not unduly lengthened, either by
deceit or contumacy.[2]

If the day set for a trial or judicial action is a *feria,*
i.e., a legal holiday, and no mention is made in the decree
of the judge that the tribunal does not sit on that day,
the term is supposed to be the next court day which is
not a *feria.*

[2] Cfr. cc. 5, 10, X, II, 14.

CHAPTER IV

CAN. 1636

Quamvis Episcopus in quolibet suae dioecesis loco, qui non sit exemptus, ius habeat erigendi tribunal, nihilominus penes suam sedem aulam statuat, quae sit ordinarius iudiciorum locus: ibique Crucifixi imago emineat, et adsit Evangeliorum liber.

CAN. 1637

Iudex e territorio suo vi expulsus vel a iurisdictione ibi exercenda impeditus, potest extra territorium iurisdictionem exercere et sententiam ferre, certiore tamen hac de re facto loci Ordinario.

CAN. 1638

§ 1. In unaquaque dioecesi Ordinarius publico decreto dies et horas definiri curet, pro loci ac temporum adiunctis opportunas, quibus tribunal adiri regulariter possit, et ab eo iustitiae administratio exigi.

§ 2. Iusta tamen de causa, et quoties periculum sit in mora, fas est fidelibus quovis tempore iudicis ministerium in sui iuris vel boni publici tutelam invocare.

CAN. 1639

§ 1. Dies festi de praecepto, et ultimi tres dies hebdomadae sanctae feriati habeantur; et in iis citationes intimare, audientias habere, partes et testes excutere, probationes assumere, decreta et sententias ferre, denuntiare et exsequi vetitum est, nisi necessitas, christiana caritas, aut bonum publicum aliud postulent.

§ 2. Iudicis autem est in singulis casibus statuere et denuntiare, an et quae acta supra dictis diebus expleri debeant.

Although the bishop may set up a tribunal anywhere in his diocese (provided it be not exempt), yet he should establish a judgment hall in his episcopal city, which shall be the ordinary place for holding trials. There the Crucifix shall occupy a conspicuous place and there must also be a copy of the Gospels. The reason for choosing the episcopal city is, according to Boniface VIII that experts may usually be found there.[1]

A doubt may perhaps arise concerning *exempt religious,* who seem to live in an " exempt place." However, a monastery or convent, as such, is not exempt, but local exemption extends only as far as, and in virtue of, personal exemption. Hence it is licit to perform civil as well as criminal jurisdictional acts, to examine witnesses, or to write the acts of a trial in a convent or monastery of exempt religious: and such acts are certainly valid. Whether they would be valid if the entire trial, inclusive of the sentence, were conducted in such a place, seems doubtful.[2] Of course, if the place itself were exempt, for instance, a territory *nullius*, the proceedings would be invalid.[3]

The Council of Vienne (1311–1313) allowed bishops

---

[1] C. 11, 6°, I, 3.

[2] Cfr. c. 8, X, II, 20; c. 2, 6°, II, 1; Wernz, *Ius Decret.*, Vol. V, n. 315, p. 267, denies the validity according to a decision of the S. C. EE. et RR., Sept. 15, 1741; Messmer, *Canonical Procedure,* 1897, p. 143, asserts the validity, and quotes S. C. Imm., Jan. 21, 1821, and July 14, 1830.

who had been forcibly driven from their dioceses, to give judgment in any strange diocese, although this was otherwise prohibited by law, according to the adage: *"Extra territorium ius dicenti non paretur impune."*[3] Our text amplifies and to some extent moderates this law. The amplification consists in that it permits any judge who is driven away from his diocese or prevented from exercising judgment there (*e.g.*, on account of being a prisoner) to exercise jurisdiction outside his own territory, provided (not for valid exercise, but as a sign of respect), he notifies the local Ordinary of the fact,— a condition of which the Clementine decretal said nothing.

Ordinaries should make known the *days and hours* when the diocesan court may be approached by those seeking justice. These days and hours (office hours) should be set as conveniently as possible. The Code abstains from fixing the hours more closely, and hence any hour is valid.

Although the appointed days and hours should form the rule for holding trials or giving audience, there may be just reasons for seeking redress of grievances at other times. *Sundays and holydays of obligation,* and also the three last days of Holy Week are *feriae* or *dies feriati*, legal holidays on which no tribunal should be in session.[4] On these days, therefore, it is forbidden to issue summons, give audiences, hear parties or witnesses or discuss their testimony, accept proofs, issue decrees or sentences, denounce or execute criminals,— except in case of necessity or when Christian charity or the public welfare demand an exception. It is the right and duty of the judge to decide in each individual case which acts performed on forbidden days need supplementation. Here

---

[3] C. 2; 6°, I, 2.
[4] S. Pius V, *"Cum primum,"* *"Ab eo tempore,"* Nov. 5, 1745. April 1, 1566, § 8; Bened. XIV,

the old law has been modified, for the Decretals [5] declared every judicial act performed on a sacred day or holiday to be null and void. A summons served on such a day did not render the party contumacious. Now it is left to the judge to determine what is valid and what not.

[5] Cc. 1, 5, X, II, 9.

CHAPTER V

The Code wishes to insure orderly procedure and correct treatment of the official acts which are drawn up for and during a trial. To procure the first, it determines the persons to be admitted.

CAN. 1640

§ 1. Dum causae coram tribunali aguntur, extranei ab aula arceantur et ii tantummodo adsint, quos ad processum expediendum iudex necessarios esse iudicaverit.

§ 2. Omnes, iudicio assistentes, qui reverentiae et obedientiae tribunali debitae graviter defuerint, iudex, etiam illico et incontinenti si coram tribunali sedente in id quis peccaverit, potest censuris quoque aliisve congruis poenis ad officium reducere, advocatos praeterea et procuratores etiam iure alias causas apud tribunalia ecclesiastica pertractandi privare.

CAN. 1641

Si alicui actui processuali interveniat persona linguae loci ignara et iudices ac partes linguam huius personae propriam non intelligant, interpres adhibeatur iuratus, et a iudice designatus, contra quem alterutra pars legitimam exceptionem non proposuerit.

The court room is not to be encumbered by outsiders whilst a trial is going on, but only those whom the judge deems necessary for conducting a trial are to be admitted. This rule might be profitably copied by our civil courts. Newspaper reporters are not required for the proper conduct of a trial.

It may happen that those who are allowed to be present cannot control their temper but profess *contempt and scorn or otherwise act in a manner injurious and offensive to the respect and obedience due to the tribunal.* The offense must be of a serious nature, but it need not consist in actual maltreatment (for instance, spitting in the face of, or making fists, at the judge); seriously contumelious words suffice.[1] In order to bring such intemperate persons to their senses, the judge may punish them there and then by inflicting censures or other suitable penalties. Lawyers and proctors guilty of such behavior may be deprived of the privilege of acting at ecclesiastical trials.

Among those to be admitted is the *interpreter,* if any person among those called to the trial does not speak the language of the place where the trial is held, and the judges and parties to the trial do not understand his language. Interpreters must be sworn and no one can be appointed to this office against whom either party has raised a legitimate exception.

THE JUDICIAL ACTS

CAN. 1642

§ 1. Acta iudicialia, tum quae meritum quaestionis respiciunt, seu *acta causae,* ex. gr., sententiae et

---

1 C. 11, X, V. 37: " *de improbi-   tionem judicis temere prorumpen-
ate constat . . . adversus asser-   tis."*

cuiusque generis probationes, tum quae ad formam procedendi pertinent, seu *acta processus,* ex. gr., citationes, intimationes, etc., scripto redacta esse debent.

§ 2. Nisi iusta causa aliud suadeat, quoad eius fieri potest, lingua latina redigantur; sed interrogationes et responsiones testium, aliaque similia, lingua vernacula confici debent.

CAN. 1643

§ 1. Singula folia processus numerentur; et actuarii subscriptio cum sigillo tribunalis apponatur in unoquoque folio.

§ 2. Singulis actis completis vel interruptis seu ad aliam sessionem remissis, apponatur subscriptio actuarii et iudicis vel tribunalis praesidis.

§ 3. Quoties in actis iudicialibus partium aut testium subscriptio requiritur, si pars aut testis hanc facere nequeat vel nolit, id in ipsis actis adnotetur, simulque iudex et actuarius fidem faciant actum ipsum de verbo ad verbum parti aut testi perlectum fuisse, et partem aut testem vel non potuisse vel noluisse subscribere.

CAN. 1644

§ 1. In casu appellationis, actorum exemplaria ad norman can. 1642, 1643 conscripta et in fasciculum religata, cum indice omnium actorum et documentorum et cum testificatione actuarii seu cancellarii de eorum fideli transcriptione et integritate, mittantur ad superius tribunal; si exemplaria sine gravi incommodo exscribi nequeant, mittantur cum opportunis cautelis acta ipsa originalia.

§ 2. Si eo mittenda sint ubi vernacula lingua non sit cognita, acta ipsa in linguam latinam vertantur, adhibitis cautelis ut de fideli translatione constet.

§ 3. Si acta debita forma et charactere confecta non fuerint, a iudice superiore repelli possunt: quo in casu illi, quibus culpa imputanda est, acta suis impensis denuo conficere et mittere tenentur.

Can. 1645

§ 1. Iudicio expleto, documenta partibus restitui debent, nisi in criminalibus, bono publico ita exigente, iudex aliquod retinendum censuerit.

§ 2. Documenta omnia, quae apud tribunal manent, in archivo Curiae deponantur sive publico sive secreto, prout eorum natura exigit.

§ 3. Notarii, actuarii et cancellarius sine iudicis mandato tradere prohibentur exemplar actorum iudicialium et documentorum quae sunt processui acquisita.

§ 4. Anonymae epistolae quae nihil ad causae meritum conferunt, et etiam subscriptae quae sint certo calumniosae, destruantur.

Writing plays a conspicuous part in every trial, yet not all things that are or must be written are of equal importance. Some concern the *merits of the case* and are styled *acta causae*. To this class of documents belong all sentences, either interlocutory or final, and proofs of every kind, even those presented orally, because they, too, must be put down in writing. Other papers (*acta processus*) touch the mode or *form* of procedure. To this class belong the summons, intimations, the oaths taken, and, perhaps, the special rules laid down for proceeding in a particular case. If one should wish to call the *acta causae* " records," and the *acta processus* " minutes," he would, we believe, not commit a grievous mistake, although the word *records* has a wider significance, though not as wide as "minutes." Which of the *acta* must be put in writing in order to be valid is determined under each heading; thus, for instance, the summons must certainly be recorded (can. 1723 f.); but if no invalidating clause is attached, a trial cannot be attacked as invalid because some portion of the proceedings was not written out.

Some ecclesiastical acts are intended not only for private use, but for the Church at large,[2] whose language is Latin, and since these records in many cases must be forwarded to Rome, which acknowledges as official languages only Latin, Italian, and French,[3] all acts should, as far as possible, be composed in Latin, unless there is a just reason for departing from this rule. However, the questions put to the witnesses, their answers, the so-called *articuli* or specified charges and counter-charges of plaintiff and defendant, and also the reports of experts[4] are to be written in the vernacular language (see, however, can. 1644, § 2). Each and every sheet of the records as well as the minutes (*folia processus*) must be paginated and signed by the secretary, who has also to put the seal of the tribunal on each. As soon as any part of the acts (for instance, the defense, or the hearing of one set of witnesses, or the report of an expert) has been completed, the secretary should sign his name to the record, which is then passed on to the judge (or to the president of the tribunal, if a board of judges is sitting) for their respective signatures. This process must be repeated every time the session is interrupted or adjourned. The Code does not prescribe that only one page

---

[2] S. C. C., Aug. 22, 1840 (*Coll. P. F.*, n. 911).

[3] *Regulae S. R. R.*, Aug. 4, 1910, § 7 (*A. Ap. S.*, II, 785).

[4] S. C. C., Aug. 22, 1840 (*l. c.*).

of the sheet be written on, but we have become accustomed to use only one page. Typewriting is not excluded, but special ink should be used at least for important documents.

If the judicial acts have to be signed by the *parties to the trial and by the witnesses,* and these are either unable or unwilling to sign — they cannot be compelled to do so — this fact must be set down by the secretary or clerk in the minutes, and the record thereof accompanied by the testimony of the judge and the acting clerk that the acts were read to the respective parties or witnesses, and that they were either unable or unwilling to sign them (can. 1643).

The acts taken down and signed in the first instance or stage of a trial may be required for the *court of appeal.* In that case the original papers should remain with the court of the first instance and *copies* forwarded to the court of appeal. Each copy must be bound so as to form a booklet and contain a list of the minutes and records, and of all other documents, together with the attestation of the secretary, or clerk, or chancellor, that the copy is a faithful and complete transcript of the original text. If copies cannot be made without great inconvenience, the original text may be sent to the court of appeals, provided there is no danger that they be lost, abused, or damaged, or fall into strange hands. We hardly believe that a carbon duplicate, provided with the necessary signature, or a photographic reproduction with the signature in handwriting (no rubber stamp!) would be refused. If the acts are written in the vernacular (for instance, English) and have to be sent to a court (for instance, at Rome, where this language is unknown, or at least not officially acknowledged) they must be translated into Latin and the faithfulness of the translation guaranteed.

Acts not composed in the proper form and style may be refused by the higher judge, and the official through whose negligence this has happened, is bound to have them redrawn and forwarded at his own expense (can. 1644).

Form refers to the condition of the sheets and the signatures.

Character may signify style, hence the expression " *stylus curiae,*" the style peculiar to judicial acts. The term " character " may also refer to the legibility of the acts and their arrangement; or to the language, which, as a rule, should be Latin, although if it is customary in a country to employ the vernacular, this fact would be a sufficient reason for composing the acts in that language. It sometimes requires an expert in both languages to translate certain terms into a dead language, and courts are not precisely intended for stylistic and linguistic exercises.

Here it may be added that a wise rule of the S. R. Rota prescribes that the written defence should not comprise more than twenty printed quarto pages, and the answers not more than ten pages of the same size.[5]

After the trial is *finished,* such documents as testimonials, deeds, letters of appointment, certificates, etc., which were required in court, must be restored to their owners. Only if the judge should deem it necessary to retain the one or other such document in a criminal case, may he keep it. But the documents which remain with the court (for instance, the charges and counter-charges, the depositions of witnesses, the defence, etc.) should be deposited in the diocesan archives, either the public or the secret archives — the latter in criminal and some secret marriage cases. The notaries, secretaries, and chan-

5 *Lex propria,* June 29, 1918; can. 29, § 1 (*A. Ap. S.,* I, 27).

cellors * *are not allowed to give out copies of any judicial acts or documents* which have been acquired by reason of trials without a commission by the judge.

Anonymous letters which have little or no bearing on the merits of the case, and manifestly slanderous letters, though signed by their authors, must be destroyed.

* What Archbishop (then Professor) Messmer wrote some twenty-three years ago (*Canonical Procedure*, 1897, p. 58) is still true: These different terms are "confoundedly confused"; neither can an adequate distinction be drawn from the Code. Hence a chancellor may act as notary and secretary, provided he can fill the office and is not otherwise employed in the same case; see can. 373.

TITLE IV

THE PARTIES TO THE CASE

CHAPTER I

PLAINTIFF AND DEFENDANT

In each and every trial or case there is one who complains and one who is complained against, one who accuses and one who is accused. The accuser may be the judge himself, who, in certain criminal cases, must proceed *ex officio*.[1]   Yet even in this instance he must have at least some knowledge of the case, gained from one source or another.

After setting forth the office of the judge and his duties, and outlining in general terms the mode and method of procedure, the Code now turns to the parties involved in a trial.

WHO MAY BE PLAINTIFF OR DEFENDANT

CAN. 1646

Quilibet potest in iudicio agere, nisi a sacris canonibus prohibeatur; reus autem legitime conventus respondere debet.

CAN. 1647

Licet actor vel reus conventus procuratorem vel advocatum constituerit, semper tamen tenetur in

---

1 Criminal action proper is reserved to the fiscal promoter; can. 1934.

iudicio ipsemet adesse ad praescriptum iuris vel iudicis.

First, the general rule is laid down that *any one* not prevented by the Canon Law may be plaintiff. This is a natural and inalienable right which can be to some extent limited or taken away only by way of a judicial penalty.

The terms used to designate the plaintiff are *actor, agere in iudicio, habere personam standi in iudicio,*[2] from which it may be seen how intimately this right is connected with the personal rights of man. Nor is it surprising that the Roman Law, which refused to acknowledge slaves as persons, should deny them the right of being plaintiffs, except in a very few cases of later date. Christianity knows no slaves in the Roman sense of the word. However, the exercise of personal rights supposes certain necessary personal faculties, of reason and will. Therefore the law provides for cases which concern persons not fully developed. Besides, some kind of a dependent will must be acknowledged in religious and moral persons or corporations which have a corporate will. Lastly, the law may, as stated, deprive certain delinquents of the right of acting as plaintiffs; as *defendants* all must be admitted, and all must answer when called to a trial, or sued, or accused, as otherwise criminals might profit by their malice.[3]

The question arises whether plaintiff and defendant, when duly and personally summoned, must appear *personally* before the judge. The answer is given in can. 1647, according to a Decretal[4] of Boniface VIII, but in a more extended form. Plaintiff and defendant may present their case by proxy or through advocates (law-

[2] This term might be rendered by *right to prosecute*.

[3] Cfr. c. 7, X, II, 1; c. 11, X, V, 1.

[4] C. 1, X, 6°, II, 1, which mentions only delegated judges.

yers; unless the law — which here means first and above all, the common law, then also a particular law which does not contradict the common law — or the judge demand their personal presence. The supreme judge, *i. e.*, the Pope may give the power to summon the parties personally in his letter of delegation in criminal cases. But even in civil cases the judge who acts by virtue of his office may demand the personal appearance of either plaintiff or defendant, for instance, to test his mental capacity or character, or whenever the *iuramentum calumniae* is to be administered.[5]

MINORS

CAN. 1648

§ 1. Pro minoribus et iis qui rationis usu destituti sunt, agere et respondere tenentur eorum parentes aut tutores vel curatores.

§ 2. Si iudex existimet ipsorum iura esse in conflictu cum iuribus parentum vel tutorum vel curatorum, aut ipsos tam longe distare a parentibus aut tutoribus vel curatoribus, ut hisce uti aut minime aut difficulter liceat, tunc stent in iudicio per curatorem a iudice datum.

§ 3. Sed in causis spiritualibus et cum spiritualibus connexis, si minores usum rationis assecuti sint, agere et respondere queunt sine patris vel tutoris consensu; et quidem, si aetatem quatuordecim annorum expleverint, etiam per seipsos; secus per tutorem ab Ordinario datum, vel etiam per procuratorem a se, Ordinarii auctoritate, constitutum.

5 Santi-Leitner, II, 1, n. 19.

Can. 1649

Nomine eorum de quibus in can. 100, § 3, stat in iudicio rector vel administrator, firmo praescripto can. 1653; in conflictu vero eorum iurium cum iuribus rectoris vel administratoris, procurator ab Ordinario designatus.

Can. 1650

Bonis interdicti, et ii qui minus firmae mentis sunt, stare in iudicio per se ipsi possunt tantummodo ut de propriis delictis respondeant, aut ad praescriptum iudicis: in ceteris agere et respondere debent per suos curatores.

Can. 1651

§ 1. Ut curator ab auctoritate civili alicui datus a iudice ecclesiastico admittatur, debet accedere consensus Ordinarii proprii illius cui datus est.

§ 2. Ordinarius potest quoque alium curatorem constituere pro foro ecclesiastico, si, omnibus mature perpensis, id statuendum esse prudenter censuerit.

To act personally at trials requires a normally developed mind and will. Personal rights cannot properly be exercised by infants or minors who lack judgment, and, consequently, to secure them from hurting themselves by improvident acts, not only the ecclesiastical, but the civil courts also, give them guardians.[6] Like unto infants are those adults who lack either the actual or the habitual use of reason. Therefore can. 1648 rules that for *minors* and those adults who lack the use of reason, parents or guardians are obliged to act as plaintiffs or defendants.

6 Blackstone-Cooley, *Comment.*, I, 464.

The text says: *"aut tutores aut curatores."* These two terms are comprised by the one English term *guardians,* although the Roman as well as ecclesiastical law draw a distinction between *tutores,* who are given ·to *impuberes,* and *curatores,* who are appointed for those who have reached *puberty,* but have not yet completed the age of twenty-one.[7] Also note the term *" tenentur ";* parents or guardians have the same obligation as the plaintiff or defendant himself, according to can. 1647.

However, it may be that parents or tutors have personal interests [8] of their own involved in a trial, and that these interests clash with the rights of the children or mentally incapacitated wards. In that case the judge should appoint a guardian. The same rule applies if the parents or guardians live so far away from the residence of their children or wards that they can not be present at the trial or can attend only with great difficulty. Attendance would be difficult if the distance were great or travelling inconvenient or expensive, or if there were danger of seriously delaying the trial.

The ecclesiastical law naturally favors *spiritual matters,* and matters closely connected with these, for instance, the Sacraments, *iuspatronatus* and beneficiary cases, pious legacies, etc. In all such cases minors who have attained the use of reason may act as plaintiffs or defendants without the consent of their parents or guardians; and after completing the age of fourteen, they may act by themselves without a procurator. But before they have completed the fourteenth year of age, minors, or rather

---

7 The *tutor* had charge of the maintenance and education of the minor; the *curator* had the care of his fortune; or in English law terms: the *tutor* was the committee of the person, the *curator* the committee of the estate (Blackstone-Cooley, l. c., I, 460).

8 This may easily happen if the religion of the minor is at variance· with that of the tutors, and these are bigots,

impuberes, must be represented at trials by a guardian appointed by the Ordinary, or by a procurator whom they have chosen with the approval of the Ordinary. Thus disputed engagements of minors may be answered in court by the parties themselves if [9] they are over fourteen, and this holds not only for young men, but also for girls, because the text does not discriminate as to sex.

Can. 100, § 3, compares *moral* or artificial persons, whether corporate or non-corporate, with minors. If such are called to judgment, their rector or administrator must represent them (can. 1653). But if the rector or administrator has a special interest in the trial, which might clash with the interests or rights of the corporation or juridical entity which he represents, a procurator must be appointed for said juridical persons.

Can. 1650 considers the case of *prodigals* (*bonis interdicti*) and *weak-minded persons*. We say prodigals, because the Roman law put spendthrifts, who were supposed to be incapable of managing their own affairs, under guardianship.[10] The reason for this is to be sought partly in the abnormal mental condition which shows itself in one who squanders his property, and partly in the fact that such a person may not be able to defray the expenses of a trial. The aforesaid persons, then, need appear personally only in criminal cases or when the judge demands their personal presence, which he may, even in civil cases, as explained under can. 1647. Otherwise their curators may appear for them.

If *curators* have been appointed by the *civil authority*, must the ecclesiastical judge admit them? Yes, answers

---

[9] C. 14, X, II, 13; c. 3, 6°, II, 1.

[10] L. 1, Dig. 27, 10: "*Lege XII tabularum prodigo interdicitur bonorum suorum administratio.*" In Scotch law, *interdict* means a legal restraint from executing deeds imposed on persons of weak mind; Stimson's *Law Dictionary*, 1911, s. v. "Interdict."

can. 1651, provided the Ordinary of the ward to whom the civil authority has given a curator, consents. But the same Ordinary may, if he deems prudent, appoint another curator.

Note that in canons 1648, § 3, 1649, 1651 the apposition *loci* is omitted, and hence, according to can. 198, the superiors of clerical exempt institutes are also competent.

RELIGIOUS AS PLAINTIFFS

CAN. 1652

Religiosi sine Superiorum consensu non habent personam standi in iudicio, nisi in casibus qui sequuntur:

1.° Si de vindicandis adversus religionem iuribus sibi ex professione quaesitis agatur;

2.° Si ipsi extra claustra legitime morentur et iurium suorum tuitio urgeat;

3.° Si contra ipsum Superiorem denuntiationem instituere velint.

Since religious have abdicated the habitual or actual right of holding property — which is the cause of most legal quarrels — and transferred it to the monastery, and since, besides, they depend on the will of their superiors, it follows that, to prosecute their rights as individual religious, they need the *consent of their superiors*.[11] But there are a number of exceptions, which the Code reduces to three, to wit:

1.° When a religious wishes to *prosecute rights which he has acquired* by reason of his *religious profession*, against the institute to which he belongs, he may proceed without the superior's permission. Thus if a sentence

11 Cfr. c. 11, C. 12, q. 1; c. 35, C. 16, q. 2; c. 7, X, I, 31; c. 6, X, III, 35.

of dismisal or expulsion was inflicted, and the religious believes he has just reason to complain against the same, he may bring the case before the superior (provincial or abbot) and also appeal to the higher court (general or abbot president) ; he may do this also in case he was deprived of the right of voting (active or passive).[12]

2. If a religious lawfully dwells outside the enclosure and is compelled to defend his rights, he may proceed to do so without the superior's permission. Thus a religious who, by reason of his studies (see can. 606, § 2), is absent from his monastery, is lawfully absent, and may defend his rights in the ecclesiastical and civil courts according to can. 120; a religious who is rector of a church, or administrator of a pious foundation, or chaplain of an institution, may defend his case, because his office involves the right of defence, and the permission of his superior is included in the appointment to office.[13]

3. Finally, individual religious may *denounce* their own *superiors* and prosecute the case at the expense of the monastery. The sources from which our text is taken [14] mention in a general way the right of accusing superiors who commit crimes, but the second text has in view especially the reformation of monasteries. A criminal charge is never or rarely to be brought against superiors; rather, as our text says, should denunciation be made to the next higher superior, who shall decide what course is to be taken.[15]

---

12 Cfr. c. 22, X, I, 3; Santi-Leitner, II, 1, n. 17.

13 C. 16, X, II, 1; c. 1, Clem. I, 2; Reiffenstuel, II, 1, n. 167.

14 Cc. 11, 26, X, V, 1.

15 Wernz, *l. c.*, V, n. 166. Besides, it must be understood of crimes, not of mere transgressions, for instance, of a rubric which perhaps cannot be carried out on account of circumstances and admits a common-sense interpretation, nor of every transgression of a minor ecclesiastical law.

ORDINARIES AND CORPORATIONS

CAN. 1653

§ 1. Ordinarii locorum possunt nomine ecclesiae cathedralis aut mensae episcopalis stare in iudicio; sed, ut licite agant, debent audire Capitulum cathedrale vel Consilium administrationis eorumve consensum vel consilium habere, quando periculo vertitur pecuniae summa pro qua alienanda ad normam can. 1532, § § 2, 3 eorundum consensus vel consilium requiritur.

§ 2. Beneficiarii omnes nomine beneficii possunt in iudicio agere aut respondere; quod tamen ut licite faciant, servare debent praescriptum can. 1526.

§ 3. Praelati ac Superiores Capitulorum, sodalitatum et quorumlibet collegiorum stare in iudicio nequeunt, nomine suae cuiusque communitatis, sine eiusdem consensu ad normam statutorum.

§ 4. Adversus eos de quibus in § § 1-3, si sine praescripto consensu aut consilio in iudicio egerint, piae causae aut communitati ius est ad refectionem damnorum.

§ 5. In casu vero defectus vel negligentiae illius qui administratoris munere fungitur, potest ipse loci Ordinarius per se vel per alium stare in iudicio nomine personarum moralium quae sub eius iurisdictione sunt.

§ 6. Superiores religiosi nequeunt nomine suae communitatis stare in iudicio, nisi ad normam constitutionum.

The right of *standi in judicio* by reason of administration, is a limited right because, like that of alienation, it is liable to restrictions or formalities set up by the law.

1. *Local Ordinaries* may prosecute for the rights attached to the cathedral church or to the *mensa episcopalis*.

But in order to act lawfully (*licite*) they must have the consent or advice of the chapter (diocesan consultors) or the board of administrators (according to can. 1532, § 2, 3 on alienation).

2. *Beneficiaries* (which name certainly comprises our pastors) may act as plaintiffs or defendants in the prosecution of beneficiary rights, but for so doing they need the written consent of the local Ordinary, or, in urgent cases, that of the rural dean, according to can. 1526.

3. Prelates and superiors of chapters, sodalities, and collegiate bodies cannot go to court in the name of their communities without the consent of the latter, as required by their statutes. The statutes may distinguish between the revenues, or property proper to the prelate or superior, or at least subject to his personal and exclusive administration, and goods which the prelate or superior administers in the name of the community. For these latter rights the superior needs the consent or advice of his chapter or council according to the rules laid down in the constitution or bylaws. Concerning the goods or property which the superior administers in his own name, he is not tied to the consent or advice of chapter or council.[16] However, in religious communities with solemn vows, this distinction has little weight, except in orders where the *peculium* still exists.

§ 6, therefore, simply rules that *religious superiors* of male and female organizations cannot go to court in the name of their community except in so far as their constitutions permit.

4. Those persons mentioned under nn. 1–3, if they go to court without the prescribed consent or advice, *are*

---

16 Cfr. c. 21, X, I, 3; c. 16; X, II, 1; Reiffenstuel, II, 1, n. 170 ff. In America, as far as we know, there is no distinction between the *mensa abbatis* and the *mensa communitatis*.

bound to make restitution of the damage caused to the *pia causa* or community by their action. The bishop is held to repair the damage to his cathedral or *mensa episcopalis,* the beneficiary to his benefice, prelates and superiors to their community. Of course, religious superiors who have no property of their own cannot be held to restitution, except as far as they are able and it is compatible with the vows, as stated elsewhere.[17]

5. If there is no administrator, or if he is negligent, the local Ordinary may himself or by proxy prosecute the case in the name òf those juridicial persons who are subject to his jurisdiction, as, for instance, diocesan congregations.

EXCOMMUNICATED PERSONS

CAN. 1654

§ 1. **Excommunicatis vitandis aut toleratis post sententiam declaratoriam vel condemnatoriam permittitur ut per se ipsi agant tantummodo ad impugnandam iustitiam aut legitimitatem ipsius excommunicationis; per procuratorem, ad aliud quodvis animae suae praeiudicium avertendum; in reliquis ab agendo repelluntur.**

§ 2. **Alii excommunicati generatim stare in iudicio queunt.**

Those who are under a sentence, either declaratory or condemnatory, of excommunication, either as *vitandi* or *tolerati,* are allowed to appear as plaintiffs in ecclesiastical trials only in case they wish to plead against the justice or legitimacy (validity) of the sentence of excommunication, and in this case they may defend *themselves.* But

17 Cfr. Vol. III, p. 273 of this Commentary.

if they wish to ward off spiritual injury or damage, they should act by *proxy*. If they are called into court in some other case, they must of course obey.[18]

All other persons, even though excommunicated, are admitted as plaintiffs. From this it would follow that non-Catholics are not excluded from ecclesiastical courts, as long as no declaratory sentence has been pronounced against them. (*De facto* they are excommunicated; can. 2314).

[18] Cfr. c. 7, X, II, 1; c. 2, 14, 6°, V, 11; a spiritual damage would be a marriage case or danger of spiritual ruin; Wernz, Vol. V, n. 168.

CHAPTER II

The difference between attorneys and counsels is explained by the commentators on Book I, tit. 38, *de procuratoribus*.[1] But much of what they say can hardly be applied to-day. We may say, broadly, that an attorney acts *ex officio,* while a counsel acts at random or upon the demand of the client. We did not get much enlightenment from perusing the English terminology,[2] in order to establish an adequate distinction between barristers, attorneys, advocates, and proctors. In the last analysis all these terms signify persons who plead the cause of others.

Our Code lays down certain conditions for a procurator which are not applicable to a counsel (see 1656, § 2). The procurator has limited power, whereas the counsel is not limited by established restrictions. Apart from this, as the Code itself admits, the distinction is but slight

CHOICE OF ATTORNEYS AND COUNSELS

CAN. 1655

§ 1. In iudicio criminali reus aut a se electum aut a iudice datum semper habere debet advocatum.

§ 2. Etiam in iudicio contentioso, si agatur de minoribus aut de iudicio in quo bonum publicum vertitur, iudex parti carenti defensorem ex officio at-

---

1 Cfr. Reiffenstüel, I, 38, nn. 7 ff.
2 Cfr. Stimson's *Law Dictionary, s. v.*

tribuat, aut, si casus ferat, parti etiam habenti alium adiungat.

§ 3. Praeter hos casus pars libere potest advocatum et procuratorem constituere, sed potest quoque in iudicio per se ipsa agere et respondere, nisi iudex procuratoris vel advocati ministerium necessarium existimaverit.

§ 4. At Episcopus, si quando in causa est, aliquem constituat, qui eius personam, procuratorio nomine, gerat.

CAN. 1656

§ 1. Unicum quisque potest eligere procuratorem, qui nequit alium sibimet substituere, nisi expressa facultas eidem facta fuerit.

§ 2. Quod si, iusta causa suadente, plures ab eodem deputentur, hi ita constituantur, ut detur inter ipsos locus praeventioni.

§ 3. Advocati autem plures simul constitui queunt.

§ 4. Utrumque munus, procuratoris et advocati, etiam in eadem causa et pro eodem cliente eadem persona exercere potest.

In *criminal* cases the defendant *must choose* a counsel, or at least accept one appointed by the judge. This is now the rule,[3] though it appears to have been discountenanced by the Decretals,[4] which, perhaps owing to a confusion of the counsel with the proctor, rather deny that right or duty.

The appointment of a counsel may be made even against the will of the defendant ("*semper debet habere.*")

In *civil* cases also a *defensor* (the same as counsel or

[3] S. C. EE. et RR., June 11, 1880, n. 30 f. (*Coll. P. F.*, n. 1534).   [4] C. 1, 6°, I, 19; Santi-Leitner, II, 1, n. 19.

advocatus) must be appointed by the judge for minors or in cases concerning the public welfare, if the parties have no counsel.　Besides, if a counsel or lawyer chosen by the parties, or by the civil authorities, proves undesirable or lacks the necessary qualities, as described in can. 1657, the judge may appoint another counsel.　This appointment, in all the cases mentioned, is *ex officio, i.e.,* the judge is in duty bound to make it.

With the exception of these cases, then (*vis.:* criminal cases, civil cases of minors or public interest, and of counsels not acceptable) it is left to the parties to the trial either to choose a counsel or defend their own case, unless the judge deems it necessary that a proctor or counsel should be chosen, as in case the defendant has not the necessary knowledge of legal procedure or the qualities of equipoise and calmness necessary to defend his case effectively.　Besides, it may also be that the person himself does not care to be dragged into court, or that his or her state of life does not permit him or her to leave home.[5]

If the *bishop* is a party to a case, he should designate a proctor or attorney to act in his name.　This rule was made to protect the episcopal dignity and to save bishops the trouble of leaving their pastoral occupations.[6]

Can. 1656 rules that only *one* attorney or *procurator* may be chosen by each party.　This one cannot be substituted by another, unless he has obtained special permission to that effect.　One reason for this ruling lies in the certainty required.[7]　We believe another reason is that the procurator is chosen *de industria personae, i.e.,* on account of personal fitness, which may not be found in the substitute.

5 Cfr. cc. 1, 3, 6°, II, 1; Messmer, *l. c.*, p. 74.

6 *Trid.*, Sess. 13, c. 6, *de ref.*

7 C. 1, 6°, I, 19; Reiffenstuel, I, 38, n. 56.

If *several proctors* are chosen, which can be done only for good reasons, these must be appointed to *act in solidum, i.e.,* the one who first takes hold of the cast must bring it to a finish.[8]

Counsels or *lawyers* are not limited as to number, and the parties to a trial may therefore choose several without restriction,

The office of proctor and counsel may be held by *one and the same person,* who may act in the same case and for the same client. In this case the limit as to number would certainly cease to be effective.

QUALITIES AND CONDITIONS OF ATTORNEYS AND COUNSELS

CAN. 1657

§ 1. Procurator et advocatus esse debent catholici, aetate maiores, bonae famae; acatholicus non admittitur, nisi per exceptionem et ex necessitate.

§ 2. Advocatus debet praeterea esse doctor vel alioqui vere peritus, saltem in iure canonico.

§ 3. Religiosus admitti potest, nisi aliud in constitutionibus caveatur, in causis tantum in quibus vertitur utilitas suae religionis, de licentia tamen Superioris.

CAN. 1658

§ 1. Quilibet pro lubitu a parte potest eligi et deputari procurator, dummodo secundum praecedentem canonem idoneus sit, quin opus sit ut Ordinarii approbatio antecesserit.

§ 2. Advocatus autem, ut ad patrocinium admittatur, indiget approbatione Ordinarii, quae aut generalis sit ad omnes causas aut specialis pro certa causa.

---

8 Reiffenstuel, *l. c.,* n. 24.

§ 3. In iudicio coram Sanctae Sedis delegato, ipsius delegati est approbare et admittere advocatum, quo pars uti se velle ostenderit.

§ 4. Procurator et advocatus, in causis quae ad normam can. 1579, § § 1, 2 aguntur in religionis tribunali, eligendi sunt ex eadem religione et ante patrocinii susceptionem approbandi ab eo, qui partes iudicis in causa agit; in causis vero quae ad normam eiusdem canonis § 3 apud tribunal Ordinarii loci pertractantur, admitti potest etiam religioni extraneus.

Attorneys and counsels must be *Catholics;* they must have completed the legal age of twenty-one years, and be of good moral standing. *Non-Catholics* are admitted only by way of exception and in cases of necessity.[9]

The text has a general bearing and requires only three qualities: religion, age, and reputation. Hence laymen and women are |not excluded. The Roman law permitted women to act for their parents when sickness or age prevented them.[10] The third qualification would seem to exclude excommunicated and infamous persons.[11] However, since heretics are excommunicated, and are nevertheless admitted in cases of necessity, a rigid exclusion of censured persons can hardly be maintained. In cases of *necessity,* which should at the same time be exceptional, non-Catholics may act as attorneys or counsels for the defence. An able lawyer of a non-Catholic denomination may be more successful in defending a case; we could give instances of this.

[9] This canon may also be applied to cases of appeal, for instance, of parishioners who have recourse from the bishop's decree concerning boundary lines to the Apostolic Delegate: the latter should not be more lenient than the law prescribes for courts, especially if Catholic lawyers or attorneys are available.

[10] L. 41, Dig. 3, 3; but the mother was not allowed to act as defender of her orphan son; l. 18, Cod. II, 12.

[11] C. 7, X, II, 1; cc. 1, 2, C. 3, q. 7.

Since juridical knowledge is also required, and the Code demands that counsel for defence be a *doctor* of canon law, or at least an expert in that science, it is evident that if this quality were wanting in a Catholic lawyer, but found in a non-Catholic lawyer, the case of necessity would be verified. The same rule may be proportionately applied to *Freemasons,* who belong to a condemned sect.

Religious may be admitted as attorneys and counsels to defend their own institute with the permission of their superiors and constitutions. If a religious has the same case to defend, according to can. 1652, he can be chosen procurator or counsel by the litigant religious; otherwise he needs the permission of his superior either for appointing, or being appointed as, or for acting as a substitute for, a procurator.[12]

Provided one has the qualities described in can. 1657, he may be chosen and appointed *procurator* without the formal approbation of the Ordinary. But in order to be chosen and admitted as *counsel for the defence* he must be approved by the Ordinary, who may grant that license once for all, *i.e.,* for all cases, or for a special case only.

In trials conducted before a *delegate of the Holy See,* the delegate himself is entitled to approve and admit the counsel desired by the defendant.

For trials which, according to can. 1579, § § 1, 2, are conducted exclusively by and for *religious,* the proctor and counsel for the defence are to be chosen from among the members of the institute in question. Before they assume the defence they must be approved by the judge. In cases to be tried by the local Ordinary, according to § 3, can. 1579, outsiders, *i.e.,* persons who are not members of the same religious institute, may be admitted as procura-

12 C. 3, Clem. I, 10.

tors or counsels, provided they have the qualifications described in can. 1657, § § 1 and 2.

MANDATE OF ATTORNEY AND COUNSEL

CAN. 1659

§ 1. Procurator ne prius a iudice admittatur quam speciale mandatum ad lites scriptum, etiam in calce ipsius citationis, mandantis subscriptione munitum, et locum, diem, mensem et annum referens, apud tribunal deposuerit.

§ 2. Quod si mandans scribere nesciat, hoc ipsum ex scriptura constet necesse est, et parochus vel notarius Curiae vel duo testes, loco · mandantis, mandatum subsignent.

CAN. 1660

Mandatum procurationis asservari debet in actis causae.

CAN. 1661

Advocatus, ut causae patrocinium suscipiat, habeat necesse est a parte vel a iudice commissionem ad instar mandati procuratorii, de qua in actis constare debet.

CAN. 1662

Nisi speciale mandatum habuerit, procurator non potest renuntiare actioni, instantiae vel actis iudicialibus, nec transigere, pacisci, compromittere in arbitros, deferre aut referre iusiurandum, et generatim ea agere pro quibus ius requirit mandatum speciale.

A proctor needs a special written commission, which is called *mandatum ad lites*. Before he has deposited this mandate with the tribunal, he cannot be admitted by the judge. The mandate must be signed by the *mandans* and note thereof must be made at the bottom of the official summons, from which fact it may be inferred that the mandate must be issued by the *mandans* before the summons, because after that proceeding the case has taken a legal turn (*res non amplius integra*).

The *mandate must mention the place where, and the day, month and year* when it was issued. If the *mandans* is unable to write, this fact must be noted, and the pastor or notary public of the ecclesiastical court or two witnesses must sign the mandate in his stead. The document by which a special mandate is issued to a proctor must be placed among the judicial acts of the trial.

A special mandate is required for all cases, for the text is general and therefore no cases or persons are excepted.[13] This is a very appropriate measure, because if no special mandate were necessary, there might be uncertainty as to the power of the mandatory and a loophole left for the party to attack the sentence by pleading incompetency of the proctor. Hence this special mandate, although given *ad lites*, and perhaps for all cases of a judiciary character, must define in clear terms the power of the proctor and its extent.

This special mandate *ad lites* differs from the one mentioned in can. 1662, which is also called a special mandate, but not included in the one named in can. 1659, unless expressly so determined and set down in writing. This special mandate concerns: foregoing actions, instances, and judicial acts; it may also concern transactions, agreements, compromises on arbiters, giving and requiring the oath of the other party,—all acts for which a special mandate is necessary.

---

13 The commentators allowed exceptions for relatives and co-litigants; Reiffenstuel, I, 38, n. 80 f.

The *counsel*, too, must have a commission, similar to the procuratorial mandate, either from the parties or from the judge, before he can take up the defence; and the judicial acts must take note of this commission.

REMOVAL OF ATTORNEY AND COUNSEL

CAN. 1663

Tum procurator tum advocatus possunt a iudice, dato decreto, repelli sive ex officio sive ad instantiam partis, iusta tamen de causa.

CAN. 1664

§ 1. Advocati et procuratores possunt ab eo a quo constituti sunt, removeri, salva obligatione solvendi honoraria ipsis debita; verum ut remotio effectum sortiatur, necesse est ut ipsis intimetur, et, si lis iam contestata fuerit, iudex et adversa pars certiores facti sint de remotione.

§ 2. Lata definitiva sententia, ius et officium appellandi, si mandans non renuat, procuratori manet.

CAN. 1665

§ 1. Vetatur uterque emere litem, aut sibi de immodico emolumento vel rei litigiosae parte vindicata pacisci.

§2. Quae si fecerint, nulla est pactio, et a iudice vel ab Ordinario poterunt poena pecuniaria mulctari; advocatus praeterea tum ab officio suspendi, tum etiam, si recidivus sit, destitui et titulo privari.

Can. 1666

Advocati ac procuratores qui ob dona aut pollicitationes aut quamlibet aliam rationem suum officium prodiderint, ab officio repellantur, et, praeter damnorum refectionem, mulcta pecuniaria aliisve congruis poenis plectantur.

The attorney as well as the counsel for the defence may be *rejected* by the judge, who in that case must issue a corresponding decree, either *ex officio* or upon demand of the party.

However, a just cause is required for such action. Such a cause would be the fact of relationship or suspicion of conspiracy or inability discovered later.

The counsel as well as the procurator may be *discharged* by those who appointed them, provided, of course, their salaries have been paid or guaranteed. Besides, since a mandate was given, the revocation must be intimated to the proctor or counsel and also to the judge and the other party, after the *litis contestatio*. After this stage it is generally supposed that a just reason is required for revocation because of the expenses already incurred and of the good name of the attorney and counsel.[14] No reason, however, is required if the party who has appointed a proctor or counsel dies before the case has taken a legal turn, *i.e.*, before the judicial summons have been issued.

After the definitive or final sentence the *attorney is entitled and obliged to appeal* the case if his client does not object.

Attorney as well as counsel are forbidden to buy the case or to *make an agreement* as to large profit or part of the disputed object. Every such agreement is null and

14 Reiffenstuel, I, 38, n. 136.

void, and the transgressor may, besides, be fined by the judge or Ordinary; the counsel may be suspended and, in case of relapse, be removed and deprived of his title.

Counsels or attorneys who allow themselves to be *bribed by gifts or promises,* or in any other way, thus betraying their trust, must be removed, condemned to repair the damage done, and fined by the court.

TITLE V.

ACTIONS AND EXCEPTIONS

IN GENERAL

CAN. 1667

Quodlibet ius non solum actione munitur, nisi aliud expresse cautum sit, sed etiam exceptione, quae semper competit et est suapte natura perpetua.

CAN. 1668

§ 1. Qui ad rem sibi vindicandam, seu ad ius suum in iudicio persequendum titulo agit iuris auctoritate subnixo, actione dimicat quae *petitoria* dicitur.

§ 2. Si vero rei possessionem vel iuris quasi-possessionem postulat, eius actio *possessoria* vocatur.

CAN. 1669

§ 1. Actor pluribus simul actionibus, quae tamen secum ipsae non confligant, sive de eadem re, sive de diversis, reum convenire potest, si aditi tribunalis competentiam non egrediantur.

§ 2. Reus non prohibetur pluribus exceptionibus etiam contrariis uti.

CAN. 1670

§ 1. Actor potest una instantia cumulare actiones possessorias et petitorias, nisi spolii exceptio ex adverso opponatur.

§ 2. Pariter fas est reo convento in petitorio, actorem reconvenire in possessorio; et viceversa, nisi res sit de spolio.

CAN. 1671

§ 1. Item fas est actori, antequam conclusum fuerit in causa, ab instituto iudicio petitorio regredi ad possessorium adipiscendae vel recuperandae.

§ 2. Imo ex iusta causa iudex etiam post conclusionem in causa, sed ante sententiam definitivam, hunc regressum permittere potest.

§ 3. Iudicis est, attentis partium allegationibus, aut utramque quaestionem unica sententia definire, aut prius uni, postea alteri satisfacere, prouti magis expedire ipsi videatur ad celeriorem et pleniorem iurium tuitionem.

What the Code sets forth in this title really forms part of the legal proceedings, because, according to the structure of the Roman trial, the *actio* as well as the *exceptio* were brought after the summons. However, they are appropriately treated here because they are remedies granted by law to redress grievances or injuries, and to reply to these by the defendant. For every right may be supported and sustained, not only by an action, but also by an exception, unless the law expressly forbids the latter.

Actio signifies the cause or legal demand of a right, either corporeal or incorporeal, spiritual or temporal. In Roman law it meant a certain prescribed form of words derived directly from the law upon which the claim was founded. To this form it was necessary to adhere strictly. The parties having appeared before the praetor, the plaintiff stated his claim (*intentio*) and asked leave to bring the suit into court (*actionem postulabat*). The defendant then either denied his liability or put in a plea in law (*exceptio*).[1] Such an exception or counter-charge is also admitted in ecclesiastical courts. It is always within the right of the defendant to put in this plea, which is by its very nature perpetual. Thus although prescription may eliminate penal action in criminal cases, yet the right of exception always remains intact ("*temporalia ad agendum, perpetua sunt ad excipiendum*").[2] This also holds good concerning possessory claims, as shall be seen under can. 1698.

There are two actions, especially in civil cases, which are here taken over from former law sources:[3] the one by which the plaintiff seeks to vindicate a thing in court or a right founded, as he believes, on the authority of law. This action is called petitory (*actio petitoria*). The other by which the plaintiff claims possession or quasi-possession of a thing (*actio possessoria*). For in every complete title to an object of right, either movable or immovable, two things are necessary: the possession or *seisin*, and the right or property, which in terms of old English law was called *iuris et seisinae coniunctio*.[4]

Possession or seisin may be severed from property, although in common parlance the two terms are used promiscuously. Possession is the retention of an object in which bodily and mental occupation concur with the law ("*rei detentio corporis, animi, iuris adminiculo suffulta*"). *Ius* here is taken, not in the subjective sense, to designate the moral faculty of holding a thing, but rather in the objective sense, to designate the law which

1 Cfr. Ramsay-Lanciani, *Roman Antiquities*, 1901, p. 32 ff.; the five *legis actiones* were: *sacramento, per judicis postulationem, per convictionem, per manus iniectionem, per pignoris captionem*; later these were superseded to a great extent by the *formula petitoria* and by *sponsio*.

2 S. C. EE. et RR., March 8, 1898 (*Coll. P. F.*, n. 1992).

3 See X, II, 12.

4 Blackstone-Cooley, *Comment.*, III, 176.

protects the possessor.[5] Of course, where there is no
title at all, either at the beginning or in the course of
occupation, the ecclesiastical law (differing here from the
Roman law) never defends possession, but the *auctoritas
iuris* ceases.

The term *quasi-possession* in our Code indicates rights
which are not properly possessed, but are incorporeal, for
instance, the right of election.   However, even in this case
a visible or manifest assertion is required, as the text in
the Decretals clearly proves.[6] Hence also in holding an
immaterial right, a tangible proof or fact is necessary,
and therefore the definition given above is to the point.

Property is a right to some thing, especially a corporeal
object, by which the holder is empowered to dispose of
it at his pleasure, to the exclusion of others.   Property
differs from possession in more than one way.   Possession means the right of retaining a thing, whereas property is the title by which one vindicates something as his
own.   Again, property may be acquired by merely mental
action, whereas possession requires actual holding, etc.,
etc.[7]

It is evident that the *causa proprietatis* is more important, but also more difficult to prove, than the *causa
possessionis*, which, even though called momentary or
transient, is more palpable.

If a plaintiff thinks he has *several cases,* either concerning the same object or different objects, he may bring
them to court together, provided, of course, the respective tribunal is competent in all and there is no conflict
between the different claims.   On the other hand, the

5 Santi-Leitner, II, 12, n. 2.
6 C. 3, X, II, 12; the lower
clergy of Sutri (in Italy) claimed
the right of voting at the election of
the bishop, and had exercised this
right at the election of three bishops,
— which was a manifestation of the
title involved and was acknowledged
by the pope; see c. 16, X, II, 2.
7 Reiffenstuel, II, 12, n. 30 ff.

defendant is allowed to put in a counterplea to all the cases brought against him. Thus an advowee may bring suit for the right of presentation and the support he thinks he is entitled to, if he was disturbed in his possession. The mere fact of such a suit could be taken cognizance of by a lay judge, but the *ius patronatus* or the right of property cannot be decided by the lay judge, who therefore lacks competency.[8]

The plaintiff may bring a possessory and a petitory claim at the same time and before the same judge. On the other hand, the defendant is allowed to oppose to the petitory claim of the plaintiff his counterclaim of possession, and conversely. This is called bulking, or *cumulatio causae possessionis cum causa proprietatis*. For instance, a pastor who has been removed for some reason, claims salary due him. To obtain full justice he may assert that he is still the lawful pastor and in possession of the parish, although removed. The petitory claim is the title to the pastorship, the possessory claim, the actual holding of the parish. His rival may be able to prove that N. is not the pastor, or that N. has never held the legal title. These two conflicting claims may be settled at the same trial. Nor is it useless to bulk both claims, because the question may thus be more speedily settled. Besides, there is question of restitution. For the plaintiff may be victorious as to the petitory claim, but not as to the possessory claim, and in that case the revenues are due to him from the time when the petitory claim was settled, but not for the previous period.[9]

Bulking is not permitted in cases of disseisin (*causae spolii*) because these require the return of the object vio-

8 Cc. 2, 3, X, II, 1; Santi-Leitner,   II, 13; Santi-Leitner, II, 12, n.
II, 12, n. 12.   13 ff.

9 Cc. 2, 3, 4, X, II, 12; c. 1, X,

lently seized to the original possessor, or at least that it be put in a safe place.

The law also allows the plaintiff *to change* the sequence of his claims. Thus if he brought the petitory cause or claim to property first, he may waive it for a time and have the possessory right settled first. However, this may concern only the right of obtaining or regaining possession, but not of retaining it, because he who claims possession in law, is not supposed to be in possession. Besides, this change is allowed only before the *conclusio causae, i.e.,* before all the proofs and depositions are given and the parties have renounced the right to produce additional evidence.[10]

The judge himself may, for a just reason, permit this change before the final sentence. Such a reason may be the quicker settlement of the disputed case and the saving of expense.

The judge may also decide a twofold controversy involving petitory and possessory claims *by one sentence,* if the allegations were such as to comprehend the whole case. Or he may first decide one claim and then the other, if he regards such action as conducive to the quicker and better defence of the rights at issue.

The Code now proceeds to consider various actions, or rather remedies of law and counterpleas, which must be settled before the final or definitive sentence can be rendered, and which tend to secure a full adjustment as well as security from damages and injuries while the case is pending.

10 Cfr. c. 36, X, II, 20.

CHAPTER I

CAN. 1672

§ 1. Qui ostenderit super aliqua re ab alio detenta ius se habere sibique damnum imminere nisi res ipsa custodienda tradatur, ius habet obtinendi a iudice eiusdem rei sequestrationem.

§ 2. In similibus rerum adiunctis obtinere potest ut iuris exercitium alicui inhibeatur.

§ 3. Sequestratio rei et inhibitio exercitii iuris a iudice decerni potest ex officio, instante praesertim promotore iustitiae aut defensore vinculi, quoties bonum publicum id postulare videatur.

CAN. 1673

§ 1. Ad crediti quoque securitatem sequestratio rei admittitur, dummodo de creditoris iure liquido constet et servata norma de qua in can. 1923, § 1.

§ 2. Sequestratio extenditur etiam ad res debitoris quae depositi causa aut quolibet alio titulo apud alias personas reperiantur.

CAN. 1674

Sequestratio rei et suspensio exercitii iuris decerni nullatenus possunt, si damnum quod timetur, possit aliter reparari et idonea cautio de eo reparando offeratur.

§ 1. Ad custodiam rei sequestrationi subiectae idonea persona, proponentibus partibus, a iudice designetur, quae sequester dicitur; si partes inter se dissentiant, iudex ex officio sequestrem deligat.

§ 2. Sequester in re custodienda, curanda et servanda non minorem diligentiam adhibere debet quam suis adhibet rebus, eamque postea, cui iudex decreverit, reddere tenetur cum omni causa.

§ 3. Iudex congruam decernat mercedem sequestri, si eam petat.

A plaintiff, under the Roman law,[1] sometimes requested the *praetor* to issue an *interdictum* or summary order to secure his rights by preventing anything from being done to deteriorate or injure the object claimed. This, in ecclesiastical language, is termed *sequestration*. It is a writ issued by the judge to take a disputed object held by any one, whether the plaintiff or the defendant, and place it in the custody of a third party, called *sequester*, in order to prevent the object from being damaged.

A kind of sequestration is that of the exercise of rights otherwise acknowledged; this is called *inhibition*. Thus a beneficiary may be commanded by the ecclesiastical judge to suspend the exercise of his rights; a husband, the validity of whose marriage is disputed in court, may be commanded to let the wife go to a place of security, or a bride claimed by two rivals may be told to go to a convent, until the question is settled.

Sequestration and inhibition (or injunction) may be decreed by the judge *ex officio* whenever the public welfare is at stake and the promoter or defender demand it. It

1 Cfr. Ramsay-Lanciani, *l. c.*, p. 327; in English law it means taking   property of the defendant in contempt; Blackstone-Cooley, III, 444.

may also be decreed in case a *creditor* has a clear and proved title to the thing which requires security. And in that case all the things which the debtor has in his custody as a deposit or pawn, or under another claim, may be sequestered.

But neither sequestration nor inhibition may be decreed if the danger of damage can be warded off otherwise and bail is given to cover possible deterioration or damage.

The *sequester* may be proposed either by the parties to the suit or by the judge if the parties cannot agree upon a fit person. The *sequester* must take care of the things entrusted to him as he would of his own belongings, *i.e.*, he must bestow ordinary (not extraordinary) care on them and in the end restore them to those to whom the judge awards them. The judge shall decide, at the request of the sequester, what recompense is due him for his trouble.

CHAPTER II

Can. 1676

§ 1. Qui ex aliquo novo opere damnum timet suae rei obventurum, potest illud iudici nuntiare ut opus interrumpatur, donec utriusque partis iura, iudicis sententia, definiantur.

§ 2. Is cui intimata fuerit prohibitio, continuo ab opere cessare debet, sed, dummodo idonee caveat se in pristinum omnia restituturum si absoluto iudicio victus discesserit, poterit a iudice continuationem eiùsdem impetrare.

§ 3. Nuntianti novum opus ad ius suum demonstrandum duo menses praefiniuntur; qui ex iusta et necessaria causa a iudice, audita altera parte, prorogari vel reduci poterunt.

Can. 1677

Si vetus opus magna ex parte immutetur, idem ius esto quod de novo opere can. 1676 constitutum est.

Can. 1678

Qui grave damnum rei suae imminere pertimescit ex alieno aedificio quod ruinam minatur, ex arbore aut ex alia re quacunque, actionem habet *de damno infecto* ad obtinendam periculi remotionem, aut cautionem de damno vel avertendo, vel compensando, si forte evenerit.

127

Under the Roman law a citizen was obliged to give notice of a new structure to the prefect of the city, who could command it to be discontinued for good reasons. This law, says a Decretal, was initiated or adopted by the Church.[1]   Hence anyone who fears that a new structure may be prejudicial to his interests, either material or spiritual (for instance, because it damages his property or curtails his jurisdictional rights or revenues), may denounce the same to the ecclesiastical judge and demand a decree ordering the work to be discontinued until the claims of both parties can be adjusted by a judicial sentence.

The one who receives notice of such a prohibitory decree must desist from the work begun.   However, he may ask to continue on condition that he give bail and restore everything to the *status quo* if he should lose the trial.

The one who objects to a new structure has two months to prove his claim; but this term may, at the demand of the other party, be either prolonged or shortened by the judge.   The same rule applies to substantial changes in an old structure.[2]

Those who are afraid that a decaying edifice may cause them damage, may institute an action *de damno infecto*, in order to have the danger removed or to obtain security against possible damage.   This strictly belongs to the competency of the civil court.

1 Cfr. cc. 1, 2, X, V, 32.
2 S. C. EE. et RR., Sept. 21,   1838.

CHAPTER III

CAN. 1679

Si actus aut contractus sit ipso iure nullus, datur ei, cuius interest, actio ad obtinendam a iudice declarationem nullitatis.

CAN. 1680

§ 1. Nullitas actus tunc tantum habetur, cum in eo deficiunt quae actum ipsum essentialiter constituunt, aut sollemnia seu conditiones desiderantur a sacris canonibus requisitae sub poena nullitatis.

§ 2. Nullitas alicuius actus non importat nullitatem actorum qui praecedunt aut subsequuntur et ab actu non dependent.

CAN. 1681

Qui actum posuit nullitatis vitio infectum, tenetur de damnis et expensis erga partem laesam.

CAN. 1682

Nullitas actus a iudice declarari non potest ex officio, nisi aut publice id intersit, aut agatur de pauperibus vel de minoribus aliisve qui minorum iure censentur.

CAN. 1683

Iudex inferior de confirmatione, a Romano Pontifice actui vel instrumento adiecta, videre non potest, nisi Apostolicae Sedis praecesserit mandatum.

An act is called null and void if its essential constituents, or any of the formalities or requisites prescribed by law under penalty of nullity, are wanting. Thus ordination performed under physical compulsion is null and void.[1] A marriage contracted under the influence of grave fear (can. 1088) is null and void. A religious profession made under similar circumstances is invalid.[2] In marriage the solemnities or conditions are manifest, because a marriage contracted without the prescribed form is null and void.[3] A division of parishes is void if made without canonical reason.[4]

However, from the fact that an act is null and void, it by no means follows that the preceding or following acts are also null and void, unless indeed they depend upon the void act itself. Thus in contracts, whatever depends on the agreement itself, must necessarily be tainted with the defects inherent therein. Independent acts, as also records and minutes, are valid if not essentially connected with the invalid act. For instance, borrowing money in view of a division of a parish would not be invalid, because not necessarily connected with the act of division.

If one of the interested parties (not a third person) wishes to bring suit against an act he considers null, he may ask the judge to declare it null and void. Take the example of a religious profession which is claimed to be null and void on account of fear. In that case the judge would have to demand proofs; for a mere assertion cannot be accepted before the law.

Under can. 1682, the judge cannot *ex officio* declare the nullity of an act, unless the *public welfare* is at stake,

1 Can. 103, § 1.   3 Can. 1096 f.
2 Can. 572.   4 Can. 1428.

and in case of minors. The public welfare is generally at stake in matrimonial cases, because marriage is a requisite of public order. The same is true of ordinations.

The judge may proceed *ex officio* in case of minors because these are under the special tutelage of the Church. Therefore, those who have not yet completed the age of twenty-one, as well as all ecclesiastical corporations and noncorporate entities,[5] enjoy the benefit of this law.

No judge who has common sense and a conscience will pronounce an act null, unless he has good reasons for doing so, for can. 1681 rules that he who acts invalidly is bound to indemnify the party injured by his invalid act.

It may be useful [6] to add that an act performed with deliberation (*i.e.*, every human act), must be considered valid until the contrary is proved or is at least notorious. The nullity of an act can be easily proved if a substantial formality has been omitted, or if the act contravenes a prohibitory statute or law, or if it exceeds the limits of a faculty or mandate, or the wording of a rescript. Otherwise an act, even if doubtful, must be regarded as valid.

If the judge is not acting in the capacity of ordinary or independent judge, but as delegate or inferior judge, the rule holds: "*Actus regulariter tribuitur ordinanti, non exequenti.*" This applies especially if the Roman Pontiff confirms an act or a document. The act of *confirmation* may concern an act of the judge (for instance, his sentence), a privilege, a contract (for instance, alienation), a statute or decree of appointment. If an inferior judge receives such a ratification from the Pope or from one of the S. Congregations or Tribunals, he must take cognizance of it, because the order of jurisdiction de-

[5] Can. 100, § 3.
[6] Cfr. Barbosa, *Tractatus Varii,* Axioma 13, *s.v.* "Actus"; cfr. can. 1625, § 1.

mands that the authority, of the inferior be silent when the superior places an act under his special protection. Hence the clause is sometimes added in rescripts: "*sublata cuilibet aliter iudicandi atque interpretandi facultate.*" Yet, since the Roman Pontiff does not claim infallibility in matters of an individual nature and of a judiciary character, and since fraud may have been committed by the petitioner, a means is needed to recognize even apostolic letters. This is expressed in our text, can. 1683 as follows: "*nisi Apostolicae Sedis praecesserit mandatum.*" It means that the judge, if he has a strong suspicion of fraud, can demand the *aperitio oris,* in order to be enabled to take cognizance of the facts and the proofs which elicited the confirmation. Thus are safeguarded on the one side the authority of the supreme judge and, on the other, the administration of justice.

CHAPTER IV

These are two actions, of which one is called ordinary, the other extraordinary, because the latter supposes, as it were, that all ordinary means for obtaining redress have been exhausted. Hence it is granted (can. 1687) only when ordinary means prove insufficient.

RESCISSORY ACTION

CAN. 1684

§ 1. Si quis motus metu gravi iniuste incusso, vel dolo circumventus actum posuerit vel contractum inierit qui ipso iure non sit nullus, poterit, metu vel dolo probato, obtinere actus vel contractus rescissionem actione quae vocatur *rescissoria*.

§ 2. Eadem actione intra biennium uti potest, qui gravem ex contractu laesionem ultra dimidium ex errore passus est.

CAN. 1685

Institui haec actio potest:

1.° Contra eum qui metum intulit aut dolum patravit, quamvis ipse non in suum, sed in alterius commodum talia peregerit;

2.° Contra quemlibet malae fidei et etiam bonae fidei possessorem, qui res metu vel dolo extortas possidet, salvo iure regressus contra quemlibet usque ad ipsum metus vel doli auctorem.

CAN. 1686

Si is qui metum intulit aut dolum patravit, urgeat actus vel contractus exsecutionem, parti laesae seu deceptae competit exceptio metus vel doli.

Broadly speaking, a rescissory action is one brought to avoid an obligation or deed which follows an act or contract. Here the term is specially applied to an action based on fear or deceit (*metus vel dolus*). Canon 1684 says that one who acted under the influence of grave fear, unjustly inflicted, or who was deceived, is entitled to demand nullification of the act thus committed or the contract made. In order to understand this law it must be remembered that even grave fear does not render an act simply involuntary, but only *secundum quid,* unless the law makes a special exception, as, for instance, in favor of freedom of religious profession and marriage.[1] The conditions of fear have been explained elsewhere.[2] But a judge cannot proceed unless he has proofs as to the existence and degree of fear,— which proofs, as stated more than once, must be solid.

This *actio ex metu vel dolo* is also at the disposal of one who has by mistake sustained a loss of more than half of what was stipulated in a contract. In that case what is required is rather *restitutio in integrum.* However, the legislator appears to compare *error* to *dolus,* and, besides, the time is here split into half, so that this action may be brought within two years from the date when one obtained knowledge of the damage sustained.

Rescissory action may be brought, not only against the one who has threatened fear or committed deceit, but also against the one in whose behalf the threat was made. Be-

1 See can. 103, §2; can. 572; can. 1087.

2 Cfr. this *Commentary,* Vol. II, p. 29 ff.

sides, it may be brought against any one who acted in bad faith or who, though in good faith, retains goods extorted by fear or deceit. However a possessor *bonae fidei* is entitled to retort the action upon the one who exercised the fear or deceit. Finally, if he who inspired fear or employed deceit should insist upon fulfillment of the contract or execution of the deed, the party who has been injured is entitled to put in a counterplea of fear or deceit (*exceptio metus vel doli*).

RESTITUTION IN INTEGRUM

CAN. 1687

§ 1. Minoribus vel minorum iure fruentibus graviter laesis eorumque heredibus et successoribus, ad laesionem reparandam ex negotio seu actu valido rescindibili, praeter alia ordinaria remedia, suppetit remedium extraordinarium restitutionis in integrum.

§ 2. Hoc beneficium maioribus quoque conceditur quos deficit rescissoria actio aut aliud ordinarium remedium, dummodo iustam subesse causam et laesionem sibi imputandam non esse probaverint.

CAN. 1688

§ 1. Restitutio in integrum peti debet ab ordinario iudice, qui competens est respectu illius, contra quem petitur, intra quadriennium ab adepta maioritate computandum, si agatur de minoribus, a die laesionis factae et cessati impedimenti, si de maioribus aut personis moralibus.

§ 2. Minoribus vel minorum iure fruentibus restitutio concedi potest a iudice etiam ex officio, audito vel instante promotore iustitiae.

CAN. 1687-1689

Restitutio in integrum id efficit ut omnia revocentur in pristinum, idest restituantur in statum quo erant ante laesionem, salvis iuribus quae alii, bona fide, ante petitam restitutionem quaesiverint.

Restitutio in integrum is an extraordinary remedy of the law, by which a party grievously damaged or injured, is restored by the authority of the judge to his original condition (*in statum quo ante laesionem*).[3] The persons who are principally benefitted by this legal remedy are *minors,* and those who in law enjoy the privilege of minors, viz., ecclesiastical corporations and non-corporate juridical entities (pious foundations, religious), their heirs and successors.

The object of this remedy is to repair damage sustained by reason of a rescindible deed or act, even though this deed or act may in itself have been valid, and therefore obligatory. This return or restitution to the original condition or status (*ante petitam restitutionem*) restores all the rights acquired bona fide before the restitution was asked. Alienation furnishes an example. An administrator has alienated a piece of church property by selling it to a layman, who paid the price demanded. The *promotor iustitiae* or fiscal attorney perceives that the bargain was detrimental to the church or community and asks the ecclesiastical court for a *restitutio in integrum*. What must be done in that case? The administrator must restore the price paid for the church property and, besides, refund whatever expenses the layman may have incurred for improvements, etc.[4] Whether the layman

---

[3] Cfr. the commentators on X, I, 41 especially Boekhn and Reiffenstuel.   [4] C. 11, X, III, 13.

has to restore the profit or interest received from the property after the expenses are repaid, is a controverted question, and therefore in the court of conscience the layman could hardly be held to restitution.

Attention may be drawn to the term: *"ante petitam restitutionem."* For it is not required that restitution be already granted, because if it was asked for, the *bona fides* of the possessor could hardly be sustained.

Can. 1688 rules that restitution must be asked from the judge who is competent with regard to the one against whom the injunction is asked, whether he be plaintiff or defendant.

In regard to the *time* within which the demand for an injunction is to be made, the text distinguishes, because, as stated under can. 1687, § 2, not only minors are granted the benefit of restitution, but also those who cannot avail themselves of rescissory action or other remedies under the law, provided they can prove that they have a just cause and have sustained injury or damage beyond their own responsibility or culpability; for instance, if one was lawfully absent, or detained by hostile forces, or deceived through ignorance.[5] *Minors* in the proper sense, *i.e.,* those who have not yet completed the twenty-first year, must put in the demand for restitution within *four years* after they have completed the aforesaid age. This period of four years is here taken in the sense of *tempus continuum*, reckoning ferial days as well as days of absence, in other words, it runs continually, regardless of any obstacle that may suspend the use of time granted.

Those who are of age and all *juridical persons* have four years' time to demand an injunction, but this term runs from the moment the injury or damage was done and from the cessation of the impediment that prevented

5 Reiffenstuel, I, 41, n. 50 ff.

them from demanding restitution. By "*dies laesionis factae*" must certainly be understood not merely the time when the damage was done, but when it was realized or perceived.[6] This interpretation seems evident from the apposition: "*cessati impedimenti,*" for one cannot realize an obstacle (for instance, absence or detention), if he does not realize or perceive the damage done.

Finally, the Code permits the judge to grant to minors and to those who enjoy the privileges of minors, the benefit of restitution also *ex officio,* upon the advice or demand of the *promotor iustitiae.* This may be favorable to religious, who in law are compared to minors; but they cannot be said to belong to those under age. When does the four years' term begin with them? Either at the same time as for those who are of age, or according to the decision of the judge.

[6] Engel I, 41, n. 11.

CHAPTER V

CAN. 1690

§ 1. Actio quam reus coram eodem iudice in eodem iudicio instituit contra actorem ad submovendam vel minuendam eius petitionem, dicitur *reconventio.*

§ 2. Reconventio reconventionis non admittitur.

CAN. 1691

Actio reconventionalis locum habere potest in omnibus causis contentiosis, exceptis causis spolii; in criminalibus vero non admittitur, nisi ad normam can. 2218, § 3.

CAN. 1692

Proponenda est iudici coram quo actio principalis instituta est, licet ad unam causam dumtaxat delegato vel alioquin incompetenti, nisi sit absolute incompetens.

An action by which the defendant endeavors to stop, or at least to curtail, the plea or demand of the plaintiff, is called counter-charge or counter-plea if made before the same judge and during the same trial. Such a counter-plea cannot be upset by another counter-plea of the plaintiff; the reason probably is not to prolong the trial unduly.

A counter-plea is permitted only in *civil matters,* and

139

in these to the whole extent, except in cases of disseissin. In criminal matters a counter-plea is permitted only where mutual injuries are charged, according to can. 2218.

The counter-plea is to be made before the judge before whom the main suit was brought, even though he may be delegated for one special case only and may not be fully competent, provided, however, he be at least relatively competent, *i.e.*, either by reason of the matter involved, or of the person.

CHAPTER VI

CAN. 1693

Qui ad possessionem alicuius rei adipiscendam, vel ad alicuius iuris exercitium obtinendum munitur titulo legitimo, petere potest, ut in rei possessionem vel iuris exercitium immittatur.

CAN. 1694

Non solum possessio, sed etiam simplex detentio praestat, ad normam canonum qui sequuntur, actionem vel exceptionem possessoriam.

CAN. 1695

§ 1. Qui annum integrum in possessione rei vel in quasi-possessione iuris manserit, si molestiam patiatur quominus suam possessionem vel quasi-possessionem retineat, habet actionem *retinendae possessionis*.

CAN. 1696

§ 1. Etiam qui vi, clam vel precario possidet, actione *retinendae possessionis* uti potest adversus quemlibet deturbatorem: non autem contra personam a qua ipse rem vi vel clam surripuit aut precario accepit.

§ 2. In causis quae ad bonum publicum spectant, iustitiae promotori ius est opponendi vitium possessionis adversus eum qui vi, clam vel precario possidet.

141

CAN. 1697

§ 1. Si inter duos controversia oriatur uter eorum possideat, ille in possessione praeferendus est qui intra annum frequentiores et potiores possessionis actus exercuit.

§ 2. In dubio iudex possessionem pro indiviso utrique parti attribuat.

§ 3. Si rei vel iuris indoles aut contentionum et rixarum periculum non patiantur ut litigantibus pro indiviso possessio interim attribuatur, iudex rem apud sequestrem deponi, aut iuris quasi-possessionem suspendi iubeat usque ad iudicii petitorii exitum.

CAN. 1698

§ 1. Qui vi aut clam quoquo modo a possessione rei vel quasi-possessione iuris deiectus est, adversus quemlibet spolii auctorem vel rei detentorem habet actionem *recuperandae possessionis* vel de spolio et spolii exceptionem.

§ 2. Haec actio non admittitur praeterlapso anno postquam spolium passus rei notitiam habuit; exceptio, contra, perpetua est.

CAN. 1699

§ 1. Spoliatus adversus spoliantem excipiens et probans spolium, non tenetur respondere, nisi prius fuerit in suam possessionem restitutus.

§ 2. Spoliatus ut in possessionem restitutatur, nil aliud probare debet, nisi spoliationem ipsam.

§ 3. Sed si in restitutione rei vel exercitii iuris aliquod occurrat periculum (ex. gr., saevitiarum, cum vir contra uxorem postulat restitutionem coniugalis,

consortii), iudex, ad instantiam partis vel promotoris
iustitiae, pro diversis personarum causarumve adiunctis decernat aut restitutionem suspendi, aut rem vel
personam apud sequestrem custodiri, donec causa
petitorio iudicio definiatur.

CAN. 1700

Iudicia possessoria absolvenda sunt, citata dumtaxat adversa parte in iudiciis retinendae vel recuperandae; citatis vero omnibus iis quorum interest, in
iudiciis adipiscendae.

Possession, as distinguished from the right of property, is the holding of a thing by the concurrent operation
of body, mind, and law. Hence either a real or fictitious [1]
apprehension of the thing itself, or at least the aid of a
law or statute, is necessary for possession. Possession
presupposes a right, *i.e.*, a just cause for possessing. But
one may claim possession without reference to the title
upon which it is based. It is this that constitutes what is
known as *actio possessoria*.

If an object is claimed by one who is not yet in possession thereof, but thinks he is entitled to it, either by a
fictitious or a statutory title, we have what is called *actio
rei adipiscendae*.

Our text appropriately adds: " or to obtain the exercise
of certain rights," for instance, that of election or presentation; and this is called *quasi-possessio*.[2]

In order to justify the act of quasi-possession three
things are said to be required: (a) the exercise of the
right through certain acts indicative of the same; (b) the

---

[1] *Fictitious* is the apprehension which by a fiction of law is con-sidered equivalent to real possession, for instance, the delivery of a docu-ment or a key.

[2] C. 3, X, II, 12.

knowledge and forbearance of the superior or those who might otherwise claim that right; (c) the intention of the one who exercises the right to claim it as his own.[3] However, it must be added that it appears unjustifiable to demand an exercise of a right (*actus illius iuris*) in order to insure the acquisition thereof, for instance, the right of presentation. This demand seems to be based upon a confusion of exercise with prescription. Electors may claim the right of voting by belonging lawfully to a chapter. Therefore the *titulus legitimus* must be sought in the fictitious or legal title which conveys the right to possession.

But not only the possession, but also the *detention* of an object or right entitles the detainer to a possessory action or exception. The one who wishes to possess the thing or right he claims, is put into possession, the detainer is detained in its possession. The plaintiff brings suit before the judge to obtain or acquire possession of the thing or right, and the judge issues an *interdict* or decree which secures possession to the claimant,[4] at least *ad interim.*

One who is in possession of a thing or right,— for instance, a beneficiary or owner of church property,— may suffer *molestation* from another. If the holder has been in possession for one full year, he may ask the judge to issue a decree " *uti possidetis* " or " *utrobi* " for either immovable or movable property. This writ has the same effect as an *actio retinendae possessionis*. But it must be brought within one year from the beginning of the disturbance, and against the disturber, so that he may stop the vexation.

---

3 Reiffenstuel, II, 12, n. 151.

4 There are five *interdicti adipiscendae possessionis: interdictum quorum bonorum, interdictum quod legatorum, interdictum possessorium, interdictum sectorium, interdictum Salvianum;* Santi-Leitner, II, 12, n.

An *actio retinendae possessionis* may also be brought by one who forcibly, stealthily, or precariously (*i.e.*, by begging), possesses a thing against the disturber, but not against the person from whom he has taken the thing in the above-named manner. This privilege was not granted formerly as an action proper, but was allowed in cases of violence or stealthy or beggarly possession. However, the legislator permits this action in order to avoid other acts of violence and fraud; but he also empowers the *promotor iustitiae* to take exception or oppose the crime of violent, stealthy, or beggarly possession against a possessor, if the public welfare demands such action.

If a controversy arises which of two possessors *actually* holds possession, that one is to be preferred who has exercised more frequent and conspicuous acts, for instance, of administration, or in acquiring a servitude or right of way.[5] If the judge is still in doubt to whom to adjudge the disputed property, he may grant it to both competitors *pro indiviso, i.e.*, to each one full possession indivisibly. If this is infeasible on account of quarrels or contentions, he may command the litigants to deposit the disputed object with a *sequester*, and suspend *quasi-possession* until the petitory cause is settled.

A third action is that of *recuperandae, i.e.*, having the possession or quasi-possession of an object adjudged to the one from whom it was forcibly or stealthily taken. To this corresponds the *edictum "unde vi"* of the judge against the author of disseissin or detainer of an object. But the latter may also put in a counter-charge of disseissin. The action proper may not be accepted after the lapse of one year, to be reckoned from the moment one has become aware of the disseissin. But the *exceptio* or counter-plea is perpetual, *i.e.*, exception can be brought

5 Cc. 3, 9, X, II, 19.

against it at any time.   The *spoliatus* or disseissined, who
puts in the counter-charge, has only to prove the fact of
disseissin and is not obliged to answer any questions until
he has been put in possession, and to obtain that he has
only to prove the fact of possession.

Sometimes the restitution of possession or quasi-possession may be dangerous.   Thus if a woman (supposed
wife) or a girl engaged to one man and claimed by another would have to be delivered to the so-called husband
or bridegroom there might be danger of maltreatment.[6]
In this case the judge shall suspend restitution or decide
that the person or object be confided to a sequester until
the petitory cause is settled.   Thus he may decide that the
woman be kept in custody by her relatives, or that the girl
claimed by two rivals go to a convent until the claims are
definitively adjudged.

Possessory actions which are *retinendae* and *recuperandae* must be settled by summoning the adversary, but
actions called *adipiscendae* require that all interested
parties be cited, because then more proofs are demanded,
and proofs are not so easily adduced.

6 Ce. 8, 3, X, II, 13; c. 14, X, II, 19; c. 14, X, IV, 1.

CHAPTER VII

CAN. 1701

In contentiosis actiones tum reales tum personales exstinguuntur praescriptione ad normam can. 1508–1512; actiones autem de statu personarum nunquam exstinguuntur.

CAN. 1702

Omnis criminalis actio perimitur morte rei, condonatione legitimae potestatis, et lapsu temporis utilis ad actionem criminalem proponendam.

CAN. 1703

Firmo praescripto can. 1555, § 1 de delictis Sacrae Congregationi S. Officii reservatis, tempus utile ad actionem criminalem proponendam est triennium, nisi agatur:

1.° De actione iniuriarum, quae uno anno perimitur;

2.° De actione ob delicta qualificata contra VI et VII divinum praeceptum, quae quinquennio perimitur;

3.° De actionibus ob simoniam vel homicidium, contra quae actio criminalis decennio perdurat.

CAN. 1704

Sublata per praescriptionem actione criminali:

1.° Non est hoc ipso sublata actio contentiosa, forte ex delicto orta, ad damna sarcienda;

147

2.° Ordinarius remediis can. 2222, § 2 statutis uti adhuc potest.

CAN. 1701–1705

§ 1. Praescriptio in contentiosis currit ex quo actio primum potuit iure proponi; in criminalibus, a die patrati delicti.

§ 2. Si delictum habeat tractum, ut vocant, successivum, non currit praescriptio, nisi a die qua delicti tractus cessaverit.

§ 3. In delicto habituali vel continuato praescriptio non decurrit nisi post ultimum actum; et conventus ob aliquem criminosum actum non praescriptum, tenetur de antiquioribus, qui cum eodem actu connectuntur, etiamsi singulatim sumpti ob praescriptionem excluderentur.

Real as well as personal actions in *civil cases* are extinguished by prescription, as set forth under can. 1508–1512. But actions concerning the status of persons are never extinguished. An action is a demand of one's right, and a *real* action is one inherent in the thing, which it follows everywhere (*actio in rem* or *vindicatio rei*). A *personal* action (*actio in personam*) is directly aimed at a person by reason either of a contract or a crime. Although an object may be claimed, yet only the person who contracted or perpetrated a crime is responsible.[1] An example is stated in can. 1534 concerning alienation, where real action is permitted in case of an alienation that is null and void by law; and personal action in case of alienation lacking the formalities required by law.

The text adds: "*actiones autem de statu personarum*

[1] Reiffenstuel, II, 3, n. 11 f.   Stimson's *Law Dictionary*, *s. v.*
The English terminology wavers; see   "*Actio*," Action.

nunquam exstinguuntur." The status of men in Roman law [2] was twofold: freedom and slavery. The Canon Law recognized a threefold status: that of *virgines, continentes,* and *conjugati.*[3] From this we may surmise that personal status here means walk of life, as we say the clerical state, the lay state, the religious state, the married state. Now, then, an action may always be brought by one living in a state which he has good reason to believe was forced upon him or which he thinks he did not enter in a lawful manner. Thus, for instance, a cleric may bring action to be released from the clerical state and a married man may attack the validity of his marriage. The reason for this is that the state of any person interests not only that person himself, but society as a whole. Hence, too, no transactions are allowed concerning the personal state.[4]

A *criminal action* is quashed by the death of the culprit, by his condemnation on the part of lawful authority, or by the lapse of an equitable period of time, granted by law for bringing a criminal suit. The *time* is determined in can. 1703, which says that a criminal suit can be brought within *three years.* But this rule is liable to some exceptions, namely:

(a) All cases belonging to the *Holy Office,* and which this S. Congregation takes cognizance of itself or through inferior tribunals, according to can. 1555, § 1.

(b) Actions against *iniuriae* are prescribed after *one year. Iniuriae* are offences of a contumelious character against the honor and respect due to one's fellowmen. They may be either verbal or real, *i.e.,* committed by word of mouth or by acts which are offensive, for instance, spitting in one's face or throwing mud. They

---

[2] See Dig. I, 5, *de statu hominum.*   [4] Wernz, *l. c.,* V, n. 41.
[3] Reiffenstuel, I, 1, n. 149.

may also amount to defamation or slander and affect a man's calling [5] or official standing.

(c) Actions arising from qualified crimes against the sixth and seventh commandments of God are quashed after *five years*.

The Code does not state which *delicta* of those named are *qualificata*. In the source [6] from which our text has undoubtedly been taken, *peculatus* (embezzlement) stands for the seventh commandment and *delicta carnis* for the sixth. One might be tempted to identify a qualified crime with one that is usually called indictable; yet the decree in question mentions special classes which belong hither: *raptus, stuprum per vim illatum, adulterium cum incestu coniunctum*, which, it says, require a prescription of twenty years. Hence it may be that these are the qualified crimes, which, according to the Code, require only five years, whilst all other crimes against the two commandments mentioned are actionable only within the space of three years, according to the general rule. This interpretation is certainly acceptable, although it spells a mitigation of the former practice.

(d) Criminal actions based on simony and homicide are not admitted after the lapse of ten years. Note, however, that *only criminal actions* in the strict sense, *i.e.*, such as directly aim at the punishment of the culprit and the satisfaction due to the public order, cease after the lapse of those various terms.

Civil actions brought in order to obtain indemnity or damages arising from a crime are not subject to prescription (can. 1704); for the main reason for admitting prescription against criminal action is the difficulty of

5 See Kenny, *A Selection of Cases Illustrative of the English Law of Tort*, 1904, p. 280.

6 S. C. EE. et RR., March 8, 1898 (*Coll. P. F.*, n. 1992).

properly proving the crime and defending the accused after a long period of time. This difficulty might prove fatal to the public authority if it condemned one not guilty of crime. Besides, criminal action has another object, *viz.,* to repair scandal and to give satisfaction for a violation of the public order. This, too, seems no longer required for the benefit of society after the lapse of a considerable time.[7] The case is different with civil action, which is a more or less private affair depending upon the good pleasure of individuals. Hence one who has suffered from a crime may always bring a damage suit, though not a criminal action, against the criminal. The clergy have other remedies which the Ordinary may employ, as stated in can. 2222, § 2, such as forbidding the reception of higher orders, suspension *ex informata conscientia,* etc.

A more important question is the *starting point* from which the term of prescription may be reckoned. Can. 1705 answers this question first as to *civil actions,* the prescription of which begins to run from the moment the law permits action to be brought. In order to complete what was merely adverted to under can. 1508–1512, something may be added here concerning prescription.[8]

Prescription broadly signifies a legitimate means of acquiring a right or ridding oneself of an obligation by possession during the time and in the manner laid down by law. Here it means particularly the quashing of civil

7 Wernz, *l. c.,* V, n. 768. Note, however, the passage in Kenny-Webb, *Outlines of Criminal Law,* 1907, p. 382: " Statutes of limitations (prescription) which bar the prosecution for certain crimes under certain circumstances, after specified periods of time have elapsed, have never been applied either in England or in the United States to the crime of murder; " instances are given where crimes were prosecuted after 30 and 35 years.

8 Cfr. the commentators on lib. II, tit. 26 *de praescript.;* Slater-Martin, *A Manual of Moral Theology,* 1908, Vol. I, p. 376 f.

action by the opposing term allowed by law. Thus a claim may become void if the creditor allows the term to expire before going to court. Our Code admits prescription according to the laws of different countries, but adds that the canons must be observed. Hence if the civil law should admit prescription in things excluded by the ecclesiastical law, or lay down a shorter time than the law of the Church, the civil law cannot be applied.

This premised, four conditions are necessary to render prescription lawful: prescribable matter, good faith, title, and continued possession.

(a) The *matter which cannot* be prescribed, according to the law of the Church, is determined by can. 1509.

(b) Good faith (*bona fides*) is required, because the one who holds a thing must be persuaded that he and none other is the owner thereof.[9] This is the *animi possessio* which cannot coexist with the conviction that the thing belongs to another. Ecclesiastical law [10] requires this persuasion, not only at the beginning, but as long as the period of prescription lasts.

But what if there is a *doubt* as to whether one has the right to the object? If this doubt is positive (not a mere scruple) and occurs at the beginning, the possessor has to relinquish the object, or at least investigate whether the other has a better title. If the doubt arises in the course of prescription, *regula juris 65 in 6°* may be applied: "*Melior est conditio possidentis*," at least until a counter-plea has been made and adjudged.

What if a prelate or administrator were under the wrong impression that he was allowed to alienate church property without observing the required formalities? In

9 Cfr. c. 2, X, II, 26; Engel, II, 26, n. 13.   10 See cc. 5, 20, X, II, 26.

this case there would be an error in law (*error iuris*), provided, of course, the law is clear and certain, and prescription would hardly be admissible because ignorance of the law cannot be effectively pleaded, and it is this ignorance of the law that proves hurtful, because who errs in regard to the law is not supposed to be in good faith.[11]

The authors solve another practical case: If a prelate of a church with a chapter is in bad faith concerning property, and nevertheless holds it; is the chapter able to prescribe? The answer is that the *mala fides* of the prelate, who is the head of the chapter, renders prescription invalid, so that the chapter cannot lawfully prescribe the property thus held.[12]

This principle is similar to that applied to *heirs* or successors in property held in bad faith by their predecessors; according to the *Regula Iuris 46 in 6°* the successor enters upon the rights and property with the same right as the predecessor.[13] However this may be, to us it seems rather queer that good faith should be denied to the successor if he has no inkling of bad faith on the part of his predecessor. Here the civil law may certainly be applied. Of course, prescription runs only from the moment of good faith.

Bona fides is also required when prescription is invoked to free one from an obligation. For instance, the Society of Jesus had a legal claim on the Olivetans of Palermo, who paid 2500 scudi interest to the Society until the latter's suppression, in 1773, and even afterwards to the *Camera Spoliorum*, until 1782, when they stopped payment. After the restoration of the Society of Jesus, in

---

11 Cfr.*Reg. Iuris 82 in 6°*: " *Iuris ignorantia in usucapione negatur prodesse, facti vero ignorantia pro-* *desse potest* "; Engel, II, 26, nn. 79 ff.

12 Reiffenstuel, II, 26, nn. 79 ff.

13 *Ibid.*, n. 131 ff.

1814, the payment was naturally claimed by the Jesuits, and the S. Congregation decided in their favor, although the Neapolitan laws favored the claim of the Olivetans. The reason for this decision was that the documents showed that their opponents were aware of their duty, as they mentioned it in 1796, 1818, and 1823. Hence the *bona fides* required by Canon Law could not be proved.[14]

This case illustrates what is called *positive liberation from an obligation*. There is also a *negative* one, which specially concerns servitudes (leases) and criminal actions. For the prescription of these the authors do not require good faith, saying that one is not positively held to bring criminal action against the culprit, because there is question of a mere tolerance or non-use of a right which may be claimed or discarded.[15] But it may be added that the duty of prosecution lies primarily with the authorities, and that many are either not in a condition, or not disposed, to institute a criminal action. This view forestalls hatred and fanaticism. That no obligation of denouncing transgressors exists in regard to merely penal laws goes without saying.

(c) The next requisite is a *titulus*, which is defined as " *causa de se habilis ad transferendum dominium.*" This is the legal evidence of one's right of property, or the legal claim to an acknowledged or alleged right. Such a title is any contract legally and lawfully entered. A title is called *just* if acknowledged by law; it is *true* when it is based upon the thing itself, without reference to the legal requisites; for instance, a donation or contract may have been made by two parties informally, *i.e.*, without the observance of formalities, as an informal engagement. There is

14 S. C. EE. et RR., Sept. 23, 1836 (Bizzarri p. 426).　　15 Cfr. Engel, II, 26, n. 18 ff.; Santi-Leitner II, 26, n. 22.

also a colorable or putative title (*titulus coloratus*) which is acknowledged by law, although it may be tainted with an intrinsic defect, for instance, if the person, being a minor, was incapacitated for acting, such a title is sufficient for lawful prescription. For although the title may not be true, it is just, and it is only for the sake of public tranquillity that the law requires a certain lapse of time for a colorable title to become true *and* just. Otherwise prescription would effect nothing, because where there is a true and just title from the very beginning, prescription is not needed.[16]

(d) The last requisite is *continued possession*. A real hold on the thing, either by the person himself or by another in his name, is required, because without a manifest and palpable sign of the will of possessing a thing, possession cannot exist among men.[17] But possession must also be *continued*, not interrupted. Interruption, either natural or civil, is an obstacle which stays prescription in such a way that the time elapsed is no longer reckoned. Thus if three years are required, and the impediment occurs in the course of the third year, the term must be commenced anew. *Natural* interruption may be caused by supervening bad faith or by loss of possession. *Civil* interruption is caused by civil action begun with the summons (see can. 1725). Entirely different from interruption is *suspension*, which may happen, for instance, when a church is deprived of its pastor or prelate by death or superior force. In that case the duration of the suspension is subtracted, but the preceding and following time are counted.[18]

The *time* required for prescription is defined partly by

[16] Engel, II, 26, n. 22 f.; Reiffenstuel, II, 26, n. 120 ff.; Santi-Leitner, II, 26, n. 23 ff.

[17] *Reg. Iuris 3 in 6°.*

[18] Santi-Leitner, II, 26, n. 31 f.

can. 1508, which admits the term acknowledged by civil law, partly by can. 1511, which establishes a period of 100 years for prescription against property and precious things belonging to the Apostolic See, and a period of 30 years with regard to ecclesiastical corporations, and partly by can. 1703, concerning criminal actions.

We proceed to can. 1705, § 1, which rules that prescription in *civil* cases runs from the moment the law permits prescription to be brought. Therefore the canons just mentioned, viz., 1508 and 1511, may be applied here, even after the time allowed by civil law for prescription has run out, except, of course, that the application of can. 1511 is a very delicate matter.[19]

Canon 1705 continues: in *criminal* cases prescription runs from the day when the crime was perpetrated, unless the crime is continuous (*habet tractum successivum;* for instance, rape or violent detention), in which case the prescription runs from the day the continuity ceases, *i.e.,* after the completion of the last of a series of acts which form a whole.

§ 3 of can. 1705 makes a special regulation concerning *habitual crimes,*[20] against which prescription runs only from the last act not followed by another of the same species. If one has been accused of a criminal act not yet prescribed, he is also held responsible for coherent acts which antedate prescription, even though these former acts could not have been prosecuted because of prescription. Take, for instance, a husband accused of violence, whose wife seeks separation; there may be other crimes connected with the one alleged, though committed years ago.[21]

---

[19] Because of the politico-religious aspects of the so-called Roman Question; cfr. can. 2345.

[20] Such would be *concubinatus,* also *non-residentia* of clergymen.

[21] For instance *abortus* resulting from acts of violence.

TITLE VI

OPENING OF THE CASE

A trial may be considered to have three stages: the opening, the defence or pleading, and the sentence with its execution.

The first stage, or opening of the case, comprises two distinct acts: the statement of the case (*libelli oblatio*) and the summons (*citatio*).

CHAPTER I

CAN. 1706

Qui aliquem convenire vult, debet libellum competenti iudici exhibere, in quo controversiae obiectum proponatur, et ministerium iudicis ad deducta iura persequenda expostuletur.

CAN. 1707

§ 1. Qui scribere nescit, aut legitime impeditur quominus libellum exhibeat, oretenus petitionem suam coram tribunali proponere potest.

§ 2. Item in causis facilioris investigationis et minoris momenti ac propterea cito expediendis, iudicis arbitrio relinquitur petitionis admissio oretenus sibi facta.

§ 3. In utroque tamen casu iudex notarium iubeat scriptis actum redigere qui actori legendus est et ab eo probandus.

CAN. 1708

Libellus quo lis introducitur debet:

1.° Exprimere coram quo iudice causa introducatur, quid petatur, et a quo petatur;

2.° Indicare, generatim saltem, quo iure innitatur actor ad comprobanda ea quae allegantur et asseruntur;

158

3.° Subscribi ab actore vel eius procuratore, appositis die, mense et anno, nec non loco in quo actor vel eius procurator habitant, aut residere se dixerint actorum recipiendorum gratia.

Can. 1709

§ 1. Iudex vel tribunal, postquam viderit et rem esse suae competentiae et actori legitimam personam esse standi in iudicio, debet quantocius libellum aut admittere aut reiicere, adiectis in hoc altero casu reiectionis causis.

§ 2. Si iudicis decreto libellus reiectus fuerit ob vitia quae emendari possunt, actor novum libellum rite confectum potest eidem iudici denuo exhibere; quod si iudex emendatum libellum reiecerit, novae reiectionis rationes exponere debet.

§ 3. Adversus libelli reiectionem integrum semper est parti intra tempus utile decem dierum recursum interponere ad superius tribunal: a quo, audita parte, et promotore iustitiae aut vinculi defensore, quaestio reiectionis expeditissime definienda est.

Can. 1710

Si iudex continuo mense ab exhibito libello decretum non ediderit quo libellum admittit vel reiicit ad normam can. 1709, pars cuius interest instare potest ut iudex suo munere fungatur; quod si nihilominus iudex sileat, lapsis quinque diebus a facta instantia, poterit recursum ad Ordinarium loci, si ipse iudex non sit, vel ad superius tribunal interponere ut vel iudex ad definiendam causam adigatur vel alius in eius locum subrogetur.

A bill of plea, or original writ,[1] is a statement of the case made to the competent judge in order to ask him to prosecute or to grant redress.

It is not *absolutely required* that this bill be *presented in writing*. It may be that the plaintiff is illiterate or unable to write on account of a lawful obstacle, such as paralysis. If so, the plea may be made *orally*. Besides, the judge is free to accept an oral plea if the case is of minor importance and easily settled, or if quick action is required.

When the bill is not presented in writing, the judge shall command the notary or clerk to put it into writing and to read it to the plaintiff, so that he may approve of it.

The *contents* of the bill are:

(a) the *name of the judge* (or at least the court) before whom the case is to be tried; because, for reasons stated above, under can. 1560–1568, it is important to know whether the judge is competent;

(b) the *object of the plea,* for instance, whether it is a civil or a criminal case; also whether possession or ownership is claimed; in matrimonial cases, whether separation or complete divorce is asked;

(c) the name of the *defendant,* or adversary, or accused party (in criminal cases), for this is necessary to summon him;

(d) the *law* or reason on which the claim is based, at least in general, because this is the directing line along which the defence shall run. Thus a clergyman who asserts that force was used in his ordination may cite can. 214; a claim against unjust alienation may be based on can. 1532–1534; a suit against division of parishes on can. 1427 f.; an invalid profession on can.

---

1 Plaint and original writ are not entirely identical, but depend on the amount involved; Blackstone-Cooley, III, 273.

572, etc., etc. But this allegation is to be made only *in general terms,* because the bill should be brief and not contain proofs and documents, etc.

The bill must contain the *signature* of the plaintiff or his proctor (attorney); the date (day, month and year), the *place* where the plaintiff or his attorney live or reside, or where they will be ready to receive judicial acts. An attorney may give his office address, so also the plaintiff, if he has one, because both may refuse to accept judicial documents in their homes for various reasons.

What is the *judge* to do with such a bill? He may either accept or reject it. After inspecting the bill he shall ask himself whether he is *competent* (can. 1560-1568) to take cognizance of and decide the case and whether the plaintiff is entitled to bring suit. Concerning the latter point he should look up can. 1646-1654.

Though the judge may be competent to accept the case and the plaintiff entitled to bring suit, the judge may reject the bill, not on account of a frivolous plea of incompetence, which is forestalled by can. 1625, but by reason of *defects in the bill.* It may be that the judge, without being a stickler or bent on "red tape," finds the bill in need of correction (*ob vitia quae emendari possunt*). "Correction" here is not identical with change, because *emendatio* means correction of an accidental mistake; thus it may be that the sum demanded is not correctly stated, or the demand is made in an obscure way, or the law is not quoted properly, or the names are illegibly written. The reasons why the bill is refused must be stated by the judge, not only if the refusal is based on purely material or formal grounds, but also if the judge believes himself incompetent or deems the plaintiff incapable of bringing suit. If the *corrected bill* is again rejected, the reasons must be restated, for after the first refusal of the bill on account of formal defects the plaintiff may offer a new, corrected bill.

Should the bill be refused a second time, the party may, within the space of ten equitable days, *have recourse* — not appeal — to the higher court which has to settle the question of refusal as soon as possible, after having heard the party, the prosecuting attorney, and the *defensor vinculi.*

But it may be that the *judge* to whom the bill was first presented, *makes no move* either to accept or to refuse it. In that case, after the expiration of *a month* from the date when the bill was presented, the plaintiff may insist that the judge perform his duty, and if he or his attorney knows the Canon Law, they may quote can. 1625 in order to make him act. If he continues inactive, the party shall wait five more days, and then have recourse to the local Ordinary. If the Ordinary himself is the judge, the plaintiff may appeal to the higher court, asking it to compel the judge to decide the case or to substitute another judge. This privilege was granted to expedite cases as much as possible.[2]

[2] *Trid.*, Sess. 24, c. 20, *de ref.*

CHAPTER II

CAN. 1711

§ 1. Libello vel orali petitione admissa, locus est vocationi in ius seu citationi alterius partis.

§ 2. Quod si partes litigantes sponte coram iudice se sístant ad causam agendam, opus non est citatione, sed actuarius significet in actis partes sponte sua iudicio adfuisse.

CAN. 1712

§ 1. Citatio fit a iudice, et libello litis introductorio inscribitur aut adiungitur.

§ 2. Denuntiatur autem reo, et, si sint plures, singulis.

§ 3. Debet insuper actori nota fieri, ut statuta die et hora ipse quoque coram iudice se sistat.

CAN. 1713

Si lis moveatur ei qui non habet liberam administrationem rerum, de quibus disceptatur, citatio denuntianda est ei qui ipsius nomine iudicium suscipere tenetur ad normam can. 1648–1654.

CAN. 1714

Quaelibet citatio est peremptoria; nec iteretur necesse est, nisi in casu de quo in can. 1845, § 2.

163

After the plaintiff has presented his bill, or stated, and the competent judge has accepted, the case, the latter shall (as formerly the proctor), summon the *defendant* to appear in court. This was and is called *in ius vocare* or the summons made by the lawful judge to the other party, either plaintiff or defendant. This is the *beginning of the judicial action.* It may be omitted if both parties appear of their own accord before the judge; but in that case the clerk must record the fact that the parties appeared spontaneously at the trial, so as to preclude a plea of dilatory exception.

The citation or summons must be issued by the *judge,* and is to be written on the bill of plea, or added to it. This, in civil cases, is done in order to give the defendant a chance to know immediately the nature of the case and to prepare his defence. In *criminal cases,* however, this insertion into, or connection with, the bill of complaint is not only not required, but generally impractical, and may therefore be omitted, according to can. 1945, § 2 n. 3.

If there are *several* defendants, the summons is issued to each, otherwise only to the one. If a corporation is the defendant in the case, the summons is issued to the lawful superior, which is entirely sufficient.[1]

Can. 1713 rules that if *minors,* or corporate persons, or non-corporate entities, such as pious foundations, are sued, the summons must be issued to the respective superiors, guardians, or administrators, in a word, to their lawful representatives.

It is also required that the *plaintiff himself be notified of the summons* as soon as it has been made, so that he, too, may present himself in court on the day and at the hour set for the case.

---

[1] Santi-Leitner, II, 3, n. 7.

Every summons is peremptory, *i.e.*, one citation suffices and is final and urgent, so that the defendant is held in contempt, or may at least be declared to be in contempt, if he ignores it. The only exception to this rule is when ecclesiastical censures are threatened, because in that case a second summons is required.

CONTENTS OF THE SUMMONS

CAN. 1715

§ 1. Citatio denuntietur per schedam, quae praeceptum iudicis parti conventae factum ad comparendum exprimat, idest a quo iudice, ob quam causam saltem verbis generalibus indicatam, quo actore, reus, nomine et cognomine rite designatus, conveniatur; nec non locum, et tempus, idest annum, mensem, diem et horam ad comparendum praefixam perspicue indicet.

§ 2. Citatio, sigillo tribunalis munita, subscribenda est a iudice vel ab eius auditore et a notario.

CAN. 1716

Citatio duplici scheda conficiatur, quarum altera remittatur reo convento, altera asservetur in actis.

As will be seen under can. 1723, the summons must comply with all the conditions prescribed by can. 1715. Hence it is important to explain the various elements distinctly:

1. The intimation must be made in writing (*per schedam*).

2. It must be a *command* of the judge to the defendant, and not a mere exhortation or friendly invitation.

3. The *name of the judge* must be clearly stated, so

that the defendant may know immediately whether the judge is competent or not; if the judge is delegated, he should have his credentials or letters-patent ready to show them to the defendant. If he does not prove his delegation, the summons is void.[2]

4. The tenor of the *complaint* at least in general terms according to the bill of plea or petition.

5. The *name* and surname of the *plaintiff* and the *defendant,* so that no mistake as to persons may void the summons.

6. The *place* where and the *date* when the defendant has to appear, giving year, day, and hour, all clearly and distinctly written.

7. The summons must be *sealed* with the seal of the court, and be signed by the judge or his auditor and the notary.

These are the essential features of the summons; the *duplicates* required by can. 1716 are not essential. One copy is to be delivered to the defendant, while the other is inserted in the records or *acta* and preserved.

INTIMATION OR CONVEYANCE OF SUMMONS

CAN. 1717

§ 1. Citationis scheda, si fieri poterit, per Curiae cursorem tradenda est ipsi convento ubicunque is invenitur.

§ 2. Ad hoc cursor etiam fines alterius dioecesis ingredi potest, si iudex id expedire censuerit et eidem cursori mandaverit.

§ 3. Si cursor personam conventam non invenerit in loco ubi commoratur, relinquere poterit citatoriam schedam alicui de eius familia aut famulatu, si hic eam

---

[2] C. 31, X, I, 29; c. 2, X, II, 8.

recipere paratus sit ac spondeat se reo convento quamprimum schedam acceptam traditurum; sin minus eam ad iudicem referat, ut transmittatur ad normam can. 1719, 1720.

CAN. 1718

Reus qui citatoriam schedam recipere recuset, legitime citatus habeatur.

CAN. 1719

Si ob distantiam vel aliam causam difficulter per cursorem tradi possit reo convento scheda citatoria, poterit iussu iudicis transmitti per tabellarios publicos, dummodo commendata et cum syngrapha receptionis, vel alio modo qui secundum locorum leges et conditiones tutissimus sit.

CAN. 1720

§ 1. Quoties, diligenti inquisitione peracta, adhuc ignoratur ubi commoretur reus, locus est citationi per edictum.

§ 2. Hoc autem fit affigendo per cursorem ad fores Curiae schedam citationis ad modum edicti per tempus prudenti iudicis arbitrio determinandum et in aliqua publica ephemeride eam inserendo; si vero utrumque fieri nequeat, alterutrum sufficiet.

CAN. 1721

§ 1. Cursor, cum in manu rei conventi citationis schedam relinquit, debet eam subsignare, adnotatis die et hora qua reo tradita est.

§ 2. Idem peragat si eam relinquat in manibus

alicuius de familia aut famulatu rei conventi, addito insuper nomine personae cui schedam tradidit.

§ 3. Si citatio fiat per edictum, cursor in edicti calce signet qua die et hora edictum affixum ad fores Curiae fuerit et quandiu affixum manserit.

§ 4. Si reus receptionem schedae recuset, cursor schedam ipsam subsignatam, addita die et hora recusationis, iudici remittat.

CAN. 1722

§ 1. Cursor quae peregit ad iudicem referat in scriptis manu propria subsignatis, quae in actis serventur.

§ 2. Si per tabellariorum officium citatio transmittatur, asservatur in actis fides eiusdem officii.

A summons, as stated, is essential and must be delivered into the hands of the defendant and proof of the delivery furnished. The summons may be conveyed by a courier, or by means of a letter, or by public edict.

1. A *courier* [3] is the most reliable means of conveying an important message. He should be a trustworthy person and deliver the summons to the defendant, wherever the latter may be. For this purpose he may enter the boundaries of a strange diocese — which act is not, properly speaking, an act of jurisdictional exercise — if the judge deems it expedient and commands him to do so. After the courier has found the defendant and delivered the summons into his hands, he must sign the summons

[3] In our ecclesiastical courts, so far at least, *apparitores* were not employed; Messmer, *l. c.*, p. 62. Although the Code does not reject the contrary custom, yet where these officers can be made use of, it should be done on account of the safety of conveyance. In England, according to Blackstone (III, 279), two of the sheriff's messengers delivered the summons either to the person himself or left it at his house.

personally with the date and hour of delivery, after the manner of a telegraphic dispatch.

If the defendant *refuses* to accept the summons, the courier shall nevertheless sign the summons, as stated above, noting the day and hour of refusal, and return it to the judge. The effect of this refusal is that the defendant is *considered as duly summoned*, and may be declared in contempt of court.[4]

If the defendant is *not at home, i.e.*, at his usual residence, office, shop, or store, when the courier arrives with the summons, the latter may leave the writ with a member of his family or one of his employees or servants, provided they are willing to accept it and promise to hand it to the defendant as soon as possible. If no such readiness is manifested, the courier must return the writ to the judge, in order that other means may be employed. But if the family or employees are willing to comply with the demand, then the courier may leave the summons in their hands, having signed it, noted the day and hour of delivery, and added the name of the person to whom the paper was delivered.

2. Another means of conveying the summons into the hands of the defendant is the *public mail service*. This may be resorted to when the distance is too great, or for other reasons, for instance, to avoid suspicion or gossip. But the letter containing the summons must be *registered*, and a return receipt must be demanded (*ricevuta di ritorno*).

3. When neither a courier nor the post office are able to locate the defendant, no other means is left than *summons by edict*. This is done by posting the summons at the outside door of the court for a period considered sufficient by the judge *and* by advertising in the public (not neces-

4 C. 5, X, II, 6.

sarily in the Catholic) press. If both of these expedients are impossible, one suffices. This is certainly the case if there is no proper court-room or established place for holding trials. If the edict is posted at the gate of the court-room, the officer who posts it must set down at the bottom of the edict the day and hour when he posted it, and later add the time during which it was publicly displayed. He must also make out a written report of the proceedings, and this document, properly signed, must be added to the judicial acts. If the summons was sent through the mail, the receipts must be kept in the records.

NECESSITY AND EFFECT OF SUMMONS

CAN. 1723

Si scheda citatoria non referat quae in can. 1715 praescribuntur aut non fuerit legitime intimata, nullius momenti sunt tum citatio tum acta processus.

CAN. 1724

Regulae superius statutae pro rei citatione, ceteris quoque iudicii actibus, pro diversa tamen eorum natura, accommodandae et applicandae sunt, ut decretorum vel sententiarum denuntiationi aliisque huiusmodi.

CAN. 1725

Cum citatio legitime peracta fuerit aut partes sponte in iudicium venerint:

1.° Res desinit esse integra;

2.° Causa fit propria illius iudicis aut tribunalis, coram quo actio institua est;

3.° In iudice delegato firma redditur iurisdictio ita ut non exspiret resoluto iure delegantis;

4.° Interrumpitur praescriptio, nisi aliud cautum sit, ad normam can. 1508;

5.° Lis pendere incipit; et ideo statim locum habet principium: *"lite pendente, nihil innovetur."*

How necessary a carefully written and lawfully conveyed summons is, is apparent from can. 1723, which says that if the summons was omitted, the entire proceedings are null and void.

The rules laid down for the summons must be adapted and applied, with due consideration of their importance, to all the other *judicial acts, e.g.,* the issuance of decrees made by the tribunal, the pronouncement of the sentence, and so forth.

The *effects* of a duly issued and legally served summons or of the spontaneous appearance of the parties in court are:

1. The case has taken a legal turn (*res non amplius est integra*).

2. The judge or court before whom the action was brought becomes *competent,* and hence incompetency cannot be asserted afterwards.

3. The delegated judge is confirmed or *perpetuated,* so that his jurisdiction does not cease even if the *delegans* dies or goes out of office.

4. *Prescription* is interrupted, not merely suspended, so that *bona fides* or title cannot be pleaded (see can. 1508).

5. The *case* or suit is now *pending,* and hence the principle: *"lite pendente, inhil innovetur"* goes into effect. How this is to be understood appears from the Decretals, which mention [5] especially: (a) change of possession, which cannot be transferred to another; (b) validity of

5 Cfr. cc. 1-4, X, II, 16; c. 17, X, I, 6; c. 9, X, III, 19.

rescripts, which are looked upon as obreptitious or subreptitious if no mention is made of the pending suit; (c) prohibition of alienation, and (d) the restitution of things to their former condition.

TITLE VII

ISSUE IN PLEADING (LITIS CONTESTATIO)

Originally the phrase *litis contestatio* seems to have meant merely the notice given by both parties to their witnesses to appear before the judge. Later, however, the term came to comprise the whole of the proceedings before the prætor, *i.e., in iure.*[1] Our Code first explains the term, then considers some intricate and doubtful cases, and, finally, describes the effects of *litis contestatio.*

DEFINITION AND REQUISITES

CAN. 1726

Obiectum seu materia iudicii constituitur ipsa litis contestatione, seu formali conventi contradictione petitioni actoris, facta animo litigandi coram iudice.

CAN. 1727

Ad litis contestationem nulla necessaria est sollemnitas, sed sufficit ut partibus coram iudice vel eius delegato comparentibus, in actis inseratur petitio actoris et contradictio conventi, unde constet qua de re agatur seu quinam sint controversiae termini.

It is supposed that the defendant has received the original writ or plaint, understands the reason for which suit has been brought against him, and is ready to " fight the

---

[1] Ramsay-Lanciani, *Roman Antiquities,* 1901, p. 342 f.

173

case," to use a common expression. Hence the issue in
pleading is nothing else but a final denial or contradiction
of the plaintiff's demand, coupled with the intention of
prosecuting the case before the judge. By this general
answer and denial of the defendant the matter of the
trial is established. We purposely use the term " general " because it is not required that the defendant contradict every particular statement in the plea. Nor is an
exception intended in the proper sense.[2] No special or
set formality is required, and the issue in pleading is
valid even if the words or terms or rejoinders are not
pronounced or composed with technical correctness. It
suffices that the plaintiff tell the judge or his delegate what
the case is, and that the defendant deny the charge or
refuse the demand of the plaintiff before the same judge
or delegate. But both the demand and the refusal must
be inserted in the records (*acta*), which must show what
the points in controversy are.

INTRICATE AND DOUBTFUL CASES

Can. 1728

In causis tamen implicatioribus, in quibus petitio
actoris nec perspicua sit nec simplex vel contradictio
conventi difficultatibus scateat, iudex, ex officio aut ad
instantiam actoris vel conventi, partes citet ad rite defi-
niendos controversiae articulos, idest ad causae *dubia,*
ut dicitur, *concordanda.*

Can. 1729

§ 1. Si die dubiis concordandis praestituta, pars in
ius vocata non compareat nec iustam absentiae

2 C. 2, 6°, II, 3.

excusationem alleget, contumax declaretur, et dubiorum formula statuatur ex officio, parte, quae praesens fuerit, id postulante. Parti autem contumaci statim id notum fiat ex officio ut quas velit exceptiones contra dubiorum seu articulorum formulam possit proponere et a contumacia se purgare, intra tempus quod iudici congruum videatur.

§ 2. Partibus praesentibus et in formula dubiorum seu articulorum concordibus, si iudex, quod ad se attinet, nihil excipiendum putaverit, eius rei fiat mentio in decreto quo formula firmatur.

§ 3. Si vero partes dissentiant aut earum conclusiones iudici non probentur, iudex ipse controversiam dirimat decreto.

§ 4. Dubiorum seu articulorum formula semel statuta mutari non potest, nisi novo decreto, ex gravi causa, ad instantiam partis vel promotoris iustitiae, vel defensoris vinculi, audita utraque vel altera parte eiusque rationibus perpensis.

If the petition, or writ, or plaint of the plaintiff is obscure and complicated,[3] or the denial of the defendant offers serious difficulties, either because the facts are doubtful or the law is indefinite, the judge shall, either *ex officio* or at the demand of either party, command both parties to define the points at issue more clearly (*ad concordanda dubia*). This is done by means of a formal summons, in the shape of a decree issued by the judge, in which the parties are ordered to appear on the day and hour and at the place appointed.[4]

If a *party* thus duly summoned *does not appear* in

[3] The Castellani-Gould case was proposed to the Roman courts three times.

[4] This is the law with the Signatura Apostolica; see *Regulae Servandae*, March 6, 1912 (*A. Ap. S.*, IV, 196 ff.).

court on the appointed day and gives no legitimate reason for his failure, he is to be declared *in contempt,* and the party who is present may demand that the doubts or doubtful positions be formulated *ex officio.* The party declared in contempt (see can. 1842 ff.) must be at once officially notified in order to be enabled to take exception to the doubts officially formulated and to "purge" himself of contumacy. For this purpose a sufficient space of time must be granted by the judge. If both parties are *present* and agree upon the disputed points, or rather on the manner in which they have been formulated, this fact must be put on record, provided the judge on his part is satisfied. If, on the other hand, there is disagreement among the parties as to the points in question, or if the judge is not satisfied, he may settle the controverted points himself, *i.e.,* formulate them by a decree. Once the controversial points have been determined, no change is admissible, except for weighty reasons and upon the demand of the parties or of the *promotor iustitiae* or the *defensor vinculi,* after these have heard the parties or party and properly pondered the reasons proposed. But every change in the *positions* or controverted points requires a *new decree.*

EFFECTS OF THE LITIS CONTESTATIO

CAN. 1730

Antequam litis contestatio locum habuerit, iudex ad testium aliarumve probationum receptionem ne procedat, nisi in casu contumaciae, aut nisi testium depositionem recipere oporteat, ne ipsa ob probabilem testis mortem, ob discessum eiusdem vel ob aliam iustam causam recipi postea nequeat, aut difficulter possit.

Can. 1731

Lite contestata:

1.° Haud licet actori libellum mutare, nisi, reo consentiente, iudex, iustis de causis, censeat mutationem esse admittendam, salva semper reo compensatione damnorum et expensarum, si quae debeatur. Libellus non censetur mutatus, si coarctetur aut mutetur probationis modus; si minuantur aut petitio aut accessoria petitionis; si facti adiuncta in libello pridem posita ita illustrentur, compleantur aut emendentur, ut controversiae obiectum idem remaneat; si in locum rei petatur pretium, foenus aut aliquid aequivalens;

2.° Iudex congruum tempus partibus praestituat probationibus proponendis et explendis; quod quiden poterit, instantibus partibus, arbitrio suo prorogare, dummodo ne lis, ultra quam aequum sit, protrahatur;

3.° Possessor rei alienae desinit esse bonae fidei; qua propter damnatus rem restituere, non solum rem ipsam, sed et rei fructus a litis contestatae tempore restituere tenetur et damna praeterea sarcire, si qua secuta fuerint.

The *litis contestatio* should establish the object or character of the suit. Therefore specified charges and answers must be preferred by both parties, at least in a general way. This purpose is served by the *articuli*, or controverted points, which must therefore be settled first and are settled by the issue in pleading, which is called the foundation and beginning of the trial. Before the trial has actually begun, the judicial procedure is not determined, nor is it certain that the defendant will prosecute. Hence:

1. *Before* the *litis contestatio* has been properly made and the controverted points have been fixed, the judge

cannot lawfully proceed to hear the witnesses or receive proofs, depositions, reports of experts, etc.

But the Code, like the old law,[5] admits *exceptions* to this rule; viz.: (a) If the defendant has been declared *in contempt,* in which case it is not required that the suit be dispatched as quickly as possible,[6] the sole fact of contumacy being sufficient; (b) If the deposition is required on account of the *condition* of the *witnesses.* A witness may be in danger of death, or advanced in age so that his memory is weak; or he may have to depart suddenly on some urgent journey; or it may be doubtful whether he will be as willing to testify later as he is now.[7]

2. *After* the *litis contestatio:* (a) It is not allowed *to change* the *original writ* (*libellus*) unless the judge, for weighty reasons, deems a change necessary and the defendant consents, provided always that the latter be indemnified, if necessary. Note well the difference between correction (*emendatio*) and change (*mutatio*). Of the former mention was made under can. 1709, § 2. Here change in the proper sense is intended. A change means a substantial alteration of the case, for instance, if a possessory is changed into a petitory cause; or in matrimonial cases, if a divorce is asked for instead of a separation, or one impediment is substituted for another; or, in ordination cases, if the invalidity of an order is pleaded instead of freedom from its obligations. But, says the text by way of example, it *is no change,* if the mode of proof is limited or altered, for instance, as to the number and quality of witnesses; if less is asked either in the substantial demand or the accessories, especially in alienation or alimony; if certain facts alleged in the writ are

[5] Title VI, Book II, is complete, amounting to a law.

[6] C. 5, X, II, 6: *celerem expeditionem.*

[7] Cfr. cc. 2, 3, X, II, 20.

made clearer, supplied and corrected, provided the point at issue, or *meritum causae,* remains the same ; if, instead of the thing itself (for instance, a precious article which has been alienated), a certain sum, or an interest, or an equivalent is demanded. These are corrections, not changes.

(b) The judge shall *set a certain term* for proposing and completing the process or proofs. This term may, however, be prorogued at the demand of the parties, but not unduly (cfr. can. 1620, 1634).

(c) The possessor of property belonging to another ceases to be *bona fide* after the *litis contestatio,* and therefore, if he should lose his case, is bound to make restitution not only of the property or thing itself, but also of the interest or profit drawn from the moment of the *litis contestatio,* and shall also be held to indemnification, if an additional loss should occur either to the defendant or to the object.

In the Roman tribunals the sum to be deposited for the expenses is determined at this juncture.[8]

8 *Reg. Sig. Apost.,* art. 37 (*A. Ap. S.,* IV, 199).

TITLE VIII

LITIS INSTANTIA OR PROCEEDINGS

There is no such title as this in the Decretals, nor could we find an adequate term for it in English law.[1] Perhaps *pleadings* would suit, but *proceedings,* if taken in the limited sense of judiciary acts which begin with the *litis contestatio,* conveys the idea of the title just as well. The text first defines *litis instantia,* and then explains the modes of interruption, abatement, and renunciation.

DEFINITION AND INTERRUPTION

CAN. 1732

Instantiae initium fit litis contestatione; finis autem omnibus modis, quibus iudicium terminatur, sed et antea non solum interrumpi, verum etiam finiri potest sive peremptione sive renuntiatione.

CAN. 1733

Si pars litigans moriatur aut statum mutet aut cesset ab officio cuius ratione agit:

1.° Causa nondum conclusa, instantia interrumpitur, donec heres defuncti aut successor litem instauret;

2.° Causa conclusa, instantia non interrumpitur, sed iudex procedere debet ad ulteriora, citato procuratore, si adsit, secus defuncti herede vel successore.

1 Cfr. Blackstone, III, 292 f.

Can. 1734

Si controvertatur cuinam ex clericis litigantibus ius
sit ad beneficium, et alter, lite pendente, moriatur, aut
beneficio renuntiet, instantia non interrumpitur, sed
contra superstitem eam prosequitur promotor iustitiae qui pro beneficii aut ecclesiae libertate dimicet,
nisi beneficium sit liberae collationis Ordinarii et hic
praeferat causam ut victam superstiti adiudicare.

Can. 1735

Procuratore aut curatore a munere cessante, tandiu
interrupta manet instantia, quandiu pars aut ii ad quos
pertinet novum procuratorem vel curatorem nomina-
verint aut per se ipsi in posterum agere se velle pro-
fessi fuerint.

The *instantia litis* begins with the issue in pleading and
ends with the final sentence. However, the whole proceeding may not only be interrupted, but also abated or
renounced.

Interruption takes place when one of the parties dies,
or changes his status, or goes out of the office in virtue
of which he was a party to the case,— provided the pleadings have not yet been closed.

Statum mutare means to change from the lay to the
clerical state, or from either the lay or the clerical to the
religious state, because the religious form a state of their
own, and, besides, are considered as minors in ecclesiastical law. This rule, however, does not apply to novices,
because they still have their own free will (*velle et nolle*)
and hence may stand judgment, at least by proxy.

Cessare ab officio in this case signifies giving up the

office which involves one in the law-suit, for instance, that of administrator or ecclesiastical superior.

However, interruption lasts only until the litigant's heir or successor in office again takes up the case. If the pleadings have been closed, the proceedings are *not* interrupted, but the judge must proceed after having summoned the defendant, if alive and present, or else his heir or successor.

Can. 1734 refers to the special case of a *benefice* which is claimed by two clergymen, one of whom dies or resigns while the case is pending. To whom shall the benefice be adjudged? It is not a vacant benefice properly speaking, nor can it be resigned except in favor of the other litigant, which is not here supposed. In this case the proceedings are not interrupted, but continued by the *promotor iustitiae*, who defends the benefice or liberty of the church. This must be understood of all benefices not reserved to the Apostolic See.[2] If the benefice is of free collation, *i.e.*, one to which the Ordinary may freely appoint, the same Ordinary may confer it upon the survivor or rather declare that the survivor has won the case and adjudge the benefice to him. If the proctor (attorney) or guardian (curator) goes out of office by death, resignation, or removal, the proceedings are interrupted until a new proctor or curator is appointed by those concerned or until the latter have formally declared that they themselves will prosecute the case.

ABATEMENT OF THE INSTANTIA

CAN. 1736

Si nullus actus processualis, quin aliquod obstet impedimentum, ponatur in tribunali primae instantiae

---

[2] Cfr. c. 1, Clem. II, 5; can. 1435, § 1, n. 2.

per biennium aut in gradu appellationis per annum, instantia perimitur, et in altero casu sententia per appellationem oppugnata transit in rem iudicatam.

CAN. 1737

Peremptio obtinet ipso iure et adversus omnes, minores quoque aliosve minoribus aequiparatos, eaque ex officio etiam excipi debet, salvo iure regressus ad indemnitatem adversus tutores, administratores, procuratores qui culpa se caruisse non probaverint.

CAN. 1738

Peremptio exstinguit acta processus, non vero acta causae; imo haec vim habere possunt etiam in alia instantia, dummodo ea inter easdem personas et super eadem re intercedat; sed ad extraneos quod attinet, non aliam vim obtinet, nisi documentorum.

CAN. 1739

In casu peremptionis, quas quisque ex litigatoribus fecerit, has ipse ferat expensas perempti iudicii.

If, notwithstanding the fact that no lawful impediment can be alleged, no processual act has been undertaken by the first tribunal or the first instance within two years, the proceeding is abated or quashed. If the higher or second court does nothing within one year from the date of appeal, although no lawful obstacle is in the way,[3] the sentence attacked becomes *res iudicata*.

Abatement holds *ipso iure* and against all, even minors and those equal to minors under the law, and must also be made a case of exception *ex officio;* but the right of

[3] See cc. 5, 8, X, II, 28 and the canons on appeal.

claiming indemnity against guardians, administrators, and procurators who cannot prove their innocence is reserved to all minors. This claim (*regressus*), we suppose, holds for the time during which the representatives of minors have been culpably idle. This would comprise the *lucrum cessans* as well as the *damnum emergens*.

Abatement quashes all acts of proceedings (*acta processus*), but not the acts of the case (*acta causae*), which remain effective for another instance (higher court), provided the case concerns the same persons and the same matter. For outsiders these *acta causae* have merely the value of documents (see can. 1812 ff.). In case of abatement the expenses must be shared by the litigants according to the measure in which they have incurred or made them.

RENUNCIATION

CAN. 1740

§ 1. In quolibet statu et gradu iudicii potest actor instantiae renuntiare; item tum actor tum reus possunt processus actis renuntiare sive omnibus sive nonnullis tantum.

§ 2. Renuntiatio ut valeat, peragenda est in scriptis, et a parte vel ab eius procuratore, speciali tamen mandato munito, debet subscribi, alteri parti communicari, ab eaque acceptari, vel saltem non impugnari, et a iudice admitti.

CAN. 1741

Admissa, pro actis quibus renuntiatum est, eosdem parit effectus ac peremptio instantiae: et obligat renuntiantem ad solvendas expensas actorum, quibus renuntiatum fuit.

The plaintiff may renounce further proceedings at any stage or in any instance; and the plaintiff as well as the defendant may surrender the *acta processus* either totally or partially. Renunciation must, however, be made in *writing* and be signed by the party or his proctor acting under a special mandate. Besides, the renunciation must be communicated to, and accepted by the other party, or at least not objected to by the latter, and admitted by the judge. Valid renunciation has the same effect as abatement with regard to the acts renounced, and obliges the one who makes it to pay all the expenses thus far incurred.

TITLE IX

QUESTIONING THE PARTIES

It is now supposed that the parties have been duly summoned or notified of the place and date of the trial, and the issue in pleading has begun. The parties may be represented by their attorneys or proctors, unless there be an injunction by the judge commanding them to be present personally according to can. 1647. The Code now proceeds to describe the questioning of the parties and the oath to be administered to them.

QUESTIONS TO BE PROPOSED

CAN. 1742

§ 1. Iudex ad eruendam veritatem facti quod publice interest ut extra dubium ponatur, debet partes interrogare.

§ 2. In aliis casibus potest unum ex contendentibus interrogare non solum ad instantiam alterius partis, sed etiam ex officio, quoties agitur de illustranda probatione adducta.

§ 3. Interrogatio partium fieri a iudice potest in quovis stadio iudicii ante conclusionem in causa; post conclusionem in causa servetur praescriptum can. 1861.

CAN. 1743

§ 1. Iudici legitime interroganti partes respondere tenentur et fateri veritatem, nisi agatur de delicto ab ipsis commisso.

186

§ 2. Si pars legitime interrogata respondere recuset,
quanti facienda sit haec recusatio, utrum iusta sit, an
confessioni aequiparanda, necne, iudicis est aestimare.

§ 3. Pars, quae respondere debet, si illegitime
respondere recusaverit aut si postquam responderit
mendax reperta fuerit, puniatur, ad tempus a iudice
pro rerum adiunctis definiendum remotione ab actibus
legitimis ecclesiasticis; et si ante responsionem
iusiurandum de veritate dicenda praestiterit, laicus
interdicto personali, clericus suspensione plectatur.

The questions asked depend, of course, on the nature
of the case. When the public welfare is at stake, the
judge *must* question the parties concerning the facts
in order that they may be ascertained. In *other cases,
i.e.,* contentious or civil or private matters, the judge
may question one party at the demand of the other, or
both *ex officio,* whenever he considers it necessary to cor-
roborate or illustrate a proof alleged. Such questioning
is admissible until the proceedings are closed; but after
they have been finished (*post conclusionem in causa*),
questioning is allowed only under the conditions mentioned in can. 1861.

In order to produce the required effect, questioning
must be followed by the answers of the parties questioned. Hence as often as the judge is entitled to in-
terrogate the parties, these are obliged to answer according to the truth. Only the criminal is not bound to
confess his own guilt, because no one is supposed to
condemn himself.

But what if the *party questioned refuses to answer?*
Does this refusal amount to a confession? Certainly
not in the case of a criminal, because he is under no
obligation to admit his guilt. Hence the text says that

it lies with the judge who lawfully questions the party
to weigh the argument of silence or refusal, whether it
amounts to a confession or not, etc. It may be that
the judge takes a refusal to answer as equivalent to a
confession,[1] except, of course, in criminal cases.

To give greater weight to his authority and to the
law the judge may *punish the party* who unlawfully refuses to answer a lawful question by denying him any
legal action or, as we say, civic rights, which denial, however in this case only concerns the ecclesiastical sphere.[2]
This punishment is to be administered by the judge according to the importance of the matter. The same
punishment may be inflicted on one whose answer is
found to be untruthful. A heavier penalty is to be inflicted upon a lay person who swears falsely: he is to be
personally interdicted. A clergyman who perjures himself is to be suspended, *i.e.*, totally, from office as well
as benefice.[3]

THE OATH

CAN. 1744

Iusiurandum de veritate dicenda in causis criminalibus nequit iudex accusato deferre; in contentiosis,
quoties bonum publicum in causa est, debet illud a
partibus exigere; in aliis, potest pro sua prudentia.

CAN. 1745

§ 1. Tum actor tum reus invicem, tum etiam
promotor iustitiae et defensor vinculi possunt iudici
exhibere articulos, seu quaesita, super quibus pars
interrogetur, quaeque vulgo *positiones* dicuntur.

---

1 The *Regulae S. R. Rotae*, § 139,
read: "*parte praecepto iudicis non
obtemperante, facta habeantur uti-
vera et confessa.*"

2 Cfr. can. 2256, n. 2.
3 Cfr. c. 15, X, I, 11; can. 2278,
§ 2.

§ 2. In positionibus exarandis, admittendis et parti proponendis regulae cum proportione serventur quae in can. 1773-1781 statutae sunt.

CAN. 1746

Ad iusiurandum praestandum vel interrogationibus respondendum partes personaliter coram iudice se sistere debent, exceptis iis de quibus in can. 1770, § 2, nn. 1, 2.

According to the Decretals [4] an oath was administered to both parties; it was called *iuramentum calumniae,* and in it the parties declared that they were prosecuting the case in good faith and merely with the intention of defending their presumptive right, without malice, vexations, or fraudulent delays. This oath was not an absolute requirement, but could be remitted by tacit renunciation. Our Code knows no such oath. The one mentioned here is an *oath* to tell the truth, and resembles that taken by the witnesses. It must not be demanded in criminal trials, lest the defendant be exposed to the danger of perjury. However, in *civil cases* which concern the *public welfare,* like matrimonial and ordination cases, the judge *must* demand this oath of the parties. Culpable or negligent omission of this requirement does not, however, affect the validity of the acts. In other cases the judge may demand this oath whenever he deems it necessary.

In order to facilitate and systematize the proceedings, the questions to be proposed should be formulated or specified; and in that form are called *positiones.* These *positiones* are to be drawn up, admitted, and presented

---

[4] Lib. II, tit. 7, *de iuramento calumniae.*

to the parties in approximately the same way as the questions put to the witnesses (can. 1773–1781).

To give oath and to answer the questions thus formulated, the *parties must present* themselves *personally* before the judge. This rule applies to all except cardinals, bishops, illustrious personages (can. 1770, § 2, n. 1) and those who are prevented from coming to court personally by sickness or their state of life.

TITLE X

PROOFS

This title is one of the most important in legal procedure, because the issue of the trial naturally depends on the validity of the evidence.

The Code first mentions three kinds of facts which need no proof; then it states who has the duty of proving, and finally regulates the delay of proofs.

PRELIMINARY RULES

CAN. 1747

Non indigent probatione:

1.° Facta notoria, ad normam can. 2197, nn. 2, 3;

2.° Quae ab ipsa lege praesumuntur;

3.° Facta ab uno ex contendentibus asserta et ab altero admissa, nisi a iure vel a iudice probatio nihilominus exigatur.

CAN. 1748

§ 1. Onus probandi incumbit ei qui asserit.

§ 2. Actore non probante, reus absolvitur.

CAN. 1749

Probationes quae ad moras iudicio nectandas postulari videntur, ceu examen testis longe dissiti, aut cuius domicilium nescitur, vel cognitio documenti quod cito haberi non potest, iudex ne admittat, nisi hae probationes necessariae videantur quia ceterae deficiant aut satis non sint.

A proof is the judicial demonstration of the truth of a disputed assertion or fact.[1] It is not concerned with texts, for these are supposed to be safe and evident, but turns about a controversial point or criminal fact which must be proved to have happened and in the manner it is alleged to have happened. Evidence and proof are not identical, for there may be evidence without proof, but there is no proof without evidence.[2]

In regard to the *weight of proof* the Code speaks of *plena* and *semiplena probatio*, or *plenam* and *semiplenam fidem facere*. Full proof is one which convinces the judge and prompts him to give sentence without further investigation. A *probatio semiplena* or half-proof is one that leaves room for reasonable doubt. In a wavering state of mind no one should pronounce judgment.

That even full proofs may differ as to degree, is clear from such terms as *probationes apertissimae, plenissimae, luce clariores, praesumptivae*, etc., used in canon law. Psychologically speaking, a full proof always excludes the contradictory proposition and therefore must be called sufficient in any case; what is full in its kind cannot be fuller. But it remains true that different *kinds of proof* carry unequal weight and may produce various states of mind, from mere presumption to absolute certainty. This truth is illustrated by the following verses:

" *Aspectus, sculptum, testis, notoria, scriptum,*
    Iurans, confessus, praesumptio, fama probavit."

---

1 See the commentators on lib. II, tit. 19 *Decretal.*, especially Reiffen- stuel, Santi-Leitner, and Werntz (*Ius Decret.*), Vol. V.

2 Messmer, *l. c.*, p. 91 f.

Of these nine kinds of evidence the Code mentions some explicitly, whereas others are implied under other species. *Confessus* or confession occurs in chapter I of this title; *iurans* (oath), *testis* (witness), and *fama* (rumor) are treated in chapter II, on witnesses;[8] *aspectus* doubtless refers to experts and ocular inspection; *sculptum, i.e.*, monumentary proof, must be combined with *scriptum* or documentary proof. *Praesumptio* is treated in ch. VI; *notorietas* is mentioned in can. 1747.

Of *notorious facts*, provided they be such as defined in can. 2197, n. 2, 3, the text says that they *need no proof*. Notoriety may be either of *law* or of *fact*. The former arises from adjudged matter and confession; the latter from that kind of publicity which no artifice can hide or law protect.[4]

No *proof* is required, secondly, for *facts which are presumed by the law;* see chapter VI, on presumptions.

Finally, proof is superseded by *judicial confession;* see chapter I of this title.

The next question that arises is: *Who is obliged to furnish proof?* It is the one who asserts a right or fact, not the one who denies it. For a mere denial is no proof.[5] Since the *plaintiff* generally is the one who asserts a right or fact, he must furnish proof, as in petitory and possessory trials.[6] However, if the *defendant* sets up an exception or makes a counter-charge, and thereby becomes a plaintiff (*reus excipiendo fit actor*), he must furnish proof of his exception or counter-charge. Those, for instance, who oppose the excommunication of witnesses, or of parties, or of the judge, must prove

8 The oath refers to witnesses; see ch. VII.

4 Cfr. cc. 8, 10, X, III, 2; c. 23, X, I, 6.

5 See l. 2, Dig. 22, 3; c. 23, X,

I, 6; c. 5, X, I, 9: "*negantis factum, per rerum naturam, nulla est directa probatio.*"

6 C. 3, X, II, 12.

that it was inflicted.[7] Those who oppose prescription must prove the title, if the law is against them as in case of titles; those who pretend exemption must prove the privilege by showing or proving prescription.[8]

If the *plaintiff fails to furnish proof, the defendant goes free.* By proof is here understood full proof (*plena probatio*), for, as will be seen from can. 1829 ff., a half-proof may be supplied by an oath. Besides, the proof must concern the action intended; for instance, if the plaintiff brings suit against disseissin, and proves only possession and disseissin, but not ownership (*petitorium*), he is victorious in the former two points, but not as to the latter.[9] The merit of the cause must be proved. Thus if a donation is attacked, the instrument of donation, or the proof that the donation has been made, is the point at issue, not some attached condition, which has perhaps been verified in the meanwhile.[10] Therefore the principle asserted in can. 1748, § 2 must be understood in this sense, that the defendant is absolved to the extent that the plaintiff fails to furnish proof (*in hac parte*).[11] Only if the plaintiff fails entirely in furnishing proof for his accusations is the defendant fully free, even though he made no use of counter-defence.[12] But a mere assertion or confession of the plaintiff, even though it may reflect on his character, is not sufficient to equal full proof. Thus if one confessed adultery with his brother's wife, and then (after her husband's death) married her, but wished to have the marriage dissolved, his confession would not be sufficient.[13]

Can. 1749 is intended to expedite trials, *i.e.*, to finish them as quickly as the case permits. Hence it ordains

[7] C. 1, 6°, II, 12; c. 2, 6°, V, 11.
[8] C. 1, 6, II, 13; c. 7, 6°, V, 7.
[9] C. 3, X, II, 12; c. 3, X, II, 19.
[10] C. 3, 6°, II, 14.
[11] C. 15, X, II, 1.
[12] C. 36, X, II, 24.
[13] C. 3, I, X, IV, 13.

that the judge *should not admit evidence* that is apparently demanded for no other purpose than to delay the sentence, unless such evidence is required because of the lack or insufficiency of the other proofs. Proofs which have this dilatory effect are the testimony of a witness who lives far away from the court or whose domicile is unknown, and the examination of a document which cannot be easily and quickly obtained. There is always room for the suspicion that such witnesses and documents are demanded with a sinister intention or frivolously, and they are therefore sometimes called *futilia documenta*, which the *ponens* may and should reject.[14]

The Code then proceeds to describe the different means of obtaining evidence. They are: confession, the testimony of witnesses, the declarations of experts, judicial inspection, documents, presumptions, and oaths.

[14] Cfr. c. 5, X, II, 14; *Les propria S. R. Rotae*, can. 27, § 3 (*A. Ap. S.*, I, 27).

CHAPTER I

CAN. 1750

Assertio de aliquo facto, in scriptis aut oretenus ab una parte contra se et pro adversario coram iudice, sive sponte, sive iudice interrogante peracta, dicitur confessio iudicialis.

CAN. 1751

Si agatur de negotio aliquo privato et in causa non sit bonum publicum, confessio iudicialis unius partis, dummodo libere et considerate facta, relevat alteram ab onere probandi.

CAN. 1752

Pars, aliquid confessa in iudicio, non potest contra confessionem suam venire, nisi aut in continenti hoc faciat, aut probet confessionem ipsam vel carere conditionibus in can. 1750 expressis vel errori facti esse adscribendam.

CAN. 1753

Confessio sive scriptis, sive oretenus, ipsimet adversario aut aliis extra iudicium facta, dicitur extraiudicialis: eaque in iudicium deducta, iudicis est, *perpensis omnibus rerum adiunctis, aestimare quanti facienda sit.*

Confession is here understood in the judicial, not in the sacramental sense. It is called judicial because given *before* the judge sitting in tribunal. If the judge delegates a notary or an auditor to receive a confession, it is nevertheless judicial, because the notary acts in the name of the judge.[1] But a confession made before a lay judge cannot be accepted as such by an ecclesiastical judge, and the latter may not pronounce sentence on the strength of it.[2]

Confession, therefore, may be defined as a statement, oral or written, made before the ecclesiastical judge by one party against itself and in favor of the other, spontaneously or upon the demand of the judge. The text allows not only spontaneous, but also elicited confession. That one may confess a deed of his own accord is evident. But fraud, deceit, or captious words are not admitted in a spontaneous confession. On the other hand, the judge may *solicit* a confession; but he must proceed lawfully, and lawful proceeding requires that the party to be questioned is under his jurisdiction, and that, in a criminal case a denunciation at least, if not a formal inquisition, was previously made. Besides, the judge is not free to act like a shrewd lawyer, extorting a confession by misleading or suggestive questions, by cross-examination, by captious and ensnaring remarks, unworthy trickery, etc.[3]

The judge being entitled to solicit a confession, it follows that the *party* is *obliged* to answer truthfully, because right and duty are correlative. Besides every one is obliged to obey his superior when he lawfully

1 Reiffenstuel, II, 18, n. 9.
2 C. 4, X, II, 1.
3 Cfr. Messmer, *l. c.*, p. 97; Santi-Leitner, II, 18, n. 14.

commands, and the judge is supposed to proceed lawfully.[4]

The plea of "not guilty," with the mental restriction, "because not convicted" or the like, is not admitted by Canon Law.

Entirely different from this is the question whether the defendant is in conscience bound to confess in reply to a true question which would condemn him in the external forum, although in the court of conscience he could not be condemned. Let us give an instance. James feigned a promise of marriage to Gemma (*ficte promisit matrimonium*), and now, at the trial, he is asked by the judge: Did you promise to marry Gemma? What is his duty? The more probable answer to this question is that James may deny the proposition, *i.e.*, he may answer negatively, because in doing so he does not tell an objective untruth, since not the material words are to be considered, but the intention, and he never intended to marry Gemma, but feigned the promise. Of course, we suppose that the judge was under the impression of a false presumption when he asked the question.[5]

Another question: Is the *proctor* allowed to make a confession for his client? Although the text mentions only the party himself, yet if the proctor would confess in the presence of his client, and the latter would not contradict him, or if the proctor had a special mandate to that effect, his confession could not be rejected.[6]

The *effect* of a judicial confession, made freely and deliberately, is very moderately stated in can 1751: "*it frees the other party from the burden of proof.*" Hence,

4 Messmer, l. c., p. 101.
5 Cfr. c. 11, C. 22, q. 5; Reiffenstuel, II, 18, n. 171 ff., who could quote Sanchez, Lugo, and others in favor of this view.
6 Cfr. C. 28, Dig. 2, 14; C. 6, § 4, Dig. 42, 2.

if the defendant confesses his obligation or guilt, the plaintiff has won the case, and, in civil or private matters ("*in negotio privato*") the judge may proceed to pronounce sentence.[7] In cases affecting the public welfare, such as matrimonial and criminal cases, the confession of the party does not produce full proof.[8]

Another effect of confession is stated in can. 1752, namely, the party who has confessed something at the trial, *is not allowed to retract his confession.* The reason is because a confession is supposed to be made deliberately and with due reflection, and without any intention of deriding the judge. However, there are exceptions to this rule. A confession may be retracted:

1. *In continenti, i.e.,* immediately after the confession has been made, and before it is taken down in writing, or before leaving the court, if the judge is willing. In this case it is not necessary to prove the mistake, but it is sufficient simply to recall the previous statement or to correct the error.[9]

2. If the party who confessed can prove that the confession was not made legitimately, according to can. 1750, for instance, that the judge proceeded unlawfully.

3. If an error in fact (*error facti*)—not in law— is proved, for instance, if an administrator or procurator momentarily forgot the exact sum or date.[10]

Can. 1753 mentions *extrajudicial confession, i.e.,* confession made privately to one's adversary or to others, say the judge or notary, or an attorney outside the court or tribunal. The proof that such a confession was made could be furnished by the free admission in court that it had been made, or by two witnesses who heard it.[11]

7 C. 10, X, I, 36; c. 6, X, I, 9.
8 C. 5, X, IV, 13; c. 5, X, V, 1.
9 See c. 7, X, II, 21; Reiffenstuel, II, 18, n. 77 f.
10 C. 4, X, II, 18.
11 C. 23, X, II, 20; Santi-Leitner, II, 18, n. 7.

The value or *effect* of such an extrajudicial confession is not judical *per se,* because it is at the most only half-proof, which does not free the plaintiff from the burden of supplying the remaining half by other means. It rests with the judge to weigh the value of such a confession, and in doing so, he shall consider all the circumstances of the case. Circumstantial evidence may often be helpful. For instance, if a boy was for a long time called the child of a certain man and acknowledged as such by the putative father, even though the latter did so only upon the insistence of the mother, the presumption is in favor of his paternity, even if the mother afterwards denies it under oath.[12]

[12] C. 10, X, II, 19.

CHAPTER II

As in the Roman,[1] so in Canon Law, witnesses have always played a conspicuous part. The *contestatio litis* already introduced witnesses, and in the course of the trial, their testimony was instrumental in deciding the case.

A *witness* is a person who has seen or knows a fact about another person, and is therefore competent to give evidence concerning the same. A testimony (*attestatio*) is a more or less solemn statement, made in court, concerning a fact seen or known by another, for no one can be a witness in his own case. Our Code in two preliminary canons regulates the admission of witnesses and defines their obligation.

ADMISSION AND OBLIGATION OF WITNESSES

CAN. 1754

Probatio per testes in quibuslibet causis admittitur, sub iudicis tamen moderatione, secundum modum praefinitum in canonibus qui sequuntur.

CAN. 1755

§ 1. Testes iudici legitime interroganti respondere et veritatem fateri debent.

1 See Dig. 22, 5; Cod., IV, 20.

§ 2. Salvo praescripto can. 1757, § 3, n. 2, ab hac obligatione eximuntur:

1.° Parochi aliique sacerdotes quod attinet ad ea quae ipsis manifestata sunt ratione sacri ministerii extra sacramentalem confessionem; civitatum magistratus, medici, obstetrices, advocati, notarii aliique qui ad secretum officii etiam ratione praestiti consilii tenentur, quod attinet ad negotia huic secreto obnoxia;

2.° Qui ex testificatione sua sibi vel consanguineis vel affinibus in quolibet gradu lineae rectae et in primo gradu alineae collateralis infamiam, periculosas vexationes, aliave mala valde gravia obventura timent.

§ 3. Testes iudici legitime interroganti scienter falsum affirmantes aut verum occultantes puniantur ad normam can. 1743, § 3; eademque poena mulctentur omnes, qui testem vel peritum donis, pollicitationibus aut alio quovis modo inducere praesumpserint ad falsum testimonium dicendum aut ad veritatem occultandam.

Canon 1754 repeats the old saying of Arcadius [2] that witnesses may be admitted in all trials, whether criminal or civil. The same jurisconsult adds that the judge should control the witness-stand and admit only as many witnesses as are necessary to bring out the truth. This is here expressed by the phrase *" sub iudicis moderatione,"* and the mode or manner is governed by the following canons.

Witnesses, when called upon legitimately by the judge, are *obliged to answer and to speak the truth.* For the office of witness is one of public interest and affects the public welfare. Therefore the ecclesiastical law per-

[2] L. 1, Dig. 22, 5; cfr. c. 13, X, II, 19. Some canonists denied that witnesses could be compelled to give testimony in criminal cases; see Reiffenstuel, II, 21, n. 18 ff.

mits the judge to employ penalties in order to compel persons to act as witnesses. But they must be warned before penalties are inflicted.[3] Besides, the judge must *question them lawfully*, *i.e.*, he must be competent and summon them according to the rules which follow.

Not all persons who are otherwise qualified, are to be *compelled to take the witness stand*. The following are excepted:

1. *Confessors*, who, according to can. 1757, § 3, n. 2, are incapable of giving testimony in regard to matters learned through sacramental confession.

2. All persons whose *knowledge is privileged*, or who are bound by official secrecy, even though this be imposed only by reason of advice. This includes *pastors* and priests who have knowledge of the matter in question only by reason of, and in connection with, their sacred ministry, even though such knowledge was gained extra-sacramentally; also civil magistrates, physicians, midwives, lawyers (attorneys), notaries, and other persons bound by official secrecy.[4] This law was made to safeguard public trust and confidence in public or semi-public persons.

3. All who *would sustain damage* if forced to give testimony. Hence all persons who reasonably fear that their testimony will render themselves or their relatives, either by consanguinity or affinity in every degree of the direct line and up to the first degree of the collateral line, *infamous*, or cause themselves or the aforesaid relatives dangerous *vexations* or other probable disadvantage, cannot be forced to give evidence. As to infamy,

---

[3] C. 1-5, X, II, 21.

[4] This also in English law, according to Blackstone, *Comment.*, III, 370; *Ibid.*, note 24, Cooley adds: "In several of the U. S. statutes have been passed extending similar protection to the communications made to physicians and clergymen."

it is certain that no man can be compelled to prove his own infamy or to answer any questions which may tend to incriminate himself, or render him liable to punishment.[5] Such vexations and evil may be of the moral or the material order.

The question may arise: Is a witness, who is otherwise capable and not excused, bound to speak the truth, if he has sworn to keep it secret (*secretum commissum et iuramento firmatum*)? The answer is, yes, because such an oath was either rash or illicit, and therefore contrary to good morals. If the oath is publicly known, the judge may publicly declare it null and void, in order to prevent danger of scandal arising from presumptive perjury.[6]

§ 3 of can. 1755 establishes the *penal sanction* against *perfidious witnesses.* The judge who proceeds lawfully in questioning witnesses, may inflict upon those *who knowingly tell an untruth,* or conceal the truth, the same penalties as are threatened in can. 1743, § 3, against the parties who tell a lie. But the untruthfulness of the testimony must be either notorious or juridically proved.[7]

The same penalty may be meted out under the same condition to those who *bribe* witnesses or experts with gifts and promises, or in any other way (for instance, by threats or fear) endeavor to induce them to make a false statement or to hide the truth. Thus in the case of a divorce obtained by perjury or false testimony, the bribed witnesses had to do penance and were no longer admitted as witnesses.[8] This, we are sorry to say, still happens in connection with affidavits and other testimony. Severe punishments were formerly visited

---

5 Reiffenstuel, II, 20, n. 22 ff.; see also Blackstone-Cooley, *l. c.*

6 Reiffenstuel, II, 21, n. 43 ff.; Santi-Leitner, II, 21, n. 7.

7 C. 17, X, I, 11.

8 C. 9, X, II, 20.

upon higher and lower clerics who perjured themselves: they were deposed, relegated to a monastery, or reduced to the lay state.[9] Perjurers were excommunicated, or declared infamous, and their testimony rejected.[10] This was done to safeguard the public welfare and the dignity and authority of the courts.

ART. I

WHO MAY BE WITNESSES

CAN. 1756

Omnes possunt esse testes, nisi expresse a iure repellantur vel in totum vel ex parte.

CAN. 1757

§ 1. Ut non idonei repelluntur a testimonio ferendo impuberes et mente debiles.

§ 2. Ut suspecti:

1.° Excommunicati, periuri, infames, post sententiam declaratoriam vel condemnatoriam;

2.° Qui ita abiectis sunt moribus ut fide digni non habeantur;

3.° Publici gravesque partis inimici.

§ 3. Ut incapaces:

1.° Qui partes sunt in causa, aut partium vice funguntur, veluti tutor in causa pupilli, Superior aut administrator in causa suae communitatis aut piae causae, cuius nomine in iudicio consistit, iudex eiusve assistentes, advocatus aliique qui partibus in eadem causa assistunt vel astiterunt;

2.° Sacerdotes, quod attinet ad ea omnia quae ipsis

9 C. 7, Dist. 50.
10 C. 9, C. 3, q. 3; c. 20, C. 24, q. 3.

ex confessione sacramentali innotuerunt, etsi a vinculo
sigilli soluti sint; imo audita a quovis et quoquo modo
occasione confessionis ne ut indicium quidem veritatis
recipi possunt;

3.° Coniux in causa sui coniugis, consanguineus et
affinis in causa consanguinei vel affinis, in quolibet
gradu lineae rectae et in primo gradu collateralis, nisi
agatur de causis quae ad statum civilem aut religiosum
personae spectant, cuius notitia aliunde haberi nequeat,
et bonum publicum exigat ut habeatur.

CAN. 1758

Non idonei et suspecti audiri poterunt ex decreto
iudicis, quo id expedire declaretur; sed eorum
testimonium valebit tantummodo ut indicium et
probationis adminiculum, et generatim iniurati
audiantur.

The general rule is that all whom the law does not
debar, either entirely or partially, may be witnesses.
The law always supposes two qualities in a witness, *viz.*,
first, *knowledge* of the facts to which he was to bear witness, and, secondly, probity or *uprightness* of character.

The Code distinguishes a threefold class of persons
who are, or may be, excluded from the witness-stand;
they are the unfit, the suspected, and the incapable. The
former two classes may be said to constitute the *relatively unfit,* and the last the absolutely unfit witnesses;
or, as the Code says, *ex parte* and *in totum.*

The difference is explained in can. 1758, which declares that the *relatively unfit, i.e.,* the unfit and suspected,
may be admitted as witnesses if the judge considers that
for one reason or another they are necessary. However, their testimony has no value except as an indi-

cation or a sign which may eventually lead to the establishment of complete evidence and to strengthen the proof by corroborating the testimony of other witnesses. Relatively unfit witnesses should, as a rule, be heard without being put under oath (*iniurati audiantur*). Thus in the case of procedure against presumptive heretics witnesses are admitted who are or were the companions and friends of the accused.[11] Thus, also, perjurers are admitted as witnesses by the S. Roman Rota, but their testimony is treated as a mere *indicium*, more especially *in causis spiritualibus*.[12] Conspirators in the same case are generally repelled.[18]

1. Unfit (*non-idonei*) to act as witnesses are boys who have not yet completed the fourteenth, and girls who have not yet completed the twelfth year of age (*impuberes*). Also the feeble-minded (*mente debiles*). To this class belong idiots, mentally deranged persons, and those who are under the influence of magic, or hypnotism, or drugs, or intoxicating liquor. Those who are merely defective in hearing, sight, or speech, are not excluded, provided that the mental condition of this class of *non-idonei* was defective at the time the fact occurred or the act was committed, regarding which they would testify.[14] That they must be mentally normal when they are called upon to give testimony goes without saying.

2. *Suspected* witnesses are:

a) All excommunicated and infamous persons as well

---

11 Cfr. cc. 5, 8, 6°, V, 2.

12 *Reg. Servandae*, Aug. 4, 1910, § 114, n. 1 (*A. Ap. S.*, II, 820).

18 C. 22, X, II, 27.

14 A loose statement is that of Santi-Leitner, II, 20, n. 15: " *quando autem testis adducitur ad probandum actum, eius idoneitas requiritur tempore probationis.*" Does that *probatio* go back to the time the act was committed? If so, all right; but if *probatio* is taken to mean the witness-stand, the statement is ambiguous; for if he was not fit to witness the act, he cannot testify regarding it.

as perjurers against whom a declaratory or condemnatory sentence has been duly pronounced. Note that *vitandi* and *tolerati are equally included* under *excommunicati*, and the Constitution of Martin V ("*Ad evitanda*," 1418) cannot be applied in this case. As to *perjurers*, a special penalty may be meted out to those who perjure themselves outside of a trial court by the Ordinary,[15] who can deprive them of the right and capacity to give testimony if he sees fit. In our case, either the Ordinary or the judge would have to issue a declaration to the effect that perjury was committed, and that the perjurer will not be admitted as a witness; the law permits the issuance of such a sentence.[16]

Concerning *infamous* persons observe that the infamy implied is infamy in law as well as in fact, but the persons in question must have sustained a condemnatory or declaratory sentence to that effect according to the penal code (can. 2293) of the Church. If the civil authorities have pronounced sentence of infamy, the sentence is valid under the ecclesiastical law if the Ordinary approves it.[17]

A special class of infamous persons (*infames infamia iuris*) are those who fight a duel and their seconds.

In all the above-mentioned cases mere notoriety is not sufficient, but a formal sentence, either declaratory or condemnatory, is required.[18]

b) Another class of "suspected" persons debarred from testifying at ecclesiastical trials are those whose *character* is such as to render them untrustworthy. This

---

[15] Can. 2323.

[16] Cfr. c. 9, C. 3, q. 5; c. 9, X, II, 20.

[17] Cfr. c. 17, C. 6, q. 1; can. 2293, § 3.

[18] S. C. C., Aug. 9, 1890 (*A. S.*

S., XXIII, 234 f.); but compare can. 2351, § 2; when this canon is verified, the so-called *Mensuren* of the Austrian and German students render the participants infamous.

is a rather vague rule, the application of which is left
to the judge. It appears to comprise the two classes
formerly [19] known as *criminosi* and *personae viles sive
pauperes*. Criminals are here understood, not such as
are infamous in fact,[20] because these are comprised under
the preceding number. However, as long as no declaratory or condemnatory sentence has been issued, even
those stained with *infamia facti* may reasonably be included here. Hence all persons who have lost the esteem
and respect of their fellowmen, and have not amended
their lives, are included in the phrase: *"qui ita abiectis
sunt moribus,"* etc., also the class formerly styled *personae pauperes et viles*, because, as the Roman law [21]
says, paupers and persons of low condition are apt to
commit a crime for filthy lucre's sake, or, in other words,
are more easily bribed than others. Yet this statement
needs some modification, for a poor man may be as honest as a rich man, and if there is no proof of his having
been bribed on former occasions, he cannot justly be
excluded. It must not be forgotten that the Christian
religion has raised the lowly (slaves, serfs, and villains)
to a higher moral standard than the Roman law could reasonably assume. But proved bribery would certainly be
sufficient to exclude one from the witness-stand.[22]

c) Still another class of persons excluded from testifying at ecclesiastical trials consists of those who have
*publicly fostered hatred and enmity against the party
against whom they are called to testify*. This exclusion is
based on common sense and has been generally adopted
by civil codes. This class of witnesses was not admitted
even in exceptional judgments, either civil or criminal,
and was excluded also in inquisitorial proceedings.[23]

19 C. 54, X, II, 20; c. 3, C. 4,
q. 2 et 3; see l. 3, Dig. 22, 5.
20 Reiffenstuel, II, 20, n. 55.
21 L. 3, Dig. 22, 5.
22 C. 9, X, II, 20.
23 C. 32, X, V, 3.

But there are three limitations established by the Code:

1) The enmity must be *public*, *i.e.*, divulged, or at least easily and readily known from the circumstances of the case.[24] Thus a former lawsuit or the threat of bodily violence, blackmail, serious quarrels or fights would be indicative of an existing enmity. This enmity must furthermore be

(2) *Deadly or grievous*, which means that the enemy would inflict a grievous mental, spiritual or physical evil on his adversary if it were in his power to do so.

(3) The enmity must finally be limited to *one of the litigant parties*, *viz.*, the one against whom testimony is to be given. For if the witness would be an enemy to both the plaintiff and the defendant, his testimony could not be rejected.[25]

3. The following are also *incapable* of being witnesses:

a) Those *who are parties to the same cause or act in the name of the litigant parties;* such as tutors in the case of their wards, superiors or administrators in the case of their communities or pious foundations, judges and their assessors, attorneys and others who assist or have assisted their clients in the same case. All these are presumed to be engaged in a common cause, and therefore to be personally interested. Hence the maxim: " No one may be plaintiff and witness or judge and witness " [26] at the same time and in the same case. However, this, too, must be taken with a grain of salt. For a prelate, either secular or regular, may testify in the case of his own church or community, as long as he is not plaintiff, defendant, or proctor; canons and capitulars may testify in civil matters concerning their chapters, provided only the chapter as such, and no personal in-

24 See can. 2197, n. 1.
25 Reiffenstuel, II, 20, n. 132 f.
26 Cfr. c. 6, X, II, 20; Santi-Leitner, II, 20, n. 9.

terests, are involved.[27] This applies to all instances (first, second, last), through which the case may run.

b) *Priests* are rejected as witnesses in *whatever concerns knowledge gained through sacramental confession*, even though the parties have given them permission to speak. This principle applies to anyone who, whether cleric or layman, has in any way acquired knowledge through sacramental confession; the testimony of such a one cannot be accepted even as a presumptive indication of truth. Thus bystanders at the confessional or chance hearers of a sacramental confession cannot be admitted as witnesses to a fact thus perceived or learnt.

c) By reason of *natural affection*, which may influence the judgment, the following are excluded: the husband in case of his wife and *vice versa*, those who are related to one another by consanguinity and affinity in every degree of the direct line and in the first degree of the collateral line, *i.e.*, brothers and sisters, brothers-in-law and sisters-in-law, whenever their relatives are concerned.[28]

Yet even these are not entirely and in every case rejected; for if relatives wish to testify to the civil or religious state of the defendant, they may be admitted, provided the required testimony cannot be obtained otherwise and the public weal demands that it be obtained. Thus parents may testify to the baptism, or to the legitimacy, or to the clerical, religious or married state, or to the age of their children; spouses are also admitted, for they are supposed to know their pedigree better than outsiders.[29] However, no full proof could be construed from the deposition of such witnesses,[30] unless no other

27 Reiffenstuel, II, 20, 197 ff.
28 Cfr. c. 3, C. 4, q. 2 et 3; c. 78, C. 11, q. 3.
29 C. 5, X, II, 20; c. 3, X, IV, 18.
30 Reiffenstuel, II, 20, n. 119.

proof were available and the public welfare required that proof be secured.

Art. II

BY WHOM, HOW, AND HOW MANY WITNESSES ARE TO BE INTRODUCED, AND WHO ARE TO BE REJECTED

Can. 1759

§ 1. Testes a partibus inducuntur.

§ 2. Possunt quoque induci a promotore iustitiae et defensore vinculi, si id ad causam intersit.

§ 3. Sed ipse iudex, quoties agatur de minoribus aliisve qui minoribus aequiparantur, et generatim quoties publicum bonum id exigat, potest testes ex officio inducere.

§ 4. Pars, quae testem induxit, potest eius examini renunciare; sed adversarius postulare potest ut, hac non obstante denuntiatione, testis examini subiiciatur.

Can. 1760

§ 1. Si quis sponte compareat testimonii reddendi gratia, iudex poterit eius testimonium admittere vel repellere prout expedire censuerit.

§ 2. Debet autem testem, qui se sponte obtulerit, repellere cum comparere sibi videatur moras iudicio nectendi causa vel iustitiae et veritati quoquo modo officiendi.

This whole article might be simply inscribed: *" De Productione* Testium,"* which is nothing else but a petition offered to the judge to admit witnesses of the party who wishes to prove an action or exception.

1. The *parties may* introduce witnesses, who are received after the issue in pleading.[31]

2. The *promotor iustitiae* and the *defensor vinculi* may also call in witnesses if they deem them necessary.

3. The judge, too, may demand witnesses, if minors and such as are compared to minors in law are concerned in the trial, or whenever the public welfare requires witnesses, as in matrimonial cases.

4. The party who produces a witness may forego the privilege of examining him, although this does not affect the right of the opponent to do so.

It may happen (can. 1760) that some one offers himself as a witness of his own accord. But since there is room for suspicion as to the motives of such a *testis ultroneus*, the judge is free either to admit or to reject him. He *must* reject him if it becomes apparent that the object of the spontaneous witness is simply to delay the trial or to obstruct justice.

HOW WITNESSES ARE PRODUCED

CAN. 1761

§ 1. Cum probatio per testes postulatur, eorum nomina et domicilium tribunali indicentur; praeterea exhibeantur positiones seu articuli argumentorum super quibus testes sint interrogandi.

§ 2. Si ne intra diem quidem peremptorium a iudice praestitutum, obtemperatum fuerit, postulatio deserta censetur.

If witnesses are demanded, their name and domicile must be indicated and the questions or points upon which they are to be examined must be handed to the tribunal.

31 Cfr. X, II, 6: " *Ut lite non contestata non procedatur ad testium receptionem;*" see can. 1730.

The obligation of making known these things, *viz.*, the names and points, lies with those who demand witnesses, either the party, or others.[32] If this obligation has not been complied with within the time set by the judge, the demand is quashed.

The litigant parties must make known to each other the names of their respective witnesses before these are examined; if this would prove a great inconvenience, the manifestation may be made before the testimonies are published (can. 1763).

The summoning of witnesses is done by the judge, who issues a decree to that effect. The summons must be served like the citation of the parties, as stated in canons 1725 sqq. When duly served, it entails the obligation of appearing in court (can. 1766); in case of inability, the judge must be informed of the reason. This rule must be understood in the light of can. 1755, § 2.

That there is a *strict obligation* cannot be denied, since the law provides a punishment for refusal. § 2 of can. 1766 states that if a witness proves recalcitrant or disobedient to the summons duly served, and fails to appear in court without a lawful reason, the judge may inflict a suitable punishment and fine him for the amount of damage caused to the parties by his unreasonable conduct. The same penalty may be inflicted upon those who appear in court but refuse to answer lawful questions put to them, or to take the oath, or to sign the witness papers.

No distinction is made on this head between clergymen and laymen. Clergymen, when summoned to the ecclesiastical court, should set an example of obedience to laymen.

---

[32] *Regulae S. R. Rotae*, Aug. 4, 1910, § 114, n. 3 (*A. Ap. S.,* II, 821).

A written excuse should be sent in if the witness summoned is unfit, suspected, or incapable of testifying, so that the judge may take note thereof in the acts.[33]

THE NUMBER OF WITNESSES

CAN. 1762

Iudici ius et obligatio est nimiam multitudinem testium refrenandi.

CAN. 1763

Partes debent sibi invicem nota facere testium nomina antequam eorum examen inchoetur, aut, si id, prudenti iudicis existimatione, fieri sine gravi difficultate nequeat, saltem ante testificationum publicationem.

In order that the trial be not unnecessarily prolonged, the judge is empowered and obliged to restrict the number of witnesses (can. 1762). The admissible number was fixed in one Decretal as fourty for each party.[34] However, the text may have another meaning, viz., as regulating the number of times a witness may be produced. An ancient law says that a witness may be produced only three times and that a special solemnity is required for the fourth time.[35] But this Decretal would rather seem to refer to the examination of witnesses. That is now regulated by can. 1781. Our text probably refers to the number of witnesses, which is left to the judge to fix, except when there is question of " seven

[33] It is quite true (see Messmer, l. c., p. 112) that certain witnesses should not be called, but courtesy as well as despatch would seem to counsel the interpretation given in the text.
[34] C. 37, X, II, 20.
[35] C. 36, X, II, 20.

·hand " testimony in case of non-consummation of mar-
·riage; this the judge is not at liberty to curtail.[36]

WHICH WITNESSES ARE TO BE EXCLUDED

CAN. 1764

§ 1. Testes debent ex officio excludi, si iudici liquido
constet eos a testimonio ferendo prohiberi, salvo
praescripto can. 1758.

§ 2. Ast etiam, postulante adversario, testes ex-
cludendi sunt, si iusta exclusionis causa demonstretur,
quae exclusio dicitur *reprobatio personae testis.*

§ 3. Pars nequit reprobare personam testis quem
ipsa induxit, nisi nova reprobationis causa super-
venerit, quamvis possit eius dicta reprobare.

§ 4. Reprobatio testis fieri debet intra triduum
postquam testium nomina cum parte communicata
fuerunt, nec postea facta admittatur, nisi a parte
demonstretur vel saltem iuramento affirmetur de-
fectum testis antea sibi notum non fuisse.

§ 5. Iudex autem reprobationis discussionem in
finem litis reservet, nisi contra testem stet praesumptio
iuris, aut defectus sit notorius vel statim ac facile
probari possit vel postea probari nequeat.

CAN. 1765

Citatio testium fit ministerio iudicis, decreto interve-
niente, et intimanda est testibus ad normam can. 1715–
1723.

1. The judge must *ex officio* exclude from the witness-
stand all *incompetent witnesses*, those entirely incapable,

36 See cc. 5, 7, X, IV, 15; can. 1975.

and the unfit and suspected, who may, however, be admitted to give presumptive evidence (can. 1758).

2. No witnesses may be admitted to whom the opponent reasonably takes exception. The *reprobatio personae testis* is a kind of exception, but neither dilatory nor peremptory in the proper sense, for it may be made at any time before the publication of the testimonies or depositions. But it properly turns about the person of the witness whose unfitness, incapacity, etc., may be objected to, according to can. 1757.

3. However, if a party has introduced a witness to testify for himself, he cannot reject that witness, because the very fact of his producing him argues that he is willing to accept him and approves of his qualifications. Only if a reason to object to the witness developed after he was summoned, would the party who produced him be allowed to put up an exception.[37] Thus if a witness called and proposed by a party should become that party's bitter enemy, or perjure himself, or become infamous, the party could take exception to him. Besides, although a witness was introduced by the party himself, and no new reason for his rejection has arisen, the producing party may contradict or reprove anything the witness may say against him, because, although the party may know the person, he may not know his intentions or what he is going to say.

4. However, the *rejection of a witness* or exception to the same must be made *within three days* after the names of the witnesses have been communicated by the parties to each other and cannot be admitted afterwards unless the party can prove, or at least affirms under oath, that some defect in the witness, *i.e.*, unfitness, incapacity, etc., was unknown to him before.

[37] C. 31, X, II, 20.

5. The *judge* may put off the discussion of exceptions taken to witnesses to the end of the trial. This is the rule, which, however, must not be applied to certain exceptional cases, namely:

a) If the *presumption of the law* is against the witness; this would be the case if a witness were unfit, as defined in can. 1757, § 3;

b) If the *defect* in a witness is notorious and could easily and immediately be proved, for instance, by producing the sentence of excommunication issued against a *vitandus;*

c) If the defect could not be proved afterwards, *i.e.,* after some delay, for instance, if the witness were dangerously ill or about to depart for a distant country.[88]

ART. III

THE OATH TAKEN BY WITNESSES

CAN. 1767

§ 1. Testis, antequam testimonium edat, iusiurandum praestare debet de tota ac sola veritate dicenda, salvo praescripto can. 1758.

§ 2. Partes earumve procuratores praestationi iurisiurandi testium assistere possunt, salvo praescripto can. 1763.

§ 3. Testibus, si de iure partium mere privato agatur, poterit iusiurandum, utraque parte consentiente, remitti.

§ 4. Sed etiam cum iusiurandum a teste non exigitur, iudex testem commonefaciat gravis obligationis, qua semper tenetur, veritatem dicendi.

---

88 Reiffenstuel, II, 20, n. 546 ff.

Can. 1768

Testes, tametsi iusiurandum praestiterint de veritate dicenda, poterunt nihilominus pro prudenti iudicis arbitrio, absoluto examine, adigi ad iusiurandum de *veritate dictorum* sive circa omnes positionum articulos sive circa aliquos tantum, quoties gravitas negotii et editae testificationis adiuncta id postulare videantur.

Can. 1769

Testes adigi etiam iureiurando possunt ad secretum servandum circa propositas interrogationes dataque interrogationibus responsa, usque dum acta et allegata publici iuris fiant; imo etiam perpetuo ad normam can. 1623, § 3.

1. All witnesses, except the unfit and suspected, must swear that they will tell the whole truth and nothing but the truth. This so-called *iuramentum veritatis* was always considered so necessary that the saying is: " A witness not sworn proves nothing." [39] The oath is to be administered before the examination, generally by the judge or his auditor.[40]

If the litigants or their proctors wish to be present at the ceremony, they are at liberty to do so, provided they come before the examination begins. But no plea of exception can be construed from their voluntary or involuntary absence.

The phrase: " *de tota ac sola veritate,*" must be understood in the sense that they bind themselves to answer truthfully the questions proposed, concealing nothing and asserting no falsehood. But they are not bound to say more than the questions imply. At least this is the pres-

---

[39] Cfr. cc. 10, 39, 51, X, II, 20.   [40] Cfr. Messmer, *l. c.*, p. 116.

ent practice of courts.[41]   But the oath includes another element, *vis.,* that they speak the truth for motives of truthfulness, that they harbor no sinister intention, and that they have not been bribed.[42]

Both parties consenting, this *oath may be omitted* in all private trials where the public weal is not at stake. The oath is administered in favor of both parties, and hence may be remitted, without the intervention of the judge, by both.   However, the text clearly states that this may be done only when private interests are at stake. In matrimonial cases, therefore, when the validity of a marriage is threatened, and in criminal and beneficiary matters the oath may never be omitted.[43]   When the oath is not administered to a witness, the judge shall not omit to warn him of the grave obligation incumbent upon him to tell the truth.

Concerning the formalities of the oath see can. 1621.

2. There is, as can. 1768 points out, another oath, called *de veritate dictorum,* which is administered after the examination, even in cases where the oath *de veritate dicenda* has already been taken.   This oath refers either to all the answers that have been given to the questions proposed, or only to certain important questions.   The judge may demand the *iusiurandum de veritate dictorum* whenever, according to his prudence and practical insight, the importance of the matter or the circumstances of the testimony require it.   This is a new regulation in ecclesiastical jurisprudence,[44] which was made necessary by intricate cases and to control the testimony of witnesses who vacillate under cross-examination.

41 Reiffenstuel, II, 20, n. 466.
42 C. 47, X, II, 20.
43 C. 39, X, II, 20; Reiffenstuel, II, 20, n. 485 f.
44 C. 5, X, II, 20 mentions two oaths, which, however, were comprised in one, *de veritate dicenda;* but the *Regulae S. R. R.* enumerate these two oaths; Aug. 4, 1910, § 114, n. 2 (*A. Ap. S.,* II, 820).

3. The witnesses may be *bound by oath to keep secret* the questions proposed and the answers given, until the whole proceedings are published, or forever, if the good name of others is endangered or quarrels and scandals are to be feared from a divulgation (can. 1623, § 3), as is generally the case in criminal procedure and where persons of the " weaker sex " are concerned.[45]

ART. IV

THE EXAMINATION OF WITNESSES

The Code now proceeds to lay down the rules for the examination of witnesses: where and in whose presence they must be examined, the character and substance of the interrogations and answers, how they must be taken down by the clerk, and, finally, repeated questioning.

THE PLACE OF EXAMINATION

CAN. 1770

§ 1. Testes sunt examini subiiciendi in ipsa tribunalis sede.

§ 2. Ab hac generali regula excipiuntur:

1.° S. R. E. Cardinales, Episcopi et personae illustres quae suae civitatis iure eximuntur ab obligatione comparendi coram iudice testificandi causa: ii omnes eligere ipsi possunt locum ubi testificentur, de quo iudicem certiorem facere debent;

2.° Qui morbo aliove corporis vel animi impedimento aut conditione vitae, uti moniales, tribunalis sedem adire nequeunt; ii domi audiendi sunt;

3.° Qui extra dioecesim degentes, in dioecesim reverti et ad tribunalis sedem accedere sine gravi in-

---

[45] Messmer, *l. c.*, p. 116.

commodo nequeunt; ii audiendi sunt a tribunali loci in quo commorantur ad normam can. 1570, § 2, secundum interrogationes et instructiones a causae iudice transmissas;

4.° Qui in dioecesi quidem commorantur, sed in locis ita dissitis a tribunalis sede, ut sine gravibus impensis neque ipsi iudicem adire, neque a iudice adiri possint. Hoc in casu iudex debet propiorem aliquem sacerdotem dignum et idoneum deputare, ut cum assistentia alicuius, qui actuarii munere fungatur, examen horum testium perficiat, transmissis pariter eidem interrogationibus faciendis, datisque opportunis instructionibus.

The general rule is that witnesses must be examined *in court*, *i.e.*, on the witness-stand. From this rule the legislator *exempts the following persons:*

1.° Cardinals, bishops and illustrious personages,[44] who, by virtue of their civic prerogatives, are exempt from appearing in court; all these may choose a place convenient to them for giving testimony, but should inform the judge to that effect.

2.° All those who are detained from personally appearing by sickness or any other physical or mental impediment, or by their state of life (for instance, cloistered nuns and the inmates of state asylums). These may give testimony at their respective residences, and the judge may send the notary or auditor or two deputies to receive their deposition.[47]

3.° Those who dwell outside the diocese and cannot conveniently return and appear in court. Their deposi-

---

[44] The *illustres* held first place in the official hierarchy of the (reorganized) Roman empire, which was composed of *illustres* or Right Honorable, of *spectabiles* or Honorable, and of *clarissimi* or Worshipful gentlemen. To the class of *illustres* belonged the thirteen cabinet ministers of the West; see Hodgkin, *Italy and her Invaders*, 1892, 2nd ed., Vol. I, p. 603 f.

[47] Reiffenstuel, II, 20, n. 506.

tions, according to can. 1570, § 2, must be received by the local tribunal in accordance with the formulary of interrogation and the instructions sent to it by the judge in case.

4.° Those who live in the diocese, but so far away from the court that it would be expensive for them to come to court, or for the judge to reach them. In such cases the judge shall appoint a worthy and fit priest who lives near the place, to take the testimony with the help of another person, who may act as clerk. To that priest must be forwarded the interrogatories and such instructions as may be deemed necessary.

IN WHOSE PRESENCE THE WITNESSES ARE TO BE EXAMINED

CAN. 1771

Examini testium partes assistere nequeunt, nisi iudex eas admittendas censuerit.

CAN. 1772

§ 1. Testes seorsim singuli examinandi sunt.

§ 2. Prudenti tamen iudicis arbitrio relinquitur post edita testimonia testes inter se aut cum parte conferre, seu, vulgo, *confrontare*.

§ 3. Id autem fieri poterit si haec omnia simul concurrant, scilicet:

1.° Si testes inter se aut cum parte in re gravi et causae substantiam attingente dissentiant;

2.° Si nulla alia facilior ad veritatem detegendam suppetat via;

3.° Si scandali vel dissidiorum periculum non sit ex collatione pertimescendum.

CAN. 1773

§ 1. Examen fit a iudice, vel ab eius delegato aut auditore, cui assistat oportet notarius.

§ 2. In examine interrogationes non ab alio quam a iudice vel ab eo qui iudicis locum tenet, testibus deferendae sunt. Quapropter si partes, vel promotor iustitiae, vel defensor vinculi examini intersint et novas interrogationes testi faciendas habeant, has non testi, sed iudici vel eius locum tenenti proponere debent, ut eas ipse deferat.

1. The *parties to the trial are not allowed* to be present when the witnesses are examined, in order that they may not be influenced or disturbed. However, the judge may give them permission to assist, especially if only questions of patrimony or money are at issue.[48]

2. *Each witness must be examined separately.* This rule must not be interpreted so strictly as if the validity of the examination were impaired in case of its non-observance.[49] If the judge deems it prudent, the witnesses may be confronted one with another and with the parties, to compare their statements. But such confrontation is permitted only when the following conditions concur:

a) If the witnesses disagree among themselves, or with the party they testify for, in a serious and substantial point;

b) If, in the opinion of the judge, no better expedient can be found to discover the truth;

c) If no danger of scandal or quarrel is likely to arise from the comparison of the various statements.

[48] *Reg. S. R. Rotae*, Aug. 4, 1910, § 114, n. 6 (*A. Ap. S.*, II, 821). June 11, 1880, n. 17; Messmer, *l. c.*, p. 117.
[49] Instructio S. C. EE. et RR.,

3. The examination of witnesses must be performed by the *judge* or his delegate or auditor, assisted by the *notary*.

Here it may not be amiss to repeat what the Holy Office [50] enjoined concerning the examination of women who have been "*sollicitatae in confessione.*" They may be heard in the sacristy or in some other unsuspected place, in the presence of the appointed judge and a clerk (both ecclesiastics). Each *sollicitata* must be examined cautiously and separately, not in company with others, because the secret is inviolable.

The *interrogatories* or *questions* are to be put to the witnesses by the judge or his *locum tenens*. If the parties, or the *promotor iustitiae*, or the *defensor vinculi* should wish to ask other questions, these questions must be proposed to the witness through the judge or his delegate, not directly.

NATURE OF THE INTERROGATORIES AND ANSWERS

CAN. 1774

Testis primo interrogari debet non modo de generalibus personae adiunctis, hoc est, de nomine, cognomine, origine, aetate, religione, conditione, domicilio, sed etiam quae ipsi cum partibus in causa sit necessitudo; deinde deferendae sunt interrogationes quae causam ipsam respiciunt et sciscitandum unde et quomodo ea quae asserit, habeat cognita.

CAN. 1775

Interrogationes breves sunto, non plura simul complectentes, non captiosae, non subdolae, non sug-

---

50 S. O., July 20, 1890 (*Coll. P. F.*, n. 1732).

gerentes responsionem, remotae a cuiusvis offensione et pertinentes ad causam quae agitur.

CAN. 1776

§ 1. Interrogationes non sunt cum testibus antea communicandae.

§ 2. Attamen si ea quae testificanda sunt ita a memoria sint remota, ut nisi prius recolantur, certo affirmari nequeant, poterit iudex nonnulla testem praemonere, si id sine periculo fieri posse censeat.

CAN. 1777

Testes oretenus testimonium dicant, et scriptum ne legant, nisi de calculo et rationibus agatur; tunc enim adnotationes, quas secum attulerunt, poterunt consulere.

1. The questions to be proposed are partly general and partly special.

a) Of a *general* character are the preliminary inquiries regarding the personal circumstances of the witness. Hence, as in our courts, he must be asked his full name (*nomen et cognomen*), parentage, age, religion, condition or profession, domicile or residence, and also about his connection with the parties in the case.

This latter question will lead to the discovery of blood relationship or any interest the witness may have in the case. Hence the witness must be asked: Do you know the parties? If so, how long? What is your connection with them? etc.

b) The *special questions* touch the merits of the case. The first is as to the source of knowledge (*unde*) and how it was obtained. The judge is entitled to know the source of one's knowledge, and if he demands it, the witness is bound to answer.[51]   Then the judge shall ask the witness whether he has *direct knowledge* of the fact he is to testify to.   If he answers yes, he must be looked upon as a first-class witness, or a witness *de scientia*, who has witnessed the fact or perceived it immediately through his senses, for instance, if he has seen homicide or adultery committed.

If the witness has no immediate or direct knowledge, then he is only an *indirect* witness, and the question *quomodo* (how he has obtained his knowledge) must be put.

a) He may say: "This is my opinion," and therefore testify *de sua credulitate*, or what he believes to be a fact or a conclusion from conjectures and circumstantial evidence, the weight of which is enhanced by presumption.[52]

b) Or he may say that he had heard a report of the fact or incident from trustworthy persons.   Witnesses of this class are called *testes de auditu* and much depends on from how many they heard the report; for if the report or story was spread by one and the same person, this amounts only to one witness, even though forty others repeat it from hearsay.   Witnesses *de auditu* can be admitted only if the original reporter or narrator is dead, absent, or not to be found.[53]

c) Finally there are witnesses who can only testify that a rumor was spread and is believed by the people; these are *testes de fama*.   Rumor itself merely creates presumption if it is spread by and among sober and

51 Reiffenstuel, II, 20, n. 511 f.
52 Cfr. c. 12, X, II, 23; see this *Commentary*, Vol. V, p. 371.
53 Cfr. c. 47, X, II, 20; see the case stated under Title XXXI, where eighty witnesses testified against a pastor, but all had heard the story from an old woman; the pastor was declared innocent.

prudent men. Therefore the origin of the rumor has to be inquired into, and if its authors cannot be found out, the rumor must be rejected. The *vox populi* sometimes is, not *vox Dei*, but *faex populi*.

2. The questions asked must be *brief* and *simple, i.e.,* not combining many things in one. The judge is not allowed to make use of *captious, cunning or suggestive questions,* to ensnare or compel the witness to answer according to a preconceived idea. This would embarrass the witness and curtail his freedom. Besides the judge must abstain from *offensive questions* and from asking questions which have nothing to do with the case.

3. The *questions* on which a witness is to be cross-examined *must not be communicated to him beforehand, i.e.,* before he has been sworn and put on the witness-stand; for this might lead to collusion and also to mental restrictions when giving oath. However, the judge may intimate beforehand some questions which depend on the memory and could not easily and truthfully be answered without due preparation, because the facts happened a long time ago, and so forth. But the danger of fraud or collusion must always be avoided as effectively as possible.

4. The answers or statements of the witnesses must be made *orally,* not read off a paper. Yet if numbers or dates or calculations of a mathematical nature are involved, the witness may make use of notes.

ANSWERS TO BE PUT IN WRITING AND READ

CAN. 1778

Responsio ex continenti redigenda est scripto ab actuario non solum quod attinet ad substantiam, sed etiam ad ipsa editi testimonii verba, nisi iudex, attenta causae exiguitate, satis habeat unam depositionis substantiam referri.

CAN. 1779

Actuarius in actis mentionem faciat de praestito, remisso aut recusato iureiurando, de partium aliorumque praesentia, de interrogationibus ex officio additis et generatim de omnibus memoria dignis quae forte acciderint, cum testes excutiebantur.

CAN. 1780

§ 1. Testi, antequam ab auditorio discedat, debent legi quae actuarius de iis quae ipse viva voce testatus est, scripto redegit, data eidem testi facultate addendi, supprimendi, corrigendi, variandi.

§ 2. Denique actui subscribere debent testis, iudex et notarius.

1. All answers must be *immediately* set down in writing by the clerk, not only substantially, but verbally, as given, unless in the view of the judge the matter is of small importance, in which case a summary note would suffice.

2. The same clerk (*actuarius*) must also state in the minutes whether the oath was taken, refused by, or remitted to, the witness, whether the parties were present, whether other questions had been officially asked, and, generally, everything that is worth putting on record, as uttered during the examination of the witness.

3. Before the witness leaves the stand the minutes of his testimony *must be read to him,* and he may, if he chooses, add, suppress, correct, or change any statement

he has made. Afterwards this is no longer permitted.
Then the witness must *sign* his name to his deposition
as recorded by the clerk, and the judge and notary should
also sign their names, after that of the witness.

REPEATED EXAMINATIONS

CAN. 1781

**Testes, quamvis iam excussi, poterunt, parte
postulante aut ex officio, antequam acta seu testificationes publici iuris fiant, denuo ad examen vocari, si
iudex id necessarium vel utile ducat, dummodo tamen
omnis collusionis vel corruptelae adsit periculum.**

Under can. 1762 it was remarked that repeated ex-
aminations of the same witnesses are permissible. The
old law [54] permitted a *tertia* and *quarta productio testium*,
but no more. The Code fixes no limit. Therefore, if
one of the parties insists, or the judge deems it necessary
or useful, a witness may be examined repeatedly, provided
no collusion or bribery is to be feared. However, in
order not to prolong the trial, such repetition should be
permitted only before the testimonies have been officially
made known (*antequam acta seu testificationes publici
iuris fiant*).

ART. V

PUBLICATION OF TESTIMONIES AND THEIR REJECTION

As soon as the witnesses in a case have been heard, or
the parties concerned have declared that they have no
more witnesses to produce, the testimonies may be published. This means that the answers or depositions of

54 C. 37, X, II, 20.

the witnesses given to the questions proposed may be publicly read. When this is to be done and what effect it produces, especially as to exceptions and the calling-in of witnesses, is the subject of Article V.

WHEN THE TESTIMONY MAY BE PUBLISHED

CAN. 1782

§ 1. Cum partes aut earum procuratores examini non interfuerunt, testimonia statim post absolutum omnium testium examen poterunt, decreto iudicis, evulgari.

§ 2. Sed poterit iudex differre testimoniorum evulgationem in tempus quo cetera probationum capitula fuerint absoluta, si id e re existimet.

If the parties or their proctors (attorneys) were not present at the examination, publication of the testimony may be made immediately after all the depositions have been taken down. It makes no difference whether the absence was voluntary or *per contumaciam.* In any case, for contempt virtually equals presence, the publication may be insisted upon by the other party, or by the judge, who should advise the litigants to renounce further examination if the points have been sufficiently cleared up. The judge must issue a *formal decree ordering the depositions published.* He himself or a notary shall read them to the parties present. However, two things must be observed:

1. This publication is not essential to the validity of the acts, hence our text simply says: "*poterunt evulgari,*" they may be published;

2. The judge may, if he thinks it advantageous, delay the publication until all the proofs have been gathered.

CAN. 1783

Post testificationum evulgationem:

1.° Cessat facultas reprobandi testis personam, excepto casu de quo in can. 1764, § 4;

2.° Sed est ius reprobandi testes sive quod attinet ad modum examinis, cum scilicet obiiciuntur regulae iuris in examine peragendo neglectae, sive quod attinet ad testificationes ipsas, cum nempe testimonia impugnantur de falso aut de variatione, contradictione, obscuritate, defectu scientiae et similibus.

CAN. 1784

Reprobationem iudex decreto suo reiiciat, si eam futili inniti fundamento aut ad retardandum iudicium factam animadvertat.

CAN. 1785

Si iudicium reprobationis admittatur, iudex brevem terminum parti postulanti praestituat ad probandam reprobationem, et deinde procedat uti in aliis incidentibus causis.

1. One of the effects of the publication of the testimony is that neither party can any longer object to the witnesses except in the case mentioned under can. 1764, § 4. However, although the witnesses cannot be rejected, their depositions may be attacked for two reasons:

a) That the examination was not conducted legally;

b) That the testimony contains falsehoods, contradictions, obscurities, etc., or betrays a change or defect of knowledge. Concerning this second point more will be said under Art. VII. As to the first point, the exceptions may be based on the assertion that the judge was not competent, or on any point laid down in Art. IV.

2. However, if the judge is aware that these exceptions are futile or only intended to protract the trial, he may issue a *decree* rejecting the exceptions.

3. If, on the other hand, exceptions are admitted, the judge shall set a brief term for proving them and in the meanwhile proceed as in other incidental questions.

REPEATED CALLING OF WITNESSES

CAN. 1786

Post evulgatas testificationes, testes iam auditi denuo super iisdem articulis ne interrogentur, neque novi testes admittantur, nisi caute et ex gravi ratione in causis quae nunquam transeunt in rem iudicatam; ex gravissima ratione in ceteris; et in quolibet casu omni fraudis et subornationis periculo remoto, altera parte audita, et requisito voto promotoris iustitiae vel defensoris vinculi, si hi iudicio intersint; quae omnia iudex decreto suo definiat.

The *general rule* is that after the publication of the testimony the witnesses should not again be asked the same questions which they have already answered,[55] and that no new witnesses should be introduced. By consenting to the publication the witnesses are supposed to have renounced further examination. Note well that the same questions only are forbidden. If a new and necessary question would occur, for instance, concerning a baptismal record which could not be obtained before, or a lately found privilege,[56] this rule would not apply.

---

[55] Cc. 19, 25, X, II, 20.   [56] Cc. 19, 42, X, II, 20.

There are two exceptions to the rule just stated:

1. In cases which never pass into the adjudged stage, witnesses already examined and new ones may be introduced cautiously and for a grave reason. Matrimonial, clerical, and religious trials never become *res iudicatae*,[57] and in all such cases a *grave reason* is all that is required to admit of repeated examination. Such a reason would be if testimonies had been lost,[58] or also, as stated above, if new proofs could be furnished, or by the common consent of the litigants.

2. In certain other cases, *e.g.*, if the reason is *gravissima*, as, for instance, if malice or negligence on the part of the judge prevented a full examination, or if one of the witnesses was convicted of perjury.[59]

But it is required that everything be done cautiously, so that no danger of fraud or subornation enters the new hearing. Besides, the other party must be heard, and the *promotor iustitiae* and *defensor vinculi* must be asked for their opinion, if they are present; and, finally, the judge must issue a decree to that effect, mentioning all important details.

Art. VI

COMPENSATION OF WITNESSES

Can. 1787

§ 1. Testis ius habet ad petendam compensationem impensarum, quas sustinuerit ratione itineris et commorationis in loco iudicii, et ad congruam indemnitatem pro interruptione sui negotii vel operis.

§ 2. Iudicis est, auditis parte ac teste, et, si opus sit,

---

[57] See can. 1902 f.
[58] C. 15, X, II, 19.

[59] See cc. 9, 48, X, II, 20; Reiffenstuel, II, 20, n. 156 f.

etiam peritis, taxare indemnitatem et impensas testi solvendas.

CAN. 1788

Si intra peremptorium terminum a iudice praestitutum congrua pecuniae quantitas de qua in can. 1909, § 2, ab eo qui testes inducere vult deposita non sit, is testium examini renuntiasse censeatur.

The Roman as well as ecclesiastical law,[60] from which modern civil codes hardly differ in this matter, demand that witnesses be proportionately recompensed for the expenses incurred.

In reckoning the sum, the distance from which they came (mileage), living expenses, and indemnity for interrupted business or work must be considered. The judge shall adjudge the expenses and indemnities. He should, however, hear the parties and witnesses, and may also, if necessary, consult experts as to the amount to be allowed. The judge may also demand that the sum for all these expenses be deposited with the clerk or that security (bail) be given guaranteeing payment.[61] If the parties refuse to comply with this demand within the term peremptorily assigned, they are supposed to have renounced the examination of the respective witnesses.

WEIGHT OF TESTIMONIES

CAN. 1789

In aestimandis testimoniis iudex prae oculis habeat:

1.° Quae conditio sit personae, quaeve honestas et an aliqua dignitate testis praefulgeat;

---

60 Cfr. c. 3, C. 4, q. 2 et 3.   61 Can. 1909, § 2.

2.° Utrum de scientia propria, praesertim de visu et auditu proprio testificetur, an de credulitate, de fama, aut de auditu ab aliis;

3.° Utrum testis constans sit et firmiter sibi cohaereat, an varius, incertus, vel vacillans;

4.° Denique utrum testimonii contestes habeat, an sit singularis.

CAN. 1790

Si testes inter se discrepent, iudex perpendat utrum edita ab eis testimonia sibi invicem adversentur, an sint dumtaxat diversa vel adminiculativa.

CAN. 1791

§ 1. Unius testis depositio plenam fidem non facit, nisi sit testis qualificatus qui deponat de rebus ex officio gestis.

§ 2. Si sub iuramenti fide duae vel tres personae, omni exceptione maiores, sibi firmiter cohaerentes, de aliqua re vel facto in iudicio testificentur de scientia propria, sufficiens probatio habetur; nisi in aliqua causa iudex ob, maximam negotii gravitatem, vel ob indicia quae aliquod dubium de veritate rei assertae ingerunt, necessariam censeat pleniorem probationem.

Now the legislator proceeds to weigh the testimonies and to state the effect of the evidence after it has been duly pondered. Let it be said right in the beginning, however, that these criteria are tentative or relative rather than absolute and not entirely conclusive in every instance. Besides these characteristics cannot be overlooked by the judge, because they are based on common and long-standing practice. The criteria or momenta by which the weight of evidence is measured, may be reduced to four: moral, mental, material, and numerical.

1. The *moral* weight refers to the *person* of the witness; hence the text says that his condition, character, and dignity should be considered. *Conditio* here means status, ecclesiastical or lay, and, in a layman, vocation.[62] But it also includes character as a witness (cfr. can. 1757, § 1, § 3). *Honestas* refers properly to the moral quality of the person, as stated in can. 1757, § 2. The testimony of a citizen whose moral reputation is beyond suspicion and that of one who has a bad name, are manifestly of unequal value.

Dignitas refers,[63] not only to ecclesiastical, but also to civic dignity. The assumption is that dignitaries are less likely to perjure themselves than ordinary mortals.

2. *Mental* or intellectual weight must be measured according to can. 1774. For *direct* witnesses, who testify to what they have personally seen or heard — also called eye-witnesses — are certainly to be preferred to *indirect* witnesses, who merely express their opinion or repeat what they have learned from hearsay or rumor.

3. The *material* weight of the testimony lies in the mode in which it is produced. Much depends on whether a witness is steady and consistent, or wavering and contradictory. A *testis varius* is one who makes different statements on the same subject in different stages or instances of a trial. A *testis incertus,* also called *contrarius,* is one who makes contradictory answers in the same instance or stage of trial. *Vacillans* may refer to the wavering, uncertain mode of answering, which seems to indicate some doubt or unbelief. Such a testimony should not be accepted at all.[64] If, how-

---

62 The testimony of slaves was formerly admitted only if given under torture; c. 7, C. 2, q. 1: *corporali discussione.*

63 C. 3, C. 4, q. 2 et 3: *utrum decurio an plebeius sit.*

64 Reiffenstuel, II, 20, n. 317.

ever, trembling or sweating is a mere concomitant or
sign of a nervous disposition, and does not create a
positive doubt, the testimony may be accepted, if fortified
by conjectures or other proofs. A testimony called contrary, *i.e.*, one which contradicts another statement of
the same witness, cannot be admitted, unless it admits
of correction. Of two contradictory answers given to
the same question it must be held that, as a rule, the first
stands, unless the error is immediately corrected and recalled, and the second appears more probable.[65]

4. The *numerical weight* of a testimony depends on
whether several witnesses agree in their depositions or
whether they differ from one another. Witnesses whose
testimony differs one from another, are called *singulares*.
If testimonies agree, their weight must be judged according to can. 1791, § 2. The depositions of single
witnesses are to be weighed according to can. 1790, to
wit:

a) If they conflict with one other, the general rule
must be applied that they prove nothing; because a
single witness is but one witness, and in the case of conflict one excludes the other; this is called *singularitas
obstativa*.[66]

b) If the witnesses testify to facts or circumstances
which, though true themselves, have no connection with
one other, their testimony is called diverse (*singularitas
diversificativa*). However, it is evident that they must
bear on the case on trial, otherwise they would be
irrelevant. Thus, for instance, the case of *sollicitatio*
mentioned in the Constitution of Gregory XV, is referred to one and the same priest, whom diverse persons

[65] *Ibid.*, 2, 326 f.
[66] C. 9, X, II, 19; Santi-Leitner,   II, 20, n. 21; Messmer, *l. c.*, p. 106 f.

accuse of different crimes.[67]   Such testimonies are accepted, if circumstantial evidence corroborates the depositions.

c) If the witnesses testify to facts or circumstances which bear on one another, like cause and effect, their testimony is called adminicular (*singularitas adminiculativa*).   This is the weightier, the more witnesses report the same fact or circumstance, and may be admitted as full proof, at least in civil matters (in criminal cases it would not be accepted fully).[68]

The numerical weight of witnesses whose evidence is concordant, neither varied nor wavering, is stated in can. 1791, according to the old rules, thus:

a) *One witness alone does not afford full proof*, because even an upright witness may err in regard to facts and be prompted by personal motives.   There is, however, an exception to the rule stated in our text: *one qualified witness* may furnish full proof when he makes deposition concerning acts which he himself performed *ex officio*.   This is called *qualification*.   Thus experts, as described in the following chapter, official couriers, public notaries, court clerks, are qualified witnesses, whose testimony concerning their official acts is accepted as full proof.[69]

b) The *testimonies of two or three persons is considered full or sufficient proof,*

a) If they have been duly sworn;

b) If they are beyond suspicion and exception;

c) If their testimony is consistent, and

d) If they make judicial (not extrajudicial) deposi-

[67] " *Universi Dominici,*" Aug. 30, 1622, § 5.

[68] C. 9, X, II, 19; Santi-Leitner, II, 20, n. 22 f.

[69] See cc. 10, 23, X, II, 20; c. 13, X, II, 26.

tion concerning a thing or fact which they themselves have witnessed (*de scientia propria*).

Yet it may happen that the matter is of exceptional importance, or that the judge has reason to doubt the truth of such testimony; in that case he may demand fuller proof.

Concerning matrimonial cases of non-consummation, the seven-hand testimony remains. On the other hand, the greater number of witnesses required by the former law against bishops and clerics [70] is no longer demanded by the Code.[71]

[70] See cc. 2, 3, C. 2, q. 4, where more than three against a clergyman, and seventy-two against a bishop are required; see also c. 19, C. 2, q. 5.

[71] Santi-Leitner, II, 20, n. 17; Messmer, l. c., p. 106.

CHAPTER III

EXPERTS

That experts, or specialists, *i.e.*, persons learned or skilled in their own science or profession, especially midwives in cases of non-consummated marriage, were not wholly unknown to the Decretals,[1] appears from the fact that proof from such persons was admitted. Now-a-days their part in settling litigation has become even more conspicuous and frequent. The Code on this head adopts most of the rules laid down for the S. Romana Rota.[2]

WHEN, BY WHOM AND FOR WHAT PURPOSE EXPERTS ARE CHOSEN

CAN. 1792

Peritorum opera utendum est quoties ex iuris vel iudicis praescripto eorum examen et votum requiritur ad - factum aliquod comprobandum vel ad veram alicuius rei naturam dignoscendam.

CAN. 1793

§ 1. Iudicis est peritos eligere vel designare.

§ 2. Hanc designationem in causis mere privatis iudex facere potest rogatu utriusque partis vel etiam alterutrius, altera tamen consentiente; in causis vero bonum publicum respicientibus, audito promotore iustitiae aut vinculi defensore.

1 C. 14, X, II, 19.
2 *A. Ap. S.*, II, 822–826; § 120–136.

§ 3. Prudenti iudicis arbitrio relinquitur unum pluresve peritos eligere pro causae natura et rei difficultate, nisi lex ipsa numerum peritorum praefiniat.

CAN. 1794

Peritorum est peritiam suam ad veritatis et iustitiae leges exigere, neque falsum affirmando neque verum occultando; in quo si deliquerint, puniantur ad normam can. 1743, § 3.

Experts are selected as often as the law (for instance, in matrimonial cases),[3] or the judge demands them, in order to prove a fact or to establish the true nature of a thing, as in the matter of reading a difficult document. Their *office and duty*, therefore, consists in applying their skill or science to the subject in dispute, according to the rules of truth and justice. Hence scientific equipment is the first qualification of an expert. From a physician, *e.g.*, we demand above all medical knowledge and experience. This, however, does not exclude, but rather implies, honesty and conscientiousness.

Experts are witnesses in the true sense of the word, and hence, if they are untruthful, may be punished like witnesses or delinquents, according to can. 1743, § 3.

WHO MAY BE CHOSEN

CAN. 1795

§ 1. Ad periti munus, ceteris paribus, deligantur, qui competentis magistratus auctoritate idonei fuerint comprobati.

§ 2. Qui a testimonio ferendo excluduntur ad

---

3 Cfr. can. 1976 ff.

normam can. 1757, ne ad peritorum quidem officium assumi possunt.

CAN. 1796

§ 1. Easdem ob causa quibus testes, possunt et periti recusari.

§ 2. Iudex suo decreto edicat utrum sit admittenda recusatio, necne, et, recusatione admissa, in locum periti recusati alium sufficiat.

All other things being equal, those should be chosen as experts who hold a certificate or diploma as to their fitness from a competent public authority. For, generally speaking — except where the evil of "graft" is deeply rooted and widely spread, and where bigotry is rampant — diplomas are a safe indication of one's skill and experience. The phrase "*ceteris paribus*" means that a Catholic who is an acknowledged authority in his branch may be chosen, even though the judge does not " favor " him.

One who is not qualified to be a witness, according to can. 1757, cannot be called in as an expert, and the parties may, therefore, *take exception;* but no exception is admissible on the one sole plea that a man has no public certificate. If an expert is lawfully refused, it becomes the duty of the judge to *issue a decree* substituting another one in his place.

DUTIES OF EXPERTS TOWARDS JUDGE AND PARTIES

CAN. 1797

§ 1. Periti demandatum munus suscipere censentur praestatione iurisiurandi de munere fideliter implendo.

§ 2. Partes non solum interesse possunt iurisiurandi praestationi, sed etiam exsecutioni muneris perito demandati, nisi aliud rei natura vel honestas exigat aut lex vel iudex statuat.

CAN. 1798

Post iusiurandum praestitum, si periti intra praefinitum tempus mandato non paruerint aut sine iusta causa exsecutionem defugiant, tenentur damnorum.

CAN. 1799

§ 1. Iudex, attentis iis quae a litigantibus forte deducantur, omnia et singula capita decreto suo definiat circa quae periti opera versari debeat.

§ 2. Tempus intra quod examen perficiendum est et votum proferendum, si necessarium vel opportunum iudici videatur, potest ab ipso iudice praefiniri et etiam, auditis partibus, prorogari.

An expert is supposed to assume his office by taking the oath to perform his duties conscientiously.

The litigant *parties* may assist not only at the ceremony of administering the oath, but also when the expert performs his duty. However, there are delicate cases, especially of a criminal nature or demanding ocular inspection, which make the presence of the parties undesirable. Hence the law itself, as, for instance, in the case of non-consummation (can. 1979) or solicitation, forbids their presence, and the judge may positively exclude them.

The judge should *define* as nearly and as clearly as possible the exact purpose for which the aid of the expert is asked; and in so doing he should take into consideration the suggestions made by the parties.

The *time* within which the examination must be made

and the report handed in, may be fixed by the judge, who, after hearing the parties, may also prorogue the term.

If the expert, after having taken the oath, does not go to work within the time established, or fails to perform his duty without reason, he is obliged to make good the loss that may be caused by his neglect or delay.

CRITICAL INVESTIGATION OF PAPERS

CAN. 1800

§ 1. Si dubitetur quis scriptum aliquod exaraverit, iudex praeter scripturam quaestioni obnoxiam assignet peritis, proponentibus partibus, scripturas cum quibus illa comparari et conferri debeat.

§ 2. Si de scripturis, quae sint inter se comparandae, partes dissentiant, iudex seligat, comparationis gratia, eas, quas pars ipsa alias recognovit, aut quas qui accusatur auctor scripturae controversae, scripsit ut persona publica et in archivis aut alio publico tabulario custodiuntur; aut eius subscriptiones quas ex fide notarii vel personae publicae constet coram ipsis fuisse exaratas.

§ 3. Quod si scripturae a partibus et a iudice pro comparatione designatae, peritorum iudicio, investigationi non sufficiant, et is cui scriptura controversa tribuitur, in vivis sit, iudex ad instantiam partis aut etiam ex officio eum citet, ut manu propria coram iudice vel eius delegato scribat quidquid periti, iudex ipse, eiusve delegatus dictaturi sint.

§ 4. Recusatio scribendi, non probata legitima recusationis causa, habetur ut confessio genuinitatis scripturae controversae in praeiudicium recusantis.

In deeds, last wills, and other documents, in fact in every kind of writing, there may be *calligraphic or palaeographic* difficulties which create doubt in the mind of the judge as to the original writer. If that be the case, the judge may command the parties to submit the doubtful writing to experts for examination.

Suppose there is a last will written in the hand of John, who is supposed to have drawn it up. The specimens of John's handwriting produced by the parties differ among themselves, the *g* or *h* or other letters not being written in the same way as in the document attacked by one of the parties. What is to be done? In that case: (a) papers which are recognized by the defendant as in the genuine handwriting of John, or (b) papers which John certainly wrote in an official capacity and which are kept on file in public places, or (c) signatures which are officially acknowledged as in John's own writing should serve as means of comparison. If the experts declare that the writings thus submitted for comparison are not sufficient to form an opinion, the judge shall, either *ex officio* or at the demand of the parties, summon the supposed author of the disputed document and command him to write in presence of the judge or his delegate, whatever the experts, the judge himself, or his delegate, shall dictate. If he refuses to write without good reason, his very refusal must be taken as a confession that the disputed writing is not genuine.

REPORTS OF THE EXPERTS AND NON-EXPERTS

CAN. 1801

§ 1. Periti votum suum vel in scriptis proferre possunt, vel oretenus coram iudice; sed si ore proferatur, statim in scriptis redigi debet a notario et a peritis subscribi.

§ 2. Peritus autem, praesertim si sententiam suam in scriptis protulerit, accersiri potest a iudice ut explicationes, quae ulterius necessariae videantur, suppeditet.

§ 3. Periti debent indicare perspicue qua via et ratione processerint in explendo munere sibi demandato et quibus potissimum argumentis sententia ab ipsis prolata nitatur.

Can. 1802

Periti suam quisque relationem a ceteris distinctam conficiant, nisi, lege non contradicente, iudex unam a singulis subscribendam fieri iubeat; quod si fiat, sententiarum discrimina, si qua fuerint, diligenter adnotentur.

Can. 1803

§ 1. Si periti inter se discrepant, licet iudici aut peritioris suffragium super relatis a primis peritis exquirere aut novos de integro peritos adhibere.

§ 2. Eadem facultas iudici est quoties periti post electionem in suspicionem inciderint vel impares atque non idonei muneri perspecti fuerint.

Can. 1804

§ 1. Iudex non peritorum tantum conclusiones, etsi concordes, sed cetera quoque causae adiuncta attente perpendat.

§ 2. Cum reddit rationes decidendi, exprimere debet quibus motus argumentis peritorum conclusiones aut admiserit aut reiecerit.

Experts must, as a rule, make their *report in writing*. If it is made orally to the judge, it should be immediately put into writing by the notary, and signed by the expert.

The latter may, however, especially after having made a written report, be called upon by the judge to give further explanations which may appear necessary.

The report shall contain an account of how the experts proceeded, what system or method they employed, and also give their reasons (*i.e.*, scientific or professional reasons) for adopting the view expressed in their report.

Each expert must write out his own report, unless, the law permitting, the judge demands one report to be made by several; in which case all experts engaged in the matter must sign this one report and, besides, carefully state wherein their views differ.

If the experts differ, the judge may ask another more skilled expert for his opinion on the report submitted, or call in an entirely new set of experts.

He has the same power whenever the experts have become suspected or rendered themselves unfit for the work in hand.

The judge shall carefully ponder, not only the conclusions of the experts, but also the other circumstances of the case. He is not, however, bound to accept the experts' view. If he decides to give the reasons for his decision (which, however, he is not bound to do, because the text only says, *cum reddit, when* or *if* he does), he should explain why he admitted or rejected the conclusions of the experts.

EXPENSES OF EXPERTS

CAN. 1805

Peritorum expensas et honoraria iudex, receptam uniuscuiusque loci consuetudinem prae oculis habens, ex bono et aequo taxare debet, salvo iure recursus ad normam can. 1913, § 1.

The expenses and salaries of experts should be fairly and squarely fixed by the judge, in conformity with local custom. Recourse, but no appeal, is permitted to the parties within ten days after the sentence has been pronounced.

CHAPTER IV

LOCAL INSPECTION

CAN. 1806

Si ad controversiae locum iudex accedere atque ipsam rem controversam inspicere necessarium existimet, decreto id praestituat, quo ea quae in accessu praestanda sint, auditis partibus, summatim describat.

CAN. 1807

Iudex recognitionem peragere potest vel ipse per se vel per auditorem aut iudicem delegatum.

CAN. 1808

§ 1. Iudex, rem vel locum recognoscens, peritos adhibere potest, si ipsorum opera necessaria vel utilis videatur.

§ 2. Si periti adhibeantur, serventur, quantum fieri potest, quae praescripta sunt can. 1793–1805.

CAN. 1809

Si iurgii vel perturbationis periculum pertimescendum iudici videatur, poterit ipse prohibere ne partes vel earum advocati iudiciali recognitioni intersint.

CAN. 1810

Iudex testes, vel ex officio accitos vel a partibus ante recognitionem rite productos, potest in ipso iudiciali accessu examini subiicere, si id expedire videatur ad pleniorem probationem aut ad removenda dubia ob quae recognitio decerni debuit.

CAN. 1811

§ 1. Notarius diligenter curet ut constet ex actis qua die et hora recognitio facta sit, quae personae interfuerint, quae, recognitione durante, aut dicta aut peracta aut a iudice decreta sint.

§ 2. Peractae recognitionis instrumenta tum iudex tum notarius subscribant.

Cases [1] have occurred and still occur which require a personal and local inspection. Hence our Code lays down rules for this judicial procedure.

1. If the judge deems local inspection necessary, he must issue a decree to that effect in which he summarily states the points to be examined. This he does after having heard the parties.

2. The judge may hold this inspection himself or entrust it to his udiator or a delegate. Besides, he may, if he deems it necessary or useful, employ experts, concerning whom the rules laid down in the preceding chapter must be observed as strictly as feasible.

3. However, if the judge should apprehend any quarrel or disturbance between the parties, he may forbid them or their attorneys to be present at the local inspection.

4. If the judge deems it expedient for fuller proof

1 Cfr. c. 9, X, II, 26: *agrimen-sores* or surveyors.

and for the dispersion of doubts, he may examine the official witnesses and the other witnesses produced by the parties on the spot where the judicial inspection is held.

5. The *notary* shall keep a careful record of the day and hour when the inspection was held, stating who was present, what was done or said during the process, and what was decreed by the judge. This record must be signed by the judge — or, we presume, by the auditor or legate, if these take the judge's place — and the notary.

CHAPTER V

Besides the oral evidence of witnesses there is another class of evidence recognized by law, namely, *written evidence,* which the Decretals (11, 22) treat under the title *"De fide instrumentorum."*

ART. I

NATURE OF DOCUMENTS

CAN. 1812

In quolibet iudicii genere admittitur probatio per documenta tum publica tum privata.

CAN. 1813

§ 1. Praecipua documenta publica ecclesiastica haec sunt:

1.° Acta Summi Pontificis et Curiae Romanae et Ordinariorum in exercitio suorum munerum authentica forma exarata, itemque attestationes authenticae de iisdem actibus datae ab illis vel eorum notariis;

2.° Instrumenta a notariis ecclesiasticis confecta.

3.° Acta iudicialia ecclesiastica;

4.° Inscriptiones baptismi, confirmationis, ordinationis, professionis religiosae, matrimonii, mortis, quae habentur in regestis Curiae vel paroeciae, vel religionis, et attestationes scriptae ex iisdem desumptae et a parochis, vel Ordinariis, vel notariis ecclesiasticis confectae aut earum exemplaria authentica.

§ 2. Documenta publica civilia ea sunt quae secundum uniuscuiusque loci leges talia iure censentur.

§ 3. Litterae, contractus, testamenta et scripta quaelibet a privatis confecta, privatorum documentorum numero habentur.

The title of this chapter is: *De Probatione per Instrumenta,* which might apply to oral as well as written evidence. But the Code plainly intends written proofs only. Hence can. 1812 simply states that proofs by documents are admitted in all kinds of trials, both civil and criminal, and that these documents may be either public or private.

A *public document* is one composed by an official in his official capacity, with due observance of the prescribed formalities, or at least in official style.[1] The official style requires the signature of an officially acknowledged person, his seal or at least that of the office (for instance, the diocesan or episcopal seal, the parish seal, the monastery seal, etc.), and the date and place of issuance.

A *private* document is a writing executed by private persons or by officials in their private capacity only. Thus a pastor or notary public may give a receipt (*apocha*), or make a bilateral contract (*syngraphum*), or write a letter, which are entirely private.

There occur in this chapter two terms which have been variously explained for various purposes; they are: *authentic* and *genuine*. *Authentic* [2] here generally oc-

---

[1] If it is stated that among the solemnities required are the invocation of the Divinity, the signature of at least three witnesses, etc. (Santi-Leitner II, 20, n. 2), this cannot be applied now-a-days in ecclesiastical courts.

[2] *Authentic* is derived from αὐθέντης or αὐτὸ εἰς, ἐς, the archaic form for *esse*, to be; hence *eum qui ipse est vel agit*, the one who has written the document. Thus by an authentic gospel we mean a gospel attributed to one of

curs in the phrase, "*forma authentica*," and therefore can only mean that the legal form in the execution of a document was duly observed. *Genuine*, on the other hand, refers to the origin or authorship of a writing, although we candidly admit that "genuine" in can. 1814 could just as well be taken for "authentic."

So far as the *juridical effects* are concerned, there is no difference between a public and an authentic document, because every public document is authentic, but not conversely.[3] Private documents may also be authentic, and if they are, they produce the same juridical effect as public documents.

It may be worth while to state some of the marks which render private documents authentic. A private document may become authentic by the signature of one's own hand, together with the signature of three living witnesses, or by affixing to it the official seal of a public (ecclesiastical or civil) magistrate, by being found in the public archives, by long-standing recognition, or by custom.[4]

This premised, let us hear what can. 1813 has to say about the chief *public ecclesiastical documents;* these are:

1.° *The acts of the Sovereign Pontiff, of the Roman Court*, and of *the Ordinaries*, when issued in authentic form in the exercise of their office; also authentic attestations or copies of such acts given by themselves or their notaries.

A perusal of the *Acta Apostolicae Sedis* shows how authentic Roman documents look. They are signed by the head of the Congregation and its Secretary with the L(oco) S(igilli), place and date of issuance. An epis-

the four evangelists. A *genuine* writing is not necessarily the work of a certain author (Epistle of Barnabas), but only one belonging to a certai age or century.

3 Reiffenstuel, II, 22, n. 14 f.

4 *Ibid.*, II, 20, n. 143 f.

copal document should be issued in the same way, signed with the bishop's name.

"*Attestationes*" may be either identic copies of the original text, or extracts therefrom. They, too, must be *authenticated* by being signed and sealed by the respective officials or their notaries.

2.° *Documents issued by ecclesiastical notaries.* Concerning these the commentators[5] are rather lavish in their demands, which may be briefly reduced to the following:

a) The *document* itself must contain the date and place of issuance according to the customary manner. The year must be reckoned not from the Incarnation, but according to the civil calendar.[6] The seal of the notary must be affixed if he has a special seal; otherwise his personal signature will suffice.

b) The *notary* must be lawfully appointed, not removed from office,[7] and should sign his name always in the same way for the sake of comparison. The notaries of exempt clerical institutes are entitled to issue authentic documents concerning their orders.[8]

3. *Judicial ecclesiastical acts,* because they possess all the requisites of authentic documents.

4. The original *records* of baptism, confirmation, ordination, religious profession, matrimony, and death, which are kept on file in the ecclesiastical courts, in the archives of parishes and religious institutes; also the *testimonies* or certificates taken from these original registers and issued by pastors, Ordinaries, or ecclesiastical notaries, as well as *copies* of these attestations; but the latter must be *authenticated*, as explained above, *i.e.*, they must

---

[5] Cfr. Engel, II, 20; Reiffenstuel, II, 20 ff.

[6] Pius X, "*Sapienti consilio*," June 29, 1908, III, 5 (*A. Ap. S.*, I, 17).

[7] Can. 373 f.

[8] Can. 503.

contain date and place of issuance as well as the official seal.

A doubt may naturally arise as to our *assistants or curates,*— whether they may issue authentic certificates of baptism or marriage, etc., because the text only mentions the pastors. To answer this question is not as simple as it would appear, and therefore we state our personal opinion only. An assistant or a curate who takes the place of his pastor (*e.g.,* during a vacation) is certainly entitled to issue such a certificate. But a merely casual or accidental absence of the pastor would not render the assistant a *locum tenens.* An assistant cannot *per se* issue a certificate, because the Decretals [9] as well as our text exclude him,— a curate not being an official in such matters. However the law [10] admits *exemplaria* or copies (certificates) made by the authority of the judge or his delegate, provided there be a just reason and at least one of the parties asks for it. Besides, as the Gloss says,[11] it is not necessary that the copy or certificate be made by a public person, if only the official seal is appended. From this, then, and considering the rules of delegation, we conclude that an assistant may in urgent cases be delegated, and even presume delegation, provided he uses the parish seal and issues such papers in the name of the pastor.[12]

We believe that if the local Ordinary or the diocesan court would call upon an assistant to issue a certificate, the latter would act officially and could therefore freely use the parish seal.

§ 2 of can. 1813 then mentions *civil public documents* which must be accepted as authentic if issued according

9 C. 16, X, II, 22.
10 *Ibid.*
11 Ad c. 16, *l. c.;* Reiffenstuel, II, 22, n. 60.

12 Of course, the assistant should also put down his own name: *v. g.,* J. J. Murphy, Pastor, per J. J. Hogan, Assistant.

to the laws of the respective country. In the U. S., as also in England, *affidavits* are frequently used as public and legal evidence. An affidavit is a written declaration or statement, made before a magistrate or other person legally authorized to administer an oath, the truth of which statement is confirmed either by an oath or a solemn affirmation. Such affidavits, and certified copies thereof, constitute *prima facie* evidence in most matters before the civil courts.

Besides, the Revised Statutes of some States, *e.g.*, Missouri, admit the registers of religious societies as evidence.[18]

§ 3 of can. 1813 states that *letters, contracts, last wills and all other writings* which are written or drawn up by private persons, as such, must be regarded as *private documents*. To this class belong the private letters written by persons in public office. *Last wills* may be drawn up by private persons, but if they are made before a notary public and two witnesses, all of whom sign their names, they are public documents.

18 Rev. Stat. Mo., 1899, Sect. 3102: "When, by the ordinance or custom of any religious society or congregation in this state a register is required to be kept of marriages, births, baptisms, deaths or interments, such registers shall be admitted as evidence." Sec. 3103: "Copies of the register referred to in the preceding section, certified by the pastor or other head of any such society or congregation, or by the clerk or other keeper of such register, and verified by his affidavit in writing, shall be received in evidence." From this law we may deduce a corollary concerning copies or certificates of baptismal registers issued by *ministers of non-Catholic denominations*. They are admitted as evidence by the civil court if issued under affidavit. Therefore they may lawfully be compared to, and treated as, civil documents, in spite of the sad fact, which a *defensor vinculi* once deplored, that the parties sometimes are not at all conscientious in stating the facts and often deceive their ministers.

CAN. 1814

Documenta publica sive ecclesiastica sive civilia genuina praesumuntur, donec contrarium evidentibus argumentis evincatur.

CAN. 1815

Recognitio aut impugnatio scripturae proponi potest in iudicio tum incidenter, tum ad instar causae principalis.

CAN. 1816

Documenta publica fidem faciunt de iis quae directe et principaliter in eisdem affirmantur.

CAN. 1817

Documentum privatum, sive agnitum a parte sive recognitum a iudice, probat adversus auctorem vel subscriptorem et causam ab eis habentes, perinde ac confessio extra iudicium facta; sed per se non habet vim probandi adversus extraneos.

CAN. 1818

Si abrasa, correcta, interpolata aliove vitio documenta infecta demonstrentur, iudicis est aestimare an et quanti huiusmodi documenta facienda sint.

Public documents, ecclesiastical as well as civil, are presumed to be genuine as long as the contrary is not evidently proved. They *prove* what is directly and principally affirmed in them. In other words, such documents afford *prima facie* evidence. The phrase, " *quae directe et principaliter in eisdem affirmantur,"* must be understood of the intention of the plaintiff or the direct object of the action to be proved by a document. For instance, a baptismal record proves that baptism has been conferred, but it does not prove the validity of the baptism, and a marriage certificate issued by a recorder proves that the parties have gone through the ceremony required by civil law, but it does not prove the validity of the marriage from the ecclesiastical point of view.

Even a public document, may, however, be attacked. Can. 1815 says: A document may be acknowledged or attacked at a trial, either incidentally, or as the principal action. It is a mere *incidental* or side issue if it only leads to establishing the main question or *meritum causae;* it is the *principal* issue, if the whole trial revolves around it. Thus a last will depends chiefly on the document, although perhaps later on the plaintiff may attack either the mental or the juridical capacity of the testator.[14]

The attack may be made on different grounds, either because the writer was not an official person, or was no longer in office when the document was drawn up; or because of a lack of the required formalities, or because the document was made fraudulently.[15]

But to prove the spuriousness or falsity of a document at least two classical witnesses (*omni exceptione maiores*) are required. These witnesses may be either instrumental or extraneous; they are *instrumental* if they are mentioned in the document as witnesses or if they assisted at the drafting of the paper or signed it. *Extraneous* witnesses are such as are mentioned in the document but did not sign it. Two witnesses, either instru-

[14] We know of a lawsuit that lasted twelve years and depended on a last will; after the will was declared authentic, the capacity of testating and accepting the legacy was attacked.

[15] Cfr. Santi-Leitner, II, 22, n. 19 f.

mental or extraneous, if they have the necessary qualities, are sufficient to render a document useless for proof. Of course, if two witnesses would testify in favor of the validity of a document, and two against it, these depositions would not affect the weight of a public or authentic document.

Since the *seal* is a strict requisite of an authentic document, this, too, may be the object of rebuttal. For the seal must be genuine, *i.e.*, it must be that of the official who is supposed to have impressed it on the paper. The inscription of the seal, or the letters around it, must be legible and as clearly expressed as possible. The seal should not be torn or broken.[16]

Private documents, says can. 1817, whether acknowledged by the party or accepted by the judge, have the weight or value of an *extrajudicial confession*,[17] which may or may not be admitted by the judge against the plaintiff, or against the signatory, or against those whose cause is bound up with that of the plaintiff and the signatory. Thus one who has gone security or furnished bail is bound up with the person in whose favor he has done so.

Can. 1818 mentions *defective documents*, viz., such as bear the signs of erasure, interpolation or correction. It is left to the judge whether and how far to accept such documents.

The *erasure*, to render a document defective, must occur in a notable or substantial place, as in the date or place when and where it was drawn up, in the name of the drafter, or in a dispositive part of the document itself. However, if it can be proved that the notary himself caused the erasure, the authenticity of the document can not be doubted.

16 Reiffenstuel, II, 22, n. 72 f.   17 Cfr. can. 1753.

Interpolation means the insertion by another than the authorized hand, of matter or names foreign to a document. This defect, too, must be judged according to what was said of erasure.

The same applies to *corrections*, whether in date, place, names, or matter. All three of these processes render a document somewhat suspect, until the doubt has been cleared away by experts or by comparison, according to can. 1800.

Art. II

EXHIBITION OF DOCUMENTS AND CLAIM THERETO

The first three canons of this Article regulate the shape and form in which the documents must be " shown," whilst the following three determine the claim and duty to exhibit them. The title of the Article styles the latter *actio ad exhibendum,* because a refusal to exhibit document may call for a judiciary settlement, which may amount to an action.

ORIGINAL AND AUTHENTICATED DOCUMENTS

CAN. 1819

Documenta vim probandi in iudicio non habent, nisi originalia sint aut in exemplari authentico exhibita et penes tribunalis cancellariam deposita, exceptis documentis quae publici iuris sunt, ceu leges rite promulgatae.

CAN. 1820

Documenta in forma authentica sunt exhibenda et in iudicio deponenda, ut a iudice et ab adversario examinari possint.

§ 1. Si dubium excitetur utrum fideliter exscriptum
sit exemplar, an non, iudex ad instantiam partis vel
etiam ex officio decernere potest, ut ipsum documentum exhibeatur, unde exemplar est desumptum.

§ 2. Si id fieri aut minime aut valde difficulter possit,
iudex potest auditorem delegare aut loci Ordinarium
rogare pro examine et collatione documenti, prae-
scribens quibus de articulis et quemadmodum fieri
debeat collatio; collationi vero utraque pars assistere
potest.

Documents furnish judicial proof only if they are exhibited in their original form, or in an authentic copy,
and are deposited with the chancery of the tribunal. An
authentic copy is one made by a notary public and sealed
with his official seal.[18] The *visum* of an official is sufficient if that official has personally inspected the original
and compared the copy with it.[19] But even in this case
his official signature and his seal would be required, testifying to the conformity of the copy with the original
document; because signature and seal are the usual signs
of an official certificate. For affidavits an oath would
be necessary.

Such formalities, says the text, are not required if the
documents have been published (*quae publici iuris sunt*)
and therefore made the common property of all, as is
the case, *e. g.*, with laws when they are promulgated.
By-laws, statutes, charters, also decisions and documents
published in the *Acta Apostolicae Sedis*, and official

18 C. 2, X, II, 22: the fact alone
that it is made by a public person
or has the authentic seal; we joined
both by the particle and, because
the official seal can be validly attached only by an official person, or
at least with his consent or by his
command.
19 C. 16, X, II, 22.

civil publications, are public documents which require neither to be authenticated nor to be deposited with the tribunal, although the latter may demand a copy of civil publications. The *Acta Apostolicae Sedis* may be supposed to be on file in every ecclesiastical court.

Documents, says can. 1820, must be exhibited in an *authentic* form and deposited in court, so that they may be inspected by the judge and the other party. This is the case also with privileges and indulgences which exempt religious may oppose to Ordinaries.[20]

If the *judge has a doubt* as to the correctness and trustworthiness of a copy exhibited in court, he may, either officially, or upon the demand of the other party, decree that the original document be produced from which the copy (*exemplar*) was made. However, if there may be great inconvenience in complying with this demand (because the original writ will not stand being exposed to the light, or because it is so frail and delicate that transportation would injure it), or if the civil authorities forbid the removal of original documents from their places (this would be a case of impossibility), the judge may delegate his auditor or ask the local Ordinary to have the document examined and collated with the copy presented in court.

¶ ACTIO AD EXHIBENDUM

CAN. 1822

Documenta communia quaeve de communi agunt negotio, ut testamenta et instrumenta quae respiciunt successiones, bonorum partitiones, contractus aliaque huiusmodi de quibus lis est inter partes, quilibet ex

20 C. 7, 6°, V, 7.

litigantibus potest postulare ut in iure exhibeantur ab ea parte quae illa possidere dicitur.

CAN. 1823

§ 1. Nemo tamen exhibere tenetur documenta, etsi communia, .quae communicari nequeunt sine periculo damni ad normam can. 1755, § 2, n. 2 aut sine periculo violationis secreti servandi.

§ 2. Attamen si qua saltem documenti particula, quam produci intersit, describi possit, et in exemplari exhiberi sine memoratis incommodis, iudex decernere potest ut eadem exhibeatur.

CAN. 1824

§1. Si pars exhibere recuset documentum de iure producendum, quod ipsa fertur possidere, iudex, altera parte postulante, auditoque, si opus sit, promotore iustitiae vel vinculi defensore, interlocutoria sententia statuat, an et quomodo eiusdem documenti exhibitio facienda sit.

§ 2. Parte parere recusante, iudicis est aestimare quanti haec recusatio facienda sit.

§3. Quod si pars documentum apud se esse neget, iudex poterit eam examini subiicere et ad iusiurandum de ea re praestandum adigere.

The question arises whether there is any obligation to exhibit or produce documents which are necessary to settle a disputed point in court. And here a distinction is drawn, not between public and private documents as such, but between the contents of such documents and the parties' mutual claim on them.

Can. 1822 mentions *documenta communia, i.e.,* docu-

ments which are the common property of both litigants.
This condition may be achieved by mutual agreement
or the common payment of the expenses incurred for
drawing up a paper, for instance, by each party paying
its share to the notary public. ·

Documents may also be common by reason of the common interest both parties have in them, as is usually the
case in legacies, last wills, and contracts. Common documents, lastly, are such as are drafted by official persons,
such as judicial acts or official documents drawn up by
notaries public which concern the two parties, also the
account-books kept by administrators of minors or corporations.[21] All such documents, not being exclusively
private property or involving a criminal or incriminating
action, are common to both parties and must, therefore,
be produced at the trial by the party who happens to be
in possession of them.

Aside from this *no one is bound to exhibit a document*
which may place him or his nearest relatives (can. 1755,
§ 2, n. 2) in danger of infamy, or cause him or them
great trouble and vexation. Neither is there any obligation of producing such documents, even though they be
common, if there be danger of violating a secret imposed
either by the natural law or by one's office.

But the judge may decree that, if these inconveniences
are not to be feared, parts at least of the documents,
which are important, be copied, and the copy presented
at the trial.

Should a party refuse to show a document in his possession, the judge shall decide whether and how the document must be exhibited, provided the other party insists
on its exhibition. In that case, therefore, the judge
issues an interlocutory decree, after having consulted,

21 Cfr. Reiffenstuel, II, 22, n. 246 ff.

if necessary, the *promotor iustitiae* and the *defensor vinculi*. A refusal by the party in possession of the document must be weighed by the judge as to its juridical value. If the party denies possession of the document, he may be cross-examined under oath.

A word concerning the *account-books* of ecclesiastical corporations. These furnish proof, not in favor of, but against these corporations,[22] unless they have been *audited* by a public auditor, in which case they deserve great credit and constitute circumstantial evidence.[23] It may be added that the fiscus is entitled to inspect these account-books and also all common documents produced at trials.[24]

22 C. un. Clem. v, 5.   24 Reiffenstuel, II, 22, n. 251 f.
23 Santi-Leitner, II, 22, n. 10.

CHAPTER VI

CAN. 1825

§ 1. Praesumptio est rei incertae probabilis con-
iectura; eaque alia est iuris, quae ab ipsa lege statui-
tur; alia hominis, quae a iudice coniicitur.

§ 2. Praesumptio iuris alia est iuris simpliciter, alia
iuris et de iure.

CAN. 1826

Contra praesumptionem iuris simpliciter admittitur
probatio tum directa tum indirecta; contra praesumptionem iuris et de iure, tantum indirecta, hoc est
contra factum quod est praesumptionis fundamentum.

CAN. 1827

Qui habet pro se iuris praesumptionem, liberatur ab
onere probandi, quod recidit in partem adversam; qua
non probante, sententia ferri debet in favorem partis
pro qua stat praesumptio.

CAN. 1828

Praesumptiones, quae non statuuntur a iure, iudex
ne coniiciat, nisi ex facto certo et determinato, quod
cum eo, de quo controversia est, directe cohaereat.

Next in value to positive proofs is presumption or
circumstantial evidence, which is here (can. 1825) de-

·fined as a probable conjecture concerning an uncertain fact or thing. From circumstances which either necessarily or usually attend a fact we conclude to the existence of the fact itself. The conclusion is, therefore, based on certain *indicia,* or signs, indications or circumstances which influence the judge's mind either for or against the party who brought suit. A presumption is called legal (*a lege*), if expressed in and admitted by law; it is called made by the judge or jury (*ab homine*), if it arises from the mental operation of the judge, but is not especially pointed out in law. It is natural for any man, and especially for a judge, to form a judgment from usual occurrences. This presumption is called natural, although it might just as well be styled ethical, whilst the *praesumptio a lege* might be named juridical or legal presumption.

Legal presumption is twofold: *iuris,* simply, when introduced and admitted and expressed as such by law; *iuris et de iure,* when not only expressed and acknowledged by law, but when the law is based upon the presumption. The legislator, perceiving that certain circumstances tend to prove an event or fact, often uses this fact as a basis for the law. There are in our Code two canons which establish a *praesumptio iuris et de iure, viz.,* can. 1904, a matter adjudged, and can. 1972, concerning a marriage not disputed during life. The *praesumptio iuris tantum* is treated in three canons, *viz.,* can. 1015, § 2, which presumes the consummation of. a marriage duly celebrated, with the added clause: " until the contrary has been proved; " can. 1086, § 1, where the internal consent to marriage is presumed in conformity with the external manifestation; and can. 1814, which presumes ecclesiastical and civil public documents to be genuine.

Can. 1826 determines the *weight of legal presumption,* stating that against a *praesumptio iuris simpliciter* direct as well as indirect proofs are admissible; whilst against a *praesumptio iuris et de iure* direct evidence only may be admitted, *i.e.*, a proof overthrowing the fact upon which the presumption is based. The Code does not define the different species of direct and indirect proofs, nor do the commentators [1] offer any light on this subject. Hence it appears rather risky to venture upon an adequate discrimination. However, some examples may illustrate the distinction. Take can. 1972, concerning a marriage not disputed, which creates a *praesumptio iuris et de iure*. What is to be done in that case? The legitimacy of the children is involved directly, whilst the validity of the marriage can be attacked only indirectly. But the question will necessarily turn about an existing impediment. For although the presumption for the validity of a marriage which has not been disputed by both or one of the parties during their lifetime is so strong that the tie cannot be directly impugned, yet if the legitimacy of a child is in question, for instance, on account of an inheritance or title, the question of validity will naturally enter the fact at issue (*factum probandum*). Therefore, the plaintiff, who attacks the legitimacy of a child on the ground that the marriage from which this child was born was invalid, must prove that either before or during the marriage there existed a diriment impediment which had never been removed.[2] Hence we may say that *direct* evidence is evidence admitted by reason of the contrary evidence which is produced against the merits of the case itself; whereas *indirect* evidence is admitted only by rea-

[1] They generally distinguish between *iudicialis* and *extra-iudicialis*, *plena* and *semi-plena*, *naturalis* and *artificialis*, *simplex* and *mixta*, *probatio* and *reprobatio*; cfr. Wernz, V, n. 594, p. 450 ff. Of all these divisions the last-named would come nearest to direct and indirect.

[2] Concerning a title-case see Kenny-Webb, *Outlines of Criminal Law*, 1907, p. 325 ff.

son of the case being connected with another. Another difference can hardly be established. For it is customary to classify evidence according to the differences in its logical bearing upon the question to be decided, and from this point of view all evidence is either direct or indirect. Direct evidence is testimonial evidence to one or more of the *facta probanda, i.e.,* those facts which, if all of them are proved, legally necessitate a decision favorable to the person producing them. All other evidence is circumstantial, which includes real as well as personal evidence.[3] From this it will be readily perceived that the *directa* and *indirecta probatio* of our text has nothing in common with this division. For the fact to be proved against a violent presumption may be produced directly as well as indirectly.

Can. 1827 lays down the *effects* of legal presumption. And if we say legal presumption, we include, because the text draws no distinction, the *praesumptio iuris tantum* as well as the *praesumptio iuris et de iure.* Legal presumption frees the party from the burden of proof, which is thus devolved on the adversary. Thus the presumption of receiving tithes is in favor of the pastor against strangers who claim the tithe in the parish subject to that pastor, for it is very unlikely (*inverisimile*) that strangers in a parish [4] are entitled to the tithes of the same. Thus also the presumption is in favor of the bishop's right to appoint to benefices in his diocese, until the contrary is proved.[5] Consequently, if either party, plaintiff or defendant, has not proved his intention against the rival, the judge must pronounce in favor of the one for whom the legal presumption stands, because the law is in his favor and as long as the contrary is not evident, the law

3 Kenny-Webb, *l. c.,* p. 322 f.   5 See can. 1432, § 1.
4 C. 2, 6°, II, 5; c. 16, X, II, 23.

must be upheld. But the judge must act altogether differently when *natural* or ethical evidence, not expressed in law, is to determine or influence his decision. For such a presumption can only be gathered from certain and determined facts which directly bear upon the *factum probandum.* This is expressed by a learned modern writer thus: The jury or judge has to depend on the cohesion of each circumstance in the evidence with the rest of the chain of circumstances of which it forms a part.[6]

Here is introduced the *praesumptio hominis,* which has been divided into three classes: *levis, gravis, violenta* or *gravissima.* Light presumption is based on indications which seldom or hardly ever permit us to conclude that a fact really happened; for instance, if one would surmise evil by seeing a clergyman talking with a woman. Such a presumption is frivolous and must be discarded. It should rather be called rash judgment. The *praesumptio gravis* occurs when the indications or circumstances are of such a nature that they permit us to infer a usual and ordinary occurrence. A case of this kind is mentioned in the Decretals.[7] A young man was seen in frequent company with a girl, " *per plana et nemora, vias et invia, pluries convagantes.*" A *violent* presumption is one which, though not expressed, creates such a firm conviction in the mind that it cannot be resisted, although perhaps a slim evasion may be possible.[8]

These evidences, then, must be weighed and compared with the fact at issue. The rule advanced by barristers, that no conviction is allowed unless the fact in question

---

6 Kenny-Webb, *l. c.,* p. 324.

7 C. 13, X, II, 23; but both swore *se carnaliter cognovisse,* therefore a case of the former illicit affinity.

8 An example in c. 12, X, II, 23; concerning adultery: *solum cum sola, nudum cum nuda in eodem lecto.*

has been fully proved,[9] may safely be accepted by the ecclesiastical court.

Here we will add some rules concerning the prevalence and weight of circumstantial evidence, as laid down by canonists.[10]

a) Legal presumptions are weightier than natural ones, and must therefore be preferred.

b) A special circumstance connected with the fact at issue has more value than a general presumption, according to *reg. juris 34 in 6°*: "*Generi per speciem derogatur.*"

c) Presumptions which are in favor of the established laws of nature and society and conformable to natural tendencies, must be preferred, as a rule, to circumstances which indicate unnatural excess; thus temperate habits in youth and manhood create a favorable presumption for old age, provided all other things are equal.

d) Presumptions in favor of the validity of an act already posted are weightier than those in favor of its invalidity. Hence the axiom: "*Baptismus valide censendus in ordine ad matrimonium.*" A violent presumption of this kind is mentioned in the Decretals,[11] where Innocent III decided that Baptism may be *violenter* presumed in one who was born of Christian parents and lived faithfully among Christians; although in case he was not baptized, he was not ordained validly.

e) Where the evidence is equally compatible with either view, the judge is not competent to leave the matter to the jury,[12] or to decide the case. For equal presumptions, like equal proofs, kill each other, and a judge cannot decide whilst he is in a doubtful frame of mind.

9 Kenny-Webb, *l. c.*, p. 329.
10 Cfr. Reiffenstuel, II, 23, 73 ff.; Santi-Leitner, II, 23, n. 13; Messmer, *l. c.*, p. 126 f.

11 C. 3, X, III, 43.
12 Cfr. Kenny, *A Selection of Cases Illustrative of the English Law of Tort*, 1904, p. 548.

CHAPTER VII

THE OATH OF THE PARTIES

The last means of proof is the oath or invocation of the Divine Name in testimony of the truth. The Code distinguishes three kinds of oaths: the supplementary, the estimatory, and the decisive oath.

THE SUPPLEMENTARY OATH

CAN. 1829

Si habeatur semiplena tantum probatio nec alia probationis adiumenta iam supersint et iudex aut iubeat aut admittat iusiurandum ad probationes supplendas, hoc iusiurandum dicitur *suppletorium*.

CAN. 1830

§ 1. Huic iuriiurando vel maxime locus est cum adiuncta, quae civilem vel religiosum personae statum respiciunt, aliter comperiri nequeunt.

§ 2. Sed eodem abstineat iudex tum in causis criminalibus, tum in contentiosis, si de iure vel re magni pretii agatur aut de facto nimii momenti, aut si ius, res, factum non sit proprium personae cui iusiurandum esset deferendum.

§ 3. Deferri autem hoc iusiurandum potest sive ex officio, sive ad instantiam alterius partis, vel promotoris iustitiae, vel defensoris vinculi, si iudicio intersint.

§ 4. Regulariter deferatur ei qui planiores habet probationes.

§ 5. Iudicis tamen est decreto definire an et quando adiuncta concurrant, cur iusiurandum suppletorium deferri debeat.

CAN. 1831

§ 1. Pars cui iusiurandum suppletorium defertur in rebus quae ad eius statum civilem vel religiosum non pertinent, potest ex iusta causa illud recusare vel in adversarium referre.

§ 2. Quanti autem haec recusatio facienda sit, utrum iusta sit, an potius confessioni aequiparanda, iudicis est aestimare.

§ 3. Iusiurandum suppletorium, ab una parte praestitum, potest ab altera impugnari.

The supplementary oath supplies a missing proof and therefore takes the place of a witness or other instrument of evidence. It may be that the plaintiff has produced one witness who was not rejected, but has none other at his disposal to prove his contention. Or the parties may grow weary of a protracted trial, and therefore resort to this last expedient. The judge, too, may have exhausted all the means of evidence. In this case he may permit, nay even command, the oath to be taken in order to supply the wanted evidence.

The *cases in which this oath may or may not be administered* are the following:

1. When the personal status of a person, either civil or religious, cannot otherwise be determined, *i.e.*, whether one is a layman, legitimate or illegitimate, a clergyman or a religious, married or unmarried, free or slave, possessed of a title or not. This is rather new legislation,

for the commentators [18] generally contended that the supplementary oath could not be administered in cases concerning the personal status, although in matrimonial cases they limited this exception to a marriage to be solved. Our text admits the oath even in these cases, provided no other evidence can be obtained.

2. In *criminal cases* the judge shall *not* admit the oath. Among these the authors also reckon the so-called *causa famosa*, which involved infamy by law.[14] The judge shall furthermore abstain from demanding this oath in *civil matters* if:

a) the right or thing involved is of great value, or the fact, *i.e.,* the case itself, is of great importance; or if

b) the right, object or case concerns, not the party to whom the oath should be administered, but another. As to a) there can hardly be any doubt that matrimonial cases fall under this heading, because of their importance; besides *magni pretii* applies to alienations, which substantially change the condition of a church or corporation. And the latter case should also be applied to b) because it concerns administrators and guardians.

3. This oath may be administered either *ex officio* or *upon the demand* of the other party, or of the *promotor iustitiae* or the *defensor vinculi,* if present at the trial.

4. As a rule this oath is administered to *the party who has furnished fuller or better proofs.* The reason for this ruling is that the oath is privileged evidence, but supplementary only. Hence on one side some proofs are required, because if no proofs at all are given, the defendant must be absolved; and on the other, even semi-proofs, which ordinarily would justify the administration of the oath, may be shaky or weakened by contrary evi-

---

18 Cfr. Reiffenstuel, II, 24, n. 219; Santi-Leitner, II, 24, n. 27.   14 Reiffenstuel, II, 24, n. 217.

dence. It does not matter whether the plaintiff or the defendant has furnished the better evidence.

5. The judge must *decide by a formal decree* whether and when the circumstances are such as to admit a supplementary oath. A slight presumption will not move a conscientious judge, who may, however, proceed according to the rules of probabilism, provided he takes into account the preceding canons. Strong evidence, and especially a violent presumption in favor of this privileged proof, would certainly suffice.[15] The next question, according to can. 1831, is the acceptance or refusal of the oath and the weight of a refusal.

The party to whom the oath is to be administered, *may refuse* to accept and rebut it, if there is a just reason, and the oath does not concern the civil or religious status of the person. Omitting this last clause concerning the status of a person, concerning which the legislator does not admit a refusal, there may be good *reasons for refusal.* Such a reason would be if the party had sufficiently proved the action or exception, or if nothing had been proved against him, or if the oath would refer to matters unknown by personal experience (*de scientia propria*) because the oath, being an accessory testimony, must have reference to one's own knowledge (*de proprio auditu aut visu*); or if one of the reasons for the matter itself, as stated in can. 1830, § 2, would exist.[16]

How *much weight* should be attributed to such a refusal, is the reason just, and may the refusal be equal to self-confession? are questions which depend on the judge.

The oath given by one party may *be attacked* by the other, for the very same reasons which prompted refusal. Besides, since this oath supplies the deficiency of wit-

15 Reiffenstuel, II, 24, nn. 174 ff.   16 Santi-Leitner, II, 24, n. 31.

nesses, the qualifications of a witness may here be brought into play.

IURAMENTUM AESTIMATORIUM

CAN. 1832

Si de iure ad damni reparationem constet, sed quantitas damni aestimari certe non possit, iudex potest parti quae damnum passa est, iusiurandum deferre, quod *aestimatorium* dicitur.

CAN. 1833

In deferendo iureiurando aestimatorio:

1.° Iudex a parte, quae damnum passa est, petat ut sub iurisiurandi sanctitate designet res sibi ablatas vel dolo perditas, earumque pretium et valorem secundum probabilem suam aestimationem exprimat;

2.° Si taxatio iudici nimia videatur, eam ad aequitatem reducat, prae oculis habens omnia indicia et argumenta usu comprobata, adhibitis etiam, si opus sit, peritis, quo magis veritati et iustitiae consulatur.

If the right to indemnity is established, but the amount of the damage cannot be ascertained, the judge may demand an oath of the injured party. This oath is called *estimatory.* The party who suffered the damage swears as to what has been taken from him either by violence [17] or fraud and states the price and value of these things according to the best of his knowledge.

If the estimate is deemed excessive by the judge, he shall reduce it according to the most probable indications and customary methods of appraising; he may also employ experts in order to find out the truth and be just to both parties.

[17] Cfr. c. 7, X, I, 40; c. 32, X, II, 24 (usury).

IURAMENTUM DECISORIUM

CAN 1834

§ 1. Non solum ante initam litem partes convenire possunt ut controversia per iusiurandum ab alterutra praestandum transigendo dirimatur, sed pendente quoque lite et in quolibet eius momento et statu, altera pars potest, iudice probante, alteri iusiurandum deferre, ea conditione ut quaestio, sive principalis sive incidens, secundum iusiurandum decisa habeatur.

§ 2. Iusiurandum huiusmodi dicitur *decisorium*.

CAN. 1835

Decisorium iusiurandum deferri nequit, nisi:

1.° De re, in qua cessio et transactio admittitur, et quae pro litigantium personis non sit nimii momenti seu pretii;

2.° Ab eo qui cedere aut transigere potest;

3.° Ei, qui cedere vel transigere valet, quique pariter pro se non habeat plenam probationem;

4.° De mera notitia facti aut de facto, quod proprium sit illius, cui iusiurandum defertur.

CAN. 1836

§ 1. Hoc iusiurandum potest a parte, a qua delatum est, revocari quousque praestitum non fuerit, et ab altera parte acceptari et praestari, vel minus, aut referri in adversarium.

§ 2. Praestito iureiurando, quaestio secundum iuratam formulam finita est, perinde ac si cessio aut transactio iudicialis intercessisset.

§ 3. Si iusiurandum recusetur nec referatur in

adversarium, iudicis est aestimare quanti facienda sit recusatio, utrum iustis innitatur causis an potius confessioni sit aequiparanda.

§ 4. Si in adversarium referatur, hic debet illud praestare, secus causa cadit.

§ 5. Ut iusiurandum in adversarium referri possit, eaedem illae concurrant conditiones necesse est, quae ad illud deferendum requiruntur, atque idem intercedat iudicis ministerium.

This oath is called decisive because it decides between victory and defeat and its effect consists in settling the trial or controversy. It may concern the principal issue or merit of the cause (*causa principalis*) or it may refer only to an incidental matter related to the point at issue. But it rests upon a mutual agreement between the parties. If the parties agree to settle their *dispute by this oath before the trial* has begun, the settlement resembles a *transactio,* on which see can. 1925 ff. If the oath is demanded *during the trial,* it can be demanded of the other party only with the approval of the judge, but may be interposed at any moment or stage of the trial.

The decisive oath *can be taken only* in the following cases:

1. In *matters* admitting cession and transaction, provided they are not of too great importance or value for the litigants. The reason is the danger of perjury.

2. When the parties are capable of making cession and transaction, they may demand and give the oath, provided full proof has not been furnished.

3. Concerning knowledge of the fact, or concerning a fact connected with the party who has to swear; because this oath is one of truth, and not of credibility. Therefore they are supposed to swear *de propria scientia.*

This oath may be *revoked* by the party who demanded it, as long as it has not been taken; it may also be accepted or rejected, given or not given by the other party, or reversed by one party upon the other.

After the oath has been given, the case is settled according to the tenor of the formula, just as if cession or transaction had taken place. If the oath is refused — it may be refused for the reasons stated above — and not retorted upon the adversary, the judge should deliberate how much weight is to be attributed to this refusal, whether it was just or amounted to a confession of guilt.

Should the competitor upon whom the oath was retorted refuse to swear, he is defeated.

An oath may be retorted upon the adversary for the same reasons for which it may be demanded.

For the rest, this oath is to be treated in much the same way as the supplementary oath.

TITLE XI

INCIDENTAL QUESTIONS

Either at the beginning or in the process of a trial there may arise questions which have either a remote or proximate bearing upon the issue. Thus at the very *beginning* exception may be taken against an incompetent or suspected judge, or against the right of the other party to go to court, or against their attorney and counsel, or against the validity of the summons, and all these matters must be decided before the trial can proceed. In the course of the trial questions may arise concerning bail and sequestration, or the admission of evidence.[1] Hence this title is logically inserted after the different kinds of evidence have been set forth.

There are certain incidental questions which are common to all trials; these concern contempt and attempts, which are comprised under the present title.

DEFINITION, PROPOSAL AND ACCEPTANCE

CAN. 1837

Causa incidens habetur, quoties, incepto saltem per citationem iudicio, ab una ex partibus aut a promotore iustitiae vel vinculi defensore, si iudicio intersint, quaestio proponitur quae, tametsi libello, quo lis introducitur, non contineatur expresse, nihilominus ita

---

1 Cfr. Lega, *Compendium de Iudiciis Eccl.*, 1906 n. 419 ff., p. 320 f. Incidental questions might also be called side issues or special demurrers; see Blackstone, III, § 313 ff.

ad causam pertinet ut resolvi plerumque debeat ante quaestionem principalem.

CAN. 1838

Causa incidens proponitur vel oretenus vel per libellum, indicato nexu qui intercedit inter ipsam et causam principalem, et servatis, quoad eius fieri poterit, regulis can. 1706–1725 statutis.

CAN. 1839

Iudex, libello vel petitione verbali receptis, auditis partibus, et, si opus sit, promotore iustitiae, vel vinculi defensore, secum deliberet num proposita incidens quaestio futilis sit et ad retardandum principale iudicium unice excitata; itemque num causa incidens talis sit naturae et tali nexu cum causa principali cohaereat, ut ante eam resolvi debeat. Si ita se res habeat, libellum vel instantiam admittat; aliter decreto suo eam reiiciat.

1. An *incidental* question is one which, though not expressly contained in the introductory bill, is so intimately conected with the point at issue that it must be settled before the principal controversy is defined, for instance, the competency of the judge. Every such question must be proposed after the trial has begun, *i.e.*, after the summons was duly made, and it may be introduced by the party himself or by the *promotor iustitiae*, or by the *defensor vinculi*, if these officials are present.

2. A side-issue may be proposed either orally or in writing. But its connection with the main issue must be pointed out and the question raised must be in keeping with the rules laid down for the bill and the summons,

as stated in can. 1706–1725. If there are several incidental questions, the *ordo cognitionum,* as set forth in can. 1627–1635, must be observed.

3. After having received the oral or written petition for a hearing of incidental questions, the judge shall first invite the parties and, if necessary, also the *promotor iustitiae* and the *defensor vinculi,* to hear their opinion. Then he shall deliberate with himself whether the side-issue raised has any solid foundation, or is futile, or only raised in order to delay the settlement of the main issue. He shall also carefully consider whether the incidental question is of such a nature and so connected with the main issue that it requires preliminary settlement. If this is the case, he shall *admit* the petition; otherwise he shall issue a *decree* rejecting it.

FORM OF SETTLING INCIDENTAL QUESTIONS

CAN. 1840

§ 1. Utrum incidens quae excitetur questio, definienda sit iudicii forma servata, an mero decreto, iudex, attenta rei qualitate et gravitate, aestimet.

§ 2. Si causa incidens sit iudicialiter definienda, regulae, quoad eius fieri poterit, servandae sunt, quae in ordinariis iudiciis obtinent; curet tamen iudex ut dilationum termini sint quam maxime breves.

§ 3. Iudex in decreto quo, non servata iudicii forma, vel reiicit vel definit quaestionem incidentem, rationes quibus innititur, in iure et in facto breviter exponat.

CAN. 1841

Antequam finiatur causa principalis, iudex interlocutoriam sententiam potest, iusta intercedente causa,

corrigere aut revocare sive ex se, auditis partibus, sive
ad instantiam unius partis audita altera parte, et requisito semper voto promotoris iustitiae aut defensoris vinculi, si adsint.

If the judge refuses to admit the incidental question
by a formal decree, no appeal from this decision is permitted, unless — which, however, is hardly imaginable
— his decision should forestall, or amount to, a final sentence.[2] But if he admits the incidental question, there
are, according to our Code, which introduces new regulations in this matter, *two ways* open to settle the side-
issue:

a) A mere formal decree may be issued by the judge,
with due regard to the character and weight of the side-
issue, or

b) The matter may be settled in judiciary form.

If the settlement is made by decree of the judge, who
has either refused to admit the incidental question or
solved it without the formality of a judiciary trial, he
must briefly state the reasons of law and fact for his
decree. The reason of *law*, or special demurrer, may be
based on the lack of a formal rule which the law would
otherwise prescribe. A reason of *fact* would be if the
fact itself were denied or disputed, for instance, the
enmity of the judge towards the other party.

If the judge, after due deliberation, has decided to
settle the incidental question in *judiciary form*, he must,
as far as possible, proceed along the lines prescribed
for ordinary trials, but should take special care that the
dilatory term be shortened as much as possible.

The text undoubtedly refers to the ordinary method

2 *Trid.*, Sess. 13, c. 1; Sess. 24, cc. 10, 20, *de ref.*; Lega, *l. c.*, n.
426, p. 221.

of procedure, *i.e.*, the *observatio solemnis ordinis judiciarii*, to the apparent exclusion of summary proceedings. It was generally admitted before the promulgation of the Code that, in settling incidental controversies, a summary procedure was sufficient. Our text seems positively to exclude it. The reason is not far to seek. The judge is ordinarily permitted to settle such issues by a formal decree, but if the matter is of great importance, the regular judiciary way should be adopted. Yet the text seems covertly to admit summary procedure, because it adds: "*quoad eius fieri poterit.*"

The *essential requisites for a summary procedure* are the following:

1. The petition or bill containing the controversy, as stated in can. 1706 ff., but no *solemnis libelli oblatio.*[3]

2. The *summons*, as described in can. 1711 ff.

3. The *means of evidence*, to which belong the questioning of the parties and all kinds of evidence; but the oath of the witnesses [4] and the *iuramentum calumniae* are not essential.

4. The *grant of dilatory terms and exceptions*, which, however, according to our Code, must be reduced to the shortest possible time, in order not to delay the final sentence unnecessarily; but no solemn closing of the procedure is required.

5. The *interlocutory sentence*, according to can. 1868 ff., which, though void of accidental solemnities, must be given in writing.

This last named *sentence*, according to can. 1841, proffered before the main issue is settled, *may be corrected or revoked* by the judge for any just reason, be-

---

[3] Cfr. Lega, *l. c.*, n. 457 f.; Messmer, *l. c.*, p. 88 f.

[4] See can. 1767, § 3. On the *iuramentum calumniae* the Code is silent.

cause it does not terminate the office of either the delegated or the ordinary judge. For this reason the judge shall hear the parties in order to learn, whether they think themselves injured or curtailed in their rights by the interlocutory sentence. If one party insists upon a change or correction in the interlocutory sentence, the other party, too, must be heard. If the *promotor iustitiae* or the *defensor vinculi* are present, their opinion must also be asked.

CHAPTER I

As stated above, there are incidental questions common to all trials. One of these is contumacy, or grave disobedience shown to the ecclesiastical judge who has legitimately summoned one to appear in court. In criminal cases contumacy is generally called *contempt of court*, and in the civil law it creates a presumption of guilt. In civil cases it is simply styled *default to appear or plead in court*, which follows the presumption that the plaintiff has renounced the right to prosecute. Contumacy may be shown by the defendant as well as by the plaintiff.

CONTUMACY OF THE DEFENDANT

CAN. 1842

Reus citatus qui sine iusta causa nec ipse per se nec per procuratorem comparet, contumax declarari potest.

CAN. 1843

§ 1. Non potest iudex reum contumacem declarare nisi prius constiterit:

1.° Citationem, legitime factam, tempore utili ad rei notitiam pervenisse aut saltem pervenire debuisse;

2.° Reum absentiae excusationem afferre neglexisse aut non iustam attulisse.

§ 2. Haec comprobari possunt sive per novam citationem reo factam ut contumaciam suam, si possit, excuset, sive alio modo.

CAN. 1844

§ 1. Ad instantiam partis vel promotoris iustitiae vel vinculi defensoris, si iudicio intersint, iudex rei contumaciam declarare potest, eaque declarata, procedere, servatis servandis, usque ad sententiam definitivam eiusque exsecutionem.

§ 2. Si procedatur ad sententiam definitivam, lite non contestata, sententia respicere tantum debet petita in libello; si lite contestata, ipsum contestationis obiectum.

CAN. 1845

§ 1. Sed potest quoque iudex ad frangendam rei contumaciam comminari ecclesiasticas poenas.

§ 2. Quod si facere velit, iteranda est rei citatio, cum comminatione poenarum; nec iam tunc licet aut contumaciam declarare aut, ea declarata, poenas irrogare, nisi probetur hanc quoque secundam citationem suo effectu caruisse.

1. A defendant who has been duly summoned, and does not appear in court either personally or by proxy, *may be declared to be in contempt:* (a) if the *summons,* as described in can. 1711 ff., was lawfully issued and reached or at least might have reached the defendant within a reasonable time; (b) if the defendant failed to excuse himself, or offered no legitimate reason for his non-appearance in court.

To prove contumacy, a *second summons* may be issued, in order to give the defendant time to excuse his non-appearance. But if the judge deems it more expedient, another course may be taken. If two witnesses testify that the summons was duly served and received by the defendant, the judge may proceed as stated in can. 1844, because in that case he is certain of his ground and he who is certain need not strive for greater certainty.[1] But if he issues a new summons, a term must be set for appearance, and only after this term has expired, may contumacy be declared.[2]

2. But the necessary declaration may also be made upon the demand of the other party, or of the fiscal promotor or defender, if present at the trial. As soon as contumacy has been declared, the judge may proceed to the final sentence and its execution, provided he observes the rest of the rules prescribed (*servatis servandis*). This means that the proceeding is regular and conducted along the general rules governing trials, with the sole omission of the parts which the defendant would play if he were present; therefore the interrogatories, the confrontation, and the self-defence are omitted; but the controversial points should be communicated to the defendant if he can be reached.[3]

If no *contestatio litis* has as yet taken place, the sentence can only be directed to the object or petition contained in the bill of complaint; *i.e.*, only so much can be granted as was asked for in the petition offered to the judge, and no more. On the other hand, if contumacy has been declared *after* the issue in pleading, the sentence shall cover all that the plaintiff pleaded for and the defendant denied, because the latter is supposed to have been present at that moment.

Can. 1845 permits the threat of *ecclesiastical penalties* in order to force a stubborn recusant or *contumax* to be

1 Reg. juris 31 in 6°.   3 Reg. S. RR., Aug. 4, 1910, § 126,
2 Regulae S. R. R., Aug. 4, 1910,   n. 6 (A. Ap. S., II, 793).
§ 26 (A. Ap. S. II, 792).

obedient, not merely, as the Tridentine Council admitted,[4] in order to make him accept the sentence and its execution. But if the judge wishes to make use of this juridico-ecclesiastical weapon, he must issue a *second summons* in which this threat is directly mentioned. However, even after the second summons, contumacy may be declared and the penalty inflicted only when proof has been given that this second summons, like the first, was ineffective or unheeded. The proof can be furnished as stated above, or by public courier.

DESISTING FROM CONTUMACY

CAN. 1846

Rei a contumacia recedentis seque in iudicio sistentis ante causae definitionem, conclusiones probationesque, si quas afferat, admittantur; caveat autem iudex ne mala fide in longiores et non necessarias moras iudicium protrahatur.

CAN. 1847

Post latam vero sententiam, contumax beneficium restitutionis in integrum ad appellandum ab ipso iudice qui eam tulit, petere potest, non ultra tamen trimestre ab ipsius sententiae intimatione, nisi agatur de causis quae non transeunt in rem iudicatam.

CAN. 1848

Regulis superius traditis etiam tum locus est cum reus, etsi primae citationi obtemperaverit, fit tamen postea, progressu iudicii, contumax.

4 Sess. 15, c. 3, *de ref.*; Messmer, p. 137.

If the contumacious defendant appears in court before
the final sentence, his claims and proofs, if he has any,
must be admitted; but the judge must assure himself that
the defendant's motive in postponing his appearance was
not to prolong the trial unnecessarily, or to wear out
the judge and the plaintiff.

:: If the defendant appears in court after the final sentence has been given in his case, the only mode of appeal open to him is by *restitutio in integrum*, which he
must ask for within three months from the date of the
sentence. A longer term is admissible only in matters
which never become *res iudicatae,* as, for instance, matrimonial cases.

The rules so far laid down also hold in case the defendant, after having obeyed the first summons, becomes
contumacious in the course of the trial.

CONTUMACY OF THE PLAINTIFF

CAN. 1849

Si die et hora, qua reus secundum citationis praescriptum coram iudice primum se sistit, actor non adsit, nullamque vel insufficientem absentiae excusationem attulerit, iudex eum ad instantiam rei conventi
citet iterum; et si actor novae citationi non paruerit vel
postea iudicium inchoare vel inchoatum prosequi neglexerit, instante reo convento vel promotore iustitiae
aut defensore vinculi, contumax a iudice declaretur,
iisdem servatis regulis quae supra traditae sunt pro
rei contumacia.

The Code has combined two apparently contradictory
Decretals [5] in such a way that no collision is possible.

5 C. 3, X, II, 14; c. 1, 6°, II, 6.

Suppose the summons was duly issued and the defendant
appears in court on the appointed day and hour, but the
plaintiff demurs. This seems to be a grievous offence,
because it was the plaintiff who caused the summons to
be issued and who is bound to prosecute the case. Therefore it might naturally be expected that the judge would
be stricter in case of contumacy towards the plaintiff
than towards the defendant, and a second summons would
be regarded as unnecessary.[6] But the Code leans towards
a more equitable treatment and orders another summons to be issued, even if the defendant demands it, and
the plaintiff had no excuse, or at least no sufficient reason, for not appearing in court. And if this second summons is unheeded by the plaintiff, or if he does not begin
or pursue his case in court, *he is declared in contempt,*
provided either the defendant or the fiscal promoter or
defender insist upon such a declaration. For the rest,
the rules laid down for the defendant in contempt cases
must be applied.

EFFECT OF CONTUMACY

CAN. 1850

§ 1. Actoris contumacia a iudice declarata perimit
eiusdem actoris ius ad suam instantiam prosequendam.

§ 2. Permittitur tamen promotori iustitiae vel vinculi
defensori instantiam facere suam eamque prosequi,
quoties publicum bonum id postulare videatur.

§ 3. Reus autem exinde ius habet petendi ut vel
libere possit a iudicio abire, vel nulla habeantur omnia
eo usque gesta, vel definitive ipse absolvatur a petitione

<hr>
6 Thus in c. 1, 6°, II, 6, whilst
c. 3, X, II, 14 seems to admit omission of summons to plaintiff; see
Santi-Leitner, II, 14, n. 6 f.; Lega,
l. c., n. 436.

actoris, vel iudicium, absente quoque actore, ad finem
adducatur.

CAN. 1851

§ 1. Qui contumax declaratus contumaciam suam
non purgaverit, sive actor sit sive reus, condemnetur
tum ad litis expensas, quae ob suam contumaciam
factae sunt, tum etiam, si opus sit, ad indemnitatem
alteri parti praestandam.

§ 2. Si tum actor tum reus sint contumaces, ad expensas litis tenentur in solidum.

If the *plaintiff* has been declared contumacious, he *forfeits* the right of prosecuting the case, because he is supposed to have renounced that right. However, if the case
concerns the public welfare, as, for instance, in criminal,
ordinational, and matrimonial matters, either the *promotor iustitiae* or the *defensor vinculi* may continue the prosecution in his own name.

The counter effect of a declaration of contempt against
the plaintiff is that the *defendant* may demand his discharge, or that all the proceedings so far have to be considered null and void, or that he be definitely freed from
the claims of the plaintiff, or that the trial be brought
to a close even during the absence of the plaintiff.

If either the *plaintiff or the defendant* has been declared *contumax* and has not purged himself of this
stain, he must be condemned to bear the expenses caused
by his contumacy, and if necessary, also to indemnify the
other party. If both, plaintiff and defendant, have been
contumacious, they are bound to defray the expenses thus
far incurred *in solidum, i.e.,* each one the whole expense
if either should be insolvent or beyond reach.

CHAPTER II

CAN. 1852

§ 1. Is cuius interest, admitti potest ad interveniendum in causa in qualibet litis instantia.

§ 2. Sed ut admittatur, debet ante conclusionem in causa libellum iudici exhibere, in quo breviter de iure interveniendi ipsum edoceat.

§ 3. Qui intervenit in causa, admittendus est in eo statu in quo causa reperitur, assignato eidem brevi ac peremptorio termino ad probationes suas exhibendas, si causa ad periodum probatoriam pervenerit.

CAN. 1853

Si tertii interventus appareat necessarius, iudex ad instantiam partis vel etiam ex officio debet interventum in causa iubere.

Intervention is perhaps best known from international law, where it means interference by one state in affairs pending between two or more other states that have either gone to war or reached a degree of tension clearly threatening war. The interest of the intervening state as well as that of international society justifies such interference.[1] Similarly, not only the plaintiff and defendant, but a third person, too, may be concerned in the issue of

---

1 Westlake, *International Law*, P. I, Peace; 1910, p. 317.

a trial, for instance, a legacy or a matrimonial case involving legitimacy.

Hence our text admits intervention by interested persons in any case and at any stage. However, in order to be admitted, the third party must, before the *conclusio in causa*, present a bill briefly stating the claim on which he bases his intervention. As intervention is permitted at any stage or instance of the trial, the judge who has been chosen by the plaintiff, either in the first instance or the court of appeal,[2] may take cognizance of and admit the intervention. The one who intervenes must be admitted only at the stage or instance which the trial had reached when he came in, for instance, after the *litis contestatio*, or at the defence of the parties, or at the *conclusio in causa*, or, finally, in the instance of appeal. And from that point onward the third party may be present at all the acts. But the text adds that brief and peremptory terms should be assigned to the third party for his evidence if the trial is near the point where the evidence is gathered in.

Can. 1853 mentions *necessary intervention*, undoubtedly to distinguish it from another, which is called *voluntary*. The latter is intervention spontaneously offered by a third person in order to help either of the litigants; whereas necessary intervention is commanded by the judge, either at the demand of a party, or *ex officio*. In the latter case the *promotor iustitiae* should, or at least may, be notified.[3]

---

2 C. 38, X, II, 20; cfr. Wernz, l. c., V, n. 177 f., p. 156 f.

3 *Regulae* S. R. R. Aug. 4, 1910, § 97, n. 2 (*A. Ap. S.*, II, 815).

CHAPTER III

CAN. 1854

Attentatum est quidquid, lite pendente, aut altera pars adversus alteram aut ipse iudex adversus alterutram vel utramque partem innovat, parte dissentiente et in eius praeiudicium; sive innovatio respiciat litis materiam, salvo tamen praescripto can. 1672, 1673, sive respiciat terminos partibus a iure vel a iudice assignatos ad ponendos certos actus iudiciales.

CAN. 1855

§ 1. Attentata sunt ipso iure nulla.

§ 2. Idcirco parti ex attentato laesae competit actio ad obtinendam declarationem nullitatis.

§ 3. Actio haec instituenda est coram ipso iudice causae principalis; quod si ob attentatum pars laesa iudicem suspectum habeat, exceptionem suspicionis potest opponere, in qua procedendum est ad norman can. 1615.

CAN. 1856

§ 1. Pendente quaestione de attentato, cursus causae principalis regulariter suspenditur, sed si iudici opportunius videatur, quaestio de attentato potest una cum causa principali pertractari et resolvi.

§ 2. Quaestiones de attentatis expeditissime sunt per-

297

tractandae et decreto iudicis definiendae, auditis partibus et promotore iustitiae vel defensore vinculi, si hi
iudicio intersint.

CAN. 1857

§ 1. Demonstrato attentato, iudex decernere debet
eius revocationem seu purgationem.

§ 2. Quod si attentatum vi vel dolo patratum sit, qui
illud commisit, tenetur etiam de damnis erga partem
laesam.

The trial, according to can. 1725, 5°, becomes *pending*
after the summons has been duly served or the parties
have appeared in court of their own accord.   The object of the quarrel is then litigious (*res litigiosa*),[1] and
any change of, or any act against, that object is called
an attempt (*attentatum*), provided it is prejudicial or
detrimental to one of the parties concerned.[2]

It is also called an *innovation* because it alters the
judicial status of the object.   Every " attempt " is against
the inhibition of the law (*inhibitio iuris*), because, as
stated above, the Code forbids any innovation while the
trial is pending.   To this general inhibition must also be
referred the terms set up by law, as, for instance, for appeals, in can. 1634.

The judge himself may fix definite terms for certain
judicial acts, for instance, for the experts (can. 1799,
§ 2).   These are *inhibitiones hominis* or *iudicis*.[3]   Hence
our Code calls an *attentatum* whatever savors of innovation attempted by one party against the other, or by the
judge against one or both parties, provided it is made
(a) pending the trial, (b) against the will of the other

1 C. 50, C. 11, q. 1.   3 Lega, *l. c.*, n. 429.
2 C. 3, X, II, 16.

party, and (c) to the detriment or prejudice of the other party.

The *object of an innovation* may be:

a) the subject of the trial (*materia litis*), or

b) the *terms* assigned either by law or by the judge.

The object may concern real as well as personal action. Thus *innovatio* is forbidden in *matrimonial cases* which are pending on the score of a diriment impediment, and the parties must not be separated, or be denied their marital rights until the case is settled.

However, this applies only to the court decision; the party who is absolutely certain of the existence of a diriment impediment would not be allowed either to ask for, or render, the *debitum*.[4] Other litigious matter which may occur in ecclesiastical courts are church property, benefices, and provisions or appointments. The Code makes an exception from can. 1672 f., which refer to sequestration of a litigious object and bailment or security, as these are not considered attempts, being permitted by law.

The *effect*, negative and positive, is stated in canon 1855, which decides (thereby settling a controversy) that *all attempts are null and void ipso iure*, and not merely rescindible.[5]

However, the term *ipso iure* is to some extent modified; for the injured party is granted the right to a *legal action* in order to obtain a *declaration of nullity of the attempt*. Therefore, if the party should take no action with regard to the attempt, we hardly believe that the judge would have to interfere. At least there is no hint that the judge

---

4 Reiffenstuel, II, 16, n. 11 f. The reader of Vol. V of our Comm., p. 327, line 10 from below, will please change the word *certain* into *uncertain*, the former being a misprint.

5 Concerning alienation of a litigious matter the authors were not agreed; some held that it was rescindible only. Reiffenstuel, II, 16, n. 20; Lega, *l. c.*, n. 430.

would have to proceed *ex officio*. On the other hand, it would hardly be advisable for the judge not to proceed *ex officio* in beneficiary cases, on account of can. 1447.

The *action* against attempts must be brought before the *judge* who is competent in regard to the main issue. However, if exception should be taken to the judge, because of suspicion, this must first be solved according to can. 1615.

Another effect of the *attentatum* is mentioned in can. 1856, which is modelled upon the civil code issued for the Papal States by Gregory XVI.[6] It says that the course of the main trial is, as a rule, suspended, unless the judge deems it expedient to treat and solve the incidental question concerning the attempt together with the main issue.

At any rate questions of attempt should be treated and settled as quickly as possible by a decree of the judge, who shall for this purpose hear the parties and also the fiscal promoter and the defender if they are present.

If the attempt has been proved, the judge must decree its revocation or purgation, which consists in the rescinding of all acts that have been performed during the inhibition, either of law or of the judge, with regard to this one incidental question.[7] Besides, if the attempt was made by violence or fraud, the perpetrators are bound to indemnify the injured party to an amount corresponding with the period beginning at the time when the action was brought up to the moment of its settlement.[8] This indemnification includes expenses as well as the revenues received or gain made during this time.

---

6 *Regolamento legislativo e giudisierio per gli affari civili,* Nov. 10, 1834, art. 880, 884, 886.

7 *Ibid.,* art. 881; cfr. c. 4, X, II, 13.

8 C. 2, X, II, 14; c. 1, X, II, 17; Lega, l. c., n. 433.

TITLE XII

PUBLICATION OF THE PROCESS, CLOSING OF THE EVIDENCE, PLEADING OF THE CASE

After all the incidental questions have been settled, or, if no such questions arose, after all the evidence has been produced, the pleading proper or defence might commence, were it not for two acts, one of which requires a formal decree. They are the publication of the process and the closing of the evidence.

THE PUBLICATION OF THE PROCESS

CAN. 1858

Ante causae discussionem et sententiam omnes probationes quae sunt in actis et quae adhuc secretae permanserunt, sunt publicandae.

CAN. 1859

Concessa partibus earumque advocatis facultate acta processualia inspiciendi petendique eorum exemplar, intelligitur facta publicatio processus.

Before the defence is put up and the sentence is pronounced, all the *evidence* contained in the acts or records (minutes) and that which has so far been kept secret, must be *published*. This is done in order to give an opportunity to the parties to defend themselves. Therefore they or their attorneys are permitted to inspect the acts of the process thus far conducted, and to obtain a copy thereof. This grant is called publication of the process (*publicatio processus*), but it is not required for the validity of the trial, nor does it necessitate a formal decree of the judge.

CLOSING OF THE EVIDENCE

CAN. 1860

§ 1. Expletis omnibus quae ad probationes producendas pertinent, ad *conclusionem in causa* deveniendum est.

§ 2. Haec conclusio habetur quoties aut partes a iudice interrogatae declarent se nihil aliud deducendum habere, aut utile proponendis probationibus tempus a iudice praestitutum elapsum sit, aut iudex declaret se satis instructam causam habere.

§ 3. De peracta conclusione in causa, quocunque modo ea acciderit, iudex decretum ferat.

CAN. 1861

§ 1. Post conclusionem in causa novae probationes inhibentur, nisi agatur de causis quae nunquam transeunt in rem iudicatam aut de documentis nunc primum repertis, aut de testibus qui antea ob legitimum impedimentum tempore utili induci non potuerunt.

§ 2. Si novas probationes admittendas censeat, id decernat iudex, audita altera parte, cui congruum tempus concedat ut novas probationes cognoscere et se defendere possit; aliter iudicium nullius est momenti.

The so-called *conclusio in causa* is nothing else but a formal declaration that the evidence is exhausted. It requires a *decree* of the judge, which may be brought about in three ways: (a) The judge may ask the parties to declare that they have no further evidence to produce, or (b) the term fixed by the judge for producing evidence may have expired, or (c) the judge may declare himself to be sufficiently informed.

The *conclusio in causa,* as a rule, forbids the bringing forth of new evidence; otherwise there might be no limit to the trial and the door would be opened to undue protraction. However, there are cases which admit exceptions, to wit:

1.° when the matter is such that it can never become *res iudicata,* as in matrimonial cases;

2.° when new documents have come to light;

3.° when witnesses are lawfully prevented from giving testimony within the term assigned.

In all these cases the judge must deliberate whether the new evidence is to be admitted or not, and if he decides to admit it, he must issue a *decree* to that effect, after having heard the other party, *viz.,* the one who has not produced new evidence. This same party must then, *under penalty of nullity of the trial,* be given sufficient time to take cognizance of the new evidence and to prepare his defence.

DEFENCE OR DISCUSSION OF THE CASE

CAN. 1862

§ 1. Facta conclusione in causa, iudex, pro suo prudenti arbitrio, partibus congruum temporis spatium praestituat ad defensiones suas seu allegationes sive per se sive per advocatum exhibendas.

§ 2. Hic terminus prorogari a iudice potest instante una parte, audita altera; vel etiam coarctari, utraque consentiente.

CAN. 1863

§ 1. Defensio in scriptis est conficienda, et regulariter tot exemplaribus conscribenda quot sunt iudices, ut singula singulis iudicibus possint exemplaria distribui.

§ 2. Sed etiam promotori iustitiae et defensori vinculi, si iudicio intersint, debet exemplar tradi; praeterea partes inter se exemplaria commutare debent.

§ 3. Tribunalis praeses, quoties pro suo prudenti arbitrio necessarium censeat, et sine nimio partium gravamine fieri animadvertat, mandare potest ut defensio typis imprimatur una cum documentis principalibus in fasciculo coniungendis, qui actorum et documentorum summarium continet.

§ 4. Quo in casu iubeat ne quidquam imprimatur, nisi prius exhibito manuscripto et venia illud publicandi obtenta; praeterea sedulo caveat de secreto, si quod sit in causa servandum.

CAN. 1864

Iudicis et in tribunali collegiali praesidis est moderari, pro sua prudentia, nimiam defensionum extensionem, nisi de hoc peculiari tribunalis lege sit cautum.

CAN. 1865

§ 1. Communicatis vicissim inter partes defensionum scripturis, utrique parti responsiones exhibere liceat, intra breve tempus a iudice praestitutum, et servatis regulis et cautelis de quibus in can. 1863, 1864.

§ 2. Hoc ius partibus semel tantum esto, nisi iudici gravi ex causa iterum videatur concedendum; tunc autem concessio, uni parti facta, alteri quoque data censeatur.

CAN. 1866

§ 1. *Informationes,* uti vocant, *orales,* quibus videlicet advocati iudicem de adiunctis iuris et facti causam respicientibus instruere satagunt, prohibentur.

§ 2. Admittitur tamen moderata disputatio coram iudice pro tribunali sedente ad aliquid illustrandum, si, alterutra vel utraque parte postulante, iudex eam utilem censeat atque admittat.

§ 3. Ad disputationem obtinendam partes exhibere debent in scriptis quaestionum capita cum altera parte discutienda, paucis verbis expressa; iudicis autem est ea cum partibus hinc inde communicare, ac diem et horam disputationi assignare et disputationem ipsam moderari.

§ 4. Disputationi assistat unus ex notariis tribunalis ad hoc ut, si iudex praecipiat aut pars postulet et iudex consentiat, possit de disceptatis, confessis aut conclusis, scripto ad tramitem iuris ex continenti referre.

CAN. 1867

In causis contentiosis, si partes parare sibi tempore utili defensionem negligant, aut se remittant iudicis scientiae et conscientiae, iudex, si ex actis et probatis rem habeat plane perspectam, poterit statim sententiam pronuntiare.

The law laid down in these canons is entirely modern, based on the practice of the S. Rom. Rota,[1] and it would be vain to look for precedents in the Decretals.

The *chief points* with regard to the defence are:

---

[1] *Lex Propria* S. R. R., June 29, 1908, can. 25 ff.; *Regulae Servandae,* Aug. 4, 1910, § 44 ff. (*A. Ap. S.,* I, 26 f.; II, 799 ff.); some old canonists mention "*de allegationibus*"; see Wernz, V, n. 661 p. 498.

1.° A *time* is to be fixed by the judge for the defence, and it may be prolonged or restricted.

2.° The defence is to be made *in writing,* and if so demanded by the judge,— who also gives the permission, — it must be printed. Each judge as well as the fiscal promoter and the defender is entitled to a copy, and the parties must exchange their defence.

3.° The *judge* or the president of the board of judges shall *direct* the defence so that it may not be unduly protracted.

4.° After the *parties* have exchanged their written defence, they shall *prepare the answers* within the time assigned by the judge. But answers are allowed *only once,* unless for weighty reasons the judge grants a *second chance for pleading.* However, both parties must be treated equally, *i.e.,* if one party is allowed a second pleading, the other must be offered the same opportunity.

The answers are to be in writing and, according to the practice of the S. R. Rota, should be ready twenty days after the written or printed defence has been distributed and exchanged.[2]

5.° Whilst *oral information* (by which attorneys try to explain circumstances of law and fact to the judge, who may thus be unduly influenced by a one-sided presentation of the case) is forbidden, a moderate oral discussion or *pleading is permitted,* if necessary to throw light on the subject. However, it is required:

a) That this pleading be made *before the court,* that it be requested by one or both of the parties, and that the judge give his consent or deem it useful;

b) That the permission be given only after the *points*

2 *Lex Propria S. R. R.,* c. 27, n. 3; *Regulae S. R. R.,* Aug. 4, 1910, § 50 (*A. Ap. S.,* I, 27; II, 801).

to be discussed have been briefly stated by the parties in writing;

c) That the judge *communicate* these points to both parties;

d) That he *set the day and hour* for the discussion of them and direct the discussion himself;

e) That a *notary* immediately take down the minutes of the discussion, including admissions and conclusions, as often as the judge commands or either party, with the consent of the judge, demands it.

6.° In *private civil matters*, if the parties do not present their defence within the time prescribed, or commit their case to the knowledge and conscience of the judge, the *latter may immediately pronounce sentence*, provided the acts and the evidence are so plain as to permit him to do so.

TITLE XIII

THE SENTENCE

After the pleading is ended by the defence, either because nothing more can be said or because the judge deems the evidence sufficient, the sentence must be pronounced. The Code first defines the sentence, then states the rules to be followed by the judge, and, finally, defines the contents of the sentence and prescribes the manner of its publication.

DEFINITION AND INTRINSIC CONDITIONS OF THE SENTENCE

CAN. 1868

§ 1. Legitima pronuntiatio qua iudex causam a litigantibus propositam et iudiciali modo pertractatam definit, sententia est: eaque *interlocutoria* dicitur, si dirimat incidentem causam; *definitiva*, si principalem.

§ 2. Ceterae iudicis pronuntiationes *decreta* vocantur.

CAN. 1869

§ 1. Ad pronuntiationem cuiuslibet sententiae requiritur in iudicis animo moralis certitudo circa rem sententia definiendam.

§ 2. Hanc certitudinem iudex haurire debet ex actis et probatis.

§ 3. Probationes autem aestimare iudex debet ex sua

308

conscientia, nisi lex aliquid expresse statuat de efficacia alicuius probationis.

§ 4. Iudex qui eam certitudinem efformare sibi non potuit, pronuntiet non constare de iure actoris et reum dimittat, nisi agatur de causa favorabili, quo in casu pro ipsa pronuntiandum est, et salvo praescripto can. 1697, § 2.

CAN. 1870

Sententia ferri a iudice debet, expleta causae disceptatione; et si causa sit implicatior et contentionum vel documentorum mole difficilior, interponi potest congruum temporis intervallum.

1. A *sentence* is the legitimate pronouncement of a judge, by which a case proposed by the litigants and judicially tried, is settled. It is called *interlocutory* if it settles an incidental question, *definitive* if it settles the main issue. All other settlements or pronunciamentos of the judge are called *decrees*.[1]

2. The *intrinsic requisites* for a sentence are the following:

a) The judge must have *moral certitude* concerning the case he settles by his sentence. Moral certitude requires sufficient proof to convince the judge of the righteousness of the cause.

b) The proofs may not be sought outside of the acts and allegations of the trial (*acta et probata*), because it is not as a private citizen, but as a judge, that he must give sentence. Hence privately gained knowledge should not influence the decision.[2]

---

1 See Appendix, pp. 485 sqq.

2 A theological question here arises: Is the judge so bound by the *acta et probata* that he would have to decide against his own pri- vate conscience. *Three* opinions are proposed; the first simply affirms, the second flatly denies, and the third, which to us appears more probable, distinguishes: in civil (to

c) Yet the judge *must weigh the evidence according to his own conscience.* He must know the law and acquaint himself fully with the evidence. The rule is that all other things being equal or the testimony being equally strong on both sides, the decision should be in favor of the possesser, *because melior est conditio possidentis.* Hence our text adds the clause: *unless the law itself should state something definite concerning the weight of evidence.* Every sentence opposed to a clear and express law text would be *ipso iure* null and void, for the judge has not to reverse, but to uphold the law.[4]

d) From this naturally follows the corollary set forth in can. 1869, § 4: If no certainty can be had, the *judge must pronounce in favor of the defendant and dismiss him;* unless the case is one of possession or contains or turns about a favor, in which hypothesis, although the law is more favorable to absolution or freedom, the favor should be upheld.

e) The *sentence must be given after the pleading has been completed.* This means immediately or soon after the defence has exhausted its arguments. However, there are *intricate cases,* rendered so by reason of the many papers or documents that must be pondered before the judge has a clear vision of the case, and the decision of these may *be delayed* for a time.

---

which they also belong matrimonial) cases, and in minor criminal cases, the judge is obliged to decide according to the *acta et probata,* but not in important criminal cases; see

Bouix, *De Iudiciis Eccl.,* I, p. 140.
3 Cfr. c. 27, X, II, 20; c. 3, X, II, 19.
4 C. 1, X, II, 27; c. 1, X, I, 2; c. 1, 6°, II, 14.

HOW A BOARD OF JUDGES OR ONE JUDGE PRONOUNCES
SENTENCE

CAN. 1871

§ 1. In tribunali collegiali, qua die et hora iudices ad deliberandum conveniant, collegii praeses constituat; et nisi peculiaris causa aliud suadeat, in ipsa tribunalis sede conventus habeatur.

§ 2. Assignata conventui die, singuli iudices scriptas afferent conclusiones suas in merito causae, et rationes tam in facto quam in iure, quibus ad conclusionem suam venerint: quae conclusiones actis causae adiungantur, secreto servandae.

§ 3. Prolatis ex ordine, secundum praecedentiam, ita tamen ut semper a causae ponente seu relatore initium fiat, singulorum conclusionibus, habeatur moderata discussio sub tribunalis praesidis ductu, praesertim ut constabiliatur quid statuendum sit in parte dispositiva sententiae.

§ 4. In discussione autem fas unicuique est a pristina sua conclusione recedere.

§ 5. Quod si iudices in prima discussione ad hanc sententiam devenire aut nolint aut nequeant, differri poterit decisio ad novum conventum; qui tamen ultra hebdomadam comperendinari non debet.

CAN. 1872

Si unicus sit iudex, ipsius tantum est sententiam exarare; in tribunali vero collegiali servetur praescriptum can. 1584.

1. When a *board of judges* has to pronounce sentence, the procedure is as follows:

a) The presiding officer determines the *day* and the *hour* when the judges shall meet for deliberation. The *place* for the meeting is the *courtroom*, unless circumstances make it advisable to choose another locality.

b) On the day appointed each judge shall bring with him the *conclusions* he has arrived at in the case together with a statement of the motives that prompt them.

All this must be done in writing and inserted in the acts of the trial, but kept secret. The *reasons for his opinion* or conclusions each judge must state *in facto et iure.* The phrase *in facto* means that the conclusions must remain within the writ of complaint, or concern precisely this case and no other; the reasons *de iure* may be applied to the law in general as well as to any specific right on which the plaintiff based his claim; this is also called *in causa et actione.* Hence the sentence must, as the canonists say, conform to the *libellus* and to the law in general.[5]

c) After the conclusions of each judge have been read by the *ponens* or referee, and then by the judges, according to precedence, a *moderate discussion* shall take place under the supervision of the presiding judge, in order to determine the dispositive part of the sentence more accurately.

d) Each judge is permitted to change his conclusion in the course of this discussion, because the discussion may convince him that he made an error, either *in facto* or *in iure.*

e) If the judges are unwilling or unable to arrive at a definite sentence, another discussion may be held, but not later than eight days after the first.

2. If but *one* judge is sitting in tribunal, he must work out the sentence for himself; but in a board the presi-

5 Reiffenstuel, II, 27, n. 70 ff.; Santi-Leitner, II, 27, n. 8.

dent may entrust one of the judges with the office of *ponens*, to draft the sentence in writing (can. 1584).

CONTENTS OF THE SENTENCE

CAN. 1873

§ 1. Sententia debet:

1.° Definire controversiam coram tribunali agitatam; hoc est reum absolvere vel condemnare quod attinet ad petitiones vel accusationes adversus eum prolatas, data singulis dubiis, seu controversiae articulis, congrua responsione;

2.° Determinare (saltem quatenus fas sit et materia patiatur), quid pars damnata dare, facere, praestare, aut pati debeat, aut a quo abstinere; itemque quo modo, loco vel tempore obligatio implenda sit;

3.° Continere rationes seu *motiva* quae dicuntur, tam in facto quam in iure, quibus dispositiva sententiae pars innititur;

4.° Statuere de litis expensis.

§ 2. In tribunali collegiali motiva ab extensore desumantur ex iis quae singuli iudices in discussione attulerunt, nisi ab ipsa iudicum maiore parte praefinitum fuerit quaenam sint motiva proferenda.

The sentence must be drafted in such a way:

1.° That it *settles* the controversy at issue, that is, it must be either absolutory or condemnatory concerning the question contained in the writ of complaint (*libellus*), and offer suitable answers to each disputed point.

2.° That, as far as the case permits, the *penalty of the guilty party is determined*. Hence the sentence should clearly and precisely state what the condemned party has to give, do, perform, or from what to abstain; also the manner, place, and time for fulfilling the obligation imposed. This is called *sententia certa*. A conditional sentence, as a rule, is invalid,[6] because a trial is supposed to settle the quarrel.

3.° That it *contain the reasons*[7] *in facto et iure,* as stated above, upon which the dispositive part of the sentence is based. The *dispositive part* is that which contains the absolutory or condemnatory sentence. Hence neither the *arenga,* nor the *narratio propria,* nor the *conclusio* are here concerned.

4.° That it state the amount of expenses incurred. The *extensor,* who is no one else but the *ponens* or referee, *i.e.,* one of the judges, may make a summary (*ristretto*) of the motives or reasons given by the judges, unless the majority has specifically determined which motives are to be advanced.

EXTRINSIC FORMALITIES

CAN. 1874

§ 1. Sententia ferri debet, divino Nomine ab initio semper invocato.

§ 2. Dein exprimat oportet ex ordine qui sit iudex aut tribunal; qui sit actor, reus, procurator, nominibus et domicilio rite designatis, promotor iustitiae, defensor vinculi, si partem in iudicio habuerint.

§ 3. Referre postea debet breviter facti speciem cum partium conclusionibus.

§ 4. Hisce subsequatur pars dispositiva sententiae, praemissis rationibus quibus innititur.

§ 5. Claudatur cum indicatione diei et loci in quibus

---

6 Reiffenstuel, II, 27, n. 87 ff.

7 The *Regulae S. R. Rotae,* Aug. 4, 1910, § 182 (*A. Ap. S.,* II, 836) state that if these reasons are not given, the sentence is invalid.

exarata est et cum subscriptione iudicis vel omnium iudicum, si plures fuerint, et notarii.

CAN. 1875

Regulae superius positae locum habent potissimum in proferenda sententia definitiva; sed applicantur etiam, quantum diversa res patitur, in proferenda interlocutoria.

1. The sentence must contain an invocation of the Divinity.[8]

2. The *following names* must be set down in order: the names of the judge or tribunal, *i.e.*, the board of judges; of the plaintiff, defendant, proctor, together with their domiciles, of the fiscal promoter and the defender, provided they took part in the trial.

2. It must contain a brief *statement of the case* together with the arguments or conclusions of the parties.

4. Then follows the *dispositive part* of the sentence, preceded by a statement of the motives which prompted it.

5. At the bottom or end of all these statements follow the *day* and the *place* when and where the sentence was drafted, and the signatures of the judge or judges and the notary.

All these rules, says can. 1875, apply chiefly to *definitive sentences,* but they should be observed also with regard to *interlocutory* sentences, if the nature of the incidental question calls for or permits it.

---

8 Examples are plentiful in the decisions of the S. R. Rota, for instance: *" Christi nomine invocato, solumque Deum prae oculis habentes,"* etc.

PUBLICATION OF THE SENTENCE

CAN. 1876

Sententia, hac ratione redacta, quamprimum publicetur.

CAN. 1877

Publicatio sententiae fieri potest tribus modis, vel citando partes ad audiendam sententiae lectionem sollemniter factam a iudice pro tribunali sedente; vel partibus denuntiando sententiam esse penes cancellariam tribunalis, unaque facultatem ipsis fieri eandem legendi et eiusdem exemplar petendi; vel tandem, ubi usus viget, sententiae exemplar transmittendo ad partes per publicos tabellarios ad norman can. 1719.

The sentence thus drafted should be *published as soon as possible*. How soon, is not expressly stated; but the phrase generally means after an interval of not more than three or eight days.

The *manner* in which the sentence may be published is threefold:

1. By summoning the parties to hear the sentence solemnly pronounced by the judge sitting[9] in court;

2. By notifying the parties that the sentence is ready at the chancery of the court and leave is granted to read it and have a copy made;

3. By sending a copy of the sentence to the parties through the public carrier, where this is customary.

[9] Whether this attitude of sitting is required for the validity of the sentence cannot positively be proved from the text, especially since a threefold mode of publication is admitted; therefore we would rather say that it belongs to the decorum or dignity of the judge to observe a sitting posture.

TITLE XIV

LEGAL REDRESS AGAINST THE SENTENCE

CAN. 1878

§ 1. Si agatur de errore materiali qui inciderit vel in transcribenda parte dispositiva sententiae vel in referendis factis aut partium petitionibus aut in ponendis calculis, errorem corrigere valet ipse iudex.

§ 2. Iudex ad hanc correctionem deveniat edito decreto ad instantiam partis, nisi pars altera refragetur.

§ 3. Si altera pars refragetur, quaestio, incidens ad normam can. 1840, § 3 decreto definiatur; et decretum ad calcem sententiae correctae referatur.

After the sentence has been pronounced, execution should follow. However the party condemned may find it too hard or unjust and therefore claim a *gravamen*. This would justify an appeal. But before the Code treats of appeals, it considers the possibility of a *merely material error*, which may have crept into the copy of the dispositive part of the sentence. A mistake may also have been made in the narration of facts, or in the writ of complaint, or in the reckoning of accounts. Such an error should be corrected by the judge himself, who shall *issue* a decree to that effect upon demand of one party, provided the other is satisfied. But if the other party refuses to accept the correction, the question must be treated as an *incidental* one, summarily disposed of according to can. 1840, § 3, and notice be given at the bottom of the sentence thus corrected.

CHAPTER I

APPEALS

Can. 1879

Pars quae aliqua sententia se gravatam putat, itemque promotor iustitiae et defensor vinculi in causis in quibus interfuerunt, ius habent a sententia appellandi, idest provocandi ab inferiore iudice qui sententiam tulit, ad superiorem, salvo praescripto can. 1880.

Appeal is here taken in the strictly judicial sense, requiring a preceding judicial sentence. Hence it is a complaint brought from an inferior judge, who pronounced a sentence, to a higher judge. The intention or purpose is to seek redress. This, of course, chiefly concerns the *party* who believes himself injured or hurt by the former sentence.

But the *promotor iustitiae,* too, as well as the *defensor vinculi,* may have a just complaint against the former sentence, not indeed personally, but officially, because they are under the impression that the public welfare has been injured. These, too, therefore, may appeal. As a rule, an appeal is permissible in all cases of grievance, except those expressly exempted by law.

WHEN AN APPEAL IS FORBIDDEN

Can. 1880

Non est locus appellationi:

1.° A sententia ipsius Summi Pontificis vel Signaturae Apostolicae;

2.° A sententia iudicis qui a Sancta Sede delegatus est ad videndam causam cum clausula *"appellatione remota";*

3.° A sententia vitio nullitatis infecta;

4.° A sententia quae in rem iudicatam transiit;

5.° A definitiva quae iureiurando litis decisorio innixa est;

6.° A iudicis decreto vel a sententia interlocutoria, quae non habeat vim definitivae, nisi cumuletur cum appellatione a sententia definitiva;

7.° A sententia in causa pro qua ius cavet expeditissime rem esse definiendam;

8.° A sententia contra contumacem, qui a contumacia se non purgaverit;

9.° A sententia lata contra eum qui in scriptis expresse professus est se appellationi renuntiare.

The Code forbids appeal in nine cases, two of which affect the person of the judge, one (n. 3) the form of the sentence, and the rest its matter. An appeal is inadmissible, therefore,

1.° *From a sentence of the Supreme Pontiff or the Signatura Apostolica.* The Roman Pontiff is the highest judge of the universal Church, and therefore an appeal from his sentence is impossible. Appeal from the *Signatura Apostolica* is impossible because of its office and power.[2] An appeal in the proper sense is inadmissible also from a sentence of any of the Roman Congregations, which, however, decide, not judiciary but disciplinary matters, and hence are not especially mentioned.[3]

2.° From the sentence of a judge who took cognizance of the case in virtue of *papal delegation* with the clause,

2 Cfr. can. 259; can. 1603.   3 Santi-Leitner, II, 28, n. 6.

"appellatione remota." For this clause forbids an appeal.

In these two cases only one remedy is open, namely, the *restitutio in integrum* (see can. 1905–1907).

Here may be mentioned the penalty incurred by those who appeal from a sentence of the Roman Pontiff to a general council: it is excommunication *speciali modo* reserved to the Holy See.[4]

3.° *From a sentence which is null and void,* as may be seen in can. 1892 f.; because an invalid sentence is no sentence at all, and an appeal always presupposes a valid sentence.

4.° From a *sentence which has passed into a res iudicata,* as seen in can. 1902 f., unless the sentence has been executed with excessive rigor.[5]

5.° From a *definitive sentence* which has been pronounced in virtue of a *decisive oath,* because of the sacredness of the oath and on account of a species of contract.[6]

6.° From a *decree or interlocutory sentence of the judge,* which is not definitive, unless coupled with an appeal from a definitive sentence, when an appeal is permitted by reason of the connection. Otherwise not, *ne procedatur in infinitum.*

7.° From a sentence pronounced in a matter for which the law provides a speedy settlement, as against non-resident clerics,[7] or in case of appointment to offices.

8.° From a *sentence against a contumacious person* who has not purged himself of his contumacy, according to can. 1842 ff. (*"quia contumax non appellat."*)[8]

9.° From a sentence pronounced against one who has

4 Cfr. can. 2532.
5 Cfr. c. 15, X, II, 27; c. 33, X, II, 28.
6 Cfr. c. 54, X, II, 28; c. 20, X,
I, 29; Santi-Leitner, II, 28, n. 12.
7 C. 4, X, III, 4.
8 Reiffenstuel, II, 28, n. 303.

given a *written declaration that he will not appeal,* because this declaration is equal to a contract.[9]

With these exceptions, appeals are admitted in every case, whether important or insignificant. But there are certain formalities to be observed regarding the judges from, and those to whom, an appeal is made.

THE JUDGE A QUO

CAN. 1881

Appellatio interponi debet coram iudice *a quo* sententia prolata est intra decem dies a notitia publicationis sententiae.

CAN. 1882

§ 1. Appellatio fieri potest oretenus coram iudice pro tribunali sedente, si publice sententia legatur, statimque ab actuario scriptis redigenda est.

§ 2. Aliter facienda est in scriptis, salvo casu de quo in can. 1707.

An appeal must be brought before the *judge who pronounced the sentence,* within *ten days* from the time the sentence became known. If the judge is still sitting in court, and the sentence was publicly read, the appeal may be made there and then; but the clerk must put it down in writing. Otherwise the party may, within ten days, put in the appeal in writing and offer it to the judge; or employ a notary public (of the ecclesiastical court) to draw it up for him. A notary public is also required if the appeal is made orally before the judge, because then the judge shall order the notary to put it down in

---

9 Cfr. c. 54, X, II, 28; c. 25, X, II, 24.

writing. But the appeal must by all means be presented
to the judge who passed the sentence, otherwise it is invalid.[10]

THE JUDGE AD QUEM

CAN. 1883

Appellatio prosequenda est coram iudice *ad quem*
dirigitur intra mensem ab eius interpositione, nisi
iudex *a quo* longius tempus ad eam prosequendam parti
praestituerit.

CAN. 1884

§ 1. Ad prosequendam appellationem requiritur et
sufficit ut pars ministerium invocet iudicis superioris
ad impugnatae sententiae emendationem, adiuncto exemplari huius sententiae et libelli appellatorii quem
iudici inferiori exhibuerat.

§ 2. Quod si pars exemplar impugnatae sententiae
intra utile tempus a tribunali *a quo* obtinere nequeat,
interim termini non decurrunt et impedimentum signi-
ficandum est iudici appellationis, qui iudicem *a quo*
praecepto obstringat officio suo quamprimum satisfaci-
endi.

CAN. 1885

§ 1. Si casus de quo in can. 1733 contigerit intra terminum ad appellandum utilem sed antequam appellatio
interposita sit, sententia debet iis quorum interest de-
nuntiari eisque concessi intelliguntur termini a iure
statuti a die denuntiationis computandi.

§2. Si contigerit postquam fuerit appellatum, appellatio interposita eisdem denuntietur, in quorum fa-

10 C. 59, X, II, 28.

vorem a die denuntiationis denuo currere incipit tempus utile ad appellationem prosequendam.

The appeal must be prosecuted *before the judge to whom* it was directed, *within a month* from the date when it was lodged.

But the judge from whom the appeal was made, may fix a longer term for the prosecution of the case appealed. The judge *ad quem* is not determined here, but the rule is that he should be the one immediately superior. Hence from the diocesan court appeal should be taken to the metropolitan court. However, this latter may lawfully be omitted if an appeal is addressed to Rome. From the vicar general to the bishop no appeal is possible.[11]

In order to prosecute the appeal it is *required and suffices* that the higher court be implored to change the obnoxious sentence. A copy of the first sentence and the writ of appeal presented to the inferior court must be sent to the higher court. In case the party cannot obtain a copy of the sentence from the judge *a quo*, the time " does not run," *i.e.*, the lapse of one month must not be reckoned as fatal. But the obstacle must be reported to the court of appeal, who shall send peremptory notice to the lower court, admonishing it of its duty. If the appellant should die, or change his personal status, or go out of office (see can. 1733) within the term (of ten days) granted for putting in the appeal, but before the appeal was actually made, the sentence must be notified to those concerned, and the term for appeal runs from the day of the notice. If the case, as stated above, occurs after the appeal has already been made, the appeal must be made known to the parties concerned, and the

---

11 Cfr. cc. 4, 6, C. 2, q. 6; c. 1, 6°, I, 4: the vicar general and the bishop form *one* tribunal.

term (of ten days) runs from the days of the notice given (and, we suppose, received).

CAN. 1886

Inutiliter elapsis fatalibus appellatoriis sive coram iudice *a quo*, sive coram iudice *ad quem*, deserta censetur appellatio.

If the parties permit the term granted for appeal (*i.e.*, ten days for putting in the appeal before the judge *a quo*, and a month or thirty days for prosecuting the appeal before the appellate court), to expire, the appeal is supposed to have been dropped. These terms are called *fatalia*, because they prove fatal to a cause if not observed.[12]

EFFECT OF APPEALS

CAN. 1887

§ 1. Appellatio facta ab actore prodest etiam reo, et vicissim.

§ 2. Si interponatur ab una parte super aliquo sententiae capite, pars adversa, etsi fatalia appellationis fuerint transacta, potest super aliis capitibus incidenter appellare; idque facere potest etiam sub conditione recedendi, si prior pars ab instantia recesserit.

§ 3. Si sententia plura capita contineat, et appellans quaedam tantummodo capita impugnet, cetera capita exclusa habeantur; si nullum determinavit caput, appellatio praesumitur facta contra omnia capita.

---

12 Cfr. c. 28, C. 2, q. 6; c. 2, Clem. II, 12.

Can. 1888

Si unus ex pluribus correis aut actoribus sententiam impugnet, impugnatio censetur ab omnibus facta, quoties res petita sit individua aut obligatio solidalis; expensas vero iudiciales ille tantum sustinere debet qui appellavit, si iudex appellationis primam sententiam confirmaverit. .

Can. 1889

§ 1. Appellatio in suspensivo exsecutionem appellatae sententiae suspendit ac propterea in suo robore permanet principium: *"lite pendente nihil innovetur"*: appellatio autem in devolutivo tantum, non suspendit exsecutionem sententiae, licet· lis adhuc pendeat circa meritum causae.

§ 2. Omnis appellatio est in suspensivo, nisi aliud in iure expresse caveatur, firmo praescripto can. 1917, § 2.

Since the cause binds plaintiff and defendant, the right of appeal benefits both. Thus, if one party appeals within the proper time concerning one point of the sentence, say in a possessory cause, the other may appeal on another point of the same sentence, say in a petitory cause, even after the lapse of the "fatal" time. And this may be done conditionally, *e.g.*, if John recedes from his appeal, Joseph shall also withdraw. The writ of appeal shall state precisely what is intended. If no special point is mentioned, the appeal is supposed to be directed against the entire sentence. Therefore, if only one article of the sentence is attacked, this fact must be properly stated in the writ.

It may also be that there are several *plaintiffs or defendants* who oppose the sentence. In this case the appeal is supposed to be made by all, provided the litigious object is indivisible or the obligation binds *in solidum*. But the expenses are to be borne by the one who appealed, provided the second sentence ratifies the first.

The proper *effect* of an appeal is twofold, *viz.*, suspensive or devolutive. The *suspensive* effect of an appeal consists in stopping the execution of the sentence or suspending its effect. It is, therefore, not a quashing of the sentence, but merely a putting off. Hence whatever is attempted against or during a suspensive appeal, is revocable and considered as *attentatum*, wherefore the axiom must be applied: "*Lite pendente nihil innovetur.*" The regular or usual *effect* of each and every appeal is *suspensive*, unless the law states the contrary, and with due regard to can. 1917, § 2.

The *devolutive* effect of an appeal consists in this, that the superior judge draws the whole case before his court and first decides whether or not the appeal is to be admitted, but the sentence takes effect or is carried out, even though the merit of the issue is still pending. An example may be taken from the division of parishes.[18]

SECOND INSTANCE OR COURT OF APPEAL

CAN. 1890

Interposita appellatione tribunal *a quo* debet ad iudicem *ad quem* actorum causae authenticum exemplar vel ipsamet originalia acta causae transmittere ad norman can. 1644.

---

18 For cases *in devolutivo* see canons 345; 513, § 2; 1340, § 3; 1395; 1428, § 3; 2243, § 1.

Can. 1891

§ 1. In gradu appellationis non potest admitti nova petendi causa, ne per modum quidem utilis *cumulationis;* ideoque litis contestatio in eo tantum versari potest ut prior sententia vel confirmetur, vel reformetur sive ex toto sive ex parte.

§ 2. Sed novis exhibitis documentis et novis probationibus poterit causa instrui, servatis regulis traditis in can. 1786, 1861.

After an appeal has been properly lodged, the court from which (*a quo*) the appeal was made must forward to the court of appeal (*ad quem*) either the original acts of the trial or a copy thereof, as stated in can. 1644.

In the second instance no *new complaint or new doubts concerning the merit of the cause* may be admitted, even if the new complaint were brought by way of valid bulking of several actions (*utilis cumulationis*).[14] Wherefore the *litis contestatio,* or issue in pleading at the court of appeal, consists either in the ratification or the partial or total change of the former sentence.[15] On the other hand, if new documents and new evidence have been found which for any good reason and without fraud were not available in the first instance, the case may be prepared or brought up, provided canons 1786 and 1861 are duly observed. Thus the *instructor causae* of the court of appeal may have to insert the new findings in the acts of the lower court.

[14] Because the judge would overstep his limits as appellate judge if he were to decide an action not yet taken cognizance of by the lower court; Lega, *l. c.,* n. 509.

[15] Hence the formula: "*an sententia in casu sit confirmanda an infirmanda?*"

CHAPTER II

CAN. 1892

Sententia vitio insanabilis nullitatis laborat, quando:

1.° Lata est a iudice absolute incompetente vel in tribunali collegiali a non legitimo iudicum numero contra praescriptum can. 1576, § 1;

2.° Lata est inter partes, quarum altera saltem non, habet personam standi in iudicio;

3.° Quis nomine alterius egit sine legitimo mandato.

CAN. 1893

Nullitas de qua in can. 1892 proponi potest per modum exceptionis in perpetuum, per modum vero actionis coram iudice qui sententiam tulit intra triginta annos a die publicationis senteniae.

CAN. 1894

Sententia vitio sanabilis nullitatis laborat, quando:

1.° Legitima defuit citatio;

2.° Motivis seu rationibus decidendi est destituta, salvo praescripto can. 1605;

3.° Subscriptionibus caret iure praescriptis;

4.° Non refert indicationem anni, mensis, diei et loci quo prolata fuit.

CAN. 1895

Querela nullitatis in casibus de quibus in can. 1894, proponi potest vel una cum appellatione intra decendium, vel seorsim et unice qua querela intra tres menses a die publicationis sententiae coram iudice qui sententiam tulit.

CAN. 1896

Si pars vereatur ne iudex, qui sententiam, querela nullitatis impugnatam, tulit, praeoccupatum animum habeat et proinde eum suspectum merito existimet, exigere potest ut alius iudex, sed in eadem iudicii sede, in eius locum subrogetur ad norman can. 1615.

CAN. 1897

§ 1. Querelam nullitatis interponere possunt nedum partes, quae se gravatas putant, sed etiam promotor iustitiae aut defensor vinculi, quoties iudicio interfuerunt.

§ 2. Imo ipse iudex potest ex officio sententiam nullam a se latam retractare et emendare intra terminos ad agendum supra statutos.

This means of redressing a grievance against a sentence was looked upon as *extraordinary*.[1] However we hardly believe that it could now be so called, for it has entered the list of regular remedies of redress.[2] The text distinguishes *two kinds of nullity* that may upset a sentence or at least retard its execution: one is a curable and the other an incurable defect.

The sentence is *incurably null* in the following cases:
1. When it has been rendered by an *incompetent judge*,

---

1 Lega, *l. c.*, n. 477.
2 See can. 1905, which corroborates our opinion.

or, if there was a board of judges, by a number less than that prescribed by law. And here it must be borne in mind and emphatically stated that according to can. 1576 *three judges* are required for ordination and matrimonial cases, and for some criminal cases of removal or excommunication; whilst *five* judges must pronounce sentence in important criminal cases of deposition and degradation.[3] The consequences involved are too serious to overlook this ruling; for a sentence in matrimonial cases may be upset by the lack of the number of judges required by law.

2. When the sentence has been pronounced on parties one of whom was not entitled to bring suit in an ecclesiastical court (" *Non habet personam standi in iudicio* "; see can. 1646–1654).

3. When one has prosecuted a case in another one's name without being commissioned to do so (*sine legitimo mandato*). Hence a proctor, counsel, or administrator (cfr. can. 1520) cannot prosecute validly without a special commission.

The *mode* by which a complaint of nullity may be interposed is by way of a perpetual exception, which amounts to a peremptory exception when the judge is opposed and stopped in the execution of the sentence, or the party is stopped in vindicating a sentence pronounced in his favor; or by way of *action*, when the judge who pronounced the sentence is petitioned to declare his own sentence null and void.[4]

A sentence has a *curable defect:*

1. If the legitimate summons was omitted;

2. If it does not contain the reasons or motives that prompted the judge; exempt from this rule are sentences given by the Signatura Apostolica;[5]

3 The Directory of 1920 does not prove the adoption of this necessary requisite in all American dioceses.

4 Lega, *l. c.*, n. 510.
5 Can. 1605.

3. If the necessary signatures are wanting;

4. If the date and place are wanting; as to date, the year, month, and day are required.

Now the question naturally arises, who is the judge before whom this complaint of nullity must be lodged; for it appears that the *querela nullitatis* should be exclusively proposed to the judge who gave sentence (*iudici a quo*). First, it must be observed that a complaint against an incurable sentence can be counteracted only by way of a *restitutio in integrum*, according to can. 1905; because can. 1895 refers only to a sentence with a curable defect. Hence it states that a complaint against a curably defective sentence may be lodged either together with the *appeal*, within ten days from date of the sentence intimated,— and in this case the complaint must certainly be placed before the appellate judge —(*ad quem*)— or the complaint may be separately and solely brought before the judge who pronounced the sentence. For this complaint a term of *three months* is granted from the time the sentence was published.

If the complaint is made not by way of appeal, but separately before the judge who gave sentence, and *this judge* is *suspected* by the party of favoritism, said party may demand that another judge be substituted. However, since there is no appeal proper and the case remains in the same stage or instance, it is plain that a judge of the same instance must be substituted.

The complaint of nullity may be brought by the aggrieved parties as well as by the fiscal promoter or the defender, if they took part in the trial. The judge may *ex officio* retract or correct his own sentence within the time stated above, *i.e.*, within ten days by way of appeal, or within three months in case of a complaint of nullity.

CHAPTER III

CAN. 1898

Si sententiae definitivae praescriptum iura aliorum offendat, hi habent remedium extraordinarium quod *oppositio tertii* dicitur, vi cuius qui ex sententia suorum iurium laesionem verentur, possunt sententiam ipsam ante eius exsecutionem impugnare eique se opponere.

CAN. 1899

§ 1. Oppositio fieri potest ad recurrentis arbitrium sive postulando revisionem sententiae ab iudice qui eam tulit, sive appellando ad iudicem superiorem.

§ 2. In utroque casu oppositor probare debet ius suum revera esse laesum aut probabiliter laedendum.

§ 3. Laesio autem oriri debet ex ipsa sententia quatenus aut ipsa sit causa laesionis, aut, si exsecutioni mandetur, oppositorem gravi praeiudicio sit affectura.

§ 4. Si neutrum probetur, iudex, non obstante tertii oppositione, sententiae exsecutionem decernat.

CAN. 1900

Admissa instantia, si oppositor agere velit in gradu appellationis, tenetur legibus pro appellatione statutis; si coram ipso iudice qui sententiam tulit, regulae servandae sunt pro causis incidentibus datae.

CAN. 1901

Causa ab oppositore victa, sententia antea lata mutanda est a iudice, secundum oppositoris instantiam.

If a third person believes himself injured or hurt by a judicial sentence, he may lodge a complaint and oppose the execution of the sentence. This is an *extraordinary means* of *redressing a grievance*. The opposition or interference may be brought before the court that gave the sentence and a revision demanded of the same; or by way of an appeal to a higher court. But in any case the opposer must prove that his right has been curtailed or will probably suffer damage in future. For instance, a bishop may suffer in the case of a monastery or convent which is declared dependent on another bishop.[1] But it may also happen, in the case of nullity of a marriage, because of the attendant legitimacy.

The damage may arise from the sentence itself or from its execution, as, for instance, in the case just mentioned of legitimacy. If no proof is given, the judge must issue a decree of execution of the sentence.

If the complaint is admitted and the opponent proceeds by way of appeal, the *rules for appeal* must be observed. If he lodges the complaint with the judge who rendered the sentence, the question must be settled as an *incidental one*. If the opponent *wins the case,* the former sentence must be changed according to the wording of the complaint lodged by the opponent.

1 C. 17, X, II, 27.

TITLE XV

RES IUDICATA AND RESTITUTIO IN INTEGRUM

'A *res iudicata,* or adjudged matter, has the same effect as a definitive sentence, because it is supposed that no appeal was made or no complaint lodged against the sentence, and that no third person interfered or opposed the same. Besides, there are sentences against which no appeal is admitted, and which, therefore, should be carried into effect. However, there is an extraordinary means even against such a sentence, *vis.,* the so-called *restitutio in integrum.*

RES IUDICATA

Can. 1902

Res iudicata habetur:

1.° Duplici sententia conformi;

2.° Sententia intra utile tempus non appellata; aut quae, licet appellata coram iudice *a quo,* deserta fuit coram iudice *ad quem;*

3.° Sententia definitiva unica, a qua non datur appellatio ad normam can. 1880.

Can. 1903

Nunquam transeunt in rem iudicatam causae de statu personarum; sed ex duplici sententia conformi in his causis consequitur, ut ulterior propositio non debeat admitti, nisi novis prolatis iisdemque gravibus argumentis vel documentis.

CAN. 1904

§ 1. Res iudicata praesumptione iuris et de iure habetur vera et iusta nec impugnari directe potest.

§ 2. Facit ius inter partes et dat exceptionem ad impediendam novam eiusdem causae introductionem.

The Code determines very clearly when a *res* becomes *iudicata*, namely:

1.° After *two uniform sentences* have been pronounced on the same case, *i.e.*, in the first and second instance, or in the second and third instance.

2.° After a *sentence which has not been appealed* within the time granted by law. The same holds good when a sentence, though appealed to the judge who pronounced it, was not prosecuted at the court of appeals.

3.° After *one sentence* in cases in which no appeal is admitted, according to can. 1880. Certain cases never pass into the stage of adjudged matter because they affect the public welfare, which can. 1903 connects with the *status personarum,* or the personal state of the litigants, which certainly affects the clerical, religious, and married state. Therefore sentences passed on the validity of ordination, of religious profession, and of marriage do not become *res iudicatae,* even though the requisites of can. 1902 are verified.[1] Yet even these cases, if a double uniform sentence was pronounced, cannot again be proposed unless new and weighty evidence or documents are

---

[1] We hardly think that other cases, such as beneficiary or sentences of excommunication (Bouix, *l. c.,* II, p. 284 f.) would now be considered; concerning criminal cases, see can. 1701-1705.

produced, because judicial sentences are safeguards of public tranquillity and must be respected.

Can. 1904 enumerates the *effect of a res iudicata,* which are:

1. That it *creates a true and just praesumptio iuris et de iure* which can be attacked or upset only indirectly. This, of course, must be understood in the light of what was said on presumption (can. 1825 sqq.). A *res iudicata* is taken for a true and just sentence because the party accepts it, and the trial must be supposed to have been conducted properly.[2] Yet if the victorious party would admit the iniquity of a sentence, or if ocular inspection would prove that it was wrong, the sentence could be impugned, although only indirectly, *i.e.,* by the *querela nullitatis* or the *restitutio in integrum.*[3]

2. The second effect is that the *res iudicata establishes right* between the litigant parties, so that they are entitled to bring action for the execution of the sentence; that furthermore the parties obtain thereby the right of opposing the *exception* of *res iudicata* to any future action brought against them in the same matter.

RESTITUTIO IN INTEGRUM

CAN. 1905

§ 1. Adversus sententiam contra quam non suppetat ordinarium remedium appellationis aut querelae nullitatis, datur remedium extraordinarium restitutionis in integrum intra fines can. 1687, 1688, dummodo de evidenti iniustitia rei iudicatae manifesto constet.

---

2 Canonists used to say: "Sententia illa quae in rem transiit iudicatam tantae est auctoritatis, ut de ente faciat non ens, et de falso verum, et de albo nigrum." Reiffenstuel II, 27, n. 106.

3 Reiffenstuel, II, 27, n. 128 ff.

§ 2. De iniustitia autem manifesto constare non censetur, nisi:

1.° Sententia documentis innitatur, quae postea fuerint falsa deprehensa;

2.° Postea detecta fuerint documenta, quae facta
nova et contrariam decisionem exigentia peremptorie
probent;

3.° Sententia ex dolo partis prolata fuerit in damnum alterius;

4.° Legis praescriptum evidenter neglectum fuerit.

CAN. 1906

Ad restitutionem in integrum concedendam competens est iudex qui sententiam tulit, nisi ea petatur ex
neglecto a iudice praescripto legis; quo in casu eam
concedit tribunal appellationis.

CAN. 1907

§ 1. Petitio restitutionis in integrum sententiae exsecutionem nondum inceptam suspendit.

§ 2. Si tamen suspicio sit ex probabilibus indiciis petitionem factam esse ad moras exsecutioni nectendas,
iudex decernere potest ut sententia exsecutioni deman-
detur, assignata tamen restitutionem petenti idonea
cautione ut, si restituatur in integrum, indemnis fiat.

This remedy of redressing an evident injustice is called
an extraordinary one and means a re-instatement or return of the case to the state in which it was prior to
the sentence. Therefore it should be employed not as a
rule, but only in case the *injustice is manifest*. This
can be proved:

1.° By showing that the sentence was based on documents which were later found to be false or forged, as may happen in last wills and in baptismal or marriage certificates;

2.° By producing documents which peremptorily establish new facts that were formerly unknown and require an entirely contrary decision;

3.° By showing that the sentence was procured in favor of one party by the artifice or deceit of the other; but since deceit must be strictly proved, this process would require at least two trustworthy witnesses;

4.° By showing that the rules prescribed by law were set aside.

The *competent judge* for granting the *restitutio* is the one who pronounced the sentence, except in cases where the regulations prescribed by law have been neglected, when the court of appeal is competent to grant it.

A re-instatement suspends the execution of the sentence, if it has not already begun. But if the judge surmises that the *restitutio* was asked for merely to delay execution, he may *issue a decree* to the effect that the execution take place, but in that case bail must be given to the party demanding the restitution in order to safeguard indemnification.

TITLE XVI

TRIAL EXPENSES AND GRATUITOUS DEFENCE

This title is divided into two chapters, of which the first treats of the expenses of a trial conducted for such as are able to defray them, while the other sets forth the rules for gratuitous trials.

CHAPTER I

CAN. 1908

In causis contentiosis possunt partes adigi ad aliquid solvendum, titulo expensarum iudicialium, nisi ab hoc onere eximantur ad norman can. 1914–1916.

CAN. 1909

§ 1. Concilii provincialis, vel conventus Episcoporum est taxarum notulam ac regulam statuere in qua praefiniatur quid partes debeant pro expensis iudicialibus; quae sit retributio pro advocatorum et procuratorum opera a partibus solvenda; quae mercedis mensura pro versionibus et transcriptionibus; pro his examinandis et fide facienda de earum fidelitate; itemque pro exscribendis ex archivo documentis.

§ 2. Potest autem iudex pro suo prudenti arbitrio exigere ut pecunia pro iudicialibus expensis, pro indemnitate testium, pro honorariis peritorum debita a parte quae petit vel, si iudex ex officio agat, ab actore, antea deponatur penes tribunalis cancellariam aut saltem congrua cautio praestetur pecuniam deinde solutum iri.

CAN. 1910

§ 1. Victus victori iudiciales expensas regulariter reficere tenetur tum in causa principali tum in incidenti.

§ 2. Si actor vel reus temere litigaverit, etiam ad damnorum refectionem damnari debet.

CAN. 1911

Si actor vel reus partialiter tantum succubuerit, aut lis agitata fuerit inter consanguineos vel affines, aut de quaestione valde ardua actum fuerit, aut quacunque alia iusta et gravi de causa, poterit iudex pro' suo prudenti arbitrio ex toto vel ex parte inter litigantes expensas compensare; idque debet exprimere in ipso sententiae tenore.

CAN. 1912

Si plures sint in causa qui condemnationem ad expensas mereantur, iudex eos damnet in solidum, si agatur de obligatione solidali; aliter pro rata.

CAN. 1913

§ 1. A pronuntiatione circa expensas non datur appellatio; sed pars quae se gravatam putat, oppositionem intra decem dies facere potest coram eodem iudice: qui de hac re cognoscere denuo poterit, et taxationem emendare ac moderari.

§ 2. Appellatio a sententia circa causam principalem secumfert appellationem a pronuntiatione circa expensas.

Unless the parties are paupers, or quasi-paupers, they are to bear the expenses of *civil trials*. The charges to be made by diocesan courts should be established at a provincial council or meeting of the bishops, who should prescribe regular fees:

a) for the counsel and proctor;

b) for translations and copies of documents;

c) for the examination and verification of documents;

d) for the copying of certificates or documents from the archives.

The *sum to cover the judicial expenses* must be deposited with the court chancery, if the judge deems it appropriate, or be demanded in the form of bond or bail, either by the party who asks for a *deposition,* or by the plaintiff, if the judge orders a deposition. This sum should include the expenses of the trial for witness fees and the honorarium to be paid to the experts.

The loser must, as a rule, pay the expenses of the trial in the main as well as in incidental issues to the winner. Rash trials, *i.e.,* such commenced and prosecuted without a semblance of justice, entail indemnification to be paid by him who caused the trial, be he plaintiff or defendant.

The judge may, if he deems it prudent, *distribute the expenses* among both parties, in the following cases:

1) If the victory of either party is only partial;

2) If the parties are related to each other by consanguinity or affinity;

3) If the case was a very difficult one, or

4) For any other just and reasonable cause.

However, this sharing of costs must be properly mentioned in the sentence.

If those condemned to pay the expenses are several, and had a common cause, the judge must condemn each for the whole (*in solidum*), otherwise, *i.e.,* if they were only co-partners without a common obligation, each has to pay his share.

Appeal from the sentence condemning one to pay the expenses of a trial cannot be made separately or distinctly from the main appeal; but the party who believes himself aggrieved may oppose the sentence within ten days before the same judge, who shall reconsider his sentence and either change or modify the tax imposed. But an appeal against the sentence in the main issue also implies an appeal from the sentence condemning the party in question to pay the expenses.

CHAPTER II

CAN. 1914

Pauperes, si in totum impares sint expensis iudicialibus sustinendis, ius habent ad gratuitum patrocinium; si ex parte tantum, ad expensarum deminutionem.

CAN. 1915

§1. Qui exemptionem ab expensis vel earum deminutionem assequi vult, eam a iudice postulare debet, dato supplici libello, allatisque documentis quibus quae conditio sit postulantis quaeve eius rei familiaris copia demonstret; praeterea probare debet se non futilem neque temerariam causam agere.

§ 2. Iudex postulationem nec admittat nec reiiciat, nisi requisitis, si opus sit, notitiis etiam secretis quibus statum rei familiaris ipsius postulantis compertum habere possit auditoque promotore iustitiae; imo concessam potest etiam revocare, si in decursu processus assertam paupertatem non adesse compertum habuerit.

CAN. 1916

§ 1. Ad gratuitum pauperum patrocinium iudex in singulis causis eligat aliquem ex advocatis in suo foro approbatum, qui ab hoc munere explendo, nisi ex causa iudici probata, sese subducere nequit, secus a iudice congrua poena, etiam suspensionis ab officio, plecti potest.

§ 2. **Deficientibus advocatis, iudex Ordinarium loci roget ut aliam idoneam personam, si opus sit, designet ad pauperis patrocinium suscipiendum.**

Paupers who are entirely unable to defray the expenses of a trial are entitled to gratuitous defence; quasi-paupers, *i.e.,* such as are able to pay something, may have the expenses lowered. But those who claim either total or partial exemption from the payment of judiciary expenses, must submit a petition to the judge, in which they prove by documents that their financial condition entitles them to this privilege and, besides, that the reason for which they are going to law is solid and not rash. The judge shall neither admit nor reject the petition before he has ascertained (by secret information if necessary) the financial status of the petitioner, and heard the advice of the fiscal promoter. He may revoke the grant if he finds out afterwards that the poverty of the petitioner was a pretence.

After granting the petition, the judge shall, in each case, choose an *approved attorney* or counsel for the defence. This lawyer is not allowed to shirk the duty unless for a reason accepted by the judge. If he attempts to evade his duty, he may be punished by the judge, even to privation from his office of court attorney. If there are no attorneys, the judge may ask the Ordinary to appoint some other capable person to assume the defence.

TITLE XVII

EXECUTION OF THE SENTENCE

The text first considers when a sentence is ready for
execution, then the duties of the executor, and, lastly,
the manner or mode of execution.

THE TIME OF EXECUTION

CAN. 1917

§ 1. Sententia quae transiit in rem iudicatam, exsecutioni mandari potest.

§ 2. Iudex tamen potest sententiae, quae nondum
transiit in rem iudicatam, provisoriam exsecutionem
iubere:

1.° Si agatur de provisionibus seu praestationibus ad
necessariam sustentationem ordinatis;

2.° Si alia gravis urgeat necessitas, ita tamen ut, concessa provisoria exsecutione, per cautiones, fideiussiones aut pignora satis consultum sit indemnitati alterius partis casu quo exsecutio revocanda sit.

CAN. 1918

Non antea exsecutioni locus esse poterit, quam exsecutorium iudicis decretum habeatur, quo scilicet edicatur sententiam ipsam exsecutioni mandari debere;
quod decretum pro diversa causarum natura vel in ipso
sententiae tenore includatur vel separatim edatur.

Can. 1919

Si sententiae exsecutio praeviam rationum redditionem exigat, causa incidens habetur, ab illo ipso iudice, servatis de iure servandis, decidenda, qui tulit sententiam exsecutioni mandandam.

Since the *res iudicata* establishes a (subjective) right and precludes appeal, a sentence may be executed *after the matter has been adjudged.*

However, the judge may command *provisional execution* even before the sentence has become *res iudicata*, if

- a) The execution concerns payments or warrants necessary for support, as in the case of alimony;

b) For other urgent reasons. However, every provisional execution pre-supposes a guarantee for the other party's indemnification in case the execution has to be repealed. This is done by bail, bonds, or securities. In order to proceed legitimately to execution, a *decree* by the judge ordering execution is required. This decree may be either inserted in the writ of the sentence itself, or published separately.

Should the execution of the sentence require the *rendering of accounts,* as in cases of alienation or benefices, an *incidental question* arises, which is to be settled by the judge who pronounced the sentence of execution.

THE EXECUTOR

Can. 1920

§ 1. **Sententiam exsecutioni mandare debet per se vel per alium Ordinarius loci in quo sententia primi gradus lata est.**

§ 2. **Quod si hic renuat vel negligat, parte cuius in-**

terest instante vel etiam ex officio, exsecutio spectat ad iudicem appellationis.

§ 3. Inter religiosos exsecutio sententiae spectat ad Superiorem, qui definitivam sententiam tulit aut iudicem delegavit.

Can. 1921

§ 1. Exsecutor, nisi quid eius arbitrio in ipso sententiae tenore fuerit permissum, debet sententiam ipsam, secundum obvium verborum sensum, exsecutioni mandare.

§ 2. Licet ei videre de exceptionibus circa modum et vim exsecutionis, non autem de merito causae; quod si habeat aliunde compertum sententiam esse manifeste iniustam, abstineat ab exsecutione, et partem ad eum qui exsecutionem commisit, remittat.

The executor has to put the sentence into effect. He may be a *merus executor* or a *mixtus*. If he is a " mere executor," like a bailiff or a constable, he simply reads the tenor of the decree of execution and carries it out literally. But if he is a *mixtus* — which must be ascertained from the wording of the decree — he may take cognizance of eventual exceptions or objections made by the losing party concerning the mode and efficacy of the execution, and if convinced that the sentence is unjust, must refrain from execution and direct the party to the judge or whoever commanded the execution.

The execution should be carried out, either personally or through a delegate, by the *local Ordinary* of the diocese in which the trial was prosecuted in the first instance. If he refuses or neglects to put the sentence into effect, the interested party may demand execution from the court of appeal, who may execute the sentence *ex officio* in case of refusal or neglect of the lower court.

Concerning *religious*, the executor is the superior who pronounced the definitive sentence or delegated the judge.

MODE OF EXECUTION

CAN. 1922

§ 1. Quod attinet ad reales actiones, adiudicata actori re aliqua, haec actori tradenda est statim ac res iudicata habetur.

§ 2. Quod vero attinet ad actiones personales, cum reus damnatus est ad rem·mobilem praestandam, vel ad solvendam pecuniam, vel ad aliud dandum aut faciendum, quadrimestre conceditur pro implenda obligatione.

§ 3. Iudex potest terminum praescriptum vel reducere vel protrahere, ita tamen ut neque infra bimestre coarctetur, neque semestre excedat.

CAN. 1923

§ 1. In exsecutione peragenda exsecutor caveat ut quam minimum damnato noceatur, eaque de causa incipiat exsecutionem a distrahendis rebus quae minus ei necessariae sunt, salvis semper quae eius victui vel industriae deserviunt; et si agatur de clerico, salva honesta eiusdem sustentatione ad norman can. 122.

§ 2. Ad exsecutionem privationis beneficii iudex ne procedat contra clericum qui Sanctam Sedem adierit; sed si agatur de beneficio, cui adnexa sit animarum cura, Ordinarius provideat per designationem vicarii substituti.

CAN. 1924

Exsecutor utatur prius monitis et praeceptis erga reluctantem; ad poenas autem spirituales et ad censuras ne deveniat, nisi ex necessitate et gradatim.

An object gained by *real action* and adjudged to the plaintiff must be delivered to the latter immediately after the *res* has become *iudicata.* But in *personal actions* [1] a term of four months is granted to the one who is condemned to hand over a movable object, or to pay a certain sum, or to give or do something. However, the judge may reduce this term to two months or prolong it to six months, neither less nor more.

In executing the sentence, care must be taken that no unnecessary damage is inflicted. Therefore, the less necessary things must be taken first, but enough must be left for a man's support and the exercise of his profession or trade. In the case of clerics the *beneficium competentiae* must be applied. [2] No cleric may be deprived of his benefice by way of execution, if he has had recourse to the Holy See. If the benefice is one to which the care of souls is attached, the Ordinary shall appoint a temporary substitute.

The executor shall *first admonish and urge,* and proceed to spiritual penalties and censures only by degrees and in case of necessity.

1 See can. 1701.
2 See can. 122, Vol. II, of our Commentary, p. 67 f.

SECTION II

SPECIAL RULES FOR CERTAIN TRIALS

TITLE XVIII

WAYS OF AVOIDING TRIALS

Christians should avoid quarrels and their evil consequences, trials.[1] Therefore the legislator exhorts dis-
putants to compose their differences peacefully. This may
be done by compromise or by arbitration.

1 Cfr. I Cor. 6, 1 ff.

CHAPTER I

COMPROMISE

A compromise may be defined as the surrender of a supposed legal claim by peaceful settlement and for a consideration.[1] The effect of this is called composition or concord. This means should always be recommended by the judge when he is approached. A compromise may be offered before the party appears in court or when the parties have appeared, or at any other time that may be propitious for such an agreement. But the proposal should be made, not by the judge himself, to safeguard his authority, but by an intermediary person, especially a priest or synodal judge.

As to the rules to be followed, the *civil law* of each country must be obeyed, provided it does not clash with the divine and ecclesiastical law. Besides, the following rules must be observed:

1. *No compromise* is admissible (a) in criminal cases, (b) in civil cases which concern the solution of a marriage, (c) in beneficiary matters when the possessory title is involved, without the intervention of the ecclesiastical authority, (d) in spiritual things, as often as the payment of temporal goods is concerned, because of the danger of simony.

2. A *compromise is permitted*, (a) if merely temporal ecclesiastical property is concerned, (b) if spiritual things are involved, but can be dealt with separately, as, for in-

[1] See Harriman, *The Law of Contracts*, 1901, § 112.

stance, burial ground. But in those two cases the formalities prescribed for alienation must be observed, if the matter requires it, as stated in can. 1530 ff.

The *effect* of a compromise is called composition or concord.

The *expenses* must be shared equally by the parties, unless otherwise stated in the compromise.

CHAPTER II

If the parties, in order to avoid a trial, agree to commit the settlement of their dispute to one or more persons, there is a *compromise by arbitration*. This is two-fold, according as the *compromissarii* proceed under the *strict rules* of the law, in which case they are called arbiters (*arbitri*), or proceed according to the *rules of equity*, in which case they are known as arbitrators (*arbitratores*). But both kinds of *compromissarii* must observe the rules laid down in can. 1926 and 1927.

No one who has been under a declaratory or condemnatory sentence of excommunication or infamy may validly act as an *arbiter* (though he may be an *arbitrator*). Religious need the permission of their superiors to act as *arbitri*.

If neither compromise nor arbitration brings about the desired settlement, the dispute must be decided according to the rules laid down in section one of this Book.

TITLE XIX

CRIMINAL TRIALS

CAN. 1933

§ 1. Delicta quae cadunt sub criminali iudicio sunt delicta publica.

§ 2. Excipiuntur delicta plectenda sanctionibus poenalibus de quibus in can. 2168–2194.

§ 3. In delictis mixti fori Ordinarii regulariter ne procedant cum reus laicus est et civilis magistratus, in reum animadvertens, publico bono satis consulit.

§ 4. Poenitentia, remedium poenale, excommunicatio, suspensio, interdictum, dummodo delictum certum sit, infligi possunt etiam per modum praecepti extra iudicium.

The Church, being endowed with judiciary power over her members, has the right to take cognizance of, and to punish, crimes committed in defiance of her laws. However, in matter of fact, as our canon explicitly acknowledges (§ 3), criminal trials are now-a-days almost exclusively reserved for clerical offenders.

Can. 120 lays down the rules to be observed when a cleric is to be summoned by a civil or lay court: if the accused is of high rank (cardinal, bishop or prelate *nullius*), the permission of the Holy See is required; if he is of inferior rank (abbot,[1] priest, cleric, religious)

---

[1] Concerning an abbot we have our doubts whether the local Ordinary is competent to give permission; but can. 120 only mentions abbot *nullius* as requiring the consent of the Holy See if he is not

the Ordinary in whose diocese the trial is to be held, must give permission, or at least be informed. But official procedure against clerics is to be conducted before the ecclesiastical court.

It is scarcely necessary to add that the rules set forth in this title are *law everywhere,* and that no particular regulations opposed to these can be safely followed in criminal prosecution. The instructions of the various S. Congregations, including that of the S. C. EE. et RR., of June 11, 1880, are no longer in force for criminal procedure.[2] This fact should be carefully noted to avoid mistakes in conducting a trial and thereby, perhaps, exposing the procedure to the danger of nullity.

1. The *crimes* subject to criminal procedure must be *public.* A crime is defined in can. 2195 as an external and a morally imputable violation of the law, to which is attached a canonical sanction or penalty, at least undetermined. The crime is *public* if it is already divulged or has been committed under circumstances which make it liable to be divulged (can. 2197, n. 1).

2. *Exempted from criminal procedure* are the cases for which other penalties are sanctioned in law. These are:

a) Procedure against non-resident clergymen; can. 2168–2175.

b) Procedure against *concubinarii clerici;* can. 2176–2181.

c) Procedure against pastors who neglect their pastoral duties; can. 2182–2185.

ordinarius proprius of a religious plaintiff. The proper way would be to apply to the next highest superior of exempt religious, *viz.,* the abbot president, and, if the accused is a provincial, to the superior general.

2 This applies also to Benedict XIV's, "*Ad militantis,*" March 30, 1742; the Instruction quoted above see *Coll. P. F.,* Vol. II, p. 134, n. 1534, also Messmer, *Canonical Procedure,* 1897, Appendix. One accustomed to the old procedure is likely to make mistakes.

d) The procedure called *ex informata conscientia;* can. 2186–2194.

These cases then are not to be prosecuted in criminal form, but in the manner established by the respective canons.

3. Against crimes which may be prosecuted either in the civil or in the ecclesiastical court (*mixti fori*) Ordinaries, should, as a rule, not proceed if the accused is a layman and the civil authority is already prosecuting him, thus safeguarding the public welfare.

Mixed crimes are such as principally offend against religion, but also concern the public welfare. Such are sacrilege, perjury, blasphemy (even though not heretical), theft of ecclesiastical property, incestuous concubinage, clandestine marriage, bigamy.[3]

Note well the conditions for proceeding: the criminal must be a layman, and the public order in need of being restored. But one essential element of criminal procedure as we regard it is the restoration of the public order (see Book V). The Church, being the divinely appointed custodian of public morality, is entitled to prosecute such cases if the civil authority fails to perform its duty. Hence the ecclesiastical authority cannot be lawfully rejected as accuser before the lay criminal court, if the public welfare is involved and the civil law provides no punishment for such crimes. Spiritism in all its forms should receive more attention from our criminal courts.[4]

4. Penances and penal remedies (can. 2306–2313) excommunication, suspension, interdict, may be inflicted by *way of a precept,* without a trial, whenever the delinquency is fully proved. This is new law, except in so

---

3 Cfr. Werhz, *Ius Decretalium,* Vol. V, P. II, n. 805, p. 44.
4 The State should provide special asylums for demented subjects, where they can be treated individually.

far as the *suspensio ex informata conscientia* is concerned. Formerly censures, being looked upon as severe punishments, were held to require an ecclesiastical trial.

How the precept is to be observed, is stated in can. 2310.

CHAPTER I

Can. 1934

Actio seu accusatio criminalis uni promotori iustitiae, ceteris omnibus exclusis, reservatur.

Can. 1935

§ 1. Quilibet tamen fidelium semper potest delictum alterius denuntiare ad satisfactionem petendam vel damnum sibi resarciendum, vel etiam studio iustitiae ad alicuius scandali vel mali reparationem.

§ 2. Imo obligatio denuntiationis urget quotiescumque ad id quis adigitur sive lege vel peculiari legitimo praecepto, sive ex ipsa naturali lege ob fidei vel religionis periculum vel aliud imminens publicum malum.

Can. 1936

Denuntiatio scriptis a denuntiante subsignatis vel oretenus fieri debet loci Ordinario, vel cancellario Curiae vel vicariis foraneis vel parochis, a quibus tamen, si viva voce facta fuerit, scriptis est consignanda et statim ad Ordinarium deferenda.

Can. 1937

Qui delictum denuntiat debet promotori iustitiae adiumenta suppeditare ad eiusdem delicti probationem.

CAN. 1938

§ 1. In causa iniuriarum aut diffamationis, ut actio criminalis instituatur, requiritur praevia denuntiatio aut querela partis laesae.

§ 2. Sed si agatur de iniuria aut diffamatione gravi, clerico vel religioso, praesertim in dignitate constituto, illata, aut quam clericus vel religiosus alii intulerit, actio criminalis institui potest etiam ex officio.

Every criminal procedure involves three essential points — the accusation, the trial, and the sentence. Without any one of these the whole procedure would be null and void.

The first and most necessary step is the *accusation*, for, "where there is no accuser, there is no accused." But there is a noticeable distinction between judicial accusation and simple accusation, which is more properly styled denunciation.[1] The judicial accusation may be most properly called an *indictment*, which ensures legal action or procedure, and is (can. 1934) reserved to the *fiscal promotor*, to the exclusion of all other persons, even the local Ordinary. Hence the judicial accusation can be lodged only by an official who is the *promotor iustitiae*.

This official character of the accusation is apparent in the older Roman Law, which permitted only a magistrate to act as accuser when a criminal case was tried before the *comitia*. However, after the standing commissions

1 The English terms: indictment, presentment, warrant, do not accurately convey the Latin terms. *Indictment* comes nearest to official accusation, which is preferred to, and presented upon oath by, a grand jury. A *presentment* is the notice taken by a grand jury of any offence from their own knowledge or observation, without any bill of indictment laid before them. A *warrant* is an official precept authorizing arrest, distress or search, under the seal of a justice or court, but solicited by private persons. Blackstone, *l. c.*, IV, 289, 301 f.

(*quaestiones perpetuae*) had been introduced, about 149
B. C., the so-called *delatores* sprang up like mushrooms.
Any Roman citizen could come forward and prefer a
charge.[2] The ecclesiastical law, being, as to formalities,
largely modelled upon the Roman law, admitted as real
and formal accusers all those not expressly prohibited
by law. This is noticeable in Gratian's Decree. However, heretical tendencies made a partial departure from
the old methods necessary and gave rise to *inquisitorial
proceedings*, especially in heresy cases. In order that
these inquisitors may not act as *judges and accusers*, at
least one of them should be a promoter.[3]

The medieval inquisitors, taken mainly from the
Friars Preachers, acted in the name of the Apostolic See.
Besides these, the Ordinaries or Bishops were regarded
as *inquisitores nati*, each for his own diocese, and the
provincial councils, which had to be held every year, were
also charged with the duty of watching over the faith.[4]

This, broadly speaking, was the status up to the publication of the Instruction of 1880. For, although a summary proceeding had been introduced by the Clementine
Decretals and the *suspensio ex informata conscientia* by
the Council of Trent, yet the handling of criminal cases
remained stationary and was somewhat neglected. The
S. C. of Bishops and Regulars, by issuing the above
mentioned Instruction, which in fact was nothing else
but a compendium of former decisions, gave a new
impetus to criminal procedure. The Instruction states
the reason why the summary procedure was promoted,
namely, because the Church was hindered on every side
in the exercise of her judiciary action. It named the

2 Ramsay-Lanciani, *Roman Antiquities*, 1900, p. 332, p. 334.

3 Wernz, *l. c.*, p. 55, n. 817.

4 Bouix, *De Iudiciis Eccl.*, II, p.
365 ff.

diocesan court, *viz.*, the bishop, the vicar-general, and the *processus instructor,* as the chief factors in criminal procedure and required the co-operation of the fiscal promoter.

Now this *promotor iustitiae* has become so important that he alone is entitled to bring criminal action against offenders. This process, as stated, corresponds to our civil *indictment.*

Different from the indictment is *simple denunciation,* or, as we may call it for brevity's sake, the *warrant.* Canon 1935 defines the right and obligation of denunciation as follows:

1. Every Catholic has the right to denounce the crime of another, either (a) to demand satisfaction or indemnity, or (b) for the sake of justice, *i.e.*, that scandal may be repaired or evil counteracted. In the first case the motive is *personal interest,* and the case should therefore be classified among torts (such as libel and damage suits). In the second case the intention of the accuser is the restoration of justice, which suffers through any crime.

" *Quilibet fidelis* " must be understood in the light of the following considerations: (a) It is a mere denunciation; (b) where private interests only are involved, every believing person, *i.e.,* every Catholic, may be admitted, though formerly laymen were not permitted to act as accusers against clergymen;[5] (c) when the public welfare is concerned, as in cases of simony and others mentioned in § 2, can. 1934, anyone is admitted as accuser,[6] but with due regard to can. 1942, § 2, which says that

---

[5] C. 14, X, II, 20.

[6] Cc. 3, 7, X, V, 3. Practically it is true what Wernz (*l. c.,* P. II, n. 835) says, that *criminosi, excommunicati, inimici, infames, anonymi, plane ignoti* are not admitted as accusers, because their denunciation is worth nothing; but theoretically our text does not discriminate against them, except as stated above.

denunciation by manifest enemies and by mean and unworthy persons should be counted as nothing.

2. The *obligation* of denouncing another becomes urgent when (a) one is obliged to do so by law, or (b) by a special precept, or (c) in virtue of the natural law, which dictates that every danger to faith and religion and every menace of public evil should be averted.

Ad a) The *common law* makes denunciation imperative:

1.° Against *confessarii sollicitantes ad turpia* (can. 904; 2368, n. 2) ;

2.° When one knows of impediments to the reception of holy orders (can. 999) ;

3.° Or of the existence of matrimonial impediments (can. 1027) ;

4.° Or of the circulation of dangerous books (can. 1397) ;

5.° Or of clergymen and religious being members of Masonic sects (can. 2336).

Ad b) By *special precept* Ordinaries and religious superiors may command their subjects to denounce certain crimes or persons suspected of wrongdoing; this, however, greatly depends on the constitution of each respective congregation or order.

Ad c) In *virtue of the natural law* theologians and canonists, though with some shades of variance, hold denunciation (judicial, not evangelical) to be obligatory on

a) One who knows of a crime that is very detrimental to the *community* and has no other means to prevent the evil arising therefrom than denunciation. Such a one is obliged to denounce the crime, even though the act will cause him inconvenience.

b) One who knows of a crime that is hurtful or detrimental to a *third person*. In this case the duty of denunciation binds only if it entails no inconvenience to the denouncer.

c) One who knows of a crime that is hurtful *only to the perpetrator* himself, is under no obligation to denounce it.[7] Sacramental knowledge and professional secrecy always excuse from the duty of denunciation.

Can. 1936 describes the *mode of denunciation*. The accusation should be made in writing and signed by the accuser, or *orally* to the local Ordinary, the diocesan chancellor, or the rural dean or pastor (assistants or curates are not mentioned, and therefore can not lawfully accept a denunciation).

If a denunciation is lodged orally, it must be put in writing by the persons to whom it is made and *immediately forwarded to the Ordinary*. The latter clause has special significance, for it means that the ecclesiastics mentioned in the text as competent to receive denunciations, are not allowed to make investigation, summon witnesses or conduct a quasi-trial. Religious superiors must keep their hands off all matters pertaining to the Holy Office. If a subject is guilty of such a violation, the religious superior must denounce him, either directly to the Holy Office, or to the local Ordinary.[8]

Since the denouncer forms, as it were, one person with the fiscal promoter, the latter is entitled to demand all the evidence and the assistance of the accuser, in order to prove the crime (can. 1937).[9]

A damage or libel suit, which is of a personal or *private character*, necessarily requires a previous warrant or complaint by the party who believes himself injured; other-

---

[7] Cfr. Bouix, *De Iud. Eccl.*, II, p. 51; Sabetti-Barrett, *Theol. Moral.*, ed. 27, 1919, p. 180, n. 181.

[8] S. O., May 15, 1901 (*Coll. P. F.*, n. 2112); our Commentary, Vol. III, p. 110; can. 501, § 2.

[9] *Regulae S. R. R.*, Aug. 4, 1910, § 41 n. 1 (*A. Ap. S.*, II, 799).

wise no criminal action can follow. This is the practice in every civilized court, based on the assumption that the damage or defamation concerns private interests only. However, since the *clerical or religious state* is a privileged one in the Catholic Church, and injury or defamation brought upon any one of its members affects the whole state, especially if the injured member holds some rank or dignity, like prelates, it is but logical that only *official criminal action* may be brought against the delinquent. This rule applies also to cases where a clergyman or religious has defamed or injured another of his class (can. 1938). Here the *percussio clericorum* might enter, provided the offence was public and perpetrated in a scandalous manner.

CHAPTER II

To justify the term *inquest* for *inquisitio*, we refer to can. 1954, for *inquisitio* forms part and parcel of the inquisitorial acts to be delivered to the fiscal promoter. Hence the term is here to be taken for *judicial inquiry*, which is a preliminary and an absolutely essential part of criminal procedure.[1] There is an inquiry mentioned in can. 1939, but this is of a general character, and therefore may be called extra-judicial. Here the Code intends *judicial inquiry*, defining when and by whom it is to be made, how it should be conducted, and what follows when it is completed.

INQUEST — WHEN AND BY WHOM TO BE MADE

CAN. 1939

§ 1. Si delictum nec notorium sit nec omnino certum, sed innotuerit sive ex rumore et publica fama, sive ex denuntiatione, sive ex querela damni, sive ex inquisitione generali ab Ordinario facta, sive alia quavis ratione, antequam quis citetur ad respondendum de delicto, inquisitio specialis est praemittenda ut constet an et quo fundamento innitatur imputatio.

§ 2. Huic regulae locus est sive agatur de irroganda poena vindicativa vel censura, sive de ferenda sententia

---

[1] This process was formerly called *inquisitio pro informando iudice* or simply *processus;* S. C. EE. et RR., June 11, 1880, n. 10; S. O., Aug. 6, 1897, n. 3 (*Coll. P. F.,* nn. 1534, 1977); Messmer, *l. c.,* p. 53.

366

declaratoria poenae vel censurae in quam quis inciderit.

CAN. 1940

Haec inquisitio, quamvis ab ipso loci Ordinario peragi possit, ex generali tamen regula committenda est alicui ex iudicibus synodalibus, nisi eidem Ordinario ex peculiari ratione alii committenda videatur.

CAN. 1941

§ 1. Inquisitor delegetur non ad universitatem causarum, sed toties quoties et ad unam causam.

§ 2. Inquisitor tenetur iisdem obligationibus quibus iudices ordinarii, ac praesertim praestare debet iusiurandum de secreto servando deque officio fideliter implendo et abstinere ab accipiendis muneribus ad normam can. 1621–1624.

§ 3. Inquisitor nequit in eadem causa iudicem agere.

CAN. 1942

§ 1. Prudenti Ordinarii iudicio committitur statuere quandonam ea, quae praesto sunt argumenta, sufficiant ad inquisitionem instituendam.

§ 2. Nihili faciendae sunt denuntiationes quae ab inimico manifesto, aut ab homine vili et indigno proveniunt, vel anonymae iis adiunctis iisque aliis elementis carentes, quae accusationem forte probabilem reddant.

1. A special inquest is required in cases (a) where the crime is neither notorious nor entirely certain, viz., uncertain as to the fact or its imputability to the person denounced, but known only (b) through rumor and

hearsay,[2] or (c) by semi-official information, *viz.*, denunciation, complaint of damage, general inquiry made by the Ordinary, or in any other strictly extra-judicial way.

2. The *time* for the inquest to be held is *before* one is summoned or judicially cited.

3. The purpose of the inquest is to ascertain whether and on what ground the crime may be imputed.[3]

4. With *regard to the penalty* § 2 of can. 1939 states that an inquest must be held whenever a vindictive penalty or censure is to be inflicted — *ab homine* — or only a declaration of sentence is required, *viz.*, a declaration that the penalty or censure has been incurred. Comparing this text with can. 1933, § 4 it might seem that there is a contradiction, but this is not the case. For canon 1933 supposes the certainty of the crime. Besides, this inquest, as stated, has already given a legal turn to the procedure, and therefore legal means are required for inflicting the penalty.

The next question is, *Who* may act as *inquisitor?* Answer: The local Ordinary, *i.e.*, the bishop or his vicar-general, may personally conduct the inquest. The law is permissive rather than preceptive in this case, but it adds that as a rule the business of holding the inquest should be committed to one of the *synodal judges.* But the Ordinary may, for special reasons, *choose another,* who, according to the instructions of the Roman Congregations, should be a learned, righteous, and capable priest, or at least a cleric.[4]

The inquisitor is a *delegate,* and hence does not remain in office permanently, but is chosen for each single

2 Cfr. can. 2197; S. C. EE. et S. O., Aug. 6, 1897, n. 6; S. C. EE. et RR., June 11, 1880, n. 12.

3 On imputability, see can. 2199 ff.
4 S. O., Aug. 6, 1897, n. 6; S. C. EE. et RR., June 11, 1880, n. 12.

case (*ad hoc*) and needs special delegation for each. The conclúsion: " N. has been delegated for this case, hence he may act also in the next case," would, therefore, be entirely wrong and would nullify the whole procedure.[5]

The inquisitor is *under the same obligations* as the judge in ordinary, and must therefore give oath that he will keep the secret, conscientiously discharge his duties, and accept no donations or bribes.

The inquisitor *cannot validly act as judge* in the same case. The consequence is that a synodal judge chosen as inquisitor cannot *pro hac vice* also act as judge.

It is hardly necessary to add that the delegation must be given expressly, since the office of inquisitor is not attached to any particular judiciary office, either that of synodal judge, or of counsel, or of auditor and that the delegate must adhere strictly to his commission or mandate, the limits of which he may not exceed, if any are drawn in the writ.

The inquisitor should not proceed with the inquest until the Ordinary has prudently judged or decided that the evidence so far obtained is sufficient to institute a formal inquest. Hence it lies *with the Ordinary to give orders for the inquest.* What if the Ordinary doubts the sufficiency of the materials thus far collected? He may order other secret information to be gathered and call in witnesses who know the incriminated person and the accusers, and make them respond under oath to the questions put to them.[6] These depositions, of course, must be diligently kept, for they may be of service in the trial.

Can. 1942, § 2 proceeds to determine negatively the sufficiency of evidence, thus: *Denunciations should be counted for nothing* if: (a) they are made by manifest

5 S. O., *l. c.*   6 S. O., Aug. 6, 1897, nn. 3, 5.

enemies or by mean and unworthy persons; or if they are (b) anonymous and lack the necessary details to render the accusation at least probable.

"*Homines viles et indigni*" are persons of ill fame,[7] and, *a fortiori*, all who are infamous in fact or by law. But *vilis* may have another meaning, *viz.*, a low character. This would be the case if the accusation were prompted by a bribe or human respect.[8] *Enemies* are those who wish one ill and are ready to injure one, materially or spiritually. The word *manifest* implies that a considerable part of a community must know of this enmity of the accuser toward the accused.[9] The word *anonymous* is here used in a somewhat restricted sense, for anonymous properly means nameless, and nameless letters should, as a rule, not be accepted. Still the text does not reject them absolutely. It may be that a person does not wish to be drawn into a trial, and yet has strong evidence against another. The details demanded are circumstances of time (day, month, year, hour), of place and person (where, when, by and with whom the crime was committed), etc. No vague and general statements or flippant assertions made in anonymous letters can be accepted.

No other persons are excluded from the right of making denunciation. All that is required is that they be *Catholics*. Hence neither excommunication, nor the interdict, nor suspension debar one,[10] provided he possesses the qualities negatively stated in can. 1942, § 2.

[7] *Ibid.*, n. 1.
[8] *Ibid.*,
[9] C. 10, X, V, 1; Engel, *h. t.*, n. 9.

[10] Consequently the old view of canonists can no longer be held as to the class mentioned in the text.

MODE OF CONDUCTING THE INQUEST

CAN. 1943

Inquisitio secreta semper esse debet, et cautissime ducenda, ne rumor delicti diffundatur, neve bonum cuiusquam nomen in discrimen vocetur.

CAN. 1944

§ 1. Ad finem suum assequendum potest inquisitor aliquos, quos de re edoctos censeat, ad se accire et interrogare sub iureiurando veritatis dicendae et secreti servandi.

§ 2. In eorum examine servet inquisitor, quantum fieri potest et natura inquisitionis patitur, regulas statutas in can. 1770-1781.

CAN. 1945

Inquisitor, antequam inquisitionem claudat, potest promotoris iustitiae consilium exquirere quoties in aliquam difficultatem inciderit, et cum eo acta communicare.

After the inquisitor has been appointed and informed that the evidence at hand is sufficient, the *inquest may begin.* But it must always be conducted so *secretly* and *cautiously* that no rumor of the crime is allowed to get abroad, and the good name of no one, delinquent, accomplice, or any other person involved, is jeopardized (can. 1944). This, of course, implies *strict secrecy,* not only on the part of the inquisitor himself, as stated under can. 1941, § 2, but also on the part of all those whose assistance he may require for conducting the inquest.

The inquisitor may call in persons who are acquainted

with the accused, or with the accusers, or with the case
in general. The number of the persons that may be
summoned is not determined. Those who appear may
and must be put under oath to speak the truth and,
as stated, to keep the whole thing secret. The *procedure* for examining these persons is much the same
as that prescribed for the examination of witnesses (can.
1770–1781).

Our text says, "*quantum fieri potest et natura inquisitionis patitur.*" Hence it would hardly be advisable to
confront the witnesses.

The place of the judge is taken by the inquisitor.

No solemn or public summons is required.

If the inquisitor deems it prudent to repair to the domicile of the witness, the law does not forbid him.

In cases of *sollicitatio,* women may be heard in the
sacristy or some other unsuspected place.

If the inquisitor should meet with difficulties, says
can. 1945, he may *counsel with the fiscal promoter* and
communicate to him what has been done. But all this
must be done before the acts of inquisition are formally
closed. The *closing of the inquisitorial acts is required*
in order to mark a stage in the procedure. It is, however, left to the inquisitor to decide when the acts of
judicial inquiry are completed, or when the *conclusio in
causa* (can. 1860) is brought about; although no special
decree to that effect need be issued.

WHAT IS TO BE DONE AFTER THE INQUEST IS COMPLETED

CAN. 1946

§ 1. **Expleta inquisitione, inquisitor, addito suffragio
suo, omnia referat ad Ordinarium.**

§ 2. Ordinarius vel de eius speciali mandato officialis suo decreto iubeat ut:

1.° Si appareat denuntiationem solido fundamento esse destitutam, id declaretur in actis et acta ipsa in secreto Curiae archivo reponantur;

2.° Si indicia criminis habeantur, sed nondum sufficientia ad accusatoriam actionem instituendam, acta in eodem archivo serventur et invigiletur interim moribus imputati, qui pro prudenti Ordinarii iudicio erit opportune super re audiendus, et, si casus ferat, monendus ad normam can. 2307;

3.° Si denique certa vel saltem probabilia et sufficientia ad accusationem instituendam argumenta praesto sint, citetur reus ad comparendum et procedatur ad ulteriora ad normam canonum qui sequuntur.

After the acts of inquisition are closed, or the finding is complete in the judgment of the inquisitor, because the evidence is exhausted, he shall formulate his opinion, which is generally styled *votum*, but is here called *suffragium*. This *votum* should, we suppose, be put into writing, although the text does not expressly say so. Together with this statement the inquisitor shall submit his findings to the Ordinary, who has to read the acts carefully in order to come to a conclusion in the three possible hypotheses with which he may now be confronted.

The Ordinary (either the bishop or his vicar-general) may entrust the *officialis* (see can. 1573) with the inspection of the acts, but it requires a *special mandate* for each and every case. The Ordinary, then, or the *officialis*, shall issue a *decree* adapted to the conclusion resulting from the inspection of the acts:

1.° If the denunciation appears *groundless*, the decree

must so declare and be incorporated with the acts, which are then to be placed in the secret diocesan archives.

2.° If the *evidence* is *insufficient* to justify criminal prosecution, the acts must also be deposited in the secret archives of the diocese and the denounced person watched as to his conduct, asked concerning his behavior, and, if necessary, be served an admonition, according to can. 2307.

3.° If the evidence is *conclusive*, or at least *probable and sufficient* for criminal prosecution, the delinquent must be summoned to appear in court and proceeded against according to the rules that follow. The sufficiency of the evidence must be judged according to can. 1789–1791 and can. 1812–1818; self-confession according to can. 1750–1753.

CHAPTER III

CAN. 1947

Si reus interrogatus delictum confiteatur, Ordinarius, loco criminalis iudicii, utatur correptione iudiciali si eidem locus sit.

CAN. 1948

Correptio iudicialis locum habere nequit:

1.° In delictis quae poenam secumferunt excommunicationis specialissimo vel speciali modo Sedi Apostolicae reservatae, aut privationis beneficii, infamiae, depositionis aut degradationis;

2.° Quando agitur de ferenda sententia declaratoria poenae vindicativae vel censurae in quam quis inciderit;

3.° Quando Ordinarius existimet eam non sufficere reparationi scandali et restutitioni iustitiae.

CAN. 1949

§ 1. Correptioni locus esse potest semel et iterum, non autem tertio contra eundem reum.

§ 2. Quare si post alteram correptionem reus idem delictum commiserit, criminale iudicium instrui aut inceptum continuari debet ad normam can. 1954 seqq.

CAN. 1950

Intra fines can. 1947, 1948 potest correptio ab Ordinario adhiberi non solum antequam gradus fiat ad formale iudicium, sed etiam eo incepto ante conclusionem in causa; ac tunc quidem iudicium suspenditur, nisi tamen prosequendum idcirco sit quia correptio in irritum cesserit.

CAN. 1951

§ 1. Correptio adhiberi etiam potest, cum interposita fuit querela damni ex delicto.

§ 2. Quo in casu Ordinarius potest de bono et aequo, partibus consentientibus, videre et dirimere quaestionem de damno.

§ 3. Sed si censuerit quaestionem de damno difficulter de bono et aequo posse definiri, licet ipsi, remissa ordini iudiciario solutione huius quaestionis, per correptionem consulere reparationi scandali et emendationi delinquentis.

CAN. 1952

§ 1. Correptio iudicialis, praeter monita salutaria, debet plerumque coniuncta habere quaedam opportuna remedia, aut poenitentiarum vel piorum operum praescriptionem, quae valeant ad publicam reparationem laesae iustitiae aut scandali.

§ 2. Salutaria remedia, poenitentiae, pia opera reo praescribenda, mitiora et leviora esse debent iis, quae in criminali iudicio per sententiam condemnatoriam ipsi infligi possent et deberent.

CAN. 1953

Correptio censetur inutiliter adhibita, si reus remedia, poenitentias et pia opera sibi praescripta non acceptat aut acceptata non exsequatur.

Since the summons can be issued upon certain, or at least probable and sufficient evidence, it is plain that by *confession* here is meant a *judicial confession, i.e.,* one made in court. The Ordinary, therefore, should ask the person summoned: "You are accused of such a crime; do you plead guilty?" He may insinuate, in general terms, that proofs are available, in order to solicit a true answer. The question then naturally arises: *Is the defendant obliged to confess his guilt,* if he is guilty and is duly questioned by the Ordinary or his official? A probable opinion obliges the defendant to confess his guilt.[11] However, some authors deny this obligation if the punishment to be expected is very severe and there is hope of escaping it.[12] It is undeniable that the confession would simplify the procedure and also lessen the punishment.

We may add that the question must be put lawfully and that the answer must be given " freely and considerately," according to can. 1751. There is also in lay criminal practice a requisite stated which to us seems very reasonable: confession should not be admitted if made in consequence of any inducement of a temporal character, connected with the accusation, held out to the accused by a person who had some authority over the accusation.[13] For the voluntary character needed for confession would certainly be diminished under these circumstances.

We said that confession would lessen the measure of punishment. This is clearly stated in can. 1947, which

11 S. Thom., II-II, q. 69, art. 1; Messmer, *l. c.,* p. 101, answers " in the affirmative without exception," upon the authority of Konings, *Theol. Moral.,* n. 1072.

12 Thus Lessius, De Lugo, etc. — weighty authorities — quoted by Reiffenstuel, II, 18, n. 163 ff.; the consequence is that the confessor could not refuse absolution *in casu, vis.,* though the penitent refused to confess the guilt judicially.

13 Kenny-Webb, *Outlines of Criminal Law,* 1907, p. 375.

says that, after the confession or admission is made, the Ordinary may administer *judicial correction* or rebuke which is not identical with judicial penalty.

But there are *exceptions* to the employment of this expedient, and these are stated in can. 1948, which *excludes judicial correction.*

1. In all crimes, even though confessed, which are punishable by *excommunication* most especially or especially reserved to the Holy See, or which are punishable in law by privation of benefice, infamy, deposition or degradation (see Book V);

2. In all crimes which require only a *declaratory sentence* for incurring a vindictive penalty or censure, because *de facto* already incurred;

3. Whenever the Ordinary deems a *judicial correction insufficient* to repair the scandal given and to restore justice. This is left to the judgment of the Ordinary.

Aside from these cases the judicial correction may be administered *twice*, but not oftener. If the second correction has proved fruitless or ineffective to restrain the delinquent from committing the same crime again, criminal procedure must be applied or continued according to can. 1954 ff. If the text uses the term "*inceptum continuari*," it is because correction may be employed not only before the trial has begun, but at any time during the trial, until the *conclusio in causa, i.e.,* before the whole material is gathered and the acts are closed.

When correction is applied, the trial is *suspended*, provided the correction was effective, *i.e.,* the corrected person behaves himself (can. 1950).

Correction may also be employed in *criminal damage suits,* in which the Ordinary may, if the parties consent, settle the question of damages according to the rules of equity. If, however, the difficulty of an equitable settlement proves too great, the Ordinary may refer the matter to the civil court and in the mean while, by judicial correction, repair the scandal and endeavor to correct the delinquent (can. 1951).

Can. 1952 tells us in what *judicial correction consists, viz.*, in wholesome *admonitions*, combined with appropriate remedies, such as penances and good works, applied to the delinquent in order that he may publicly repair the disturbed order of justice and the scandal given. Of these penances mention is made in can. 2313, where special prayers, pilgrimages, fasts, alms, and retreats are recommended.

However, these remedies do not bear the character of a judicial punishment because the criminal trial has not yet begun, and hence they should be milder than those meted out after a condemnatory sentence.

From this it is apparent that the *monita salutaria* spoken of in our text must not be taken in the sense of a canonical or judicial admonition, equal to a triple or one peremptory admonition.[14] They are simply wholesome admonitions, but should not be made light of, because can. 1953 shows that, if spurned, they will pave the way for a criminal trial. Hence this canon states that if the delinquent refuses to accept or to use these remedies (penances and pious works imposed upon him) the *correction must be looked upon as ineffective* and the trial is to proceed.

14 See Messmer, l. c., p. 145, note 3.

CHAPTER IV

CAN. 1954

Si correptio iudicialis vel insufficiens sit ad reparationem scandali et restitutionem iustitiae, vel adhiberi
nequeat quia reus delictum denegat, vel inutiliter
adhibita fuerit, Episcopus, aut officialis, de eius
speciali mandato, praecipiat ut acta inquisitionis
tradantur promotori iustitiae.

CAN. 1955

Promotor statim conficiat accusationis libellum
eumque exhibeat iudici secundum normas in Sectione
Prima statutas.

CAN. 1956

In delictis gravioribus, si Ordinarius censeat cum
fidelium offensione imputatum ministrare sacris aut
officio aliquo spirituali ecclesiastico vel pio fungi aut
ad sacram Synaxim publice accedere, potest, audito
promotore iustitiae, eum a sacro ministerio, ab illorum
officiorum exercitio, vel etiam a publica sacrae Synaxis
participatione prohibere ad normam can. 2222, § 2.

CAN. 1957

Pariter si iudex censeat accusatum posse testibus
timorem incutere aut eos subornare, aut alio modo

iustitiae cursum impedire, potest, audito promotore iustitiae, decreto suo mandare, ut ille ad tempus deserat oppidum vel paroeciam quandam, vel etiam ut secedat in praefinitum locum ibique sub peculiari vigilantia maneat.

CAN. 1958

Decreta de quibus in can. 1956, 1957 ferri nequeunt, nisi reo citato et comparente vel contumace, sive post primam eius auditionem seu constitutum, sive postea in decursu processus; et contra eadem non datur iuris remedium.

CAN. 1959

In reliquis serventur regulae in Sectione Prima huius Libri traditae et in inflictione poenarum sanctiones in Libro Quinto statutae.

The Bishop or his *officialis,* provided the latter has obtained a special mandate to this effect, shall command that the *inquisitorial acts be handed to the fiscal promoter in the following cases:*

1. If judicial correction was considered insufficient to repair the scandal or to restore justice (can. 1948);

2. If the defendant denies the crimes imputed to him, in which case the judicial correction may not be employed;

3. If judicial correction was ineffective, according to can. 1953.

When any one of these three cases is verified, the fiscal promoter must immediately draw up a bill of complaint or accusation and present it to the judge according to the rules laid down in the first section of this Book (IV).

It will not have escaped the attentive reader that, in chapter III, on correction, there is not one word that

would insinuate any special formalities, such as writing
or decrees, of which we hear so often in civil procedure,
or even of keeping a record of the judicial correction
and its effect. Neither do we read of any formal canonical injunction after the admonitions have proved fruitless.[1] Are all these formalities to be omitted? It must
be remembered that a trial is based on an inquisition,
either by denunciation or formal complaint or by a general and special inquiry. The records of these proceedings must certainly be kept on file for further procedure.
In addition to this we believe that the judicial correction
must be so administered that it can be proved at the trial.
For the defence is undoubtedly entitled to ask whether
and how the judicial correction was made use of. Besides, the fiscal promoter, who receives the inquisitorial
acts and an abstract thereof, needs an official statement
that the judicial correction was duly served.[2] Hence we
conclude that the Ordinary or his *officialis* must put the
fact that judicial correction was made, on record, or give
a written statement why, in virtue of can. 1948, it has
been omitted. If the correction has proved fruitless, according to can. 1953, there is some similarity between the
former injunction and our admonitions. As the violation of injunctions was proved by simply producing the
writ and the record of its having been served, so may the
violation or non-acceptance of correction be proved. But
this requires either a written document or two witnesses,
ecclesiastics or laymen, because at least moral certainty is
required.[3]

The text says that the writ of complaint or accusation
must be exhibited according to the rules for procedure

---

[1] *Instructio S. C. EE. et RR.*,
June 11, 1880, nn. 6-8; Messmer,
l. c., p. 144 f.

[2] *Instructio cit.*, n. 32 f.
[3] *Ibid.*, nn. 15, 16, 8.

in general. These rules are contained in canons 1706–1710.

Here we may also draw attention to the fact that the term *judge* occurring in the singular by no means excludes what can. 1576 establishes concerning a board of judges, either three or five, as the nature of the case requires. For there can be no doubt that, if the case requires a collegiate body of judges, the whole trial would be null and void were this rule set aside.

After the bill of complaint has been presented, the *next step is properly and legally to summon* the accused or defendant. Here, again, canons 1711–1725 must be recalled. The accused, when duly summoned, will either appear or not appear. In the latter case he must be declared in contempt, according to can. 1842–1851. If he appears, he shall be granted a first hearing, as stated under can. 1742–1746, but the oath cannot lawfully be demanded of him. For the rest, says can. 1959, the rules laid down in the first section of this book, and for inflicting penalties the canons of the fifth book, must be observed.

There are two canons, one of which provides for the dignity of the sacred ministry and the other for a just procedure. If the *crime is of a very serious nature*, and the Ordinary is of the opinion that the faithful would be scandalized if the incriminated cleric should exercise the sacred ministry or perform spiritual functions or pious exercises or publicly receive holy Communion, he may, after having heard the promoter's advice, forbid the exercise of the sacred ministry or of spiritual ecclesiastical functions, and the public reception of Communion. This is a kind of suspension, but without penal character,[4] and therefore irregularity would not follow its

4 See can. 2222, § 2.

violation.   Note the terms, *spiritual* functions and *public* reception, which indicate that neither temporalities nor secret reception are forbidden.

Justice and safety require that witnesses be not intimidated or bribed.   Hence if the judge fears that this is being done, he may consult with the fiscal promoter, and then issue *a decree* commanding the defendant for the time being to leave the town or parish or to repair to a place assigned to him, and there remain under suspension.   In the meantime, of course, if the defendant should be a pastor, a substitute must be furnished at his expense.

Title XX, On Matrimonial Trials, has been treated in Vol. V of this Commentary, pp. 400–439.

Title XXI, On Ordination Trials, has been explained in Vol. IV, pp. 550–557.

PART II

THE PROCESSES OF BEATIFICA-
TION AND CANONIZATION

INTRODUCTION

Since these processes are exclusively reserved to the Holy See and are conducted by the S. Congregation of Rites, which alone is competent in this important matter, it would be presumptuous to comment on these canons.[1] Therefore, a brief summary must suffice. The canons referring to *the ordinary power* of the *local Ordinary* will be pointed out as they occur. The *Vicar-General needs a special mandate* (can. 2002) for each and every case.

Canonization is an act by which the Sovereign Pontiff definitely and, we may add, infallibly declares an individual who died in communion with the Church to be a Saint and deserving of the veneration of the universal body of the faithful.

Beatification is a preliminary step to this solemn act and localizes, as it were, the veneration to the individual who is declared *beatus*.

The *mode* of *procedure* in both cases is twofold: *viz.: per viam ordinariam non cultus* or *per viam extraordinariam casus excepti seu cultus,*— the difference being that the *ordinary* method presupposes, before any discussion on the heroic virtues is admitted, that no veneration has been

1 Neither do we desire to copy the classical work of Benedict XIV, *De Servorum Dei Beatificatione et Beatorum Canonizatione*, 4 Vols.

given to the person in question, or, if such was given *per abusum*, that it has been lawfully abolished. The *extraordinary* process consists in proving the existence of a standing public and ecclesiastical cult bestowed upon the person or persons in question. But each individual case must be individually examined, unless martyrs are under discussion who suffered in the same persecution and at the same place. An instance are our English martyrs, some of whom were put to death at the same time and in the same place.[2]

Historically the earliest was, of course, the veneration of the martyrs, two classes of whom are already mentioned in the fourth century: *martyres vindicati et non vindicati*, according as they were recognized or not by the ecclesiastical authority. St. Augustine briefly describes[3] the process of recognition. The bishop in whose diocese a martyr died, began the investigation by collecting the documents and forwarding them to the primate or metropolitan. The latter took cognizance of the acts, heard the bishop's view, and, after due deliberation, declared his own opinion as to whether or not the martyr should be publicly honored. It goes without saying that the veneration of martyrs as well as the celebration of their anniversaries were at first purely local festivals. But soon one church adopted the commemorations of another, and thus the festivals of the most distinguished saints came to be celebrated outside their own dioceses.[4] An investigation was required, so that the honors due to Saints were not given to heretics and schismatics.

In course of time there came to be associated with the martyrs certain *holy confessors*, that is, *ascetae* or

2 Cfr. Bede Camm., O.S.B., *The English Martyrs*.

3 *Breviculus Collationis cum Donatistis*, l. III, n. 11 ff. (Migne, P. L., 43, 629 ff).

4 Duchesne-McClure, *Christian Worship*, 1903, p. 284.

solitary monks, whose life was regarded as a continuous martyrdom (St. Martin of Tours, St. Antony the Great, St. Simeon Stylites, etc.).[5] Whether this custom of venerating confessors was prevalent already in the fourth century or arose only in the eight, as some believe, is immaterial for our purpose.[6]

From the tenth century onward canonization came to be reserved to the Apostolic See, although some bishops continued to "canonize" until the pontificate of Alexander III (1159–1181), who issued the well-known Decretal on the Relics and Veneration of the Saints,[7] summarized in the words: "Without the permission of the Pope no one may be venerated as a Saint." Ever since this has been law in the Church, and subsequent papal constitutions[8] merely determined the method of procedure, which is now cast into legal form. We will give a brief conspectus:

4. Extraordinary trial *per viam cultus* or *causus excepti*.
5. Trial of Canonization.

From this sketch it will be seen that the activity of the Ordinaries is limited to the preliminaries of the ordinary trial.

The *persons* who hold special offices are (1) the *actor*, or petitioner, who may be any faithful Catholic or congregation (women must be represented by proxy); (2) the *postulator*, who promotes and treats the case at the competent tribunal; he must be a priest, either secular or religious, and have his residence in Rome; (3) vice-postulators are admitted, but require a special mandate.

One of the Cardinal-consultors of the S. Congregation of Rites, designated by the Pope, acts as *cardinal relator*.

5 *Ibidem*, and *Le Ceremonie della Canonizzazione*, Rome, 1897, p. 11 ff.
6 See *Cath. Encycl.*, Vol. II, 365.
7 C. 1, X, III, 45.
8 Especially Urban VIII, "Coe-

lestis Hierusalem," July 5, 1634; Bened. XIV, "Ad sepulchra," Nov. 23, 1741; also S. Rit. C., *Instructio*, 1878.

1. Persons at the Trial
{
Petitioners, Postulators, Cardinal Relator, Promotor fidei, Subpromotores, Notary, Secretary, Advocates
}

2. Evidence Required
{
Evidence in General, Witnesses and Experts, Documents.
}

3. Ordinary Trial of Beatification

a) Process to be instituted by the Ordinary *iure proprio*.
{
Inquiry into the writings, Informative process
Inquest into non-cultus
Transmission of the acts.
}

b) Introduction of the trial at the S. Congregation.
{
Revision of the writings
Discussion of the informative process
Discussion of the non-cultus
}

c) Apostolic trial.
{
Instructio Processus
Validity of the Apostolic process
Heroic virtues or martyrdom, miracles.
}

The *fidei promotor* is appointed to defend the law and must always be summoned. The one employed by the S. Congregation is appointed by the Roman Pontiff, goes by the name of *promotor generalis fidei,* and is assisted by the assessor of the S. Congregation; he is called *subpromotor generalis fidei*. But a *promotor fidei* may also be appointed by the Ordinary.

Besides these persons, a *notary* must be appointed from among the protonotaries apostolic for trials at the S. Congregation, and a diocesan notary for the inquiries to be made by the diocesan court. *Religious* cannot be notaries except in case of necessity, and in trials concerning their own order they cannot be notaries at all.

A secretary or *cancellarius, advocates* (counsels), and *proctors* must or may also be employed, but the latter two must be doctors in Canon Law and at least licentiates in theology.

The next title of the Code treats of *evidence;* first in general. The proofs must be full (*plenae*) and no others are admitted. Four *witnesses* are required to establish the fact that no worship was paid to the Servant of God; at least eight are necessary to prove the fame of his virtue, his martyrdom and his miracles. To give evidence of virtue and martyrdom eye-witnesses are required, and historical documents are admitted only as aids. However, in ordinary trials concerning ancient cases, and in extraordinary trials, hearsay and public rumor are admitted together with authentic contemporary documents.

Any one who was acquainted or familiar with the Servant of God, also his relatives and servants, including non-Catholics and infidels, may be admitted as witnesses; but the confessor, the postulator, the *advocatus*, and the judge are excluded.

All the faithful are obliged to submit whatever evidence they may have against the virtues, miracles, and martyrdom. *Religious* of both sexes must forward such information under seal directly to the Ordinary, and their superiors are not allowed to inspect such letters. The superiors should take care that their subjects present themselves for deposition, but should not compel them to testify favorably or unfavorably.

Experts are principally the physicians who examine miraculous cures; they must submit a written report under oath.

The *documents* demanded by the postulator must be presented in full and must contain a declaration as to their origin and authenticity. Extra-judicial documents furnish no proof of sanctity or martyrdom; neither do eulogies and funeral sermons, and much less testimonies solicited by the friends of the Servant of God, even though given by illustrious persons. Neither are historical accounts sufficient proof, *per se,* unless inserted in the acts proper.

Title XXIV details the *process of beatification per viam non-cultus.* The preliminary requisite is that of *giving oath.* This must be administered to the local Ordinary as well as to the Apostolic delegate, also to the judges, the *promotor fidei,* the notary, the secretary, and to the witnesses, experts, translators, and interpreters. The object of this oath is to insure strict secrecy and to induce all participants to do their duty conscientiously.

The *postulator* and *vice-postulator* must swear that they will tell the whole truth and employ no fraudulent means. The formula for this oath is a special one, prescribed by the S. Congregation of Rites.[9]

[9] S. Rit. C., Oct. 5, 1678, § 1, n. 5.

CHAPTER I

Chapter I of this title (canons 2038–2064) refer particularly to the *duties of the local Ordinary*.

The *petition* for introducing a cause of beatification must be directed to the Apostolic See. But before it is admitted, the truth must be juridically established concerning the purity of doctrine of the deceased Servant of God, the fame of his sanctity, the virtues and miracles he wrought, the fact of martyrdom, and the absence of any peremptory obstacle; finally concerning the fact that no public worship has been paid to him. Hence the *postulator* must petition the Ordinary: 1. To see to it that the *writings* of the Servant of God be requisitioned, *i.e.*, seized and examined; 2. To arrange the formal inquiry (*processus informativus*), into his fame of sanctity, his virtues in general, or his martyrdom, the cause of his martyrdom, and his miracles; 3. To institute an inquiry as to the *non-cultus*.

The competent Ordinary in this matter is he in whose diocese the Servant of God died, or in whose diocese the miracles have happened. If the Ordinary himself is related to the Servant of God, he shall delegate another to conduct the trial.

If an inquiry was instituted within the past thirty years into the fame of sanctity or martyrdom of the Servant of God, but was interrupted before the case was introduced at Rome, the Ordinary or his successor must inquire into the continuation of the fame.

The *judge* is the Ordinary himself, or a priest delegated by him. If a delegate conducts the trial, two other judges, taken from the college of synodal judges, must be chosen by the Ordinary. All this must be done by a formal *decree.*

The *acts* must be closed and sealed after every session.

Art. I

INQUIRY INTO THE WRITINGS OF THE SERVANT OF GOD

1. The term "writings" comprises all published and unpublished works, sermons, letters, diaries, autobiographies and manuscripts of every kind left by the Servant of God.

2. The *faithful* must be publicly exhorted to deliver up all his writings which they may have in their possession. If a religious is concerned this publication must be made in every religious house, and the superiors are obliged to see to it that it is properly done.

The *promotor fidei* shall see to it that the publication is also made in other places, where any writings may be found.

3. The Ordinary, urged by the *promotor fidei*, shall *officially search* for all such writings. If writings of the Servant of God are likely to be found in *another diocese,* he shall ask the Ordinary of that diocese to do the same, according to law (especially can. 2043) and forward anything he may find.

4. Those who wish to *retain autographs* of the Servant of God must allow the notary to take an authentic copy thereof, to be sent to the S. Congregation. Writings found in *libraries or archives,* whence they cannot be withdrawn, should be faithfully copied or photographed,

and authenticated by the notary; if no copy can be obtained, the matter must be referred to the S. Congregation.

5. The notary must carefully describe the *number and quality* of the writings, and the acts must be *signed* by the Ordinary or his delegate, and the *promotor fidei*, and *sealed* with the Ordinary's seal.

6. The *postulator* must give oath that he will make a careful requisition. If the Servant of God is a *religious* of a female institute, the Mother General must give the same oath and testify that all the writings of the Servant of God have been delivered up by her and her subjects.

7. In case of a *martyr*, the requisition may be made after the commission has been appointed by the S. Congregation.

Art. II

THE INFORMATION PROCESS

1. The *processus informativus* is to be instituted by the *Ordinary*. If it was not begun until thirty years after death of the Servant of God, no further procedure is allowed except after proof is furnished that the delay was not due to fraud, deceit, or culpable negligence.

2. The *witnesses* to be examined (can. 2019 f.) concerning the fame of sanctity, martyrdom, or miracles, are not required to testify specifically, but general testimony as to the growth and existence of the rumor among honest and serious persons is sufficient.

The witnesses are to be queried by the judge as to their knowledge of the life, virtues, miracles, and martyrdom of the deceased, how they obtained their knowledge, and whether it is of the nature of public rumor.

Then they must answer to the questions put by the promoter of faith.

3. The acts of the inquiry may not be closed before all the letters and papers of the faithful and the friends and acquaintances of the deceased (see can. 2023-2025) have been inspected by the *promotor fidei*. After all the testimony has been gathered the tribunal shall, upon having heard the *promotor fidei*, give notice to the postulator to bring forward whatever he has within a fixed term.

4. The *judge*, then, if the *promotor fidei* is satisfied, shall command the notary to publish the acts of the inquiry, which shall be copied by a clerk designated by the tribunal. The copy shall be in hand-writing (typewriting forbidden). It is to be collated with the original in the presence of one of the judges and of the *promotor. fidei*, and then signed by the notary, the judge, and the promotor, and sealed.

After the collation, the *original* acts are closed and sealed, and placed in the diocesan archives, never to be opened without the permission of the Apostolic See. The *abstract* is closed and sealed with the seal of the Ordinary. The notary shall make two copies of it, one of which is to be forwarded to Rome, the other to be kept in the diocesan archives.

ART. III

INQUIRY INTO THE NON-CULTUS

Besides the two witnesses produced by the postulator, the tribunal shall introduce two more, who shall testify whether or not the Servant of God ever received a *public worship*. Besides, the tribunal shall carefully inspect his grave, the place (or house) where he lived and died, and other places where indications of a cult may be suspected.

If the inquiry brings to light indications which show that public worship was paid, the *promotor fidei* must insist upon further investigation and the tribunal *must give sentence* as to the existence of such worship.

ART. IV

TRANSMISSION OF THE ACTS TO ROME

1. As soon as the Ordinary has obtained the *writings,* he must *forward them to Rome,* together with a judicial report as to the care with which the requisition was conducted. If other writings are found while the trial is going on in Rome, they must be immediately forwarded and inspected there before any further progress can be made.

2. The *abstract of the informative process* must be delivered by the Ordinary to the postulator, who shall send it to the S. Congregation. At the same time he (the postulator) shall forward *letters from the judges* addressed to the S. Congregation, and *letters of the (diocesan) promotor fidei* to the promotor general of faith, in order that the S. Congregation may be informed of the trustworthiness of the witnesses and the legal formalities of the acts. For this purpose the Ordinary shall also send a description or copy of the seal with which the abstract was sealed.

3. Finally the Ordinary shall have the postulator to send the complete result of the inquiry into the fact of *non-cultus* to the S. Congregation.

CHAPTER II

INTRODUCTION OF THE CASE AT ROME

1. The *first* investigation to be made is the *revision of the writings* of the Servant of God. The *revisors,* chosen by the *Cardinalis ponens,* must be priests and doctors of divinity, and must give their opinion in writing. This examination is made to ascertain the purity of doctrine with regard to faith and morals and the virtues or defects that may be gathered from these writings. The final judgment, whether further procedure is permitted, lies with the Supreme Pontiff.

2. The second investigation concerns the *processus informativus* sent by the Ordinary through the postulator. The papers are to be examined materially and formally, and objections brought up by the *promotor fidei generalis* to be answered. The final judgment is pronounced at a congress of Cardinals, by the *Cardinalis ponens,* in the form of a doubt: "*An signanda sit commissio introductionis causae in casu et ad effectum de quo agitur.*" If the answer of the Cardinals is favorable, a commission for the introduction of the case is appointed. After that the *local Ordinaries* can do nothing more without the permission of the S. Congregation, and it is *strictly forbidden* to call the Servant of God whose case has been introduced, "*Venerable.*"

3. The third investigation regards the *non-cultus,*—whether the sentence of the diocesan court is to be ratified or not. If traces of worship have been found, the case is suspended until every vestige has been removed.

396

CHAPTER III

If a decree of *non-cultus* has been issued, the *Sovereign Pontiff* is asked for the *litterae remissoriales,* which are given by the Cardinal Prefect and permit the trial to be instituted.

Art. I

INSTITUTION OF THE TRIAL

Two *distinct trials* are to be arranged: one concerning the *fame* of sanctity, miracles, or martyrdom; the other concerning the *virtues and miracles* in particular, or concerning the *martyrdom.* The first trial may be omitted if the Cardinal Prefect and the *promotor fidei generalis* deem it superfluous or inexpedient to inquire anew into the continued fame of sanctity.

Here the services of the *Ordinary* may again be required. If important eye-witnesses are in danger of death, or cannot be obtained at the time the trial concerning the virtues and miracles or the martyrdom is to be conducted, so-called *litterae remissoriales* are sent out to at least five judges (if possible, dignitaries), one of whom is the Ordinary, who shall act as presiding officer — now no longer *iure ordinario,* but *delegato.*

In the trial concerning the miracles an expert must be chosen. Besides the *promotor fidei generalis* shall by letters patent choose *two subpromotors* and send the interrogatories to these, who, however, shall not open the envelope until the examination begins. The delegated judge must present their credentials to the Ordinary.

After all these preliminaries are completed, the presiding officer shall convoke the tribunal within at least three months after notice was received, and the trial should be finished within two years. Before it is closed, the remains of the deceased Servant of God must be juridicially examined. The acts must then be forwarded to Rome.

Art. II

JUDGMENT OF THE VALIDITY OF THE TRIAL

After these acts have been forwarded to Rome, the S. Congregation shall judge of the validity of the procedure, hear the promoter general, and finally give judgment. This is done in the presence of the Cardinal Prefect, the *Cardinalis ponens,* and three other Cardinals of the same Congregation, the Secretary, the protonotary apostolic, the promoter general, and the subpromoter.

Art. III

JUDGMENT ON THE HEROIC VIRTUES

The discussion of the virtues cannot be begun before *fifty years have elapsed since the death of the Servant of God.* The discussion concerns his practice of the theological virtues and of the four cardinal virtues (prudence, justice, temperance, fortitude), especially whether he possessed them in a heroic degree.

In the case of *martyrs,* the question is concerning the cause of their martyrdom, and the signs and miracles wrought. Difficulties are raised by the promoter general and answered by the advocates. Everything has to be taken down in writing. The Supreme Pontiff is informed of the result of the discussion, and afterwards a general congregation is held by the Cardinals of the S. Congregation, its prelates, officials, and consultors. The judgment whether the heroic degree of these virtues is verified, remains with the Pope, who commands the Secretary of the S. Congregation to issue a decree if the judgment was favorable. After the issuance of this decree the Servant of God may be called *Venerable*.

ART. IV
JUDGMENT ON THE MIRACLES

1. Besides heroic virtues or martyrdom, *miracles* wrought through the intercession of the Servant of God are required. As a rule *two* suffice, if testified to by eye-witnesses at the informative as well as at the Apostolic process. *Three* are demanded if eye-witnesses testify only at the informative trial, whilst at the Apostolic trial only hearsay evidence is presented; *four* are demanded if at both trials only hearsay witnesses and documents are produced.

2. Since *miraculous cures* are under discussion, two medical and surgical experts, who enjoy a good name and fame in their profession, must be consulted.

3. The discussion takes place at *three distinct congregations*, the last of which is a general one, held in the presence of the Sovereign Pontiff. After the miracles have been acknowledged, the doubt is formulated as follows: "*An tuto procedi possit ad beatificationem Servi Dei.*" If the answer of the consultors and Cardinals is favorable, the Pope issues a decree to that effect.

TITLE XXV

EXTRAORDINARY TRIAL PER VIAM NON-CULTUS OR CASUS EXCEPTI

1. A positive approbation of the Roman Pontiff may be asked for the cult bestowed on Servants of God who enjoyed a tolerated cultus after the pontificate of Alexander III (1159–1181) and before the time determined by the decrees of Urban VIII (1623–1644). It may be recalled that Urban VIII strictly forbade any authorization of public worship to be granted to anyone except such whose veneration had been established from time immemorial or at least a hundred years previous to the publication of the Constitution " *Coelestis Hierusalem* " (July 5, 1634), with the knowledge and approbation of the Apostolic See or the local Ordinary. The same constitution admitted as lawful a veneration of such *Beati* or Saints based upon a special indult or decree of the S. Congregation of Rites, or the writings of the Holy Fathers and other holy men.[1] Now Can. 2125 rules that, in order to obtain the approbation of the Roman Pontiff, a trial (*processus*)[2] is required. The regulations for this trial are laid down in the following canons. The competent Ordinary for conducting the inquiry is he in whose diocese the cultus was given, or the documents were found, or who has the right of pre-occupation if several Ordinaries are concerned. There-

---

[1] Cfr. *Coll. P. F.,* n. 77.
[2] We suppose, however, that the necessity of this trial must be un- derstood in the light of the Const. of Urban VIII.

fore the Ordinary who first summons witnesses is entitled to complete the preliminary trial.

2. The *postulator* then demands of the Ordinary:

a) to requisition the writings of the Servant of God, and

b) to institute an inquiry concerning the fame of sanctity and virtues, or martyrdom and miracles. This is required in order to answer the following questions: Whether there was in the place a constant and general fame and persuasion of the saintly life of the Servant of God, or of his martyrdom, and the reason thereof, also of the miracles wrought by his intercession; and whether this veneration still exists at present and in what manner it asserts itself.

3. Then the acts and results of the inquiry are sent to the S. Congregation, where the *dubium* is proposed: " *An signanda sit commissio introductionis causae.*"

4. After this the *litterae remissoriales* are dispatched to the diocesan judges, in order to arrange for the (delegated) apostolic process on the *casus exceptus*, the result of which is again forwarded to Rome, where the final sentence is given, investigation into the virtues or martyrdom ordered, and finally, the so-called decree of equivalent beatification (*aequipollens beatificatio*) is issued.[3]

---

[3] Cfr. can. 1277.

TITLE XXVI

THE PROCESS OF CANONIZATION

1. A document establishing formal or equivalent beatification is required to introduce the process of canonization, or else an inquiry must be made as to the positive permission of the cult on the part of the Roman Pontiff.

2. To proceed to the canonization of a formally beatified Servant of God, *two miracles* wrought through his intercession after beatification, and *three* miracles in case the beatification was *aequipollens*, are required. The discussion of these miracles takes place as stated under beatification (can. 2116–2124).

3. Then the Roman Pontiff issues a decree of solemn canonization, the ceremonies and solemnities of which are those approved by the Roman Court.[1]

---

1 Booklets are generally distributed on such occasions, which give all the information as to the solemnities; these require costly preparation and for those admitted to witness them — *esperientiâ loquimur* — a good dose of patience.

402

PART III

MODE OF PROCEDURE IN CER-
TAIN CASES AND THE APPLI
CATION OF PENALTIES

This last part of the Book on Ecclesiastical Procedure treats of seven particular cases which apparently call for a formal trial (*strepitus iudicii*) but in course of time have been made the object of special legislation, and hence are considered separately.

The legislator first lays down certain general rules, which apply equally to all seven cases, unless expressly modified, and then proceeds to determine each case in particular.

GENERAL RULES

CAN. 2142

In processibus de quibus infra, adhibeatur semper notarius, qui scripto consignet acta quae ab omnibus subscribi debent et in archivo servari.

CAN. 2143

§ 1. Quoties monitiones praescribuntur, hae fieri debent vel oretenus coram cancellario aliove officiali Curiae aut duobus testibus, vel per epistolam ad normam can. 1719.

§ 2. Peractae monitionis eiusque tenoris documentum authenticum in actis servetur.

§ 3. Qui impedit quominus monitio ad se perveniat, habeatur pro monito.

CAN. 2144

§ 1. Examinatores et consultores ac notarius debent, interposito ab initio processus iureiurando, servare secretum circa omnia quae ratione sui muneris noverint ac praesertim circa documenta occulta, disceptationes in consilio habitas, suffragiorum numerum ac motiva.

§ 2. Si huic praescripto minime paruerint, non solum a munere amoveri debent, sed alia etiam condigna poena ab Ordinario, servatis servandis, plecti poterunt; ac praeterea damna, si quā inde secuta sint, sarcire tenentur.

CAN. 2145

§ 1. In iis processibus summarie procedendum est; at duo vel tres testes sive ex officio arcessiti sive a parte inducti audiri non prohibentur, nisi Ordinarius, auditis parochis consultoribus seu examinatoribus, existimaverit partes eos inducere ad moras nectendas.

§ 2. Testes et periti, nisi iurati, ne admittantur.

CAN. 2146

§ 1. A definitivo decreto unicum datur iuris remedium, idest recursus ad Sedem Apostolicam.

§ 2. Quo in casu ad Sanctam Sedem omnia acta processus transmittenda sunt.

§ 3. Pendente recursu, Ordinarius paroeciam vel beneficium quo clericus privatus sit, alii stabiliter conferre valide nequit.

1. In all these trials a *notary* should be employed. He should put the acts in writing and see to it that they are signed by all concerned and preserved in the archives. Although the text commands the participation of a notary, we hardly believe that the absence of a notary would invalidate the procedure. For the chief and essential point is the writing, which, as the "*Maxima cura*" clearly; states, can be done by a clerk, called *actuarius*.[1] Those who have to sign their name to the documents or acts before they are filed away in the archives, are all who took an active or passive part in the trial.

2. *Admonitions,* if necessary, may be made orally or in writing. If they are administered *orally*, this must be done by the Ordinary in the presence of the chancellor, or some other official of the diocesan court, or two witnesses. If by *letter*, the latter should be registered and receipted for by the post office.[2]

Here the question arises whether the notary mentioned in can. 2142 is required. It appears to us that his presence is superfluous. For, as § 2 of canon 2143 states, the main point is to have a document to the effect that the admonition or warning was duly administered. This can be drawn up and filed equally well by the chancellor. If the notary were absent and inconveniences might follow, it would certainly be advisable and permissible to have the diocesan chancellor act as notary (can 372, § 3).

Whoever prevents the admonition from reaching him is regarded as having been admonished. Thus one who would refuse to accept a registered letter, of which the postmaster must have a receipt from the addressee, would be considered as having received it. The same is true

---

1 Pius X, Motu proprio of Aug. 20, 1910, § 10, n. 1 (*A. Ap. S.,* II, 641).   2 See can. 1719.

if he would not open the letter or destroy it unread.

3. *Examiners, consultors*, and the *notary* must at the very beginning of the trial promise under oath to keep the secret.[3]

This *secret* comprises all the knowledge gained in virtue of their office, especially secret papers, the debates or discussions held at the meetings, the number of the votes, etc. If any of these officials violate the law of secrecy, they *must* be removed from office. The Ordinary *may* also, *servatis servandis*, mete out other suitable or proportionate punishments. Besides these officials are bound to restitution if any damage results from the revelation of a secret.

The *oath*, says the text, must be given *ab initio processus*, which has been declared [4] to be the first session or meeting held for each and every case (but not every session of the same case). However, since the notary appears to act at the admonition in his official capacity for this whole procedure,[5] it would be more logical to refer the beginning of the trial to the administration of the canonical warning, at least for the notary. Of course, for a merely paternal admonition this oath is not required. The *secret* is the official one, or *secretum commissum*,

---

3 The *formula* for taking this oath (published in the *A. Ap. S.*, IV, 142) is as follows: "*Ego N. N. examinator (vel parochus consultor) synodalis (vel pro-synodalis) spondeo, voveo ac iuro munus et officium mihi demandatum me fideliter, quacumque humana affectione postposita, et sincere, quantum in me est, executurum: secretum officii circa omnia quae ratione mei muneris noverim, et maxime circa documenta secreta, disceptationes in consilio habitas, suffragiorum numerum et rationes religiose servaturum; nec quidquam prorsus, occa-*

sione huius officii, etiam sub specie doni, oblatum, nec ante nec post, recepturum. Sic me Deus adiuvet et haec sancta Dei Evangelia, quae meis manibus tango."

4 S. C. Consist., Feb. 15, 1912 (*A. Ap. S.*, IV, 141): "*singulis vicibus, in prima sessione, sub poena nullitatis actorum.*"

5 *Maxima cura*, can. 1, says: "*Monitio . . . ut peremptoria sit et proximae amotionis praenuntia, fieri ab Ordinario debet, non paterno dumtaxat more, verbotenus et clam omnibus; sed ita ut de eadem in actis Curiae legitime constet.*"

which is based upon an explicit or implied contract, and may safely be styled "privileged knowledge." Therefore, *in general*, it comprises every kind of knowledge gained in virtue of that office; *especially*, as the text says, all that proximately concerns the case under discussion.

That the obligation is a grave one (*sub gravi*) is evident not only from the importance of the official secret itself, but also from the *penalties threatened to violators*.

1.° The Ordinaries are commanded to punish and therefore are not at liberty to apply or not to apply this penal sanction. They must (*debent*) *remove the transgressors*. But when? As soon as the violation is proved, or as soon as the bishop is morally certain that an examiner or consultor or notary has revealed a secret. No formal procedure is required,[6] otherwise an indefinite proceeding would ensue.

2.° Other penalties *may* be inflicted. Here no obligation is stated, but it is left to the prudent judgment of the Ordinary. In case he should decree further penalties, besides removal, he is bound by the conditions of common law required for inflicting certain punishments.[7] This is the meaning of *servatis servandis*.

3.° There is a *moral* obligation to *indemnify the injured party*. If we say moral obligation, we do not mean to exclude justice, nor to deny that juridical means could be employed, but use the phrase in order to convey the idea that conscience itself dictates the obligation. The amount of indemnification is guaged by the damage done. The manner of indemnification depends on the circumstances of each case. Broadly it may be said that the Ordinary should decide upon the measure and mode of

6 F. Cappello, *De Administratione Amotione Parochorum*, 1911, p. 86 f.   7 Cfr. can. 2222 f.; also 2291, 2297.

indemnification. If a criminal case ensues, it must be
determined according to can. 1935 ff. All of which goes
to show that officials should keep the secret strictly, in
order not to injure anyone's good name, and avoid being
impeached.

4.° Can. 2145 rules that *summary proceedings* should
be employed in the trials now under discussion. However, two or three witnesses, either called officially or
by the party, may be admitted, unless the Ordinary, upon
consultation with the consultors or the examiners, should
come to the conclusion that these witnesses are simply
brought to delay the trial.

What summary proceeding involves is indicated in can.
1840 f. It is evident that, though it is a summary trial,
the following canons must be followed. *Witnesses and
experts must all be sworn in,* otherwise they cannot
be admitted. It is not stated what kind of witnesses
are to be called. Therefore can. 1756–1758 should be
consulted. It is but natural that the witnesses mentioned
in can. 2143, § 1, should be of clerical rank, although
laymen (*sexus virilis*) are not debarred, provided they
are trustworthy and of good reputation.

5.° No appeal, but only a *recourse* to the Holy See
(S.C. Concilii) is open from a definitive sentence in any
of these trials. If recourse is had, all the documents
must be forwarded to Rome. This recourse must be
treated like an appeal, of which can. 1881 says that it
should be made within ten days by notifying the judge
who has given the sentence. Pending the recourse, the
Ordinary *cannot validly* confer the parish or benefice of
which the clergyman has been deprived on another, except
temporarily. Therefore no permanent appointment can
validly be made pending a recourse. This follows from
the very nature of the case.

TITLE XXVII

PROCEEDINGS FOR THE REMOVAL OF IRREMOVABLE PASTORS

Our text is part of the well-known decree "*Maxima cura*," which was issued by the S. Consistorial Congregation, Aug. 20, 1910, at the special request of Pius X. The full title of said decree is: "*Decretum S. C. Consistorialis de amotione administrativa ab officio et beneficio curato.*"[1] The formal law established by this decree changed the former procedure in removing pastors from their parishes. The intention of the lawgiver was, on the one hand, to formulate more accurately the already existing but scattered decisions which in the course of a century had emanated from the Roman Court for a more expedient and less obnoxious removal of inefficient pastors, and, on the other hand, to safeguard and promote the welfare of the Church (*salus reipublicae suprema lex est*).[2] There is no doubt that the so-called *desservants*, who were introduced by the organic articles of Napoleon I, influenced the ecclesiastical legislation in changing the application of former laws. For these were based on the old view of the beneficiary system, which regarded a pastor as so closely connected with the benefice itself, that it seemed a hazardous task to remove him. It is quite true that some allusions to a change or transfer

[1] Cfr. *A. Ap. S.*, II, 636 ff.
[2] See the preface to the decree; also Hilling, *Die Amtsenthebung der Pfarrer im Verwaltungswege*, Mainz, 1911, p. 2 ff.

409

from one place to another are found in the Decretals; but a permanent removal, such as the "*Maxima cura*" and our Code contemplate, cannot be discovered in the old law.[3]

This is quite intelligible if we recall that canonists established two kinds of perpetuity: one called *objectiva*, attached to the benefice, and the other one styled *subjectiva*, following the person of the holder. This double perpetuity and the feudal idea of a benefice rendered a pastor irremovable, unless criminal procedure or privation of benefice was set in motion.

A decisive step, which paved the way for the present discipline, was taken by the Council of Trent, when it established a kind of temporary removal by giving the bishops power to appoint vicars or coadjutors to illiterate and inexperienced pastors.[4] A further development was brought about in the nineteenth century, in consequence of the appointment, in France and Belgium, of *desservants*, who were pastors according to ecclesiastical law, but according to the Napoleonic Code mere ministers dependent on the civil prefects. It cannot be denied that conditions have changed decidedly and that the "*salus reipublicae*" really requires a more up-to-date method of providing competent and efficient pastors, making the office more prominent than the benefice. Hence it is not surprising that the German Bishops prepared a *postulatum* at the Vatican Council, asking for an involuntary transfer of pastors, or a dismissal with a sufficient pension, if the pro-synodal examiners pronounced a sen-

---

[3] C. 5, X, III, 19. Card. Gennari (*Sulla privazione del beneficio e sul processo criminale dei chierici*, 1905, p. 215 f.) thinks he has found allusions to administrative removal, but the decisions of the S. C. C. up to the middle of last century only mention transfer or privation (see Richter, *Trid.*, p. 119). "*Potuit prius inveniri*," a famous Roman theologian would say.

[4] Sess. 21, c. 6, *de Ref.*

tence of unfitness against them.[5] Although this *postula-tum* could not be acted upon on account of the troublesome events in Rome, the Codification Commission in 1904 took up the subject. The result of its debates was laid down in the "*Maxima Cura*," a part of which has entered the Code. The decree also applied to the United States, as was formally declared to the late Apostolic Delegate, Msgr. Falconio, on March 13, 1911, by the Consistorial Congregation.[6]

It is not necessary to defend this new legislation. Only one remark may be added. The pastors have no reason to complain of the change, because the law guarantees orderly procedure and requires canonical reasons, which the bishops are not allowed to overlook or stretch beyond due limits, thereby binding the Ordinaries to the common law and protecting the pastors against arbitrary removal. The bishops cannot complain, because they have the law on their side and are sustained in the exercise of their pastoral right. The faithful have no grounds for complaint because the supreme law, namely, their own welfare, is fully safeguarded and promoted.

Note that this removal must not be confused with privation from office or benefice, because privation is strictly an ecclesiastical penalty, which requires the formalities of criminal procedure, and therefore presupposes a crime in the proper sense of the word, proved and declared.

REASONS FOR REMOVAL

CAN. 2147

§ 1. Parochus inamovibilis a sua paroecia amoveri potest ob causam, quae ipsius ministerium, etiam citra

5 *Coll. Lac.* V, II, 875; Grande-rath-Kirch, *Geschichte des Vatik. Konzils*, 1906, I, 444.

6 *Eccl. Review*, Vol. 44, 590.

gravem suam culpam, noxium aut saltem inefficax reddit.

§ 2. Hae causae sunt praesertim quae sequuntur:

1.° Imperitia vel permanens infirmitas mentis aut corporis, quae parochum suis muneribus rite obeundis imparem reddit, si, iudicio Ordinarii, per vicarium adiutorem bono animarum provideri nequeat ad normam can. 475;

2.° Odium plebis, quamvis iniustum et non universale, dummodo tale sit, quod utile parochi ministerium impediat, nec brevi cessaturum praevideatur;

3.° Bonae existimationis amissio penes probos et graves viros, sive haec oriatur ex levi vivendi ratione parochi, sive ex antiquo eius crimine quod nuper detectum eximatur iam poena ob praescriptionem, sive ex facto familiarium et consanguineorum quibuscum parochus vivit nisi per eorum discessum bonae parochi famae sit satis provisum;

4.° Probabile crimen occultum, parocho imputatum, ex quo Ordinarius prudenter praevidet magnam in posterum oriri posse fidelium offensionem;

5.° Mala rerum temporalium administratio cum gravi ecclesiae aut beneficii damno, quoties huic malo remedium afferri nequeat sive auferendo administrationem parocho, sive alio modo, quamvis aliunde parochus spirituale ministerium utiliter exerceat.

An irremovable pastor may be removed from his parish for any reason which renders his ministry harmful, or at least inefficient, even though there be no grievous fault implied on his part.

What an irremovable pastor is has been stated in can. 454, to which we may add the decree of the S. C. Con-

sistorialis, Aug. 1, 1919; where it is stated that three
things are required to establish a parish: (a) a decree
or order of the Ordinary assigning the boundaries, (b)
a parochial residence, and (c) a sufficient endowment for
the maintenance of the pastor and of divine worship.
But to make a parish irremovable, it is furthermore
required that a declaration be made to that effect, at least
negatively; for the Ordinary may, for just reasons, declare it to be a *removable* parish. This declaration is
absolutely necessary, because otherwise, according to can.
454, § 3, the parish is presumed to be an irremovable
one.[7] We do not, however, wish to deny that a former
declaration made according to the IIId Plenary Council
of Baltimore (n. 32 ff.) would be sufficient.[8] Hence
where there are irremovable pastors to the amount of
one-tenth of all the pastors of the diocese, this custom
may be followed, unless the Ordinary wishes to declare
still other parishes as irremovable, which he may do
without asking the Holy See.

The text says that the removal may be made for reasons which do not imply grievous guilt (*citra culpam
gravem*). Guilt presupposes a transgression, and
grievous guilt a violation of a serious law, and, since we
are speaking of the law, it means an external violation,
no matter what the theological guilt may be. Here the
difference between removal and privation as stated above
becomes clearly manifest. All the five reasons stated
under § 2, really may involve either no guilt at all or
only a slight fault, although some may entail grievous
guilt.

However, these reasons must bear upon the *sacred
ministry*, or rather, they must affect it in such a way that

[7] A. Ap. S., XI, 346.
[8] See Vol. II, p. 519 f. of this Commentary.

its exercise becomes either hurtful or ineffective (*noxium vel saltem inefficax*). These two adjectives, which substantially occur in the "*Maxima Cura*," are a general indication of the five following reasons. "Hurtful" involves more of personal cooperation, whilst "inefficient" or "ineffective" points to facts over which the pastor has no control, or in regard to which he might plead "not guilty."

§ 2 of can. 2147 then enumerates (not *taxative*, but *demonstrative*), five reasons which chiefly (*praesertim*) may necessitate a removal. That the enumeration is to be taken *demonstrative* only, *i.e.*, as a proximate, not exclusive enumeration, the word *praesertim* sufficiently proves.[9] These reasons are:

1. *Inexperience or permanent mental or bodily infirmity which render the pastor incapable of discharging his obligations properly,* provided, however, that the Ordinary is convinced that the welfare of the souls in his charge cannot be provided for by the appointment of a coadjutor, according to can. 475.

This reason comprises the first three of the "*Maxima cura*," which document is, therefore, helpful for the interpretation of the Code.

a) *Imperitia* is not identical with ignorance, for the latter signifies defect or lack of knowledge, whilst inexperience rather means incapacity for, or inability to exercise, the sacred ministry. A priest may be a good theologian, but a poor manager. Ignorance is now-a-days hardly conceivable among those who have passed "*laudabiliter*" through a regular seminary course. Hence *imperitia* rather concerns the method of handling a parish; lack of tact and awkwardness in the confessional or pulpit, in dealing with the parish officials, etc. This

---

[9] The reasons in "*Maxima Cura*" were understood *taxative*.

greatly depends on the place and surroundings.[10] A boorish priest may be a scandal to city people, but create little disturbance in a distant country place. To inexperience, of course, belong ignorance of the language of the country, and an offensive lack of familiarity with pastoral and moral theology.

b) *Mental infirmity* here comprises all kinds or forms of *insanity*, which is described in *"Maxima cura"* as incurable, or, at least, of the kind which is always apt to recur, and which causes loss of esteem and authority even after the recovery of the pastor. Serious fatuity, stupidity, or weakmindedness, also belong hither.

c) *Bodily infirmity* includes all diseases which are of a serious and lasting character. Just how long an infirmity, either mental or bodily, has to last in order to render one unfit for the sacred ministry, is not stated in our text, except by the word *permanens*,[11] which may be rendered by habitual, durable, or incurable. A physician's verdict is required, but we do not, of course, exclude a miraculous cure.

Very noticeable is the *clause* added to all three reasons: *if a coadjutor should not be able to provide for the welfare of the souls.* An accurate rule that would tell us when the weal of the parish requires the appointment of a new pastor *in casu*, cannot be established. For much depends upon the qualities of the coadjutor and the condition and attitude of the parish. At any rate, since the clause sets up this condition, the Ordinary must try a coadjutor.

2. The second reason is *popular hatred, even though unjust and not general*, provided it is such as to prove

---

10 Hilling, *l. c.*, p. 12.

11 Can. 155 and 465 prescribe a six months' term for provision, which, however, may be prolonged in case of pastors.

an obstacle to the pastor's useful ministry and is not likely to cease within a short time. *Odium* is more than aversion, and must manifest itself by outward signs, for instance, insults, demonstrations, injuries done to parish property. Serious and prolonged newspaper attacks may also betray a sufficient degree of hatred. Such hatred is *unjust* if the pastor has given no plausible or solid reason for it; it is *just*, if the pastor has caused the hatred, either by imprudence or imputable sinful provocation. The text admits any kind of hatred. It is *not universal* if only a portion of the parish is hostile. One or two families, or a few individuals should not cause alarm if the parish is of any size. However, one influential family with a widespread relationship may create a rather extensive hatred. In that case the condition added in our paragraph would solve the question.[12] For this hatred is supposed to impede the useful exercise of the sacred ministry and to be of some duration. The sacred ministry *would be impeded* if the reception of the sacraments and attendance at divine service would decrease considerably, if the financial condition of the parish would be seriously imperilled and factions would arise. The *duration* would be of from six months to a year. It may be added that the hatred must be directed against the *person of the pastor,* not against religion as such.

3. The third reason is *loss of esteem among righteous and serious-minded men.* Esteem is paid to the office and authority of the pastor, and the loss of it necessarily renders the exercise of the sacred ministry ineffective, if not detrimental. The persons whose esteem the pastor has lost must be *men of character,* not garrulous women, even though of the " upper " class.

12 Cappello, *l. c.,* p. 37.

The text then states how this loss may be brought about.

a) It may arise from the pastor's conduct. The phrase, "*ex levi vivendi ratione parochi*," is wider than the corresponding passage of the "*Maxima cura*," which reads: "*sive haec procedat ex inhonesta aut suspecta vivendi ratione parochi.*" The Code simply speaks of levity of conduct, which must be interpreted in the light of canons 138, 140, and 142.[13] Custom and actual conditions should also be taken into consideration.

b) The loss of esteem may be caused by the belated *discovery of a former crime which is no longer punishable by reason of prescription.*[14] Concerning prescription of crimes and criminal action see can. 1703–1705. The civil-criminal law, too, must be consulted; for the priest's good name is here concerned.

c) Lastly, a pastor may lose the esteem of his people through the conduct of his *dependents and blood relations who live with him.* This is a rather obscure text. The reading itself is not quite certain, whether *familiarium* or *familiarum;* the edition of Gasparri reads *familiarium,*[15] which includes servants who live in the parsonage. *Consanguinei* here includes blood relations and *affines.* Therefore if a *factum* — which is a very wide term — of a scandalous nature has been perpetrated by one of these persons, which would compromise the pastor, the obnoxious person or persons should be dismissed from his service or household. But it may be

13 See Vol. II, p. 86 ff. of this Commentary.

14 Whether this goes back to the time before ordination is not clearly stated, but seems implied, because the loss of esteem may follow even such crimes as were committed before ordination if the pastor is well known in the place.

15 There seems little doubt that the correct reading is *familiares*, not *familiae*, because the latter are included in the term *consanguinei.*

that dismissal would cause greater disturbance, in which case removal might be decreed.

4. The fourth reason is a *probable crime imputed to the pastor, which, though secret, in the bishop's judgment may create great scandal among the faithful*. On crime and its public or occult nature see can. 2195–2197. The text adds "*probabile*," a probable crime, *i.e.*, one that has at least the semblance of having been committed by the pastor and must be imputed to him. A great deal depends on the persons who know about the crime. Then the offence the people would take at such a discovery must be really great, and not be limited to the one or other fanatic or puritan. Some people have a very strange idea of the Decalogue. But where honesty and justice are involved, people are justly sensitive. The judgment must be left with the bishop.

5. The fifth reason *is faulty administration of the temporalities, to the great damage of the church or benefice*. This is *culpable* if it involves a misappropriation or embezzlement of public funds, *i.e.*, funds belonging to the church or diocese, diocesan collections, etc., or risky speculations, which are a sort of illegal gambling. It may not involve moral fault, but simply result from *financial incapacity* or inability to keep books and collect the revenues of the church or benefice. The faultiness of the administration is to be reckoned according to the gross amount of the revenues involved and the amount lost, for the text says, "*cum gravi damno*."

But this reason is a limited one, as removal is indicated only *if no other remedy is left to counteract the evil and the temporal administration cannot be taken away from the pastor in some other way*. Hence the bishop may entrust the administration of the temporalities of the parish to the trustees, or to the curates or assistants or *alio modo,* by giving the delinquent pastor practical lessons in administration or sending him an auditor once in a while, teach him the necessity of keeping his books properly. All these means are applicable even in cases where the pastor *performs his spiritual duties properly.* For temporal loss often entails spiritual disadvantages, since it may burden the church or even bring law suits upon the pastor, the trustees, or the diocese.

INVITATION TO RESIGN

CAN. 2148

§ 1. Quoties, prudenti Ordinarii iudicio, in unam ex causis de quibus in can. 2147 parochus incidisse videatur, ipsemet Ordinarius, auditis duobus examinatoribus et veritate gravitateque causae cum eis discussa, parochum scripto vel oretenus ad paroeciae renuntiationem intra certum tempus faciendam invitet, nisi agatur de parocho vitio mentis laborante.

§ 2. Invitatio, ut acta valeant, continere debet causam quae Ordinarium movet et argumenta quibus ipsa innititur.

CAN. 2149

§ 1. Si parochus intra praestitutos dies nec renuntiet nec dilationem postulet neque causas ad amotionem invocatas oppugnet, Ordinarius, postquam constiterit et invitationem ad renuntiandum, rite factam, parocho innotuisse et ipsum quominus responderet legitime impeditum non fuisse, eum statim a paroecia amoveat, quin teneatur praescripto can. 2154.

§ 2. Quod si non constet de superius indicatis duobus adiunctis, Ordinarius opportune provideat aut iterando invitationem ad renuntiandum aut prorogando tempus utile ad respondendum.

After setting forth the reasons which may advise a removal, the Ordinary is told how to proceed. First he shall invite the delinquent pastor to resign. This invitation may produce no effect, because the pastor does not answer, or it may produce the desired effect, *i.e.*, cause him to resign.

If the pastor refuses to resign and offers reasons for his refusal, the way is opened to legal procedure proper, as seen in can. 2151 ff.

1. Whenever the Ordinary is convinced that a pastor is guilty of mismanagement for one of the reasons stated in the preceding canon, then he himself, or his Vicar-General,[16] must proceed as follows:

a) He must *call in two of the examiners*, either synodal or pro-synodal, and hear their *advice*, though he is not bound by their consent (can. 105, n. 1.°).

b) With these two examiners he should *discuss* the truth and seriousness of the charges made against the pastor, because discussion may remove doubts and clear up the case.

c) After the discussion he shall *invite the pastor to resign*. This invitation may be made orally or in writing, but should always be accompanied by the indication of the term within which the resignation is expected. Although our text does not prescribe that the *oral invitation* be made in the presence of the chancellor, or of some other diocesan official, or of two witnesses, yet, since it amounts to an admonition, it seems to us that can. 2143, § 1, 2 must be applied.[17] A *written* invitation to resign must be sent by registered mail.

d) This invitation may be *omitted* only in case the

16 According to the "*Maxima cura*," can. 32, the Vicar General needed a special mandate; but the Code omits this condition.

17 "*Maxima cura*," can. 10, § 1, strictly required it.

pastor suffers from a mental defect which in the "*Maxima cura*" (can. 9) is simply styled "insanity." But the term *vitium mentis* is somewhat broader than insanity. It may include habitual melancholia (this is now regarded by scientists as a form of insanity) and even the so-called *determinatio ad unum*, which is a mental attitude rendering the person incapable of reasoning in any other way than along the lines of a certain preconceived idea. However we believe that the legislator means insanity in all its species. Of course the Ordinary may not presume that such a condition exists, but must have definite proof, either in the form of a medical certificate or from trustworthy witnesses.

e) In order to render not only the invitation itself, but all the following acts, juridically *valid*, the Ordinary is bound to state in the invitation the *reason* that prompted him to issue the invitation and the *evidence* which supports the reason.

The "*Maxima cura*" contains some more elaborate instructions, which, though omitted in our text, do not militate against it, and may, therefore, find a place here; with due regard to the fact, however, that they do not affect the validity of the proceedings. If the crime that prompted the invitation is secret (*crimen occultum*), and the invitation is in writing, the reason for the invitation is to be stated only in general terms;[18] for instance (can. 2147, § 2), that the respective pastor has exercised the sacred ministry less effectively and usefully than was expected. Then when the pastor appears personally, the specific reason and the evidence may be communicated to him orally, in the presence of one examiner, who at

18 The reason for this general statement is to keep the crime secret and to prevent the impeached pastor from devising excuses or destroying evidence; Hilling, l. c., p. 23.

the same time acts as secretary, and takes down the minutes. In communicating the evidence orally, great care must be taken to keep secret the names of the accusers and witnesses, especially if these persons demand secrecy, or if circumstances are such that they have reason to expect vexations. Papers referring to the crime should not be communicated in writing whenever their communication is apt to cause scandal to the faithful, or breed quarrels and contentions because other persons are involved.

But even the oral communication of such papers must be made very cautiously if inconvenience is to be feared.

As may be seen, these observations of the *"Maxima Cura"* are intended to safeguard the good name of others and to avoid unnecessary publicity.

2. If the *pastor ignores the bishop's invitation* to resign within the appointed time,[19] *i.e.*, if he neither resigns, nor asks for delay or dilatory terms, nor rebuts the reasons alleged,— what is the Ordinary to do? He must make *two inquiries*, one touching the juridical formalities, and the other concerning a mere fact; to wit, he must inquire whether, and be morally certain that,

a) The invitation to resign has been properly made and reached the pastor and that

b) The pastor had no lawful excuse for not answering the same.

As to a), it is evident that if the oral invitation was made according to can. 2143, § 1, 2, there is no difficulty to prove the juridical fact and formality; the same is true if it was made in writing, *i.e.*, by registered letter with return receipt. Therefore we believe that what was said above, under can. 2148, should be adhered to.

---

[19] *"Maxima cura,"* can. 10, § 4, grants ten days; but the Code leaves it to the Ordinary to fix the time.

As to b), a legitimate excuse for not answering might be advanced, for instance, absence, sickness, or ignorance of the invitation. However, the last-named reason could hardly be accepted in case of a registered letter.[20] Neither should the bishop be too hasty in refusing plausible excuses, for accidents sometimes happen over which individuals have no control. But if the bishop is really satisfied in conscience that the invitation was duly made and reached its destiny, and that no legitimate excuse was offered for not answering it, he may *immediately proceed to remove the pastor,* and if he does so (can. 2152, § 2), should inform him of his decision. The *pastor* on his part, because of his contempt or stubbornness, *forfeits* the *prerogatives* granted in can. 1254.

If, on the other hand, either the formal invitation was defective, or the pastor advanced a lawful excuse for not answering it, the Ordinary shall make *opportune provisions.* These consist in either repeating the invitation to resign or prolonging the time for answering the charges or reasons given in the invitation, either orally or in writing.

RESIGNATION ACCEPTED

Can. 2150

§ 1. Si parochus paroeciae renuntiet, Ordinarius paroeciam ex renuntiatione vacantem declaret.

§ 2. Potest vero parochus, loco causae ab Ordinario invocatae, aliam ad renuntiandum afferre sibi minus molestam vel minus gravem, dummodo vera et honesta sit, ex. gr., ut obsequatur Ordinarii desideriis.

§ 3. Renuntiatio fieri potest non solum pure et

[20] Though it may happen that interested persons in the household of the pastor signed the receipt and kept or destroyed the letter.

simpliciter, sed etiam sub conditione, dummodo haec ab Ordinario legitime acceptari possit et reapse acceptetur, et firmo praescripto can. 186.

If the pastor resigns his parish, the Ordinary shall declare the same *vacant by resignation*. This fact must be expressly mentioned because of the formalities required for the bestowal of the vacant parish on another, according to can. 184–187, and also on account of can. 1485. Formerly no office or benefice made vacant by resignation could be bestowed on relations of the *resignans;*[21] but the Code is silent on this condition.

A pastor who is asked to resign, may do so for another reason than that set forth by the Ordinary; this reason may be less offensive or irksome or aggravating, but it must be true and honest. Such a reason is, "to obey the wishes of the Ordinary." He may also simply say: "For reasons of my own," or "For the welfare of the parish," etc.

The *resignation may be made purely and simply, or conditionally*, provided the Ordinary is entitled to accept, and does accept, the conditions. A resignation is *pure and simple* if no simoniacal or other condition enters into the transaction; *conditional*, if a clause is attached in the act of resignation. Such a condition would be present if the pastor resigned in favor of a certain priest, which is inadmissible.[22] Neither can any resignation be admitted on the condition of *regressus, ingressus, or aggressus* (see can. 1486). Hence there remains only exchange (*causa permutationis*). A resignation conditioned upon this clause is called *resignatio sub pensione*.

Both kinds are tacitly admitted in this case by reason

21 Wernz, *Ius Decret.*, II, n. 499. , tit. 9, *Decretal.*, v. g., Reiffen-
22 See the commentators on lib. stuel, Wernz, *l. c.*, II, n. 493 ff.

of can. 2154 and under the conditions set forth in this title. What other conditions might enter it is hard to say, except they be temporary, for instance, to leave the pastor in his place for a certain time. But the Code has touched even this possibility in can. 2156.

Resignation, lastly, to be valid, must be made according to can. 186, *i.e.*, either in writing or orally, in the presence of two witnesses, and be accepted by the Ordinary.

REBUTTAL OF THE PASTOR

CAN. 2151

Parochus, si oppugnare velit causam adductam in invitatione, potest dilationem ad probationes afferendas postulare, quam Ordinarius pro suo prudenti arbitrio concedere potest, dummodo ne sit cessura in detrimentum animarum.

The pastor may *oppose the reason* alleged in the invitation if he is convinced that it has no foundation except gossip. In that case he is entitled to demand *dilatory terms* — the extent of which is not determined in the Code [23] — in order to prepare his defence. Whether and how long delay may be granted depends on the Ordinary's judgment, which, however, should be guided not only by charity towards the pastor, but also and chiefly by consideration for the *bonum commune*.

PROCEEDING OF THE ORDINARY

CAN. 2152

§ 1. Rationes a parocho contra invitationem adductas Ordinarius, ut valide agat, auditis iisdem

---

[23] "*Maxima cura*," can. 12, allowed from 10 to 20 days.

examinatoribus de quibus in can. 2148, § 1, perpendat, approbet aut reiiciat.

§ 2. Decisio, sive affirmativa fuerit sive negativa, parocho significetur decreto.

CAN. 2153

§ 1. Contra decretum amotionis potest parochus intra decem dies recursum interponere apud eundem Ordinarium, qui, ne invalide agat, debet, auditis duobus parochis consultoribus, novas allegationes ab eodem parocho intra decem dies ab interposito recursu producendas, simul cum rationibus primo allatis, examinare, approbare aut reiicere.

§ 2. Parochus potest eos testes inducere ad normam can. 2145, § 1, quos prima vice se inducere non potuisse probaverit.

§ 3. Decisio decreto nota parocho fiat.

CAN. 2154

§ 1. Amoto parocho Ordinarius, examinatoribus vel parochis consultoribus, qui partem habuerunt in amotione decernenda, in consilium adscitis, pro viribus consulat sive translatione ad aliam paroeciam vel assignatione alius officii aut beneficii, si ad haec idoneus sit, sive pensione, prout casus ferat et adiuncta permittant.

§ 2. Ceteris paribus, in provisione favendum magis renuntianti quam amoto.

1. The pastor then shall duly prepare *his defence*, for which purpose he may produce two or three witnesses, according to can. 2145, and also papers referring to the

case. Here, of course, much depends on the reason that prompted the invitation. In case of mental or bodily infirmity, the physician's verdict should be procured under affidavit. Concerning the hatred of the people, we believe local inspection, either by the Ordinary or by the examiners, would be the proper way, otherwise the pastor or bishop might have to call the whole parish. As to the loss of esteem, the men who testify to it must be examined as to their character, and it is also necessary to prove the approximate number of those in whose eyes the pastor's reputation has greatly suffered. In case of an occult or secret crime, the main investigation should turn about the probability of divulgation and the means of proving it. In that case a clever and conscientious lawyer and a detective might render good services. Finally, in case of mal-administration, the account books may be submitted to an auditor assisted by the trustees and the diocesan board. We add that, if the matter is of a delicate nature, little writing should be done and the examination carried on with as few witnesses as possible.

2. After the defence has been produced, or if it is made orally, during the hearing, the Ordinary, *for valid procedure*, is bound to call the *two examiners, in order to hear their advice*. As said above, the examiners should, or at least may, be present when the oral defence is made. After that the pastor, who may be represented by proxy,[24] shall retire, in order to permit the Ordinary and the two examiners to discuss the case freely.

The *decision is left entirely to the Ordinary*, who is not bound by the consent, much less, of course, by the advice, of the examiners. We draw special attention to

---

24 "*Maxima cura*," can. 18, 2, admits proxy, who, however, must be a priest approved by the bishop for that purpose.

this fact because the "*Maxima cura*" (can. 19) requires secret balloting, which is no longer needed now.

The *result* of the bishop's decision may be either positive or negative, *i.e.*, he may either *accept* the defence of the pastor as sufficient to clear him or he may *reject* it as insufficient. In either case the decision must be communicated to the pastor in the *form of a decree*. The text may be usefully complemented from can. 20 f. of the "*Maxima Cura*," which says that if the decree is *negative*, the reason for removal may be stated in general terms, as, *e.g.*, the welfare of souls. Special or particular reasons may be alleged if the Ordinary deems it expedient and feasible; but mention must be made of the invitation tendered to resign, of the counterplea of the pastor, and of the vote of the examiners. However, this last addition must now be formulated differently, for instance, having heard the advice of two examiners according to can. 2152, § 1. An *affirmative* decree, *i.e.*, one admitting the defence of the pastor, must also be communicated, but in this case the Ordinary should not omit to add wholesome admonitions and precepts, which may serve for future procedure.

3. The next stage in the procedure is a possible recourse on the *part of the pastor*. Note the term *recursus*, which is not equivalent to appeal, and consequently does not *suspend* the effect of the decree. The proceeding is as follows:

a) The recourse against removal must be lodged within *ten days* from the date of receiving notice of the decree.

b) The recourse is to be presented to the *same Ordinary* who issued the decree of removal. If he should have gone out of office in the meantime, either by death, resignation or transfer, etc., the recourse may be sent to the

vicar-capitular (administrator). However, we believe
that in this case the equitable time should be suspended
until the new Ordinary's arrival, unless the scandal is too
great.[25]

c) Then the Ordinary grants the pastor *another ten
days*, within which he may produce his new defence.
Thus the pastor has twenty days in all from the date
when he receives the notice of his removal, in order to
prepare his second defence.

d) The Ordinary must call in two *pastors who are
consultors*,[26] in order to proceed *validly* in the examination of the new allegations. These new allegations may
be accompanied by new *witnesses*, whom the pastor could
not produce at the first trial. But the pastor must prove
that the new witnesses could not be brought to the witness-stand before. To prove that, it would be sufficient
for the witnesses to affirm it, because they are under
oath according to can. 2145.

Together with these two consultors the Ordinary shall
discuss the case, as he did before with the examiners.
However, in order fully to enlighten the consultors, the
allegations and depositions made in the first pleading in
presence of the examiners must again be examined. The
consultors have no decisive vote.

e) Then comes the *decision, in the form of a decree*,
wherein the presence of the consultors together with the
reasons in general (as above) is mentioned.

f) Finally this *decree* must be *communicated to the
pastor*.

3. Supposing now that the *decree insisted on removal*
and was duly notified to the pastor, it appears but logical
that the parish is declared vacant, at least *de iure;* al-

---

25 Our view is based on can. 436:
sede vacante nihil innovetur.

26 Concerning these, see can.
385 ff.

though no declaration to that effect is required by the Code. But there can be no doubt that from the moment the pastor has received the decree of removal he is *no longer pastor*. The consequences are too serious not to be mentioned. The parochial rights, the ordinary jurisdiction for hearing confessions, the claim to the revenues cease from the moment of removal.[27] Therefore, in order to remedy these inconveniences, the decree of removal should contain a clause to the effect that the pastor is left in the enjoyment of all his pastoral rights until the new pastor or temporary vicar has arrived, or until further notice. In case of doubt or probable error, can. 209 may be applied. This premised, after the removal has been decreed and the decree communicated, the Ordinary must proceed as follows:

a) If the invitation was accepted or obeyed after the first plea for defence, without recourse, *the examiners* must be called to a meeting, the purpose of which is to provide for the removed pastor;

b) If recourse was had, and a second defence is therefore required, the *consultors* must be called in for the same purpose;

c) The *debate* concerns the mode of providing for the removed pastor, either by transfer to another parish, or by appointment to another office or benefice, provided he is fit for any of these places, or by a pension. The correct mode must be determined by the nature of the case and the circumstances.

d) All other things being equal, one who has *resigned is to be favored* more than one who was removed.

The Code leaves it to the prudent judgment of the Ordinary how to provide for the removed pastor. Yet,

---

27 See can. 462 f.; can. 873, § 1;   can. 1095 can hardly be applied here.

though not juridically, at least morally, he is bound by various conditions. For besides the advice of the examiners or consultors he should follow this dictate: "*pro viribus consulat*," as far as lies in his power, he should make provision for the pastor who has been removed. He must take into consideration the *fitness* of the priest for the respective place (parish, office, benefice). Furthermore he should weigh the case decided, because the five reasons advanced in can. 2147 are not all of the same nature (*prout casus ferat*). Besides, the circumstances of the parish, of the pastor (his health, good name, etc.), and of the diocese should also be taken into account (*prout adiuncta permittant*). After having weighed all these conditions, if there are several competitors for a parish, office or benefice, one who has resigned is to be preferred to one who was removed: *ceteris paribus,* or, as the "*Maxima cura*" (can. 257, § 3) says, "*in pari conditione.*" For if the resignee is not fit for the place, the Ordinary cannot conscientiously assign it to him.

The next question that arises is, whether the bishop is bound to give the resignee a *better parish* than the one he has resigned. But what is a better parish? The former law considered a parish with a richer income (*pinguiores reditus*) a better parish. The "*Maxima cura*" (can. 27, § 1) simply distinguishes between parishes of inferior and superior rank or order,— which admits of a wide interpretation and the play of personal tastes. For to some a small city parish seems preferable to a large country parish. Therefore, with the exception of a cathedral or collegiate parish, we believe that the old view of a richer income is still a safe index of superior rank. Besides, the irremovable character should be considered. This premised, the answer to the foregoing question is that a pastor who has resigned voluntarily for reasons which he himself has not brought about (for instance, on account of hatred), should be promoted to a better parish, or one of equal rank and income, provided he is fit for it, and the place is open, or the Ordinary can give it to him without inconvenience. Another question connected with this canon is this: Has a resigned or removed pastor *a right to demand a pension* instead of accepting another parish, or office, or benefice? in other words: Is he entitled to choose between a parish, office, or pension? Neither the wording of the "*Maxima cura*" [28] nor the text of the Code grants such a right. Of course, if the bishop leaves him the choice, the pastor is entitled to choose what he pleases. But there are very few, if any, dioceses in our country which could furnish pensions sufficient to provide for all cases of resignation or removal. If, then, the pastor refuses another place, offered to him by the Ordinary, the latter is not obliged to provide him with a pension.

Concerning pensions attention must be called to can. 1429, which is not affected by canon 2154.

Can. 2155

Negotium novae provisionis parochi amoti potest Ordinarius sive ipso amotionis decreto sive postea, quamprimum tamen, expedire.

Can. 2156

§ 1. Sacerdos a paroecia amotus debet quam primum liberam relinquere paroecialem domum, et omnia quae

---

28 Thus Hilling, *l. c.*, p. 32.

ad paroeciam pertinent novo parocho vel oeconomo ab
Ordinario interim deputato tradere.

§ 2. Si autem de infirmo agatur qui e paroeciali
domo sine incommodo nequit alio transferri, Ordinarius eidem relinquat eius usum etiam exclusivum,
eadem necessitate durante.

Provision for the removed pastor may be made in the
decree of removal itself or, at least, should be made as
soon as possible thereafter. The "*Maxima cura*" (can.
28) permitted insinuation of the provision to be made in
the invitation to resign, and pending the case of removal.
These two points are not mentioned in the Code. But
one thing stated in said decree, *viz.*, that the question of
removal and the question of provision should not be mixed
up, in order not to impair the welfare of souls, applies
also to the decree of removal. And here again attention
must be drawn to the necessity of mentioning the dura‑
tion of parochial rights and duties.

After removal, what has the removed pastor to do?
He must, as soon as possible, *leave the parochial residence* and hand all the belongings of the parish to the
new pastor or administrator *pro tempore*, appointed by
the Ordinary. *Omnia quae ad paroeciam pertinent* signifies all the parish books, all the account books, and all
the utensils or *sacra suppellex* [29] belonging to the parish.
Concerning the *furniture of the residence* this is generally
provided by the parish and therefore must be left in the
residence. However, if there should be a piece of family furniture to which the pastor has a claim, he may take
it along; also the books which he bought out of his
patrimony or salary.

---

29 Chalices or vestments which were given to the pastor for per-sonal motives, *intuitu personae*, be-long to him and may be taken away.

Next the Code provides for the case of a *sick priest* who can not be lodged elsewhere. This evidently supposes either a bedfast or crippled or paralytic person, who cannot conveniently be transported to another place. If he can travel, the favor extended here cannot be claimed. This favor consists in that the Ordinary should *leave the sick priest* in the (if necessary exclusive) enjoyment of the pastoral residence *as long as need requires.* Of course in that case the new pastor or administrator would have to look out for another residence within the parish limits, unless the two priests would agree to live peacefully in the parochial residence.

If a pastor who has been removed and told to leave the pastoral residence, obstructs the execution of the bishop's decree by having recourse to a *higher ecclesiastical court,* he must remember that this recourse has only devolutive, not suspensive, force,[30] and that, consequently, he must leave his residence. If the pastor should be tempted directly or indirectly to impede the execution of the episcopal decree by having recourse to the *civil power,* he should read can. 2334, which renders him liable to excommunication specially reserved to the Apostolic See. Besides, our civil law holds that a clergyman is entitled to the possession of a parsonage only as long as his connection with the congregation continues, and that one who is deposed (removed) but nevertheless stays in possession of the parsonage, becomes liable for rent.[31]

EXCURSUS ON DISABLED PRIESTS' FUNDS

The question of making provision for priests in case of removal is intimately connected with the general problem of raising funds for the support of disabled priests.

30 See Can. 2155, as compared with can. 1889, § 1.

31 Zollmann, *American Civil Church Law,* 1917, p. 342.

It is not an easy task to solve, and the Code makes no attempt to solve it; but it is worth while to compare some texts which bear on the subject. For the rest we refer to other sources.[82]

1. It must be remembered that every clergyman is incardinated in a diocese, to which he belongs and to which he is (can. 111) under obligation. A clergyman receives his support, not precisely in virtue of the office he holds or the services he renders to the diocese at large, but for the attention he gives to a determined function, or pastoral office, or benefice. This is expressed by the well-known adage: "*Beneficium propter officium.*" From this it follows that the *bishop cannot be held responsible* for the salary or support of a pastor. Attempts made to that effect have met with no favor in our civil courts.[88] And if the bishop cannot be held.

82 See *Eccl. Review*, Vols. XIX, 645 ff., XXIII, 458 ff., XXIV, 20 ff., 339 ff.

88 K. Zollmann, *American Civil Church Law*, 1917, p. 350, says: " It has been held that the relation between bishop and priest is not that of hirer and hired, but rather that of superior and inferior agents of the same church. The bishop is the priest's superior and according to the established order of things in the economy of church government regulating the degrees of subordination and the methods of administration, it is his province to designate the place for the priest to exercise his functions and to prescribe, under certain limitations, the rules for his guidance and control. To hold the bishop personally liable at law for the priest's services would be as unjust as holding the general agent of a railroad company liable for the pay of the railroad employees engaged by him in the course of his agency. Men are constantly going into positions under appointments by superior agents who are universally understood not to assume any personal liability by such appointment. Since there is no contract relation between priest and bishop after the priest has been assigned to a charge, there can be none before such assignment. Whatever duty a bishop may have to appoint a priest to some charge is a religious duty only. For its performance or nonperformance he is answerable only *in foro conscientiae* or to his ecclesiastical superior. It is a matter in which the ecclesiastical discretion of the bishop is, and must be the determining factor. In the exercise of that discretion he is answerable only to the laws of the church. If for a breach of this clearly ecclesiastical duty there should be a remedy by law, it must follow that a man may have an action for the

responsible for the salary of a working priest neither can he be obliged to provide personally for relief or support in case of disability.

2. How then may funds be raised to support disabled priests? On the one hand there is the universal conviction, emphatically expressed in the well known decretal of Innocent III, that affliction is not to be added to affliction but rather pity to be shown.[34] The tender solicitude of the Church has always been shown in the succor granted to the helpless and the poor. How much more it should be applied to the "*portio Domini*" needs no proof. Where the cooperation of the State could be invoked, the difficulties were to a great extent solved by pensions. But where Church and State are completely separated, the ecclesiastical authorities had necessarily to call upon the clergy and the faithful to mitigate the lot of helpless priests. The Third Plenary Council of Baltimore enacted that each bishop should establish a fund for the maintenance of indigent priests under his jurisdiction. This fund was to be raised either by a tax levied upon the *parishes,* or, if these were al-

refusal of a clergyman to baptize him. If there is a contract duty on the part of the bishop to assign a priest to a charge, it must follow that there is a similar obligation on the part of the priest to accept such charge. No one will contend that a bishop has any such civil right. The priest, so far as the courts are concerned, can lay down his office and its duties at pleasure. For doing so he can be visited only with ecclesiastical censure and such punishment as the church canons prescribe. The priest, so far as the courts are concerned, is thus completely without remedy as against his bishop. The bishop may appoint him or not in his discretion. He may, after he has appointed him, assign him to another charge. He may even enjoin him from exercising priestly functions and remove him absolutely without trial, and the courts will be in no position to afford him any relief. Since he has no contract with his congregation and with his bishop, the question arises whether he has any remedy against the church as a whole. Even this must be answered in the negative. The church, even if it is capable of being sued, has assumed no legal liability for his support."

[34] C. 5, X, III, 6.

ready too heavily taxed, *on the clergy,* who were to contribute pro rata from their personal income. A third method also was suggested, *viz.,* that the clergy organize themselves into a *mutual benefit society,* administered by the members themselves, with the bishop as *ex officio* president.[35] The two first methods may work well in larger dioceses, but smaller dioceses are hardly able to raise sufficient funds for the purpose.[36] There a *provincial* system might supply the shortcomings of the individual dioceses. More efficient, and, we believe more pleasing to sensitive priests and more businesslike, is the third method suggested by the Council, which entitles each priest to a share in the general fund in case of disability, regardless of his personal revenues. The only drawback we can see in this system consists in the danger of unjust distribution and of fostering an indolent, and perhaps insolent, spirit among the clergy. However, the constitutions or by-laws could be framed in such a way as to counteract these evils.

3. The next question is: *What does the Code say in this matter?* We could find only three canons that bear on the subject. They are 1429, 1505, and 2154.

Can. 1429, as explained in Vol. VI, permits the Ordinary to impose a *pension* upon parochial benefices or parishes, in favor of the pastor or assistants of the same. The amount of this pension is not to exceed one-third of the net revenues of the parish.

Canon 2154 permits a pension to be paid to a removed or resigned pastor.

Canon 1505 empowers the Ordinary to impose a *charitable subsidy* on all beneficiaries, secular as well religious, provided the needs of the diocese impel him

35 *Acta et Decreta Conc. Plen. Balt.* III, n. 71.
36 *Am. Eccl. Rev.,* XXIII, 473.

thereto and the taxation be extraordinary and moderate.

Of these texts two only refer to pastors and curates of parishes, because the pension is intended only for these. A *pastor emeritus* or a *vicarius emeritus* may be benefited by such a pension, but regular funds destined for all disabled priests cannot be construed into these two canons.

Can. 1505 is broader because the condition "*dioecesis necessitate impellente*" undoubtedly exists when there is question of providing for needy priests. But the *exactio* is to be only *extraordinaria*. This would seem to exclude regular yearly contributions. The most a private interpreter could admit is that a contribution could be demanded whenever the diocesan treasury is at a very low ebb. When this condition exists, all the *beneficiaries*, but not the parishes, may be taxed, and religious who hold parishes in the diocese would have to contribute their share to this fund.

4. This observation calls for another. Suppose the case of a *clerical aid society*, of the type found in some dioceses. Is the Ordinary or the Board of such a Society entitled to tax *religious* entrusted with congregations in the diocese? We hardly believe so, for, first of all, whatever is not connected with the care of souls is withdrawn from the episcopal jurisdiction,[37] and consequently the bishop is not entitled to exact contributions which have nothing to do with the congregation itself. Secondly, it does not appear just that religious, who are taken care of by their respective communities in case of disability, should be forced to contribute to a fund from which they derive no benefit. This reason, of course, holds only if the religious claim no subsidy from the aid society in case of sickness or other impediment.

5. Another question is, *whether the bishop is entitled*

---

[37] Cfr. can. 533, § 1, n. 4; can. 630, § 1, 3.

to levy a contribution on the personal income of (secular)
*priests under his jurisdiction to meet the expenses of a
clerical aid fund?* The Third Plenary Council of Baltimore, in the text already quoted (n. 71), not only permits, but obliges Ordinaries to establish a fund for the
support of indigent priests. The Code, while it does not
favor extraordinary charitable subsidies except moderately
and extraordinarily, does not prohibit the institution of
benevolent societies. Since the Code does not explicitly
provide for disabled priests — a canon to that effect
would have been opportune — it is certainly left to the
Ordinaries to supply this defect; because the Ordinaries
are allowed to legislate within the range of common law,
except where they are explicitly prohibited.[38] Hence the
right of making laws for the purpose of raising clerical
funds and distributing them justly cannot be denied to the
Ordinaries. And if this is true of such laws in general,
it must also apply to by-laws or constitutions that may
be necessary for the just or equitable administration of
these funds. Thus diocesan statutes concerning prompt
payment, or the prorating of contributions, or conditions
for receiving aid, are entirely justifiable.[39] The diocesan
statutes should contain the by-laws of such aid societies,
in order that they may become diocesan laws. The by-
laws themselves should clearly set forth when and under
what conditions a disabled priest is entitled to draw on
the diocesan fund or the Clerical Aid Society. Priests
who have means of their own from patrimonial or other
revenues should be excluded from the privilege of receiving such aid, which is destined for those unable to
procure a decent support.[40]

[38] Bened. XIV, *De Syn. Dioec.*, XIII, 1, 3; *Am. Eccl. Rev.*, XXIV, 26.

[39] Such statutes exist in various dioceses; see *Am. Eccl. Rev.*, XXIV, p. 29 f.; p. 339 ff.

[40] Concerning culpably — *ex delicto* — disabled priests we refer to

6. A last question: *May the Ordinary command the congregations or parishes of his diocese to contribute to the clerical aid fund?* He may do this in a friendly, but not in a domineering or threatening way. The reason lies in can. 1505 f. and can. 1186 and 1297. If the legislator would have the Ordinaries use their power in favor of the repairs required for the cathedral and other churches by persuasion rather than coercion, it is certainly not too much to argue *a pari*. The same rule of mitigation and moderation occurs in can. 1297 with regard to the *sacra utensilia*. Of course, we do not deny that Ordinaries may have collections taken up at irregular intervals for the purposes of a clerical relief or aid society.

In conclusion attention may be drawn to *life insurance for the clergy*, which may be handled, not only by responsible private companies, but also by provincial or interprovincial clerical companies, under the supervision of the ecclesiastical authorities.

can. 2303, § 2. The legislator there tells the Ordinary that he should provide for an indigent, though deposed, clergyman, lest he should have to beg, to the disgrace of the clerical state. But the obligation is merely one *ex titulo caritatis*.

TITLE XXVIII

PROCEDURE IN REMOVING REMOVABLE PASTORS

Can. 2157

§ 1. Parochus quoque amovibilis a sua paroecia amoveri potest ex iusta et gravi causa ad normam can. 2147.

§ 2. Ad parochos religiosos quod attinet, servetur praescriptum can. 454, § 5.

Can. 2158

Si Ordinarius aliquam ex his causis adesse existimaverit, parochum paterne moneat atque hortetur ut paroeciae renuntiet, causam indicans, quae paroeciale ipsius ministerium fidelibus noxium aut saltem inefficax reddit.

Can. 2159

Firmo praescripto can. 2149, si parochus renuat, rationes in scriptis reddat, quas Ordinarius, ut valide procedat, perpendere debet una cum duobus examinatoribus.

Can. 2160

Si, auditis examinatoribus, Ordinarius allatas rationes legitimas non iudicaverit, paternas iteret hortationes ad parochum, comminata amotione, si intra congruum definitum tempus paroeciam sponte non dimittat.

CAN. 2161

§ 1. Expleto praefinito tempore, quod pro sua prudentia prorogare potest, Ordinarius decretum amotionis emittat.

§ 2. Parocho autem renuntianti aut amoto providere tenetur ad normam can. 2154–2156.

The procedure for removing a removable pastor has been modified. The modification consists in the provision that no formal invitation to resign is required and no legal rebuttal or recourse against the decree of removal is admissible. Hence the consultors need not be called in, but the cooperation of the examiners is sufficient.

1. The removal of a removable no less than of an irremovable pastor requires a *just and grave cause, i.e.,* one of those stated in can. 2147.

If a *religious pastor* is to be removed, the procedure is very simple. See can. 454, § 5, where it is said that pastors belonging to a religious community may be removed *ad libitum* either by the local Ordinary or by the religious superior. The one has only to notify the other of the removal, without stating the reasons. Recourse to the Holy See is admissible, but with devolutive effect only.[1]

2. If the local Ordinary is convinced that one of the reasons stated under can. 2147 can be advanced against a removable pastor, he shall *paternally warn and exhort* the latter to resign his parish, and state the reason why his pastoral ministry has become detrimental or at least useless. No special formality is required for this ad-

1 Cfr. Vol. II, p. 520 f. of this Commentary.

monition, which is expressly styled paternal, *i.e.*, not canonical. But a certain and fixed term must be given the pastor for answering the Ordinary's demand.

If the warning is given in writing, it should be sent by registered mail, because can. 2149 also applies in this case.

3. *If the pastor does not act* upon being thus warned, he may be removed at once without the benefit granted by can. 2154. If he answers *negatively, i.e.,* if he refuses to resign, he must state the reasons for his refusal in writing. The Ordinary shall then *discuss these reasons with two examiners.* This discussion is required for *valid* procedure.

4. If the Ordinary, after having heard the advice of the examiners — which he is *not* bound to follow [2] — deems the reasons brought against the removal groundless or unlawful, he shall repeat the exhortation to resign under *threat of involuntary removal* in case the pastor refuses to leave the parish within the time appointed.

5. After the expiration of this term (which may, however, according to the prudent judgment of the Ordinary, be prolonged) the Ordinary shall issue *the decree of removal.* This, of course, must be *intimated* to the pastor. This is the last phase and requires no recourse and no calling in of the consultors. But provision is to be made just as for irremovable pastors, and therefore canons 2154–2156 apply to this case.

[2] See can. 105.

TITLE XXIX

PROCEDURE IN THE TRANSFER OF PASTORS

Can. 2162

Si bonum animarum postulet ut parochus a sua, quam utiliter regit, ad aliam paroeciam transferatur, Ordinarius eidem translationem proponat ac suadeat ut eidem pro Dei atque animarum amore consentiat.

Can. 2163

§ 1. Parochum inamovibilem Ordinarius invitum transferre nequit, nisi speciales facultates a Sede Apostolica obtinuerit.

§ 2. Parochus vero amovibilis, si paroecia *ad quam* non sit ordinis nimio inferioris, etiam invitus transferri potest, servatis tamen praescriptis canonum qui sequuntur.

Can. 2164

Si parochus consilio ac suasionibus Ordinarii non obsequatur, rationes in scriptis exponat.

Can. 2165

Ordinarius, si, non obstantibus allatis causis, iudicet a proposito non esse recedendum, debet, ut valide agat, super eisdem causis audire duos parochos consultores, et cum eisdem perpendere adiuncta in quibus versatur tum paroecia *a qua*, tum paroecia *ad quam*, et rationes quae translationis utilitatem aut necessitatem suadent.

CAN. 2166

Si, auditis parochis, Ordinarius translationem peragendam censeat, paternas exhortationes iteret ut parochus voluntati sui Superioris morem gerat.

CAN. 2167

§ 1. His peractis, si parochus adhuc renuat et Ordinarius adhuc putet translationem esse faciendam, parocho praecipiat ut intra certum tempus ad novam ac conferat paroeciam, eidem in scriptis significans, elapso praefinito tempore, paroeciam, quam in praesens obtinet, ipso facto vacaturam esse.

§ 2. Hoc tempore inutiliter transacto, paroeciam vacantem declaret.

By *transfer* is understood an exchange of parishes made with the consent of the legitimate superior. Reasons, at least in general, are required for lawful transfers, because they are generally looked upon as odious, unless they involve promotion.[1] The Code admits the welfare of souls (*bonum animarum*) as a valid reason. Our text says that the *competent superior* may decree a transfer, and draws a distinction between irremovable and removable pastors. Besides, as admitted by the old and the new law, there is a difference between voluntary and involuntary transfers, and transfers to a better or to a worse parish. It may also be noted that the practice of the Roman Court concerning transfers extends almost exclusively to the so-called *desservants* of France, who were considered *rectores ad nutum amovibiles*.[2]

1. The Code states that if the welfare of souls requires

---

1 Cfr. Vol. II, p. 167 f. of this Commentary; A. S. S., XIX, 53 ff.

2 The decisions quoted by Card. Gasparri regard France and confirm what we stated in the beginning of can. 2147.

that a pastor be transferred from a parish which he has governed with success, to another parish, the Ordinary shall propose the matter to the pastor and persuade him to accept the transfer for the love of God and of souls. The reason [3] for the transfer is here supposed to exist in the parish to which (*ad quam*) the pastor is to be transferred. It may be that this parish is financially or spiritually neglected, or that factions or parties are tearing it up to the detriment of souls.[4]

2. The Ordinary, however, must duly consider the character of the pastor, whether he is removable or irremovable, and whether he is willing or not to accept the transfer. For the Ordinary (*iure ordinario*) *has no right to transfer an irremovable pastor* against his will to another parish. To do this, special faculties are required from the Apostolic See. Whether our Ordinaries have obtained such faculties, is unknown to us; the former formularies contained no such faculty.[5] The Ordinary should beware of making threats, because a transfer made under threats, or by deceit, would be rescindible by a sentence of the diocesan court.[6] Therefore the Ordinary is not allowed to conceal the real condition of the parish to which an irremovable pastor is to be transferred, though he may emphasize its advantages.

3. A *removable pastor* may be transferred to another parish *even against his will*, provided the parish to which he is to be transferred is not of too low a rank, and pro-

---

[3] Cfr. cc. 37, 39, C. 7, q. 1; c. 5, X, VIII, 19, mentions *utilitas et necessitas*.

[4] S. C. C., March 27, 1886 (*A. S. S.*, XIX, 53).

[5] Not even the faculties (*Formula III, maior*) granted lately to the Vicars Apostolic by the S. C. P. F. contain such a faculty. The faculties just mentioned were kindly communicated to us for inspection by the Rt. Rev. Leo Haid, O. S. B., Vicar Apostolic of North Carolina, for which favor we wish to express our heartfelt thanks.

[6] Cfr. can. 103; *A. S. S* XI, 387.

vided the Ordinary proceeds according to the following canons.

What *inferioris ordinis* means has been touched upon above. The inferiority may be owing to a smaller income or to less importance or smaller size. The pastor, as stated before, may have his own ideas about the superiority or inferiority of a parish. If he accepts the parish offered to him no further formality is required, except that he declare his willingness to accept, in order that the Ordinary may declare the parish vacant,— but not by resignation. For it is a transfer, not a resignation.

4. If the removable pastor thinks he has reasons for *not following the advice of the Ordinary,* then

a) He must *state in writing* the *reasons* for not accepting the transfer, *e.g.,* his health, his mental qualities, his financial condition, etc.

b) The Ordinary shall then ponder the reasons given and consider the status of the parish. If, after due deliberation, he insists upon the transfer, he is bound, for *valid procedure,* to hear the opinion of *two pastors-consultors* on the reasons advanced, on the condition of both parishes (*viz.,* the one from which and the one to which the removable pastor is to be transferred), and, finally, on the reasons of necessity or utility which apparently demand a transfer.

Here may be added *some remarks as to the conduct of the pastor while the case is pending.* He should keep silent and above all not stir up or arouse the congregation, or create factions, or, what is still worse, have recourse to civil authority in order to bring pressure to bear upon the Ordinary.[7] Such methods are not only

[7] S. C. C., March 23, 1878; March 27, 1886 (*A. S. S.,* XI, 382 ff.; XIX, 53 ff.).

unbecoming to a priest, but may exasperate the lawful authority and cause scandal.

c) After having heard the consultors, if the Ordinary still insists on the transfer, he may *renew his paternal* (not canonical) admonition to move the pastor to acceptance.

d) If this proves fruitless, and the Ordinary remains unmoved in his former decision, he *shall command* the removable pastor (*parocho praecipiat*) to repair to the new parish within a certain time. This is a formal precept, to be served *in writing*, wherein the Ordinary declares that, after the expiration of the time granted the pastor for going to his new parish, the parish which he holds at present will *ipso facto* be vacant. But a reasonable time should be given. Twenty-four hours is not considered reasonable.[8] Ten days is more acceptable.

e) After the expiration of the appointed time, if the removable pastor has not gone to the parish assigned to him, his *old parish must be declared vacant.*

Here the procedure ends. No recourse is mentioned. It would be useless to have recourse to the Holy See, because it would cause expenses without any practical result. This whole legislation is modern and, as stated, has grown out of the conditions of the present time.

8 See *A. S. S.*, XI, 387.

TITLE XXX

PROCEDURE AGAINST CLERGYMEN TRANS-GRESSING THE LAW OF RESIDENCE

Can. 2168

§ 1. Parochum, canonicum aliumve clericum, qui residentiae legem, qua ratione beneficii tenetur, negligat, Ordinarius moneat, et interim, si agatur de parocho, eiusdem impensis provideat ne salus animarum detrimentum patiatur.

§ 2. In monitione Ordinarius recolat poenas quas incurrunt clerici non residentes itemque praescriptum can. 188, n. 8, et clerico significet ut intra congruum tempus ab eodem Ordinario definiendum residentiam instauret.

Can. 2169

Si intra praestitutum terminum clericus nec residentiam instauret nec absentiae causas afferat Ordinarius, servato praescripto can. 2149, declaret paroeciam aliudve beneficium vacare.

Can. 2170

Si clericus residentiam instauret, Ordinarius, non modo debet, si absentia illegitima fuerit, ei infligere privationem fructuum pro tempore absentiae, de qua in can. 2381, sed potest etiam, si casus ferat, pro gravitate culpae eum congrue punire.

Can. 2171

Si clericus residentiam non instauret, sed absentiae causas afferat, Ordinarius, accitis duobus examinatoribus et institutis, si opus fuerit, opportunis investigationibus, videre debet num causae sint legitimae.

Can. 2172

Si, auditis examinatoribus, Ordinarius censeat adductas causas non esse legitimas, rursus clerico praefigat terminum intra quem redire debet, salva semper privatione fructuum pro tempore absentiae.

Can. 2173

Si parochus amovibilis intra praescriptum tempus non redierit, Ordinarius statim procedere potest ad paroeciae privationem; si redierit, Ordinarius det ei praeceptum ne rursus discedat sine scripta sua licentia sub poena privationis paroeciae ipso facto incurrenda.

Can. 2174

§ 1. Si clericus, qui beneficium inamovibile obtinet, residentiam non instauret, sed novas alleget deductiones, Ordinarius eas cum eisdem examinatoribus ad examen revocet ad norman can. 2171.

§ 2. Si nec ipsae legitimae habitae fuerint, posthabitis quibusvis aliis deductionibus, Ordinarius clerico praecipiat ut intra tempus praescriptum vel iterum praescribendum redeat sub poena privationis beneficii ipso facto incurrenda.

§ 3. Si non redeat, Ordinarius eum beneficio privatum declaret; si redeat, Ordinarius idem det praeceptum de quo in can. 2173.

CAN. 2175

Neutro in casu Ordinarius beneficium vacare declaret, nisi postquam, perpensis una cum examinatoribus discessus rationibus quas clericus forte allegaverit, eiusdem Ordinarii licentiam in scriptis ab eodem clerico peti potuisse constiterit.

The obligation of a cleric to reside at the place of his office or benefice, if this requires permanent residence, was set forth in previous canons.[1] Here the Code lays down rules for the treatment of those who violate this divine-human law. It is evident that a canon who has the obligation of choir service or other residential duties cannot be punished for a lawful absence of three months each year. The pastor may enjoy a two months' vacation, during which he should not be unnecessarily vexed by a recall from the Ordinary. Outside this lawful absence pastors and canons, unless urgent need calls them away, must remain within the limits of their parishes, though during a few days of the week they may sometimes absent themselves for good reasons, provided they stay at home on Sundays and holydays of obligation. Unqualified, however, and liable to the penalties enacted in the following canons, would be regular absence from the parish on all weekdays, as if the pastor were pastor only on Sundays. The Code provides the Ordinary with rules that should be observed in proceeding against clergymen who infringe upon the laws of residence.

1. The first question naturally turns upon the *persons* whom the law intends. They are (a) *pastors*, *i.e.*, all who go by this name, either removable or irremovable, incumbents of true or holders of quasi-parishes, also those

1 Cfr. Vol. II, p. 546 f. of this Commentary.

who govern parishes as vicars of chapters or religious
corporations; for instance, the religious called *expositi*,
for these are bound by the same obligations as other
pastors.[2] Temporary substitutes or *oeconomi* are bound
by the same duty.[3] Also the *coadjutors* of disabled pastors, if they take the place of the pastor in all things.[4]

b) *Canons* of cathedral and collegiate chapters must
observe the law of residence if they are obliged to daily
choir service and are not allowed to engage a substitute.[5]

c) *Alius clericus, qui residentiae legem ratione beneficii
tenetur*, or, in other words all clergymen possessing a
residential benefice, *i.e.*, one which, either by its nature,
or by reason of a charter or particular law, requires
residence.[6] Our assistants or curates (*cooperatores*)
are not obliged to residence by reason of the beneficiary
character of their office, because the notion of benefice
can hardly be applied to the same, but can. 476, § 5 obliges
them to reside within the parish to which they are attached, according to the diocesan statutes and praise-
worthy custom. There can be no doubt whatsoever that
a priest incardinated and engaged at a certain church
as assistant to the pastor, must stay at that church according to the orders of his Ordinary.[7] *Rural deans*,
who are not at the same time pastors, must nevertheless
reside in the territory of their deanery.[8]

2. The *procedure* against clerics who seriously trans-
gress the law of residence, is as follows:

a) The Ordinary shall first give a *canonical warning*
or *admonition* and in the meantime, in the case of a negligent pastor, provide as well as he can for the welfare

2 Can. 471, § 4.
3 Can. 472, § 1.
4 Can. 475, § 2.
5 Can. 418 f.
6 Can. 1411.

7 S. C. C., May 8, 1756 (*Richter, Trid.*, p. 207, n. 3); Aug. 4, 1880 (*A. S. S.* XIV, 113 ff.).
8 Cfr. can. 448, § 2; also consultors, see can. 425, § 1.

of his subjects. The expenses of this temporary provision must be borne by the careless pastor.

If we say, a canonical warning, not merely a paternal admonition, it is because the warning here intended has all the features of a canonical basis of procedure. Therefore it should be given in *writing*, or in presence of two witnesses, according to can. 2143, § 1. The canonical nature of the warning also appears from its *contents*. For in it the Ordinary must (a) mention the penalty (loss of income according to the time of unlawful absence),[9] (b) recall to the cleric's mind that contumacious absence means tacit resignation of the office or benefice he holds,[10] and (c) appoint a certain time within which the cleric should again take up his residence.

b) The admonition may or may not produce the desired effect. *Three hypotheses* are conceivable: Either the cleric does not heed the warning at all, or he takes up his residence without further ado, or he give reasons for his absence.

(1) If the cleric *neither takes up his residence nor gives reasons* for his absence within the term appointed in the admonition, the Ordinary shall declare the parish or benefice vacant.[11] However, to do this validly, he must first make certain that the canonical warning was duly served and that there was no reason for not answering.

(2) If the cleric *returns* to his residence, the Ordinary *must*,—if the absence was entirely unlawful (of which the Ordinary is the judge),—deprive him of a pro rata share of his income, and *may* also inflict other punishments proportionate to the guilt incurred. The pro rata

9 Can. 2381.
10 Can. 188, n. 8.
11 *Trid.*, sess. 6, c. 2; sess. 23,

cc. 1, 16, *de ref.* (Richter, *Trid.*, l. c.).

share of the income is to be reckoned by the time of the unlawful absence. Thus, if the yearly salary is $1000, and the unlawful absence was six months, the fine would be $500. However, this would be excessive. For even a delinquent clergyman, as long as he is incardinated and has not forfeited every claim to a decent livelihood, must be allowed the necessary support. Therefore he may subtract the expenses for his maintenance during the six months, say, about $250 or $300, and, as required by can. 2381, give the rest to the Ordinary, who shall devote it to charitable purposes.

The bishop is not entirely free to remit the fine, because the text says *debet,* whereas the other punishments may or may not be inflicted, *ad libitum.*

(3) If the cleric does not return to his residence, but *submits the reasons* for his absence, the Ordinary must call in two examiners, hear their advice, and investigate whether the reasons are acceptable and lawful. Lawful would be sickness, or necessary business transactions connected with the parish or benefice, or other reasons which Christian charity or necessity dictate.[12] Should the Ordinary, after having heard the examiners, think the proffered reasons unacceptable or unlawful, he must assign *another term for the cleric's return* to his residence. The fine for unlawful absence runs in the meanwhile.

At this stage, *i.e.,* after the second warning, with a new term appointed for the absentee clergyman, another distinction is introduced and must be duly considered, *viz.,* the difference between a removable and an irremovable pastor.

---

[12] See can. 338 and Vol. II, p. 361 of this Commentary. But private business of merely personal interest cannot be called lawful; these personal interests are not in keeping with clerical obligations.

a) A *removable* pastor, who does not return after the second canonical warning, *may* (not must) *be deprived* of his parish immediately after the appointed time has elapsed. If he returns within the time set, the Ordinary shall *issue a precept* to the effect that if he again leaves the parish without a written permission, he shall *ipso facto* be deprived of the parish. It is not only advisable, but necessary, that a copy or abstract of this precept be kept in the archives of the diocese for further use. We may also add that a written permission is needed for protracted absence. But it does not mean that a removable pastor can not leave his parish for one or two days a week, provided this absence does not occur too frequently.

(b) If a cleric who holds an *irremovable benefice* (our irremovable pastors are here included) does not return to his residence after being duly warned, but brings forward new excuses for his absence, the Ordinary shall *discuss them with the examiners* to see whether they may be admitted as lawful. If not, he shall not demand other proofs, but simply command the cleric to return within the time already appointed or a new term now fixed, under penalty of privation of his benefice, to be incurred *ipso facto*.

If the cleric does not return within the prescribed time, the Ordinary shall *declare* him deprived of his benefice; if he returns, the Ordinary shall give him a *precept* like that issued in the case of removable pastors, *viz.*, not to leave the place a second time without a written permission, under penalty of *ipso facto* incurring privation of benefice.

However, in neither case (whether the cleric be removable or irremovable), should the Ordinary declare the benefice vacant unless he has first discussed the reasons alleged with the *two examiners* and ascertained for himself that the cleric was unable to obtain a written permission or leave of absence. For it may be that the pastor or beneficiary was retained unlawfully in a place and had no means of communicating with the bishop, or that communications were interrupted for a long time. Besides, it sometimes happens that the secretary or chancellor makes a mistake in opening or reading the mail. The same may happen to the bishop. Hence it is advisable that clergymen ask for leave of absence by registered letter.

TITLE XXXI

DE MODO PROCEDENDI CONTRA CLERICOS CONCUBINARIOS

Can. 2176

Ordinarius clericum qui contra praescriptum can. 133 mulierem suspectam secum habeat aut quoquo modo frequentet, moneat, ut eam dimittat vel ab eadem frequentanda sese abstineat, comminatis poenis in clericos concubinarios can. 2359 statutis.

Can. 2177

Si clericus neque praecepto pareat, neque respondeat, Ordinarius, postquam sibi constiterit id clericum praestare potuisse:

1.° Eum suspendat a divinis;

2.° Parochum praeterea statim paroecia privet;

3.° Clericum vero qui aliud beneficium sine animarum cura habet, si, exacto bimestri tempore a suspensione, sese non emendaverit, privet dimidia parte fructuum beneficii; post alios tres menses, omnibus beneficii fructibus; post alios tres menses, ipsomet beneficio.

Can. 2178

Si clericus non obediat, sed causas excusationis adducat, Ordinarius debet super eisdem audire duos examinatores.

Can. 2179

Si, auditis examinatoribus, Ordinarius existimaverit allatas causas non esse legitimas, id clerico quamprimum significet eique det formale praeceptum ut intra breve tempus a se definiendum pareat.

Can. 2180

Parochum amovibilem inobedientem Ordinarius statim ad normam can. 2177 coercere potest; si vero agatur de clerico qui, beneficium inamovibile obtinens, non paret, sed novas allegat deductiones, Ordinarius eas ad examen revocet ad normam can. 2178.

Can. 2181

Si ne eae quidem iudicentur legitimae, Ordinarius clerico rursus praecipiat ut intra congruum tempus mandato obtemperet; quo tempore inutiliter transacto, procedat ad normam can. 2177.

Can. 133 determined the right of the Ordinary concerning the conduct of clergymen towards suspected women. If the bishop's injunction goes unheeded, the cleric may be presumed to be a concubinarian. Can. 2176 states that the Ordinary may issue a *canonical warning* to such a cleric, asking him to dismiss the suspected woman from his house, or to abstain from visiting her. The warning should contain the *threat* of penalties as established by can. 2359.

Concubinatus is generally defined as "*illicitus consuetudinarius concubitus cum aliqua foemina corrupta et soluta, in domo sua vel alibi commorante.*"[1] There is

---

[1] Schmalzgrueber defines *clericus concubinarius* as one "*qui concubinam vel domi suae vel extra illam instar uxoris continuo retinet et as-*

no doubt that the term implies a number of transgressions, at least two.[2] Besides, the woman must, according to general opinion, be the same, because concubinage imitates the marital state.[3] *Quo modo* frequented
seems to imply any kind of suspicious conversation or
intimacy or visits to a suspected house, for instance, a
theatre of ill fame, etc., wherever this may be. Epistolary
converse cannot be styled *frequentatio;* there must be
personal visits. The woman must be suspected, *viz.,*
suspecta de incontinentia vel lascivia.[4] Suspicion is a
kind of doubt which does not permit reason to form a
judgment, but inclines it to admit one statement rather
than another. Hence, in this case a suspected woman
would be one to whom a *mala fama* had been attached.
That there should be a careful investigation of such
rumors and the persons who start them goes without
saying.[5]

Two things must be absolutely certain, *viz.,* that the
woman is really suspect, and that the clergyman retains
or visits her against the command of the bishop. If
the *concubinatus* is not notorious, strong proofs are required, *i.e.,* such as are furnished by two first-class witnesses or by authentic documents.

The text requires a *canonical warning,* which is to be

siduam cum ea tenet consuetudi-
nem;" l. III, tit. 2, n. 9; see also
Reiffenstuel, III, 2, n. 13; Wernz,
Ius Decret., II, n. 208.

2 Reiffenstuel, *l. c.,* n. 13;
Schmalzgrueber, *l. c.,* n. 11; *simplex
fornicatio* cannot be called *concubinatus.*

3 The S. C. C., quoted by Garzia,
De Benef., P. II, c. 10, n. 185,
however, held (sess. 24, c. 14, *de
ref.*): "*quod habeat locum* [*sc. hoc
decretum*] *etiamsi clericus modo cum
una, modo cum alia deprehendatur.*"

4 Reiffenstuel, *l. c.,* n. 15, see
also *A. S. S.,* VII, 414 f.

5 *Ibid.,* II, tit. 20, n. 363, relates
the following: A pastor was accused of such a misdeed, but denied
it, although eighty witnesses were
produced. He was condemned, but
upon a second hearing had to be
absolved, because he could prove
that all the witnesses testified from
hearsay, and the story had been
started by one garrulous old
woman. Caution, therefore, is required.

administered according to can. 2143 and is called personal and special, *i.e.*, directed to the clergyman himself, with special mention of the imputation.[6] Besides, the admonition must also contain the threat of the penalties, *ferendae sententiae*, which are mentioned in can. 2359. This canon refers to clerics in higher or sacred orders only.

The Code now goes on to lay down the rules of procedure after the canonical warning has been issued. Here, again, as under Title XXX, three hypotheses are possible.

The cleric *neither obeys* the command or precept given by the Ordinary to dismiss the suspected woman, or to abstain from visiting her, *nor does he answer at all*. In that case the Ordinary must make certain that the clergyman was in a condition to answer the charge. If the admonition was given orally in the presence of two witnesses, there will be no trouble concerning this requisite. If it was sent by registered letter and the receipt kept, it will be a relatively easy matter to find out whether the letter reached its address. There remains only the case where an impediment or obstacle prevents the clergyman from answering, but such cases are rare. Besides, excepting absence, there may be another person asked to answer in general, *viz.*, that the clergyman addressed is at present indisposed and will answer later. Of course, if the letter should have been intercepted by a third person, the clergyman may not know of it.

Provided the warning or precept was duly made and no answer returned, the Ordinary shall proceed as follows:

(a) He shall *suspend* the cleric *a divinis*, *i.e.*, from ex-

6 Schmalzgrueber, *l. c.*, III, 2, n. 9; Barbosa, *Summa Decisionum Apost.*, 1698, p. 148, *s. v.* "Concubinatus."

ercising the acts of the power of ordination (can. 2279, § 2, n. 2°).

(b) If he is a *pastor*, he shall be immediately deprived of his parish;

(c) Against a *beneficiary* without the care of souls the Ordinary shall proceed with the privation of half the income if he does not amend within six months from the date of the suspension; after three more months of all the income, and after three more months of the benefice itself, again provided, of course, that no emendation has followed.

There is but one difficulty in this rather categorical procedure,[7] *viz.*, concerning *suspension*. Is it a censure or a merely provisional penalty? The commentators were divided as to the character of this suspension, some holding that it was a censure, others (the more weighty ones) denying it.[8] The question is rather important, because if there is a censure involved, its violation would render the clergyman irregular. If a pastor, therefore, would say Mass while thus suspended, he would incur irregularity. Is this the intention of the lawgiver? Great canonists, like Reiffenstuel and Schmalzgrueber, maintain that it is not a suspension proper, because not expressed in law, and therefore no censure involving irregularity. However, *pace tantorum auctorum*, it appears to us that, even if it were not a censure, irregularity would nevertheless be incurred in case of violation. The reason for this assertion lies in can. 985, 7°, where irregularity from crime is attached to any violation of either a personal, medicinal, or vindicative penalty. And that the suspension here mentioned has

7 C. 15, Dist. 81, also threatened a so-called suspension for the faithful who would assist at ecclesiastical functions of *clerici concubinarii*; which suspension is now out of date.

8 Schmalzgrueber, III, 2, n. 14 f.; Reiffenstuel, III, 2, n. 40 f., deny it.

the character of at least a personal penalty, can hardly be denied. The only way of avoiding this consequence would be found in can. 1933, § 4, where it is said that suspension may be inflicted by way of *a precept* in an extrajudicial manner. However, according to can. 2306, even a precept belongs to the class of penal remedies, wherefore the penal character of such a suspension must, in our view, be maintained. On the other hand, it is argued that penalties must be interpreted benignly, and since irregularities *ex delicto* savor, at least indirectly, of penalties, it appears more conformable to the benign spirit of the Church to exclude irregularity. However, this argumentation is specious rather than solid. Therefore, until an authentic interpretation settles the controversy we are bound to cling to the severer opinion.

Whether the Ordinary is *obliged* to proceed in this manner is solved by can. 2223, which states that, when the law employs preceptive terms, the penalty should, as a rule, be inflicted, but admits delay or postponement to a more opportune time, also mitigation or change of penalty, or even abstaining from infliction, if emendation is achieved and scandal repaired.

2. It is possible that the cleric does not obey the injunction of the Ordinary, but *proffers excuses*. In that case the Ordinary must call in *two examiners* and discuss with them the validity or lawfulness of the reasons alleged. This discussion is absolutely required, although the Ordinary is not bound to accept the views of the examiners. But, as stated above, the reasons must be impartially discussed, as also the testimonies on the strength of which the cleric was charged with this offence.

3. The third *hypothesis* is that the Ordinary, after discussing the proffered reasons with the examiners, finds them *unfounded* or unlawful, either because they

are insufficient or because the evidence is too weak. The *result of this negative finding* must as soon as possible be *communicated* to the suspected cleric, together with a formal precept to obey the injunction given in the former warning within a term appointed by the Ordinary. The length of time is not precisely determined except by the adjective brief (*breve*), which may be interpreted as meaning ten days, more or less, according to circumstances or persons and the danger of scandal.

This last hypothesis has different judicical consequences, according to the difference between removable and irremovable rectors. For can. 2180 rules that a *removable* cleric who has disobeyed the second warning or formal injunction to dismiss the suspected women or to quit her company, may be punished as *contumax* (can. 2177) *i.e.*, the Ordinary *may* (though he is not obliged to) suspend him, and if he is a removable pastor, deprive him of his parish, or if a beneficiary, of the pro rata revenues, and, finally, of the benefice itself.

But an *irremovable* pastor or beneficiary must be treated somewhat more considerately. He may, after the formal precept, have discovered more and stronger excuses for not obeying the first canonical warning. These new reasons or allegations must again be discussed by the Ordinary with the two examiners. No ballot is required, since the examiners need only be heard.

If these new reasons are rejected by the Ordinary, the latter must issue *another precept* (which might be called the third canonical warning) bidding the accused cleric to abide by the injunction of the Ordinary, or rather to carry it into effect within the time appointed for that purpose. If the irremovable clergyman does not dismiss the obnoxious woman, or give up her company, the Ordinary shall proceed as stated in can. 2177, *i.e.*, he shall inflict suspension, and deprive the culprit of his parish, of the income, and of the benefice.

Note that can. 2180 permits the Ordinary to proceed, after the third warning, against a removable cleric in the same way as against an irremovable one. *Recourse* indeed is *admitted*, but it has no suspensive, but only a devolutive, effect.[*]

[*] Bened. XIV, "*Ad militantis,*" March 30, 1742, §§ 12, 23; *Archiv für K.-R.*, 1910, Vol. 90, 697 ff.

TITLE XXXII

PROCEDURE AGAINST PASTORS NEGLECTING THEIR PASTORAL DUTIES

Can. 2182

Parochum qui officia paroecialia de quibus in can. 467, § 1, 468, § 1, 1178, 1330–1332, 1344, graviter neglexerit aut violaverit, Episcopus moneat, in memoriam eius revocans et strictam obligationem qua eius conscientia oneratur et poenas in haec delicta iure statutas.

Can. 2183

Si parochus sese non emendaverit, Episcopus eum corripiat et aliqua congrua poena pro gravitate culpae puniat, postquam, auditis duobus examinatoribus et facta parocho sese defendendi facultate, probatum iudicaverit praedicta paroecialia officia etiam atque etiam per notabile tempus in re gravis momenti pratermissa aut violata fuisse et eorundem omissiones aut violationes nulla iusta causa excusari.

Can. 2184

Si et correptio et punitio in irritum cesserint, Ordinarius, probata, ad normam can. 2183, perseverante ac culpabili officiorum paroecialium omissione vel violatione in re gravi, parochum amovibilem sua paroecia statim privare potest; parochum vero inamovibilem

465

beneficii fructibus, pauperibus ab Ordinario distribu-
endis, pro gravitate culpae in totum vel ex parte
privet.

CAN. 2185

Mala voluntate persistente ac probata, ut supra,
Ordinarius etiam parochum inamovibilem e sua
paroecia removeat.

The *neglect* here mentioned concerns:

1. The *administration of the Sacraments*, pastoral correction and charity, care of the sick and dying (can. 467,
§1; 468, § 1);

2. *Catechetical instruction* and personal preaching,
especially on Sundays and holydays of obligation (can.
1330-1334; 1344);

3. *Neatness and decorum in the house of the Lord*,
which includes care that no profanation occur (can.
1178).

If a *pastor*, who is personally responsible for all the
things mentioned, *grossly neglects or violates* the regulations laid down by the law, the bishop shall *warn* him,
recall to his memory the strict and grievous obligation
imposed on his conscience, and remind him of the penalties with which the law visits such offences.

Although at first blush this admonition seems to be a
merely paternal one, yet can. 2143, § 3 makes it certain
that it is intended as an *official warning*. It must be
given either in writing, by registered letter, or orally, in
the presence of two witnesses. Note that the *bishop* is
mentioned here, which means that the bishop himself, and
not the vicar-general or *officialis*, should administer this
warning.

Gravis neglectus must be judged in proportion to the

detriment or spiritual damage that results to souls, but the judgment whether or not it is serious enough to call for a warning is left to the bishop. Besides, according to can. 447, the rural deans are called upon to watch in their respective territories over the fulfillment of these duties.

The *penalties* mentioned in law are those set forth here, because can. 2382 expressly refers to this title.

If the pastor, after the warning has been duly administered, does not amend his ways, the bishop shall rebuke him and mete out a punishment commensurate with the gravity of his neglect. *Corripere* and *punire* says the text. *Correptio* is a public admonition, to be administered before the ecclesiastical notary or two witnesses, or by letter, but always in such a way that the pastor is really reached.[10] It is a personal *reprimand* which no doubt has a canonical bearing. *Punire*, to punish, is a general term embracing all kinds of ecclesiastical punishments, not excluding suspension, as is evident from can. 1933, § 4. Only there should always be a due proportion between guilt and punishment.

However, rebuke and punishment may be inflicted only *after* the bishop has heard the advice of two examiners *and* after the pastor has been given a chance to defend himself. This defence may be made personally or by proxy, orally or in writing. If the pastor does not succeed in purging himself of the charge, rebuke and punishment may follow, and are deserved. The defence shall, of course, turn about the fact and about the reasons or excuses that the accused may offer for his neglect. The *fact* concerns the neglect of pastoral duties, especially if this lasted for a considerable time and affected matters of importance, such as omitting the teaching of

10 Can. 2309, § 2.

catechism for months, or not preaching on many Sundays, or not saying Mass on one or more holydays of obligation, neglecting to hear confessions on the days required, keeping the sacred vessels in an unclean condition, etc. Torn vestments and dirty or disorderly sacristies also belong here. Such neglect may easily be found out at the time of the visitation or through the rural deans.

But the pastor may plead not guilty, in other words, he may *offer an excuse*. There may indeed be an excuse for not preaching or teaching catechism, for instance, inborn timidity or physical impediments. But there can hardly be an excuse for tolerating filth or disorder. If the pastor is too lazy, he can at least get the altar society to attend to these matters. A prudent Ordinary will weigh personal and local circumstances with justice and impartiality, and if he deems rebuke and punishment necessary, will not fail to administer it cautiously, so that the delinquent's reputation is not jeopardized and the admonition produces its effect.

If neither rebuke nor punishment proves effective, the Ordinary shall again call in the examiners and discuss the facts and excuses with them. If the same culpable neglect continues, and concerns a serious matter, he *may* remove a *removable* pastor from his parish without further ado. An *irremovable pastor* he shall deprive of either a part, or the whole of his income, according to the gravity of the neglect, and distribute the money among the poor. If the misconduct should continue, the Ordinary may remove also an irremovable pastor from his parish. We suppose, however, that can. 2154–2156 should here be taken into consideration, as these dispositions were applied to this case by the " *Maxima cura*," although the Code is silent about their application. Equity, however, appears to require it.

TITLE XXXIII

PROCEDURE IN INFLICTING THE SUSPENSION EX INFORMATA CONSCIENTIA

Up to the time of the Council of Trent the general rule was that no one could be sentenced except he was first tried according to the forms of a properly conducted trial.[1] An apparent exception was admitted in crimes of homicide and heresy, for which, even though occult, a cleric could be judged and suspended. However, even these crimes called for at least the semblance of a trial, because justice requires that every one accused of a crime be given a chance to defend himself and demanding an investigation. Besides the adage: *"De internis non iudicat praetor"* is applicable to all occult crimes which escape evidence and the courts. However, some kind of a conscientious suspension was, according to a decretal of Lucius III, permitted to regular prelates, who could prohibit their subjects from ascending to higher orders if they had committed a secret *delictum* known to the superior.[2] This was a partial suspension and strictly reserved to prelates regular.

The *Council of Trent* ushered in a new era by establishing the suspension called *ex informata conscientia.*[3] It permitted bishops to inflict suspension on their subjects

1 Cfr. cc. 4, 7, X, I, 11; Bouix, *De Iudiciis Eccl.*, II, 315 ff.; Werns, *Ius Decretalium*, Vol. V, P. II, n. 887 ff.; Smith, *Elements of Eccl. Law*, 1893, Vol. II, 315 ff.

2 C. 5, X, I, 11; Bouix, *l. c.*, II, 317.

3 Sess. 14, c. 1, de ref.

for an occult crime in an extrajudicial manner. This was extended also to regular confessors found guilty of a crime in connection with confession.[4] That the Jansenists and Regalists were incensed at this extension of the episcopal power is not surprising;[5] but the various ways of interpreting the resp. decree of the Council and the manner in which this power was extolled by a few writers is a surprise indeed.[6] The Code lays down rules which are apt to disperse many misconceptions and misgivings, and also warns the Ordinaries against a too liberal use of this dangerous power. The text first establishes the right to use this power, then sets forth the rules for proceeding, declares for what crimes the suspension *ex informata* may be inflicted, and, finally, admits recourse to Rome.

THE POWER OF ORDINARIES

CAN. 2186

§ 1. Ordinariis licet ex informata conscientia clericos suos subditos suspendere ab officio sive ex parte sive etiam in totum.

§ 2. Extraordinarium hoc remedium adhibere non licet, si Ordinarius potest sine gravi incommodo ad iuris normam in subditum procedere.

Ordinaries are allowed ex informata conscientia to suspend their clerical subjects from office, either partly or totally. This simple text raises various questions, which call for an answer:

1. What is meant by the phrase, "*ex informata con-*

---

[4] Clem. X, "*Superna,*" June 21, 1670.

[5] Pius VI, "*Auctorem fidei,*" Aug.

28, 1794, prop. 49 f. (Denzinger, *l. c.,* n. 1420 f.).

[6] Cfr. Bouix, *l. c.,* II, 359 ff.; Wernz, *l. c.,* n. 891.

scientia"?[7] No doubt stress is to be laid on conscience, not on *informata,* because information is required to form the conscience. Negatively, as is evident from the Tridentine text, the meaning is that the bishop, in inflicting this sentence of suspension, need not observe the proceedings of a full and solemn, or even of a summary trial, but may suspend one as soon as his conscience is informed of the crime. However, it must be added that this information is not merely a matter of personal conviction or moral certitude, but must be based upon objective and reliable information. Bouix[8] justly observes that the bishop must have in hand such proofs as would move a judge to give sentence. Therefore, even if a clergyman would confess his guilt privately to the bishop — not in confession, because sacramental knowledge could not be used at all — or if the bishop himself, alone, without other witnesses, would have seen the clergyman commit the crime, he could not make use of this power, because his information would be merely private. The proof must be such as would convince the public. This is evident not only from can. 2190, but also from the fact that recourse (can. 2194) may be had from this sentence, and the S. Congregation (Concilii) would not ratify a sentence not based on objective evidence.

2. The object of this sentence *ex informata conscientia* is *suspension* from *office.* This suspension is described in can. 2279. If the suspension is *ab officio,* without further determination or limitation, it forbids every act of order, jurisdiction, and administration implied in the office itself, except the administration of the benefice as such. Hence a pastor in our country, when suspended

---

[7] The term does not occur in the conciliar text, but was coined by canonists.

[8] *L. c.,* II, 346 ff.

from office *ex informata conscientia,* cannot licitly exercise any priestly functions nor validly perform any acts of jurisdiction, nor administer ecclesiastical property, because this administration is attached to his pastoral office, the parish income not being a distinct entity, as if it were a benefice. Can. 2281 says that a suspension *ab officio* includes all offices which a clergyman may hold in a diocese.

On the other hand, this suspension *does not include the benefice,*[9] wherefore the administration and enjoyment of the benefice is not taken away from the beneficiary. Much less does our text permit sentence of excommunication or interdict to be pronounced *ex informata conscientia.*[10] Does it include ascent to, or *reception of, the higher orders?* According to the decree of the Council of Trent and all commentators up to the promulgation of the Code, this suspension could be inflicted upon a cleric who wished to receive higher orders. However, the Code *only mentions* suspension *ab officio, i.e.,* an office which one is supposed to hold. Consequently, since penalties must be strictly interpreted, suspension from receiving a higher order can no longer be inflicted *ex informata conscientia.* Neither is such a measure required, inasmuch as the irregularities and impediments cover the field sufficiently.[11]

The suspension may be either *partial or total.* It is *total,* if all the effects of suspension are intended, *i.e.,* all acts of the power of order and jurisdiction as well

---

9 Some authors, *v. g.,* Santi (V, 1, n. 22) held this, but it was justly rejected by others, *v. g.,* Wernz, *l. c.,* n. 897.

10 Bouix, II, 341.

11 This seems more probable also on the ground that the new law requires for every office of any importance the priestly character. Therefore only the prelacies might be considered or, more correctly speaking, the episcopate. But the *processus informativus* and S. C. Consist. will settle this point quite effectively.

as of administration. It is *partial*, if only the one or
the other effect is clearly indicated — because these must
according to can. 2188, 3°, be pointed out expressly —
as, for instance, from hearing confessions, *a divinis*, etc.,
as enumerated in can. 2279.

3. The prelates who may inflict this suspension are
here simply called *Ordinaries, i.e.*, all those who go by the
name of Ordinary, according to can. 198: residential
bishops, abbots and prelates *nullius*, vicars and prefects
apostolic, administrators, and religious superiors of exempt clerical orders. The vicar-general is excluded, unless he has obtained a special commission from his bishop,
because can. 2220, § 2, certainly must here be applied, as
was held before.[12] As to the *superiors of exempt clerical
institutes*, it is certain that they may suspend their subjects from office. This power is vested in all provincials
and such as hold their places, hence also in conventual
priors or guardians. According to can. 199, § 1, this
power may, either partially or totally, be delegated to
others. Thus an absent abbot may delegate this power to
a cloistral prior, a guardian to the vicar, etc. But can.
519 must always be observed. Hence, though a religious
may have been suspended by his superior *ex informata
conscientia* from hearing confessions, he could absolve
validly if he had obtained jurisdiction from the local Ordinary.[13]

4. Who is the *passive subject* of this power? The
text says: "*clericos suos subditos*," i. e., all their clerical
subjects. Therefore, laymen do not fall under this penalty.[14] On the other hand, any one who has received

12 Thus Wernz, *l. c.*, V, P. II, n.
892, and others, quoted by him
ibidem.

13 S. C. EE. et RR., July 2, 1627;

March 2, 1866 (Bizzarri, *Collect.*,
p. 24, p. 755).

14 Formerly they could, because
of the prohibition of receiving orders.

the tonsure, is a cleric, and may therefore be suspended *ex informata*. Besides, the Ordinary can inflict this sentence on all who hold an office in his diocese, whether with or without a dignity. Therefore the vicar-general, canons, consultors, and officials are subject to such a sentence.[15] Concerning offices which one holds in a strange diocese, can. 2282 must be observed. This sentence follows the clergyman affected by it everywhere.[16] Ordinaries may also suspend regulars from hearing confessions, even though they had obtained faculties from the local Ordinary without limitation; nor is the latter bound to indicate the reasons for this suspension.[17]

In order, however, to remind Ordinaries of the *extraordinary character of this power*, they are warned to make use thereof for no frivolous reasons; in other words, they *should not inflict suspension ex informata conscientia when they can proceed in the judiciary way without great inconvenience* (can. 2186, § 2). For the procedure *ex informata conscientia* involves a severity which is justified only by very strong reasons, such as the public welfare, scandal to be avoided, or very serious guilt.[18] Thereby, however, we do not mean to say that the sentence would be invalid if the reasons were not entirely strong enough, because the text merely says: *" adhibere non licet."*[19]

15 Wernz, *l. c.*, n. 893.

16 See can. 2226, § 4.

17 Clem. X, " *Superna*," June 21, 1670, § 6.

18 Bouix, *l. c.*, II, 344; a case of this kind was solved by S. C. C., Feb. 25, 1875 (*A. S. S.*, VII, 547 ff.).

19 Bened. XIV, *De Syn. Dioesc.*, XII, 8, 6, says that a bishop who would declare at a synod that henceforth he would proceed only *ex informata conscientia* would deserve to be rebuked, because his action would savor of ambition and ostentation and breed hateful tyranny, or autocracy, as we would now style it.

PROCEDURE IN INFLICTING THIS PENALTY

CAN. 2187

Ad ferendam hanc suspensionem neque formae iudiciales neque canonicae monitiones requiruntur; sed satis est si Ordinarius, servato praescripto canonum qui sequuntur, simplici decreto declaret se suspensionem indicere.

CAN. 2188

Huiusmodi decretum detur in scriptis, nisi adiuncta aliud exigant, designato die, mense et anno; in eoque:

1.° Expresse dicatur suspensionem ferri ex informata conscientia seu ex causis ipsi Ordinario notis;

2.° Indicetur tempus durationis poenae; abstineat autem Ordinarius ab ipsa infligenda in perpetuum. Potest vero infligi etiam tanquam censura, dummodo hoc in casu clerico patefiat causa propter quam suspensio irrogatur;

3.° Clare indicentur actus qui prohibentur, si suspensio non in totum sed ex parte infligatur.

CAN. 2189

§ 1. Si clericus suspensus sit ab officio in quo alius in eius locum substituendus est, ut, ex. gr., oeconomus in cura animarum, qui substituitur mercedem ex fructibus beneficii percipiat secundum prudens Ordinarii iudicium determinandam.

§ 2. Clericus suspensus, si se gravatum senserit, potest imminutionem pensionis petere ab immediato Superiore qui in via iudiciaria esset iudex appellationis.

CAN. 2190

Ordinarius, qui fert suspensionem ex informata conscientia, debet ex peractis investigationibus tales collegisse probationes, quae eum certum reddant clericum delictum revera perpetrasse et quidem adeo grave ut eiusmodi poena coercendus sit.

It was stated above that *informata conscientia* means absence or lack of judicial procedure, either summary or solemn. This is clearly indicated in can. 2187, which states that *neither judiciary formalities* (such as summons, *contestatio litis*, hearing of witnesses, defence, sentence), *nor canonical warnings* are required to inflict a suspension *ex informata conscientia;* all that is *required* is that the Ordinary observes the rules here laid down and simply declares that the suspension is hereby inflicted.[20]

Can. 2188 rules that the *decree of suspension* must be issued *in writing,* unless the circumstances should advise another mode, for instance, when there is a well-founded suspicion that the clergyman or others are bent on causing trouble in any shape or form. The decree must contain the *precise date, i.e.,* day, month, and year of issue. Besides, it must contain the following statements:

1.° That the suspension is inflicted *ex informata conscientia,* or for reasons known to the Ordinary;

2.° That it is inflicted for a certain clearly expressed period of time;

20 The following formula may be used (see Smith, *l. c.,* II, p. 331, according to Monacelli): " *Constito nobis; presbyterum N. esse reum criminis, eum ob causas quae animum nostrum digne movent, et de quibus Deo et Sedi Apostolicae, cum habuerimus in mandatis, rationem* reddere debemus, et ex informata conscientia, a divinis [ab audiendis confessionibus a dicenda Missa] suspendimus per sex [tres] menses, et suspensum declaramus, ac ei decretum suspensionis intimari mandamus. N. Episcopus N., N. Actuarius."

3.° A specification of the *acts* forbidden if the suspension is partial only.

The reason for 1° is that the clergyman may know immediately that no appeal to a higher instance or court is admitted. On recourse to Rome, see can. 2194.

To n. 2 the text itself adds that the Ordinary *should abstain* from inflicting a *perpetual suspension.* However, this does not mean that a suspension inflicted *in perpetuum* would be null and void; because the text itself has no invalidating, but only a warning clause. Therefore, to assert the invalidity of such an indefinite or perpetual suspension would be against the wording of the text.[21] If the Ordinary should suspend one "*ad bene-placitum nostrum,*" this would be an indefinite suspension, but would expire with the death or removal of the Ordinary who issued the sentence.[22]

The text adds to n. 2 that the suspension *ex informata conscientia* may also be issued as a *censure,* provided the reason for which it is inflicted is made known to the cleric in the case. Although the effect would be the same, yet absolution in case of repentance and repair of scandal could not be withheld (can. 2242, § 3).

It was said that the *effect* is the same, no matter whether the suspension is inflicted as a vindictive penalty or as a censure. This effect consists in prohibiting the clergyman from exercising the functions attached to his office, either partially or totally. If notwithstanding this suspension the clergyman would perform the forbidden acts, he would become *irregular.*[23]

21 Smith, *l. c.,* II, p. 323, maintained invalidity, for which he could refer to S. C. C., Feb. 24, 1853 (*A. S. S.,* VII, 574 f.; he might have added S. C. C., Dec. 20, 1873, *A. S. S., ib.*); but Bouix, *l. c.,* II, 334 f., defended the validity and could also allege decisions of the S. C. C. Wernz, *l. c.,* n. 898 simply says: "*non potest infligi*—"; answer: "*licite, concedo; valide, nego.*"

22 Bouix, *l. c.,* II, 336; Wernz, *l. c.,* n. 900.

23 Cfr. can. 985, n. 7; S. C. C.,

If one is suspended from office in such a way that another must take his place, as, for instance, when a pastor is suspended from his pastoral office, the *substitute must be paid* from the income of the benefice or the pastor's salary, respectively. The *amount* of the renumeration to be paid to the substitute is to be determined by the Ordinary according to his own prudent judgment. In our country, where no state funds can be resorted to, this will depend on the wealth or income of the parish. This may cause some trouble. For the suspended clergyman may think himself unjustly treated if too much is subtracted from his salary. There may not be enough left to support him. Therefore, the Code permits him to appeal (in the widest sense of the word) to his immediate superior. The scope of this quasi-appeal is to ask for a *diminution of the amount of compensation* decreed by the Ordinary for the substitute. To the metropolitan court, therefore, or the court of appeal in the second instance, a clergyman who thinks himself aggrieved should have recourse. But note well that this is no recourse from the sentence inflicted *ex informata conscientia*, but merely concerns the material question of support or remuneration.

Can. 2189 rules, what was already explained above, that the Ordinary who suspends a cleric *ex informata conscientia*, must have *evidence* sufficient to be certain:

1.° That the cleric really perpetrated the crime with which he is charged, and

2.° That the crime is of a nature to deserve such a severe punishment.[24]

April 8, 1848, ad IV (*A. S. S.,* XIV, 314); Wernz, *l. c.,* n. 901.

[24] Some cases may be seen in *A. S. S.,* VII, p. 569 ff. (*turpissimi criminis*); VIII, 547 ff. (of the same nature); XIV, 299 ff. (*prave vivendi ratio et corrupti mores,* also embezzlement of church funds).

CAN. 2191

§ 1. Suspensioni ex informata conscientia iustam ac legitimam causam praebet delictum occultum ad normam can. 2197, n. 4.

§ 2. Ob notorium delictum suspensio ex informata conscientia nunquam ferri potest.

§ 3. Ut delictum publicum suspensione ex informata conscientia plecti possit, occurrat necesse est aliquod ex adiunctis quae sequuntur:

1.° Si testes probi et graves delictum quidem Ordinario patefaciant, sed nulla ratione induci possint ut de eo testimonium in iudicio ferant, neque aliis probationibus delictum iudiciali processu evinci possit;

2.° Si ipsemet clericus minis aut aliis adhibitis mediis impediat ne processus iudiciarius instituatur aut inceptus perficiatur;

3.° Si processui iudiciali conficiendo ferendaeque sententiae impedimenta exoriantur ex adversis civilibus legibus aut gravi scandali periculo.

CAN. 2192

Suspensio ex informata conscientia valet si ex pluribus delictis unum tantum fuerit occultum.

The two canons settle the controversy as to which crimes can be punished with suspension *ex informata conscientia*. The Council of Trent really intended and mentioned only a "*crimen occultum*," as is manifest from the preface to Sess. 14, *de ref*. For public and notorious crimes the bishops needed no extension of their power, since they could prosecute these in the judiciary way.[25]

25 Wernz, *l. c.*, n. 896.

The text itself, ch. 1 of session 14, explicitly states: "occult crime." Nevertheless some authors extended this suspension to public crimes.[26] The Code takes the golden mean between the two extremes.

1.° *A just and legitimate cause* for suspending one *ex informata conscientia* is an *occult crime, i.e.*, one which is not yet divulged or has been committed under, or is involved in, circumstances which render it unlikely that it will become known. "*Occultum, quod non est publicum,*" says can. 2197.

Hence, if the crime is not liable to be divulged on account of the secret circumstances under which it was committed, it is supposed to remain secret. This is somewhat similar to a secret impediment, which is one that cannot be fully proved in court. However, if a case has been tried in court, although without result, it can no longer be called occult, and in that hypothesis the Ordinary would act wisely if he abstained from inflicting suspension *ex informata conscientia.*[27]

2.° Suspension *ex informata conscientia can never be inflicted* for a *notorious crime* because such a crime requires judiciary procedure, in order to safeguard public welfare and justice and the authority of the law. This was generally admitted.

3.° The Code makes some concessions to those who hold that this suspension may be inflicted *also for a public crime*, but it requires that at least *one of the* three following *conditions* be present:

a) That trustworthy and serious witnesses made the

26 Thus Bouix, *l. c.*, II, 325 f.
27 S. C. C., Dec. 20, 1873 (*A. S. S.*, VII, 569) granted an appeal proper, because the case had been brought before the civil court, which could not find sufficient proof for condemnation, and then twice before the ecclesiastical court, from which the pastor appealed, but was in the meanwhile suspended by the bishop *ex inf. consc.*, in order to cause less noise.

crime known to the Ordinary, but cannot in any way be induced to make depositions at a trial, and no other evidence is at hand which would prove the crime in a judiciary way;[28]

b) that the clergyman would use threats or other means to impede or stop a judiciary trial;

c) that the civil law or a serious scandal stand in the way of a formal trial or judicial sentence. This is possible in countries where the *brachium saeculare* not only does not assist but directly opposes the Church.[29]

Suspension *ex informata conscientia is valid* if *only one* crime of several imputed to the same party is occult. Thus if a clergyman should be publicly accused and tried for embezzlement of church funds, but has also been guilty of a crime which is not provable in court, he may be suspended *ex informata conscientia.*[30]

MANIFESTATION OF REASONS AND RECOURSE

CAN. 2193

Prudenti Ordinarii arbitrio relinquitur suspensionis causam seu delictum clerico patefacere aut reticere, pastorali tamen adhibita sollicitudine et caritate, ut, si delictum clerico manifestare censuerit, poena, ex paternis quae interposuerit monitis, nedum ad expiationem culpae, verum etiam ad emendationem delinquentis et ad occasionem peccati eliminandam inserviat.

---

[28] This was the case narrated in *A. S. S.*, VII, 570; *puella honesta et sincera, quae turpia passa est a clerico*.

[29] As to b) and c) see S. C. C., April 8, 1848 (*A. S. S.*, XIV, 300); the witnesses were serious and re-spectable citizens, but afraid of the pastor, and the civil court seemed to favor the priest.

[30] S. C. C., April 8, 1848; Feb. 27, 1875 (*A. S. S.*, XIV, 299 ff.; VIII, 547 ff.).

Can. 2194

Si clericus recursum a suspensione sibi inflicta interponat, Ordinarius ad Sedem Apostolicam mittere debet probationes quibus constet clericum delictum revera perpetrasse quod extraordinaria hac poena puniri queat.

The Tridentine decree permitted Ordinaries to inflict this suspension *quomodolibet, etiam extraiudicialiter.* Since, then, there is no judiciary procedure involved, it is left to the prudent judgment of the Ordinary to manifest or conceal the reason for the suspension. If he deems it prudent to make the reason known to the suspended cleric, he should use pastoral care and charity, in order that the penalty inflicted and accompanied by paternal admonitions, will not only procure an atonement of the transgression, but also better the delinquent and eliminate further occasions of sin. For the Ordinaries, as our Code,[81] following the Council of Trent, says, should remember that they are "*pastores, non percussores.*" Of course, the admonitions referred to are not canonical, but purely paternal, and hence destitute of the judiciary character.

The lawgiver, however, in order not to leave the suspended clergyman entirely defenceless, which would be against every dictate of justice, allows him to *have recourse to the Apostolic See* (S. C. Concilii). Hence there is no appeal to the metropolitan or second instance. This recourse has no suspensive, but only a devolutive effect, and the suspended clergyman must therefore conduct himself as one suspended, and abstain from every act prohibited by the suspension, whether specifically or generally stated.

---

81 Can. 2214, § 2; Trid., Sess. 13, c. 1, de ref.

The *Ordinary* must forward the papers to the same S. Congregation. They must contain the evidence or proofs that the clergyman really committed the crime for which he was suspended *ex informata conscientia*. These must be sent in trustworthy and correct abstracts bearing the official seal and signature. If the witnesses do not object, the original documents may be sent, provided a faithful translation accompanies the vernacular text. Besides, we may reasonably suppose that if the sentence was inflicted for a public crime, at least one of the three conditions mentioned above should be added and testified to; otherwise there might be delay in deciding the case.

APPENDIX I

(*To Canon 1990*)

The Papal Commission for the Authentic Interpretation of the Code has decided the following cases:[1]

1. If two Catholic parties have contracted marriage before the civil magistrate only, without observing the "*Tametsi*" or the "*Ne temere*," in places where these laws are binding, and wish to contract marriage anew *in facie Ecclesiae,* or to have their civilly contracted marriage revalidated, the local Ordinary (or the pastor after having consulted the local Ordinary) may declare the first marriage null and void without a formal trial and without the intervention of the *defensor vinculi*, after having made the investigation prescribed in can. 1019, *i.e.*, after having ascertained the free status of the couple, — that no other impediment except the formerly clandestinely and therefore invalid contracted civil marriage is in the way.

2. The same rule is to be applied in cases of *mixed marriage* contracted invalidly in a non-Catholic Church under the same condition, provided the Catholic party wishes to contract a new marriage with a Catholic.

3. The same rule applies in cases where apostates from the Catholic faith have contracted an invalid civil marriage for the same reason, and, now repentant, wish to contract a new marriage with a Catholic party *in facie Ecclesiae*.

But in each and every one of these cases a *civil divorce* must have first been obtained.

---

[1] Cfr. *A. Ap. S.*, Vol. XI, 479 (Oct. 16, 1919). We add this decision here for the convenience of those who have the first edition of Vol. V of this Commentary.

APPENDIX II

Canon 1868 states that " all other settlements are called decrees," and hence it seems worth while to give a list of these contained in the Code. We shall do so by quoting the respective canons and mentioning the topics treated therein.

1. Can. 1570, § 2   Intimation of decrees.
2. Can. 1577, § 2   Official's administration method.
3. Can. 1591, § 1   Beadle.
4. Can. 1601   No recourse from decrees.
5. Can. 1604, § 4   Signatura decrees acceptance of petitions.
6. Can. 1607, § 2   Bishop decrees extraordinary ministers.
7. Can. 1627   Order of taking cognizance.
8. Can. 1635   Dilatory terms.
9. Can. 1638, § 1   Hours of trial.
10. Can. 1639, § 1   Days of trial.
11. Can. 1663   Removal of procurator and advocate.
12. Can. 1672, § 3   Sequestration.
13. Can. 1674   "
14. Can. 1675, §§ 2, 3   "
15. Can. 1699, § 3   Spoliation.
16. Can. 1710   *Oblatio libelli.*
17. Can. 1724   Summons.
18. Can. 1729, §§ 2, 3, 4   *Litis contestatio.*
19. Can. 1758   Suspected witnesses.
20. Can. 1765   Summons of witnesses.
21. Can. 1782, § 1   Publication of witnesses.
22. Can. 1784   Rejection of witnesses.
23. Can. 1786   Readmission of witnesses.
24. Can. 1796, § 2   Experts.
25. Can. 1799, § 1   "

26. Can. 1806 Local inspection.
27. Can. 1810 " "
28. Can. 1811, § 1 " "
29. Can. 1821, § 1 Documents.
30. Can. 1823, § 3 "
31. Can. 1830, § 5 Oaths.
32. Can. 1839 Incidental questions.
33. Can. 1840, §§ 1, 3 " "
34. Can. 1856, § 2 Attempts.
35. Can. 1857, § 1 "
36. Can. 1860, § 3 *Publicatio processus.*
37. Can. 1861, § 2 *Conclusio in causa.*
38. Can. 1868, § 2 Decrees.
39. Can. 1878, §§ 2, 3 Correction of errors.
40. Can. 1880, n. 6. Appeal.
41. Can. 1899, § 4 Opposition of Third Person.
42. Can. 1907, § 2 *Restitutio in integrum.*
43. Can. 1918 Execution of sentence.
44. Can. 1946, § 2 Denunciation.
45. Can. 1957 Removal from a place.
46. Can. 1958 " " "
47. Can. 1988 Matrimonial cases.
48. Can. 1992 " "
49. Can. 2040, § 2
50. Can. 2073
51. Can. 2078
52. Can. 2083, § 2
53. Can. 2084
54. Can. 2087, §§ 1, 3 Beatification
55. Can. 2100, § 3 and
56. Can. 2110, § 1 Canonization
57. Can. 2115, §§ 1, 2 Decrees.
58. Can. 2124, § 1, 2
59. Can. 2134
60. Can. 2139
61. Can. 2140
62. Can. 2141
63. Can. 2146 Removal of pastors.
64. Can. 2152, § 2 " " "
65. Can. 2153, §§ 1, 3 " " "
66. Can. 2154, § 1 " " "

7. Can. 2155   Removal of Pastors.
8. Can. 2161, §1   "   "   "
9. Can. 2187   Suspension *ex informata conscientia.*
0. Can. 2188   "   "   "   "